# GCSE AQA A
# Religious Studies

There's a lot to learn for AQA A Grade 9-1 GCSE Religious Studies —
but this brilliant all-in-one CGP book has it under control.

It's packed with study notes and exam-style questions covering Christianity,
Catholic Christianity, Islam and Judaism. We've even included a full practice exam
at the end to make sure you're 100% ready for the real thing.

What's more, there's a free Online Edition to read on your PC, Mac or tablet. Amazing!

## How to access your free Online Edition

This book includes a free Online Edition to read on your PC, Mac or tablet.
You'll just need to go to **cgpbooks.co.uk/extras** and enter this code:

1855 8121 8073 1514

By the way, this code only works for one person. If somebody else has used
this book before you, they might have already claimed the Online Edition.

# Complete
# Revision & Practice
Everything you need to pass the exams!

# Contents

Published by CGP

*Editors:* Charles Kitts, Sam Mann, Caley Simpson, Ruth Wilbourne

*Contributors:* Jill Hudson, Helen Norris, Duncan Raynor, Paul Smith, Rebecca Tate, Ben Wallace, Philip West

*Proofreading:* Glenn Rogers

ISBN: 978 1 78908 092 6

*With thanks to Ana Pungartnik for the copyright research.*

## Sacred Text References

References from the Bible always go in the order: Book Chapter:Verse(s). So whenever you
see something like: Genesis 1:14, it means it's from the book of Genesis, Chapter 1, verse 14.

Similarly, references from the Qur'an are shown with the Surah (Chapter) followed by the Ayah (Verse).

For all collections of hadith, we've used the English referencing system.
This gives the book number followed by the hadith number, e.g. Sahih al-Bukhari 1:3.

Scripture quotations [marked NIV] taken from the Holy Bible, New International Version Anglicised
Copyright © 1979, 1984, 2011 Biblica,
Used by permission of Hodder & Stoughton Ltd, an Hachette UK company
All rights reserved
'NIV' is a registered trademark of Biblica
UK trademark number 1448790.

Holy Qur'an quotations taken from the Holy Qur'an, Sahih International Version. https://quran.com/

Quotations from the Catechism of the Catholic Church © Libreria Editrice Vaticana
Quotations from Lumen gentium on page 13, Gaudium et spes on page 17, Evangelii Gaudium on pages 18 and 19, Humanae Vitae on
pages 58 and 80, Familiaris Consortio on pages 65, 66 and 68, and a speech by Pope Francis on page 73 © Libreria Editrice Vaticana

Quotes on pages 2, 5, 6, 7, 14, 59, 73 and 125 from The Church of England, https://www.churchofengland.org.
© The Archbishops' Council.

With thanks to Alamy for images on page 35 and 80.

Quotations from Mishnah Sanhedrin reproduced under Attribution-ShareAlike 3.0 Unported (CC BY-SA 3.0).
https://www.sefaria.org/Mishnah_Sanhedrin.4?lang=en

Quote on page 90 from The Guide of the Perplexed, Volume 1 by Moses Maimonides, translated by Shlomo Pines.
Published by The University of Chicago Press, 1963.

Sahih Muslim 16:4152 quote on page 120 from https://muflihun.com

Quotes on pages 127 and 130 from Islam and the West: A Rational Perspective by Mohammed Jabbar,
published by Mereo Books, an imprint of Memoirs Publishing, 2014.

Quotation on page 128 © www.cbcew.org.uk

Data about wealth inequality on page 133 contains public sector information licensed under the Open Government Licence v3.0.
http://www.nationalarchives.gov.uk/doc/open-government-licence/version/3/

Quotes from Hadith from https://muflihun.com/

Quote on page 204, by Maimonides, Sefer Hamitzvot, Negative Commandment no. 290, reprinted with permission of www.sie.org

Every effort has been made to locate copyright holders and obtain permission to reproduce sources. For those sources where it has
been difficult to trace the originator of the work, we would be grateful for information. If any copyright holder would like us to make
an amendment to the acknowledgements, please notify us and we will gladly update the book at the next reprint. Thank you.

Printed by Elanders Ltd, Newcastle upon Tyne
Clipart from Corel®

Based on the classic CGP style created by Richard Parsons.

# Introduction to Christianity

Christianity is based on the belief in <u>Jesus Christ</u> being the <u>Son of God</u>. It is the <u>main</u> religion in Britain.

## The **Bible** is the Christian **Sacred Text**

The Bible is divided into two main parts — the <u>Old</u> and <u>New Testaments</u>:

1) Depending on the version, the <u>Old Testament</u> has at least 39 books, which include the <u>Creation</u> story (see p.3) and the <u>Ten Commandments</u>. These 39 books are the <u>Jewish scriptures</u> — they are also considered <u>sacred</u> by Jews.

2) The <u>New Testament</u> is the <u>specifically Christian</u> part of the Bible. Its 27 books include the <u>4 Gospels</u> (Matthew, Mark, Luke and John), which are accounts of <u>Jesus's life</u>. The <u>Acts of the Apostles</u> and the <u>letters of St Paul</u> describe the <u>early years</u> of Christianity.

## Christianity is Divided into **Different Traditions**

The different branches of Christianity are called <u>denominations</u>. They share key beliefs, but interpret some points of the faith differently and worship in different ways (see p.11).

1) <u>Roman Catholics</u> respect the authority of the <u>Bible</u> and <u>Church tradition</u>, plus the authority of the <u>Pope</u> and his teachings. The <u>seven sacraments</u> (which include the Eucharist — see p.13) are an important part of their faith.

2) <u>Protestants</u> base their beliefs and practices on the <u>Bible</u>, rather than Church tradition or the teachings of the Pope. In England and Wales, Protestant denominations that are not part of the 'Anglican Communion' are often called '<u>Nonconformists</u>'. These include Methodists, Baptists, Pentecostals, the Society of Friends (Quakers) and the Salvation Army.

> The <u>Church of England</u> has both Roman Catholic and Protestant features. Its beliefs are set out in the <u>39 Articles</u>. <u>Anglicanism</u> is the worldwide 'communion' of Churches in fellowship with the parent Church of England.

3) <u>Orthodox Christians</u> are found mainly in Eastern Europe, Russia and Greece. They also have <u>7 sacraments</u>, and honour (but don't worship) <u>icons</u> — pictures of Saints.

## There are Many **Beliefs** About the **Nature of God**

Christianity is a <u>monotheistic</u> (one God) religion. The Ten Commandments say "you shall have no other gods" (Exodus 20:3 NIV). Christians believe God has the following <u>characteristics</u>, though they <u>differ</u> in the <u>emphasis</u> placed on each, e.g. some focus more on God's loving nature than his role as judge.

1) **OMNIPOTENT** — God is <u>all-powerful</u>, although he still allows each person <u>free will</u>.

2) **BENEVOLENT** — God is <u>loving</u> and <u>caring</u>: "For God so loved the world that he gave his one and only Son" (John 3:16 NIV). Christians try to <u>follow</u> his example in their actions.

3) **JUST JUDGE** — God <u>judges</u> people's actions fairly. Those who reject him and live sinful lives will be <u>punished</u>, as shown in the story of the sheep and goats in Matthew 25:31-46 (see p.19). But God <u>forgives</u> people who are sorry for what they've done and become faithful to him — the story of the <u>prodigal son</u> (Luke 15:11-32) shows God will forgive anyone who returns to his ways.

4) **OMNISCIENT** — God <u>knows</u> everything — in the past, present and future.

5) **ETERNAL** — God has always existed, and he will continue to exist forever.

6) **TRANSCENDENT** — God is <u>beyond</u> this world — he doesn't depend on it to exist.

7) **IMMANENT** — But God is <u>present</u> in the human world, and takes an <u>active role</u> in humanity.

8) **PERSONAL** — God is a '<u>person</u>', albeit an almighty and <u>divine person</u>. If God is personal, then a relationship is possible through <u>prayer</u> — which can be a '<u>conversation</u>' with God.

---

REVISION TASK

## Omnipotent or omniscient? Get them the right way round

Cover this page and see how many characteristics of God you can write down. No peeking now...

# The Trinity

Although Christians believe in <u>one God</u>, they also believe that God has <u>three parts</u>.

## Christians Believe in God as the **Trinity**

The <u>Trinity</u> is the idea that God exists in three '<u>persons</u>' — the Father, the Son (Jesus) and the Holy Spirit.
The <u>importance</u> of all three is shown in the Bible:

> Matthew 3:16-17 describes how at Jesus's baptism, Jesus "...saw the Spirit of God descending like a dove and alighting on him. And a voice from heaven said, 'This is my Son, whom I love; with him I am well pleased.' " (NIV)

> In Philippians 2:6, St Paul described Jesus as having "equality with God" (NIV).

## The **Trinity** is Explained in the **Nicene Creed**

1) In 325 AD, Church leaders from around the world gathered at the <u>Council of Nicaea</u>. They produced a <u>creed</u> — a statement of beliefs. This was further developed at the <u>Council of Constantinople</u> in 381 AD, and is known as the <u>Nicene Creed</u>. It describes how Christians see God:

> "We believe in one God, the Father, the Almighty, maker of heaven and earth... We believe in one Lord, Jesus Christ, the only Son of God... of one Being with the Father... was made man... he suffered death and... he rose again... We believe in the Holy Spirit... the giver of life, who proceeds from the Father and the Son... who has spoken through the prophets."

2) Before this, not everyone had <u>agreed</u> that the Son of God (Jesus) was <u>one with God</u>, rather than having been <u>made by God</u>. Now they agreed that he was <u>equally</u> important.

3) The <u>importance</u> the <u>early Church</u> placed on the <u>Trinity</u> in the Nicene Creed means it is a <u>key belief</u> for most Christians — but some groups, such as <u>Christadelphians</u>, don't believe in the Trinity.

4) Christians see the three parts of the Trinity as having <u>different characteristics</u> and <u>roles</u>:

### The Father

- For many Christians, <u>God the Father</u> is the God of the <u>Old Testament</u>. He <u>created</u> Heaven and Earth and <u>sustains</u> them. <u>God the Father</u> might be described as the <u>transcendent part</u> of God.
- The title 'Father' is a mark of <u>respect</u> for God, and is used by <u>Jesus</u> in the Gospels: "Be perfect, therefore, as your heavenly Father is perfect." (Matthew 5:48 NIV)

### The Son

- Christians believe <u>Jesus</u> (see p.6-8) is the <u>incarnation</u> of God in human form. He is seen as both divine and human — the <u>immanent</u> and <u>personal</u> part of God, who understands human suffering.
- Christians believe that Jesus provides a <u>model</u> for Christian behaviour in <u>obedience</u> to God the Father. The <u>Gospels</u> contain a record of his life and teachings, and are an important source of <u>guidance</u> for Christians on how they should live their lives.

### The Holy Spirit

- Christians believe that the <u>Holy Spirit</u> is the <u>presence</u> of God in the world. Before his death, Jesus promised his disciples: "I will ask the Father, and he will give you another advocate to help you and be with you for ever — the Spirit of truth" (John 14:16-17 NIV).
- The Holy Spirit is seen as the <u>immanent yet impersonal</u> part of God — it continues to <u>guide</u> the <u>Church</u>.
- Some Christians feel that the Holy Spirit also guides them <u>personally</u> in being good Christians. The Catechism of the Catholic Church 736 says "By this power of the Spirit, God's children can bear much fruit."

## The Trinity means one God in three persons

For the 5-mark exam questions, you need to refer to sacred texts to get full marks. You can write quotes, or just paraphrase what is said. Say where it comes from, e.g. the Bible or the 39 Articles.

# Creation

The story of creation can be understood in different ways.  Some take it <u>literally</u>, for others it's a <u>metaphor</u>.

## The Bible Describes how **God Created** the **Universe**

1) <u>Genesis</u> chapter 1 says that <u>God</u> created everything.
The process took <u>six days</u>, and on the seventh day God <u>rested</u>.

2) On day one, <u>light</u> and <u>darkness</u> were made, and on day two the <u>sky</u>.  On the third day <u>oceans</u>, <u>land</u> and <u>plants</u> on the land were created, and on the fourth day the <u>sun</u>, <u>moon</u> and <u>stars</u>.  On the fifth day it was the creatures of the water and sky (e.g. <u>fish</u> and <u>birds</u>) and on the sixth day, <u>land animals</u> and <u>people</u>.

3) Christians see God the Father as the <u>creator</u>, but the Bible also describes how the other <u>beings</u> of the Trinity were involved.  God created the world by acting <u>through</u> the Holy Spirit.

> "...the Spirit of God was hovering over the waters.  And God said, 'Let there be light,' and there was light." Genesis 1:2-3 NIV

4) The role of the <u>Son of God</u> is described in the Gospel of John.  He uses the phrase '<u>the Word</u>', but it is clear he is referring to <u>Jesus</u> as he later says "The Word became flesh and made his dwelling among us" (John 1:14 NIV).  John makes it clear that Jesus was <u>vital for creation</u>.

> "In the beginning was the Word, and the Word was with God, and the Word was God.  He was with God in the beginning.  Through him all things were made; without him nothing was made that has been made." John 1:1-3 NIV

## It Explains how **Human Beings** were **Created**

1) The creation of human beings is described in <u>Genesis</u> chapters <u>1</u> and <u>2</u>.  The first two humans were <u>Adam and Eve</u>, and they lived in the <u>Garden of Eden</u>.

2) <u>Genesis</u> chapter 1 says "So God created mankind in his own image, in the image of God he created them; male and female he created them" (Genesis 1:27 NIV).

3) Genesis chapter 2 says "the Lord God formed a man from the dust of the ground" (Genesis 2:7 NIV) and "made a woman from the rib he had taken out of the man" (Genesis 2:22 NIV).

4) The fact that God created humans in <u>his image</u> is important.  Because of this, Christians believe that humans are <u>special</u>.  They think humans should <u>behave</u> like God by being <u>loving</u> and <u>fair</u> (see p.1).  It also shows that humans are <u>important to God</u>, and so <u>everyone</u> should be treated with <u>respect</u>.

5) In Genesis 1:28, God told Adam and Eve to "Rule over the fish in the sea and the birds in the sky and over every living creature that moves on the ground" (NIV).  Some Christians believe God gave humans '<u>dominion</u>' (power) over his creation and they can <u>use</u> it as they like.  However, Genesis 2:15 says "The Lord God took the man and put him in the Garden of Eden to work it and take care of it" (NIV).  Many Christians interpret this as humans having '<u>stewardship</u>' of the Earth — God expects them to <u>care</u> for it.

## There are **Different Ways** to **Interpret** the Creation Story

1) Some Christians take the creation story <u>literally</u> — they are known as <u>creationists</u>.  They believe that the process took six days, and humans are descended from Adam and Eve.

2) Other Christians are more <u>liberal</u> in their understanding of the Bible's events. They view Genesis as more of a <u>parable</u>, or a <u>symbolic</u> description — they acknowledge God as the creator, but are open to <u>other theories</u>, such as the <u>Big Bang theory</u> and <u>evolution</u>.  These theories can offer more <u>information</u> to Christians about how <u>God</u> made the universe.  The Roman Catholic Church has <u>accepted</u> both theories.

3) The creation story can help Christians further understand <u>God's nature</u>.  God is <u>eternal</u> as he made time, and was present 'prior' to it.  He is <u>omnipotent</u> as he created the universe through words.  God's <u>benevolence</u> can be seen through creation too as he brought humankind to life and gave them the world.

## The creation story can be seen as literal or a metaphor

Grab a pen and paper and see if you can quickly summarise what Genesis says about the story of creation.  Once you've done that, try jotting down some different interpretations of creation.

4

# Evil and Suffering

Evil comes in different forms, and can have an impact on a person's relationship with their faith.

## Free Will Led to Evil Entering the World

1) Christianity teaches that evil entered the world as a result of Adam and Eve giving in to temptation in the Garden of Eden — they disobeyed God by eating the fruit of the tree of knowledge. This switch from a perfect world to one containing evil is known as 'The Fall'.

2) After the Fall, every human being was born with a flawed nature, capable of causing suffering — this is the idea of original sin.

3) Christians believe God created humans with free will — it's up to them to choose whether they perform evil deeds or not, just as it was up to Adam and Eve whether to give in to temptation or not. Good is the opposite of evil, and since God is good, Christians try to follow his example.

"When the woman saw... the fruit of the tree... she took some and ate it. She also gave some to her husband... and he ate it." Genesis 3:6 NIV

## Evil can be Either Human-Made or Natural

Evil and suffering can be divided into two types:

### Moral (human-made) Evil

1) This is when suffering is brought about by the cruel actions of people.

2) This includes things like murder, war, rape and torture.

3) The person causing the evil is able to make a choice about what is morally right or wrong.

### Natural Evil

1) This kind of evil, and the suffering that comes with it, is caused by the world in which we live, and is no one's 'fault'.

2) This includes things like disease, floods, earthquakes and hurricanes.

3) However, many recent natural disasters may have been caused by human interference in the natural world, raising the question of whether that makes those events human-made.

## Evil can Lead People to Question their Faith

1) Evil and suffering may lead some people to question their belief in God — or even to reject their faith.

2) Some might say that since suffering exists, God can't be both benevolent and omnipotent — a loving and all-powerful God wouldn't allow it to happen. They might argue that he doesn't exist, or that he can't have the characteristics that believers say he has.

"the Lord is compassionate and gracious, slow to anger, abounding in love... he does not treat us as our sins deserve..." Psalm 103:8-10 NIV

3) But others would say that although God has these characteristics, he gave people free will and so doesn't interfere. Or some may say that he wants to help, but isn't powerful enough.

4) Christians react to evil and suffering in various ways. Suffering is often seen as a test of faith — God has his reasons (even if we don't know what they are). Many believe that God is with people in their suffering, and that it can bring people closer to him.

"I know, Lord, that your laws are righteous, and that in faithfulness you have afflicted me. May your unfailing love be my comfort..." Psalm 119:75-76 NIV

5) Others say life on Earth isn't meant to be perfect — the focus should be on reaching heaven.

6) The Book of Job tells of the terrible suffering Job endures and how he questions God. In the end, Job comes to the conclusion that God is all-powerful and knows what he is doing — and that suffering must be accepted because people can't really understand the world or God's plan: "Though he slay me, yet will I hope in him..." (Job 13:15 NIV).

7) Christians believe they should try to help people who are suffering — practically (charity) and by praying. Jesus said that "...whatever you did for one of... these brothers and sisters of mine, you did for me" (Matthew 25:40 NIV).

## Evil is the cause of suffering for humans

Cover this page and write down as many ways Christians respond to suffering as you can think of.

# The Afterlife

What people believe will happen to them after <u>death</u> can influence the way they <u>live</u> their lives.

## Christians Believe in **Heaven** and **Hell**

1) <u>Life after death</u> is the idea that, although your <u>body</u> may die and decay, your <u>soul</u> can live on.

2) Christianity teaches that the <u>soul</u> lives on after death (<u>immortality</u> of the soul), and that the body will be <u>resurrected</u> (brought back to life) for Judgement Day, just as Jesus was resurrected after his crucifixion.

3) Christians believe that God will judge you, and you'll go to either <u>heaven</u> or <u>hell</u>:

Heaven is often portrayed as a place of great beauty and serenity, a <u>paradise</u> where you'll spend eternity with God — as long as you believe in <u>Jesus</u> and have followed his <u>teachings</u>, you can be saved by <u>God's grace</u> (see p.8). The <u>soul</u> can go to heaven even though the body ('earthly tent') is gone.

"I am the resurrection and the life. The one who believes in me will live, even though they die..." John 11:25 NIV

"For we know that if the earthly tent we live in is destroyed, we have a building from God, an eternal house in heaven, not built by human hands." 2 Corinthians 5:1 NIV

Hell, on the other hand, is often portrayed as a place of <u>torment</u> and <u>pain</u> — the final destination of <u>nonbelievers</u> and those who have led <u>bad</u> lives.

"Then they will go away to eternal punishment, but the righteous to eternal life." Matthew 25:46 NIV

4) However, not all Christians believe that heaven and hell are <u>real</u> places — many Christians see heaven and hell as <u>states of mind</u>. In heaven you'll be <u>happy</u>, and know God — in hell you'll be <u>unable</u> to know God's love. Pope John Paul II said that hell was a <u>metaphor</u> for how people who've <u>rejected</u> God will <u>feel</u>.

5) Some Christians, for example Roman Catholics, believe that going to hell means that any <u>connection</u> they have to God will be <u>severed</u> forever: "This state of definitive self-exclusion from communion with God... is called 'hell' " (Catechism of the Catholic Church 1033).

6) Some believe God <u>wouldn't</u> punish people for eternity. A few believe that those who God finds <u>unacceptable</u> will be <u>annihilated</u>. In a report called 'The Mystery of Salvation', senior members of the <u>Church of England</u> said that for those people "the only end is <u>total non-being</u>".

7) Some believe that a loving God <u>wouldn't</u> allow anyone to go to hell.

### Purgatory

*Read this if you're studying Catholic Christianity.*

Roman Catholics believe in a place, or state of existence, called <u>Purgatory</u>. Here <u>sins</u> are punished and the person must "undergo purification" (Catechism of the Catholic Church, 1030) before the soul can move on to heaven. Protestants believe this isn't in the Bible, so they <u>reject</u> it.

## Christians Believe **Resurrection** Happens at the **Last Judgement**

1) Many Christians believe that Jesus will return to Earth in the <u>Second Coming</u> (<u>Parousia</u>), and everyone who has died will be <u>resurrected</u>: "in Christ all will be made alive" (1 Corinthians 15:22 NIV).

"Christ... ascended into Heaven, and there sitteth, until he return to judge all Men at the last day." 39 Articles IV

2) Some believe that all of humanity will then be judged at the <u>Last Judgement</u>. Those that God finds <u>acceptable</u> will enter <u>heaven</u> — the rest will go to hell, as in the story of the sheep and the goats (Matthew 25:31-46).

"For we must all appear before the judgment seat of Christ, so that each of us may receive what is due to us for the things done while in the body, whether good or bad." 2 Corinthians 5:10 NIV

3) Some Christians, e.g. <u>Roman Catholics</u>, believe in a <u>personal</u> day of <u>judgement</u> straight after a person <u>dies</u> — their actions will be judged and they'll go to heaven or hell <u>straight away</u>. Some think they'll be <u>judged again</u> at the Last Judgement, and will <u>re-enter</u> heaven or hell in their <u>resurrected forms</u>.

4) Others don't believe in a personal judgement — the soul must <u>wait</u> to be judged at the <u>Last Judgement</u>.

## The examiners will be judging your answers

Catholics and other Christians have different ideas about heaven and hell — make sure you know which is which. Only Catholics believe in Purgatory (you don't need to learn about this if you're doing Christianity).

**Christianity & Catholic Christianity**

# Jesus Christ and Salvation

Christians believe that Jesus Christ, the second Person of the Trinity, is the <u>Son of God</u>.

## God Became **Human** at the **Incarnation**

1) The <u>incarnation</u> was the act by which <u>God</u> became a <u>human being</u> as Jesus Christ.
An <u>angel</u> told a woman called <u>Mary</u> in Nazareth that she would have a <u>son</u> —
and that "the holy one to be born will be called the Son of God" (Luke 1:35 NIV).

2) This belief is stated in the <u>Nicene Creed</u>: "he... was incarnate
from the Holy Spirit and the Virgin Mary and was made man".

3) Christians don't believe that Jesus was 'half God and half man' — he was <u>fully
both</u>. The Bible describes how God "appeared in the flesh" (1 Timothy 3:16 NIV).

4) Jesus is referred to as '<u>Christ</u>' or '<u>Messiah</u>' — the '<u>Anointed One of God</u>'.

5) Christians see Jesus's time on Earth as God's way of showing how much he <u>loves</u> the world.
They study the <u>Gospels</u> to find out about <u>Jesus's life</u>, and to see how they should live their own.

> "The Word became flesh and made his dwelling among us. We have seen his glory, the glory of the one and only Son, who came from the Father, full of grace and truth." John 1:14 NIV

After being baptised by John the Baptist, Jesus began <u>teaching</u>. He had many followers,
including <u>12 chosen disciples</u>. Some of his key teachings are in the <u>Sermon on the Mount</u>
(Matthew 5-7) — he taught how the poor and meek are <u>highly valued</u> by God, and how
<u>peacemakers</u> are blessed. He also taught the importance of <u>kindness</u>, such as in the story of the
<u>Good Samaritan</u> (Luke 10:30-37). He performed miracles such as <u>healing</u> the sick and bringing
people <u>back to life</u>, showing that he was the <u>Son of God</u> and demonstrating God's <u>love</u>.

## Jesus was **Arrested** and **Crucified**

### The Last Supper, Jesus's Arrest and Trial

1) Shortly before his death, Jesus and his disciples ate their <u>Passover</u> meal in Jerusalem.
It was their <u>final meal</u> together and became known as the <u>Last Supper</u>.

2) At the meal, Jesus gave the disciples <u>bread</u> saying "this is my body" and <u>wine</u> saying "This is
my blood" (Mark 14:22-24 NIV). Luke's Gospel tells us he said "do this in remembrance of me"
(Luke 22:19 NIV). These words are important to many Christians today who remember Jesus
with bread and wine through the <u>Eucharist</u> (see p.14).

3) At the Last Supper, Jesus also <u>washed</u> his disciples' <u>feet</u>, which teaches
Christians about how important it is to <u>serve</u> others.

4) After the Last Supper, Jesus went to pray in the <u>Garden of Gethsemane</u>, where he was <u>arrested</u>.
The authorities felt <u>threatened</u> by Jesus — earlier that week, crowds had called him the '<u>King of Israel</u>'.

5) He was put on <u>trial</u> before the Jewish <u>high priest</u> and found guilty of <u>blasphemy</u>. Then Jesus
was tried before the Roman governor, <u>Pilate</u> — he offered to release Jesus, but the crowd said
"<u>Crucify him!</u>" (Mark 15:13 NIV). He was <u>flogged</u>, before being sent to die.

### Crucifixion

1) Jesus was <u>crucified</u> at a place called <u>Golgotha</u>, next to two robbers. A sign was fixed to
Jesus's cross that read 'The King of the Jews', to record the <u>charge</u> against him. Passers-by
threw <u>insults</u> at Jesus, saying that he could <u>save others</u>, but couldn't <u>save himself</u>.

2) In his suffering, Jesus cried out, "My God, my God, why have you forsaken me?"
(Mark 15:34 NIV). This shows that Jesus understands how people can feel
abandoned in their <u>suffering</u>.

3) Christians also believe the crucifixion helped to <u>repair</u> the <u>relationship</u>
between God and mankind — the <u>atonement</u> (see p.8).

---

## Jesus was God in human form

Draw a timeline and fill it in with details of Jesus's last supper, arrest, trial and crucifixion.

# Jesus Christ and Salvation

For Christians, Jesus's <u>resurrection</u> and <u>ascension</u> are some of the most <u>important parts</u> of Jesus's story. His resurrection <u>confirms</u> for Christians that he was the <u>son of God</u>.

## Jesus was **Resurrected**

1) After the crucifixion, Jesus's body was put in a tomb. But he was <u>resurrected</u> (brought back to life), and his tomb was found <u>empty</u>.

> Roman Catholics refer to the crucifixion, resurrection and ascension of Jesus as 'The Paschal Mystery'.

> "...Why do you look for the living among the dead? He is not here; he has risen!" Luke 24:5-6 NIV

2) Jesus talked to two women and told them "Go and tell my brothers to go to Galilee; there they will see me" (Matthew 28:10 NIV).

3) The resurrection is important to Christians as it shows them that there is <u>life after death</u> — <u>death</u> becomes <u>less frightening</u>.

4) It shows them just how <u>powerful</u> God is. This power that raised Jesus from the dead gives people the <u>strength</u> to live Christian lives.

5) Christians also see the resurrection as further <u>proof</u> that Jesus is the <u>Son of God</u> as he was "...appointed the Son of God in power by his resurrection from the dead..." (Romans 1:4 NIV). This strengthens people's <u>faith</u>.

## **Jesus** Going to **Heaven** is Called the **Ascension**

1) Over the <u>40 days</u> after the resurrection, many of Jesus's disciples said they had met him <u>alive</u> in various places around <u>Jerusalem</u>.

2) Then, Jesus '<u>ascended into Heaven</u>' to be with God the Father once again. He had <u>done</u> what he was sent to <u>Earth</u> to do, and it was time for him to <u>go back</u> to God.

> "While he was blessing them, he left them and was taken up into heaven." Luke 24:51 NIV

3) In John 14:2, Jesus tells his disciples he will "prepare a place" (NIV) for them in heaven. 1 John 2:1 says that, in Jesus, Christians have an 'advocate' with God (someone who will look out for them).

4) <u>Pope Benedict XVI</u> said that since <u>Jesus</u> was <u>human</u> and went to be with God, the <u>ascension</u> shows there's a <u>place</u> for all human beings <u>with God</u>.

5) The ascension shows <u>Jesus's power</u> — he is now "at the right hand of the mighty God" (Luke 22:69 NIV).

---

## Jesus "was made man... he suffered death... and he rose again"

This is stated in the Nicene Creed (p.2), which shows how important it is — it demonstrates God's love for man. So make sure you know all the details about Jesus's incarnation, arrest, crucifixion, resurrection and ascension — as well as key quotations from the Bible and the Nicene Creed.

# Jesus Christ and Salvation

Salvation is needed before Christians can go to Heaven, and Jesus's actions made it possible. His death meant that anyone could go to heaven — as long as they have faith in him.

## Jesus **Died** to **Save** Humanity

1) 'Original sin' (see p.4) means that everyone is born capable of sin. Many Christians believe that Jesus's suffering and death won forgiveness for everyone and ensured their redemption (freeing them from sin).

2) They believe that Jesus was perfect (without sin), but God placed all the sins of the world on him at his crucifixion. Romans 3:21-26 teaches that his sacrifice paid for their sins, so long as they have faith in him.

3) Jesus's actions brought about the reconciliation between God and humanity — known as the atonement.

> "For God so loved the world that he gave his one and only Son, that whoever believes in him shall not perish but have eternal life. For God did not send his Son into the world to condemn the world, but to save the world through him." John 3:16-17 NIV

4) His power and goodness were so great that after he was crucified, death couldn't keep hold of him.

5) However, not all Christians believe that Jesus had to die to pay for people's sins:

- 1 Corinthians 13:5 says that love "keeps no record of wrongs" (NIV). Many Christians think that Jesus's death wasn't required for a loving and merciful God to be able to forgive people's sins.
- Some people argue that it was Jesus's ministry that showed people how to be free from sin — he showed them how to live their lives in a Godly way.
- Some say Jesus's death shows God's love for humankind through his willingness to suffer and die as humans do. His resurrection showed how God could triumph over sin and death, so people don't have to fear evil.

## Christians Must Seek **Salvation** to Get to **Heaven**

1) Salvation means the soul being saved from death and sin, allowing it to reach heaven. For this to happen, Christians believe they must have faith in Jesus: "Salvation is found in no one else..." (Acts 4:12 NIV).

2) Salvation is only possible through God's grace — God showing favour to those who haven't earned it: "For it is by grace you have been saved, through faith... it is the gift of God" (Ephesians 2:8 NIV).

3) But people can't just say they believe — if they're a true believer they'll try to live a Christian life. The Bible contains many laws, such as the Ten Commandments (see p.42), which provide Christians with guidance on how they should behave. Everyone will sin, but the laws mean they'll "become conscious of ... sin" (Romans 3:20 NIV) and "turn to God in repentance" (Acts 20:21 NIV).

4) The Holy Spirit helps Christians to follow the teachings of God and his laws and keep their faith, helping them to find salvation.

## Jesus showed his love for humanity through his suffering

Not all Christians agree that Jesus had to die so that the world could be freed from sin — some think it just showed his compassion for us. But all Christians agree that salvation can be gained through Jesus. Make sure you know both sides of the argument and can argue and give evidence for both points of view.

# Worked Exam Questions

Here are some questions similar to the ones you'll get in your exams. First, there are some that have the answers written in so you can see what you should be aiming for, then there are some for you to have a go at.

**1** Which of the following occurred during the creation story?
Put a tick (✓) in the correct box.

**A** The moon and the oceans were created on the same day. ☐

**B** People were created on the third day. ☐

**C** Land animals were created on the same day as people. ✓

**D** The sun was created on the first day. ☐

*[1 mark]*

**2** Which of the following means to be present in the physical world, or to interact with humanity? Put a tick (✓) in the correct box.

**A** Omnipotent ☐

**B** Transcendent ☐

**C** Benevolent ☐

**D** Immanent ✓

*[1 mark]*

**3** Give the names of two Christian denominations.

**1)** Methodism

**2)** Orthodox

*[2 marks]*

**4** Explain two Christian teachings on heaven.
Your answer should refer to specific Christian teachings or sacred texts.

If someone believes in Jesus and follows his teachings, their soul will not die but will live forever in heaven: "The one who believes in me will live, even though they die" (John 11:25 NIV).

Some Christians believe that heaven is not a real place, but a state of mind. Heaven is closeness to God, whereas hell is separation from him.

*[5 marks]*

# Exam Questions

5  Which of the following means love from God which mankind doesn't deserve?
   Put a tick (✓) in the correct box.

   A   Salvation   ☐

   B   Redemption   ☐

   C   Grace   ☐

   D   Reconciliation   ☐

   *[1 mark]*

6  Give two Christian beliefs about evil found in the story of Adam and Eve.

   *If you're studying Catholic Christianity, you don't need to answer this question.*

   1) ..........................................................................................................................

   ..........................................................................................................................

   2) ..........................................................................................................................

   ..........................................................................................................................

   *[2 marks]*

7  Explain two ways in which beliefs about the creation of humans influence Christians today.

   ..........................................................................................................................

   ..........................................................................................................................

   ..........................................................................................................................

   ..........................................................................................................................

   ..........................................................................................................................

   ..........................................................................................................................

   ..........................................................................................................................

   *[4 marks]*

8  'A belief in the Trinity is the most important Christian belief.'

   SPaG MARKS

   Evaluate this statement. Your answer should include the following:
   • examples from Christian teachings
   • arguments that support the statement
   • arguments that disagree with the statement
   • a conclusion.

   *Write your answer on a separate sheet of paper.*

   *[12 marks]*

# Different Forms of Worship

Worship is a Christian's way of expressing their <u>love</u> of, <u>respect</u> for, and <u>devotion</u> to God.

## Christian Denominations have **Different Forms** of **Worship**

*If you're studying <u>Catholic Christianity</u>, just read the <u>green</u> box on this page.*

For Christians, Sunday is the '<u>Lord's Day</u>', when they celebrate the <u>Sabbath</u> (the holy day of rest). Most churches have their main service on a <u>Sunday morning</u>. Worship often includes prayers, readings from the Bible, a sermon and the Eucharist (see p.14) — the different denominations place varying amounts of <u>importance</u> on each, creating <u>differences</u> in worship.

## Some Worship is **Liturgical**...

*'Liturgical' means that services follow a set pattern written out by the Church.*

1) Anglican Sunday morning services <u>usually</u> include the Eucharist, and Catholic Sunday morning services <u>always</u> do (Catholics call the Eucharist '<u>Mass</u>'). For Catholics, the '<u>Roman Missal</u>' sets out the contents of the service. Anglican worship is guided by the '<u>Common Worship</u>' book, based on the Book of Common Prayer from 1662. The main <u>Orthodox</u> Sunday service is the 'Divine Liturgy', which centres on the Eucharist — it's usually based on the liturgy of <u>St John Chrysostom</u>.

<u>Anglican</u> and <u>Catholic</u> Eucharist services share many similarities:

- A <u>confession</u> of sin and a request for God's mercy is said by everyone (called the '<u>penitential rite</u>' by Catholics).
- There are readings (including one <u>gospel</u> reading) and a sermon — this part is known as the '<u>liturgy of the Word</u>'. The <u>Nicene</u> or <u>Apostle's Creed</u> is then recited.
- The priest says prayers over bread and wine — this is called the '<u>liturgy of the Eucharist</u>'.
- Then the congregation says the <u>Lord's Prayer</u> (see p.15) and 'shares the peace' by shaking hands. They receive the bread and wine. Catholics call this the '<u>rite of Communion</u>'.

- <u>Orthodox</u> services contain <u>similar</u> elements to Anglican and Catholic ones: a sermon, Bible readings, the Nicene Creed and blessing of bread and wine.
- They include the '<u>Litany</u>', where the priest says <u>prayers</u> and the congregation responds with 'Lord have mercy'. Worshippers <u>sing</u> or <u>chant</u> for most of the service.
- Services are often <u>longer</u> than most Anglican and Catholic services, and people <u>stand</u> for the majority of the time.

2) For many, public worship helps them to feel involved in a <u>wider Christian community</u>. It can also help them feel <u>closer</u> to <u>Jesus</u> as they believe he is there in the church with them: "For where two or three gather in my name, there am I with them" (Matthew 18:20 NIV). Following <u>traditions</u> also helps Christians to feel <u>connected</u> to other worshippers throughout <u>history</u>.

## ...and Other Worship is **Non-Liturgical**

The worship of the <u>Society of Friends</u> (Quakers) is non-liturgical, and it is usually <u>unstructured</u>. Worshippers sit together in <u>silence</u>, but they are free to pray or speak <u>out loud</u>.

<u>Methodist</u> services <u>don't</u> have to follow a set structure, but there is a 'Methodist Worship Book' with suggested liturgy for parts of worship, e.g. the <u>Eucharist</u>. Services feature <u>hymns</u>, <u>readings</u>, a <u>sermon</u> and <u>prayers</u>. The <u>Eucharist</u> also takes place, but <u>not every week</u>.

Worship in <u>Evangelical</u> Churches (e.g. <u>Pentecostals</u>) is often <u>spontaneous</u>. Worshippers believe they're inspired by the <u>Spirit</u> — this is called '<u>charismatic</u> worship'. It might inspire them to pray, clap, dance or shout. Sometimes they '<u>speak in tongues</u>' — praying in an unrecognisable language.

Some Christians prefer the <u>freedom</u> of worshipping God in a <u>less-structured</u> way. Others view non-liturgical worship as <u>unsuitable</u> for the level of <u>respect</u> that religious services require.

## Some Christians also Engage in **Private Worship**

1) Many Christians worship informally <u>at home</u> (not just on Sundays). This can be anything from saying <u>grace</u> before a meal to singing <u>worship songs</u> with family, to reading the <u>Bible</u> or praying (see p.15).
2) Lots of Christians worship <u>both</u> publicly and privately — private worship can help them keep God in mind throughout their <u>everyday lives</u>. Some also find greater <u>freedom</u> in private worship — they decide how they worship God and so feel a <u>better connection</u> with God.

# The Sacraments

Sacraments play a key role in <u>worship</u> and <u>belief</u> for many Christians.

## Different Denominations Believe in **Different Sacraments**

1) A <u>sacrament</u> is a ceremony (usually carried out by a <u>minister</u> or <u>priest</u>) through which Christians believe they receive God's <u>grace</u>. It's a sign of God's grace <u>working</u> within them.

2) Roman Catholic and Orthodox Churches believe in <u>seven sacraments</u> (see p.13), but most Protestants accept only <u>baptism</u> and the <u>Eucharist</u> as sacraments — they believe only these two were <u>prescribed</u> by Jesus in the <u>Gospels</u>. Many believe that the sacraments bring people <u>closer to God</u>.

3) Quakers and the Salvation Army don't celebrate the Eucharist or any other sacraments, seeing them as <u>unnecessary symbols</u> for the inward acceptance of God's grace.

## **Baptism** is an **Important Sacrament** for Many Christians

1) Baptism is seen as a sacrament because <u>Jesus</u> was <u>baptised</u>. After his resurrection, he told his <u>disciples</u> to go out and <u>baptise people</u>.

"...go and make disciples of all nations, baptising them in the name of the Father and of the Son and of the Holy Spirit" (Matthew 28:19 NIV).

2) Jesus also said "no one can enter the kingdom of God unless they are born of water and the Spirit" (John 3:5 NIV).

3) Baptism makes someone a member of God's <u>family</u> and <u>welcomes</u> them to the Church. Some Christians believe that <u>baptising</u> cleanses people from the <u>original sin</u> that everyone is born with.

4) <u>Babies</u> are baptised in many denominations, e.g. Anglican, Catholic and Methodist. (They will also baptise <u>adults</u> if they <u>weren't</u> baptised as children and want to join the Church.)

5) A sign of the <u>cross</u> is made on the baby, and in many Churches <u>holy water</u> is poured <u>three</u> times over the forehead (in the name of the <u>Father</u>, <u>Son</u> and <u>Holy Spirit</u>). Orthodox Christians baptise babies by <u>total immersion</u>.

6) Denominations that baptise babies also usually have <u>confirmation</u> — a person 'confirms' their faith when they reach an age that they can <u>declare</u> it <u>themselves</u>.

7) But some denominations — for example Baptists and Pentecostals — believe you <u>shouldn't</u> be baptised until you're old enough to accept Christianity for <u>yourself</u>. They hold <u>believers' baptisms</u>, when adults who wish to join the Church are baptised by <u>total immersion</u>.

## Immerse yourself and learn all about baptism

Close the book and jot down the beliefs of the different denominations about baptism.

# The Sacraments

Catholics believe there are <u>seven</u> specific sacraments through which God can communicate his <u>grace</u> directly. Some see the <u>whole world</u> as <u>sacramental</u> — they can experience <u>God's grace</u> through his creation.

## The **Seven Sacraments** — God Shows His **Grace**

### 1) Baptism

This marks a person's official <u>entry</u> into the Church (see p.12).

> "The seven sacraments touch all the stages and all the important moments of Christian life..." Catechism of the Catholic Church, 1210

### 2) Confirmation

In this ceremony, a Christian (often a teenager) <u>renews</u> the vows made on their behalf at baptism. <u>Confirmation</u> is believed to <u>strengthen the ties</u> of the confirmed to the Church and to God. In Catholic confirmations, the bishop anoints the believer's forehead with holy oil called <u>chrism</u>.

### 3) Reconciliation

This involves <u>confession</u> of a sin, following by <u>contrition</u>, <u>penance</u> and <u>absolution</u>. This is how Catholics seek to obtain <u>forgiveness</u> for the sins they commit. They must <u>tell</u> a priest about any <u>sinful</u> things that they've done. The priest will give a <u>penance</u> (a certain number of prayers to be said, or an action to be done) and will then pronounce <u>absolution</u> (God's forgiveness).

### 4) Anointing the sick

A priest or bishop anoints a <u>seriously unwell person</u> with the <u>oil of the sick</u>. Catholics believe that, through this, the <u>Holy Spirit</u> renews the person's <u>faith</u> and <u>strength</u> to <u>cope</u> with their illness and <u>accept</u> their suffering. The anointing is also believed to <u>link</u> the person's suffering to <u>Christ's</u> suffering, allow their <u>sins</u> to be forgiven and to <u>heal</u> them, if that is <u>God's will</u>.

### 5) Matrimony

Catholics believe Jesus performed his <u>first miracle</u> at a <u>wedding</u>. They believe that God is <u>present</u> at the ceremony and <u>promises</u> are made before him — couples joined in <u>Holy Matrimony</u> should be together for <u>life</u>. As it's a sacrament, the union is a way that God <u>blesses</u> the couple, and he also blesses them <u>through</u> one another.

### 6) Holy orders

This is the process by which men are ordained as <u>deacons</u>, <u>priests</u> or <u>bishops</u>. Like matrimony, it is a <u>commitment</u> for life.

### 7) Eucharist

The Eucharist (Mass) is seen as "the source and summit of the Christian life" (Catechism of the Catholic Church 1324). Receiving the <u>body</u> and <u>blood</u> of Christ (see p.14) <u>joins</u> people together in their faith and gives them the <u>strength</u> to live Christian lives and face any <u>problems</u> they may encounter.

Some of the bread and wine that is <u>blessed</u> but <u>not</u> <u>consumed</u> is kept in the church — people believe <u>Jesus</u> is still <u>present</u> in it, and <u>focus</u> on it as they pray and express their love for Jesus. This is known as 'eucharistic adoration'.

> "...in the breaking of the Eucharistic bread, we are taken up into communion with Him and with one another." Lumen gentium Chapter 1 Paragraph 7:53

# The Sacraments

Christians celebrate the Eucharist by sharing bread and wine as Jesus did at the Last Supper. The Eucharist is incredibly important to some Christians, but is less so for others — every denomination has different beliefs about it.

## There are Many Different Understandings of the Eucharist

The Eucharist is where Christians remember the Last Supper (see p.6) with bread and wine.
Many denominations see it as a sacrament, but have different beliefs about the bread and wine:

- Roman Catholics believe in transubstantiation (i.e. the bread and wine used at Mass become the flesh and blood of Christ), and every Mass is a re-enactment of Christ's sacrifice (see p.6). They believe that they receive the saving power of Jesus into themselves through the bread and wine.

- Lutherans, Methodists and most Anglicans believe Holy Communion is more than just an 'intellectual' commemoration of the Last Supper — it's a re-enactment. They believe that there is a 'real presence' of Christ in the bread and wine, but they don't believe that transubstantiation occurs.

  "Transubstantiation... in the Supper of the Lord, cannot be proved by holy Writ..." 39 Articles XXVIII

- Baptists view the bread and wine as symbols, but believe that God is present through the act of Christians coming together to share Communion. The bread and non-alcoholic wine are set out on a simple table. The bread is later offered from person to person, and the wine drunk from small individual cups.

- Denominations which place more meaning on the bread and wine (e.g. Catholicism and Orthodox) hold Eucharists more often — they believe it's essential for sustaining their relationship with God. They tend to use a more ornate table (an altar), and have more ritual surrounding the Eucharist (e.g. using incense). Catholics will be given bread by the priest and drink wine from a shared cup. Orthodox Christians are given the bread and wine together on a special spoon.

## Catholic Funerals have Three Parts

Read this if you're studying Catholic Christianity.

The funeral rite isn't a sacrament, but it's important. It has three parts to it:

1) The Vigil of Prayer takes place the day before the funeral and is sometimes held at home. Readings and prayers form the service, which aims to help family and friends prepare to say goodbye.

2) Attending a funeral allows Catholics to join together in praying to God to take care of the person. The Funeral Liturgy often includes Holy Communion (the 'Requiem Mass'). Its purpose is to pray for the soul of the dead person. The coffin is covered with a white cloth (a pall) as it is carried into the church. The coffin is sprinkled with holy water and the priest says, "In the waters of baptism [name] died with Christ, and rose with him to new life. May s/he now share with him in eternal glory." The coffin is later sprinkled again and perfumed with incense. The Paschal candle sits beside it.

3) The Committal is a short ceremony that happens at the cemetery (or the crematorium if the person wished to be cremated). The priest says "ashes to ashes, dust to dust" as the body goes back to the earth.

**EXAM TIP**

## Each denomination treats the Eucharist differently

In your exam, if you can't remember the names of which denomination believe what you can just say "some denominations believe..." and "other denominations believe...". But if you can remember the denominations put them down — it'll show you have a greater understanding.

# Prayer and Pilgrimage

Prayer and pilgrimage are both ways in which Christians might strengthen their relationship with God.

## Prayer Puts People In Touch with their God

1) Prayer is when believers mentally or vocally communicate with God — it should be part of daily life. The Catechism of the Catholic Church (2559) says that "Prayer is the raising of one's mind and heart to God". During prayer people might thank God (thanksgiving), worship God (adoration) or admit sins (confession). They might ask God for something (supplication) or to help other people (intercession).

2) Believers draw comfort from the fact that God is listening to them. They also listen for what he is saying to them — many believe prayer helps them to find out what God wants them to do in life.

3) Most denominations have formal, set prayers that are Church tradition — they can be said during acts of worship in church, and also in private.

4) The Lord's Prayer is very important. It's based on the words Jesus used when he told his disciples how to pray. It covers key themes — e.g. the idea that God is 'Our Father' and he provides for people's physical needs.

> "This, then, is how you should pray: 'Our Father in heaven, hallowed be your name, your kingdom come, your will be done, on earth as it is in heaven. Give us today our daily bread. And forgive us our debts, as we also have forgiven our debtors. And lead us not into temptation, but deliver us from the evil one.' " Matthew 6:9-13 NIV

5) Informal prayers are where the individual talks to God in their own words. They're sometimes called 'extempore' prayers, and can be used in worship and privately. Informal prayers are more personal and show the individual's connection with God — many Christians prefer them to set prayers.

*Read this box if you're studying Catholic Christianity.*

### Catholic Forms of Popular Piety

1) Catholics use the Rosary (a string with a cross and beads) when praying. The cross is held when reciting the Apostles' Creed, and prayers are said as the beads are moved through the fingers, e.g. Ave Maria (Hail Mary). The beads represent the key events in Christianity (known as mysteries), such as the birth, death and resurrection of Jesus — the rosary helps people think about these while praying.

2) The 'Stations of the Cross' are pictures in church of Jesus's suffering — Catholics use them as a focus for contemplation on these events.

3) Some disagree with these forms of 'popular piety'. Some Protestants think the rosary encourages prayers to be repeated without giving thought to the words themselves. Many Protestants wouldn't say the Hail Mary prayer, as most don't believe in praying to Mary. Some people might argue that praying while focusing on the Stations of the Cross creates a danger of worshipping idols.

## Pilgrimages can help Believers feel Nearer to God

1) Pilgrimages aren't compulsory in Christianity, but many see them as important. The Catechism of the Catholic Church (2691) says that "Pilgrimages evoke our earthly journey toward heaven...". Luke 2:41-43 tells the story of the pilgrimage Jesus and his parents made to Jerusalem.

2) Christians make pilgrimages to seek healing or forgiveness, to connect to God or to deepen their faith. Pilgrimages also provide the chance to escape normal life and to concentrate more on religion. Pilgrims can learn from each other. The journey reflects the path they're trying to follow towards God.

3) People may visit places that are significant in Christianity — such as Jerusalem, where they can visit key places in Jesus's life and death. Roman Catholics often visit Rome, the home of the Pope.

4) Some Christians, especially Catholics, make pilgrimages to shrines where Mary has appeared. These include Walsingham (which is popular with some Anglicans as well as Catholics) and Lourdes. The water in Lourdes is said to have healing properties which can cure ill health, and lots of people believe miracles take place there. Catholics also visit shrines to saints.

5) Protestants are more likely to visit places they can find peace to study the Bible and pray — e.g. the quiet island of Iona (which has a long history of Christianity), or Taizé where they can join worship at the monastery. Some Christians see shrines such as Lourdes as being too commercialised, with too many people. Some regard pilgrimage as unnecessary — the journey inside is what matters.

# Christmas and Easter

Christmas and Easter are the two most important <u>celebrations</u> in the Christian calendar.

## Christmas is a Celebration of Jesus's Birth

1) Christmas is celebrated by most Christians on <u>25th December</u> (for <u>Orthodox</u> Christians it's <u>7th January</u>). It celebrates how Jesus was born in <u>Bethlehem</u> — there he was worshipped by <u>shepherds</u> after an <u>angel</u> told them that "a Saviour has been born to you; he is the Messiah, the Lord" (Luke 2:11 NIV).

2) Christmas comes after a period called <u>Advent</u>, which begins four Sundays before Christmas. Advent is significant for many Christians as it's time they spend <u>getting ready</u> to celebrate <u>Jesus's birth</u> — a time for <u>prayer</u> and <u>reflection</u>. <u>Advent candles</u> are lit in homes and churches, and children may use <u>Advent calendars</u> to count off the days until Christmas.

3) Lots of Roman Catholic, Orthodox and Anglican churches have a '<u>Midnight Mass</u>' to welcome Christmas Day, and most Christians go to church on <u>Christmas morning</u> to <u>celebrate</u>.

4) Many churches hold services in the days <u>after Christmas</u>, carrying on to <u>Epiphany</u> (6th January) — the day that the <u>Magi</u> (wise men) went to see Jesus in Bethlehem.

5) Customs <u>vary</u> around the world. <u>Gifts</u> are exchanged to symbolise the fact that Jesus was <u>God's gift</u> to the world, and to remember how the <u>Magi</u> "presented him with gifts of gold, frankincense and myrrh" (Matthew 2:11 NIV).

6) Some Christians dislike modern Christmas <u>traditions</u> and <u>customs</u>, e.g. <u>Santa Claus</u> (Father Christmas), giving <u>expensive presents</u>, and <u>excessive eating</u> and <u>drinking</u>. They believe that some of these modern traditions <u>devalue</u> the <u>true meaning</u> of Christmas. Others feel that it has retained too much <u>pagan</u> influence, such as Christmas trees.

## Easter celebrates Jesus's Resurrection

> 1 Corinthians 15:14 outlines how important the Resurrection is for Christians and their beliefs: "And if Christ has not been raised, our preaching is useless and so is your faith" (NIV).

1) Easter is the most <u>important</u> festival for Christians, since it celebrates <u>Jesus's victory</u> over death, when God raised him <u>back to life</u> after his crucifixion (see p.7). This reminds people that God <u>loves</u> them so much that he was <u>willing</u> to suffer death on the cross and gives them hope of <u>eternal life</u>.

2) <u>Lent</u> is the <u>40 days</u> before Easter. On <u>Ash Wednesday</u> (the first day of Lent), ash is put on believers' <u>foreheads</u> to show they're sorry for their <u>sins</u>. Some Christians <u>fast</u> (<u>eat less</u> and have only <u>simple food</u>) during Lent to mark when Jesus fasted for 40 days in the desert. They <u>stop fasting</u> on <u>Easter Sunday</u>.

3) The lead-up to <u>Easter Day</u>, the day of resurrection, is marked by a number of important events:

- <u>Palm Sunday</u> is the Sunday before Easter, when Christians remember Jesus's <u>triumphant entry</u> into Jerusalem. This marks the beginning of <u>Holy Week</u> — Jesus's final week before his <u>crucifixion</u>.
- <u>Maundy Thursday</u> commemorates the <u>Last Supper</u> held on the night before Jesus died.
- <u>Good Friday</u> recalls Jesus's <u>crucifixion</u> — special services are held, particularly on Friday afternoon. Some services last <u>three hours</u> to mark Jesus's final three hours on the <u>cross</u>, when the sky became <u>dark</u>.

4) <u>Easter Day</u> is a <u>joyous</u> occasion when Jesus's resurrection is celebrated.

- Some churches hold services on the Saturday night, and most have <u>special services</u> on the Sunday morning.
- The <u>Paschal candle</u> is lit during services in Anglican and Catholic churches. Worshippers light their own candle from its flame, which represents Jesus as the <u>Light of the World</u>.
- Some churches hold <u>sunrise services</u> to remember how Mary Magdalene discovered at daybreak that Jesus's tomb was empty. The rising of the <u>sun</u> is symbolic of <u>God's Son</u> rising from the dead.
- <u>Eggs</u> are associated with Easter as a symbol of <u>new life</u>. Some view chocolate Easter eggs as <u>commercialisation</u> of the festival.

## It's time to celebrate...

Working from Lent to Easter Sunday, draw a timeline of Christian Easter celebrations.
Next to each day, scribble down what happens and then check your answers against this page.

# The Work of the Church

Churches aren't just about holding services.  They're active in the local community too.

## Churches play an **Important Role** in the **Local Community**

Most communities in the UK have access to at least one church.  The role of the local church is to put the Christian faith into action — this includes caring for the community, as seen in lots of Christian teaching:

> In 1 Peter 5:2-3, the leaders of the church are asked to set an example for the congregation through their actions: "...be shepherds of God's flock that is under your care, watching over them... being examples to the flock" (NIV).

> In Mark 12:31, Jesus said that the second most important commandment is "Love your neighbour as yourself" (NIV).

> Paragraph 26 of Gaudium et spes, a key Catholic document of the Second Vatican Council, states: "Every social group must take account of the needs and legitimate aspirations of other groups, and even of the general welfare of the entire human family."

Churches put this into practice in many different ways:

1) By providing regular services and a place for quiet reflection — most churches hold a Sunday service and may also have other acts of worship throughout the week.
2) By providing rites of passage such as baptisms, confirmations, weddings and funerals (see p.12-14).
3) By running youth groups and Sunday Schools to engage young people in the local community.
4) By offering support and advice to people in need — e.g. visiting and praying for people in hospital.
5) Some churchgoers work as Street Pastors — they volunteer in towns and cities on Friday and Saturday nights to support anyone in need of help. This demonstrates Christian love.
6) Some foodbanks in the UK are run by churches.  People donate food which the foodbank then distributes to those who need it the most.
7) Many churches also raise money for charity.

*Different denominations might work together, e.g. through community projects or joint services. This is called 'ecumenism'.*

## **Reconciliation** works Towards **Peace** and **Unity**

1) Christians believe in justice — all people are equal in God's eyes, so they should be treated fairly. Christian organisations help people being treated unfairly due to war, religious persecution or poverty.
2) In Matthew 5:9 Jesus said "Blessed are the peacemakers" (NIV).  Christians believe that reconciliation (coming together and making peace) is needed between people who have been in conflict with one another — just as Jesus brought God and humankind together through the atonement (p.8).
3) These are two examples of organisations that work for reconciliation:

> The Corrymeela Community in Northern Ireland was founded to help heal the country's political and religious divisions.  It works with people in areas where there is tension and strives to help people understand each other and reconcile through group activities and discussions.

> Pax Christi is an international Catholic organisation working for human rights, disarmament and peace.  They believe violence should be avoided, and they work to create a world where people can live in harmony.

## Churches work to help people both locally and globally

See if you can write down seven ways that churches play a role in local communities.

# The Work of the Church

The Church works to <u>protect</u> Christians and to spread Christianity <u>around the world</u>.

## Organisations and Churches help **Persecuted Christians**

1) Millions around the world <u>suffer</u> for being Christians — some endure <u>prison sentences</u> or even <u>death</u>.

2) Organisations give support by providing <u>Bibles</u> so people can continue worshipping in secret. They offer <u>training</u> to church members and <u>support</u> people who have lost their homes.

3) Churches <u>pray</u> for the persecuted and may send <u>money</u>. Christians might <u>petition</u> for <u>government</u> help.

## **Evangelism Tells** People about Christianity

1) <u>Evangelism</u> means spreading the Christian <u>message</u> with the aim of <u>converting</u> people.

2) In Mark 16:15, Jesus told his disciples to "Go into all the world and preach the gospel to all creation" (NIV). Many Christians believe that they should be prepared to do the same.

> "As the Father has sent me, I am sending you." John 20:21 NIV

3) They believe that by evangelising they can help people <u>discover</u> their <u>real purpose</u> in life and find <u>salvation</u>. They feel <u>excited</u> to tell other people about <u>Jesus's love</u> — Pope Francis said "The primary reason for evangelizing is the love of Jesus which we have received..." (Evangelii Gaudium 264).

4) For some, evangelism is about telling people <u>directly</u> about God. This can sometimes cause problems — people may feel <u>offended</u>. Others try to <u>demonstrate</u> God's love through their actions, to bring people <u>closer</u> to God. Here are a few different types of evangelism:

- <u>Gideons</u> distribute copies of the <u>Bible</u> in places like hotels and care homes.
- Churches might ask the congregation to <u>bring</u> along a <u>friend</u> who wouldn't normally go to church.
- The <u>Salvation Army</u> helps people by providing <u>hot meals</u> and <u>beds</u> for homeless people. They also attend <u>emergencies</u>, such as floods.

5) As church attendance falls, evangelism is increasingly important. The Church of England and Church in Wales are finding ways to interest <u>new people</u> in churches that <u>don't</u> follow the <u>traditional model</u> — for example worshipping in alternative venues like <u>cafés</u>, or creating a café <u>atmosphere</u> in church. Through initiatives called '<u>Fresh Expressions</u>' and '<u>Pioneer Ministry</u>', they offer a new approach for modern society.

6) <u>Missionaries</u> spread the Christian message <u>abroad</u>. Many aren't there to preach, but to use their <u>skills</u> to help <u>disadvantaged people</u> — e.g. a doctor might choose to work in a poor country. These people demonstrate the message of Christianity through their <u>actions</u>.

## Christians work to spread the message of Christianity

There are a lot of different ways to spread the message of Christianity — make sure you've read this page thoroughly and can give a few examples of evangelism. It would also be helpful if you remembered some quotes from the Bible or other sacred texts which demonstrate why evangelism is so important.

# The Work of the Church

Helping the <u>less fortunate</u> is an important part of Christianity — this is shown through the work of <u>Christian charities</u>.

## Christian **Charities** Help Those in Need

1) In the story of the <u>sheep</u> and <u>goats</u> (Matthew 25:31-46), Jesus explains that people who have been <u>good</u> (the sheep) and have helped others will be <u>looked after</u> by God. People who <u>haven't</u> (the goats) will <u>suffer</u>. The story tells Christians that they are <u>helping Jesus</u> when they help others.

2) Because of this, <u>charity</u> is very important to many Christians. But it's <u>not</u> all about giving <u>money</u> — it must be done with <u>love</u>. In 1 Corinthians 13:3, St Paul said "If I give all I possess to the poor... but do not have love, I gain nothing" (NIV).

3) Here are some <u>examples</u> of Christian charities and the work they do:

> <u>Christian Aid</u> works <u>globally</u> to relieve poverty. They set up projects in the developing world, drawing on the skills of <u>local people</u>. The organisation also aims to change <u>government policy</u> to help reduce the suffering of the world's poor, e.g. through <u>debt relief</u>, and <u>fair-trade</u> products.

> <u>CAFOD</u> (Catholic Agency for Overseas Development) works to fight <u>poverty</u> and <u>injustice</u> around the world. They work through churches, helping in <u>emergencies</u>, but also giving people the <u>skills</u> to help themselves.

> Christian Aid and CAFOD believe in <u>development</u> — 'helping people to help themselves', <u>whatever</u> their faith.

> <u>Tearfund</u>® is an <u>evangelical</u> organisation — it helps communities with projects run <u>through</u> their <u>churches</u>. Their work includes trying to end <u>hunger</u>, resolving <u>tension</u> in conflict zones and helping <u>refugees</u>. They also help areas hit by <u>natural disasters</u>.

## There are many **Catholic Charities**

*Read this if you're studying <u>Catholic Christianity</u>.*

Evangelii Gaudium (187) says that Catholics should strive to <u>help</u> the <u>poor</u> "to be fully a part of society". <u>CAFOD</u> (see above) is a Roman Catholic organisation, and there are many others that help those in need:

- <u>Trócaire</u>, part of the Irish Catholic Church, <u>provides aid</u> abroad. They help people <u>escape poverty</u>, but also help in <u>emergencies</u>.

- The <u>St Vincent de Paul Society</u> (SVP) helps people in <u>poverty</u>. They provide support by <u>visiting</u> the isolated and ill, helping them with <u>daily tasks</u>, providing <u>schemes</u> and <u>clubs</u> to help the disabled, and <u>donating food</u> to the homeless.

- <u>Missio</u> is an organisation that <u>supports churches</u> abroad that are <u>struggling</u> to fund themselves, e.g. by <u>training</u> church leaders. It also runs projects to provide <u>education</u> and <u>healthcare</u> for children living in poverty.

**REVISION TASK**

## Christian charities help people in need all over the world

Cover the page and write down all the Christian charities you can remember, giving details of the work each of them does, and explain why charity is important to Christians.

# Worked Exam Questions

On this page there are some more exam-style questions with model answers.
And on the next page there are some questions for you to answer yourself.

**1**   Which of the following is an international Christian organisation?
Put a tick (✓) in the correct box.

|  |  |  |
|---|---|---|
| **A** | WaterAid | ☐ |
| **B** | UNICEF | ☐ |
| **C** | CAFOD | ✓ |
| **D** | Plan UK | ☐ |

*[1 mark]*

*⌐This question is only for students studying Catholic Christianity.⌐*

**2**   Give two reasons why Catholics pray with a rosary.

**1)** Using the rosary helps them to think about events in Jesus's life while praying.

**2)** Catholics use the beads to count the number of prayers they have said.

*[2 marks]*

**3**   Explain two contrasting views about infant baptism.

Some Christians believe infant baptism is a good thing because all humans are born with original sin, and baptism cleanses them of it.

However, other Christians believe that adults, not children, should be baptised since Jesus was baptised as an adult, so Christians should follow his example.

*[4 marks]*

**4**   Explain two reasons why Christian organisations work to promote reconciliation.
Your answer should refer to specific Christian teachings or sacred texts.

Reconciliation means making peace between people. Jesus said, "Blessed are the peacemakers" (Matthew 5:9 NIV), so Christians believe that they should work to promote peace in the world in order to be blessed.

Christians also believe that people are all equal, and part of one community, so we should try to live in harmony together and promote peace.

*[5 marks]*

# Exam Questions

**5**  Which of the following is **not** regularly included in a weekly church service?
Put a tick (✓) in the correct box.

A  Bible readings ☐

B  Prayers ☐

C  A baptism ☐

D  A sermon ☐

*[1 mark]*

**6**  Explain two ways in which Christians mark the approach and celebration of Easter.
Your answer should refer to specific Christian teachings or sacred texts.

*If you're studying Catholic Christianity, you don't need to answer this question.*

..............................................................................................................................

..............................................................................................................................

..............................................................................................................................

..............................................................................................................................

..............................................................................................................................

..............................................................................................................................

..............................................................................................................................

..............................................................................................................................

*[5 marks]*

**7**  'Pilgrimage is not important for modern Christians.'

Evaluate this statement. Your answer should include the following:
• examples from Christian teachings
• arguments that support the statement
• arguments that disagree with the statement
• a conclusion.

*Write your answer on a separate sheet of paper.*

*[12 marks]*

# Revision Summary

That's the section on Christianity and Catholic Christianity finished — now it's time to see if you can remember it all.

- Try these questions and <u>tick off each one</u> when you <u>get it right</u>.
- When you've done <u>all the questions</u> for a topic and are <u>completely happy</u> with it, tick off the topic.

## Beliefs (p.1-8) ☑

1) Which books of the Bible give accounts of Jesus's life?
2) What word, often used to describe God, means all-powerful?
3) What word is used to describe how God knows everything?
4) Name the three persons in the Trinity.
5) What is the name of the statement of Christian beliefs that was written in the 4th century?
6) How many days does the book of Genesis say it took God to create the world?
7) What two words are used to describe the power humans were given over creation, and their duty to look after it?
8) What phrase describes evil entering the world when Adam and Eve disobeyed God?
9) What phrase describes the belief that every human being is born with a flawed nature?
10) Name two different types of evil, and give a brief definition of each.
11) What do Catholic Christians believe happens in Purgatory? ← *Only answer Q11 if you're studying Catholic Christianity.*
12) What do Christians believe will happen at the Last Judgement?
13) What is the name of the final meal that Jesus shared with his disciples before his death?
14) What did the sign on Jesus's cross say?
15) What word describes Jesus coming back to life?
16) What word describes the reconciliation between God and humanity enabled by Jesus's death?
17) What do Christians believe they must do to get to heaven?

## Practices (p.11-19) ☑

18) What is meant by 'liturgical' worship?
19) Name three elements of an Anglican or Catholic Eucharist service.
20) Give an example of non-liturgical worship.
21) Give a reason why some Christians might prefer liturgical worship to private worship.
22) Describe the sacraments of Baptism and the Eucharist.
23) Name the five other sacraments in Catholic Christianity.
24) Name the three parts of a Catholic funeral. ← *Only answer Q23, 24 and 26 if you're studying Catholic Christianity.*
25) Name the prayer that Jesus taught his disciples.
26) What is a Rosary?
27) Name a place to which Christians might make a pilgrimage.
28) What is Advent?
29) What is the 40-day period before Easter called?
30) What events are remembered on Palm Sunday, Maundy Thursday, Good Friday and Easter Day?
31) Give three ways in which a church might try to help the local community.
32) What does reconciliation mean?
33) What is evangelism?
34) Name two Christian charities that help those in need.

## Introduction to Islam                                    Islam

Islam was founded in the 7th century.  It shares some ideas with Judaism and Christianity.  Muslims believe in one god, Allah.  The Qur'an is the Muslim holy book — Muslims also follow the prophet Muhammad's teachings.

## Islam is Divided into Two Main Traditions — Sunni and Shi'a

1) About 85-90% of Muslims are Sunni Muslims — most of the rest are Shi'a Muslims.

2) Muhammad was the founder of Islam — Allah revealed the Qur'an to him.  After Muhammad died, Muslims had to choose a new leader (caliph).  The next four caliphs were Abu Bakr, Umar, Uthman and Ali.

3) However, some Muslims had wanted Ali to be the first caliph, and thought the first three caliphs shouldn't have been given the role.  Others said Ali shouldn't be the caliph at all.

4) After Ali died, two groups formed — the Sunnis and the Shi'as.  Each group followed a different line of caliphs.  The Sunnis accepted the next caliph after Ali, but the Shi'as (Shi'at Ali or Party of Ali) followed Ali's descendants.  Sunnis and Shi'as have been separate groups ever since.

## Sunnis and Shi'as have Many Similar Beliefs

Sunnis and Shi'as share many beliefs, but have some different ideas.  Their basic beliefs — articles of faith — are slightly different, but they share beliefs in Allah, the holy books, prophets and a day of judgement.  These, along with a belief in angels, are mentioned in the Qur'an (4:136) and other teachings, e.g. Sahih Muslim 1:4.

There are six articles of faith in Sunni Islam:
1) belief that Allah is the one and only god (Tawhid)
2) belief in angels (Malaikah)
3) belief in the holy books
4) belief in Allah's prophets (Nubuwwah)
5) belief in the Day of Judgement
6) belief that Allah knows and decides everything that's going to happen (predestination — al-Qadr)

There are five articles of faith in Shi'a Islam.  They're known as the Usul ad-Din — foundations of faith:
1) belief that Allah is the one and only god (Tawhid)
2) belief in divine justice (Adalat)
3) belief in prophethood (Nubuwwah)
4) belief in the authority of imams (Imamah)
5) belief in the Day of Resurrection (Ma'ad)

### Key Sunni beliefs

1) No one after Muhammad received knowledge from Allah.  Muslims should focus on Muhammad and his way of life (sunnah — see p.27) rather than paying too much attention to Ali and his sons.

2) Muslims should be guided by the consensus (majority view) of the community.

### Key Shi'a beliefs

1) Ali was the first true caliph.  Allah gave him knowledge to ensure his teaching and actions were right.

2) There are many branches of Shi'a Islam.  They share a common belief in a line of imams after Ali, who all had the same knowledge from Allah as Ali.  Shi'a imams are leaders and figureheads of the religion.  They're all descendants of Muhammad.  In Sunni Islam, the word 'imam' simply means 'prayer leader'.

3) The different branches of Shi'a Islam split off from each other after disagreements about the line of imams.  The Twelvers are the largest branch, but there are many others.

4) Twelver Shi'as believe in a line of 12 imams, the last of whom is in hiding and will eventually return.  The Twelvers are led by religious scholars while they wait for the last imam's return.

5) Isma'ili Shi'as (often called 'Seveners') thought the seventh imam should be Isma'il, the elder brother of the one chosen by the Twelvers.  The biggest group of Isma'ilis today, the Nizaris, think each imam can select the next and are still led by an imam now, known as the Aga Khan.

## Sunni is the biggest denomination in Islam
Grab a piece of paper and see if you can write down the articles of faith for Sunni and Shi'a Islam.

# Key Beliefs in Islam

Islam is a <u>monotheistic</u> religion — Muslims believe in only <u>one god</u>, <u>Allah</u> (this concept is known as <u>Tawhid</u>).

## Tawhid is Central to Islam

"Say, 'He is Allah, [who is] One.' " *Qur'an 112:1*

1) The word <u>Allah</u> is from the Arabic <u>al-ilah</u>, meaning 'the god', i.e. the <u>only</u> god. Several of the <u>ninety-nine</u> <u>names</u> of Allah (see below) make this clear, including <u>al-Ahad</u> (the one and only) and <u>al-Wahid</u> (the one).

2) Saying Allah is the <u>only god</u> is the first part of the <u>shahadah</u>, the Muslim <u>declaration of faith</u> (see p.31).

3) <u>Shirk</u> — believing in <u>other gods</u> as well as Allah, or that anyone or thing could share in Allah's <u>oneness</u> — is seen as the <u>worst sin</u>. Muslims therefore disagree with the <u>Christian</u> idea of the <u>Holy Trinity</u> (see p.2) and <u>polytheism</u> (believing in <u>multiple gods</u>). <u>Images</u> of Muhammad aren't allowed, in case of <u>shirk</u>.

> "Allah does not forgive association with Him, but He forgives what is less than that..."
> Qur'an 4:116. 'Association with Him' is worshipping other gods as well as Allah.

4) According to a <u>hadith</u> (see p.27), <u>Muhammad</u> said that when telling <u>non-Muslims</u> about Islam, the <u>first thing</u> Muslims should mention is <u>Tawhid</u>.

"let the first thing to which you will invite them, be the Tauhid [Tawhid] of Allah." *Sahih al-Bukhari 93:469*

## Allah has Many Characteristics

### 1) Merciful

Muslims believe Allah shows <u>mercy</u> and <u>compassion</u>. <u>All but one</u> of the Qur'an's chapters <u>begin</u> by saying this — it's known as the <u>bismillah</u>. They believe Allah is <u>kind</u> and <u>forgives</u> people's <u>sins</u>.

"In the name of Allah, the Entirely Merciful, the Especially Merciful" (Qur'an 1:1) is the phrase known as the <u>bismillah</u>.

### 2) Omnipotent

Allah is <u>all-powerful</u>. He <u>created</u> the <u>universe</u> and is in <u>control</u> of everything. He has <u>predetermined</u> people's lives (decided <u>what will happen</u>), though people do have <u>free will</u> (see p.28).

### 3) Benevolent

Allah is <u>all-good</u> — he can do no evil. He <u>cares</u> for his people — this is seen in his <u>intervention</u> in the world, e.g. his <u>revelations</u> to the prophets were to show people how to live a <u>good life</u>.

### 4) Just

Muslims believe Allah will <u>judge</u> people's behaviour in a <u>fair way</u>. This concept is particularly <u>important</u> to <u>Shi'a</u> Muslims — known as <u>Adalat</u>, it's one of the <u>Usul ad-Din</u> (see p.23).

### 5) Immanent

Allah is <u>present</u> and <u>involved</u> in the world. He's <u>close</u> to every human and <u>knows</u> them.

"And We have already created man and know what his soul whispers to him, and We are closer to him than [his] jugular vein." *Qur'an 50:16*

### 6) Transcendent

Allah's also <u>above everything</u> — he can't be thought of in <u>human</u> terms. He has <u>no equal</u>.

There are <u>ninety-nine names</u> for Allah listed in the Qur'an. Each refers to one of his <u>characteristics</u>. Points <u>1-4</u> above are <u>each</u> English translations of one of these names (originally in <u>Arabic</u>). Muslims recite them in <u>daily prayers</u>.

---

## You don't need to learn all ninety-nine names of Allah

Cover this page and see if you can write down the six characteristics of Allah with their definitions.

# Key Beliefs in Islam

The <u>prophets</u> were how Allah sent his <u>message</u> to humanity, ending with <u>Muhammad</u> — the <u>seal of the prophets</u>.

## Adam and Ibrahim were Prophets...

Belief in the prophets is an article of faith for both Sunnis and Shi'as (p.23).

1) Allah's <u>compassion</u> means he can't leave people to <u>sin</u> without <u>helping</u> them. So he sends <u>messages</u> about how to live a <u>good</u> life. He almost always does this via <u>angels</u>, who pass on his words to human <u>prophets</u> (<u>rasuls</u>). <u>Risalah</u> is the concept of <u>messengership</u> — the way Allah <u>communicates</u> with <u>humans</u>.

2) Allah <u>chose</u> many people as <u>prophets</u>. <u>25</u> prophets are mentioned in the Qur'an, although some believe there have been <u>124 000</u>. Some prophets were given <u>holy books</u> to pass on to humankind.

3) Muslims believe the prophets taught the <u>same basic ideas</u>, most importantly belief in <u>one god</u>. They see all the prophets as <u>equal</u> to each other — "We make no distinction between any of them" (Qur'an 2:136).

4) Muslims believe the <u>prophets</u> performed <u>miracles</u> — they did so to <u>prove</u> they were really prophets.

5) The first prophet was <u>Adam</u>, who was also the <u>first man</u>, created by Allah in his image. Others were <u>Ibrahim</u> (Abraham), <u>Isma'il</u> (Ishmael), <u>Musa</u> (Moses), <u>Dawud</u> (David), <u>Isa</u> (Jesus) and <u>Muhammad</u>.

6) <u>Adam</u> was sent to <u>Earth</u> after eating fruit <u>forbidden</u> to him by Allah. Allah <u>forgave</u> him his sin though. Adam is considered to have been the first <u>Muslim</u>. Some believe he first built the <u>Ka'aba</u> (p.34).

7) <u>Ibrahim rejected</u> the idea of <u>many different</u> gods and was a <u>holy</u> man. He proved his <u>faith</u> by being willing to <u>sacrifice</u> his own son, <u>Isma'il</u> (see p.35). Ibrahim is thought to have rebuilt the <u>Ka'aba</u> and he and his family's story plays an <u>important role</u> in the <u>hajj</u> rituals (see p.34).

## ...Isma'il, Musa, Dawud, Isa and Muhammad were Prophets too

1) Ibrahim's son <u>Isma'il</u> was also a prophet and helped him build the <u>Ka'aba</u>. It's believed many Arabs, including <u>Muhammad</u>, are <u>descended</u> from Isma'il — he's known as <u>Abul Arab</u>, the father of the <u>Arabs</u>.

2) <u>Musa</u> is the <u>only prophet</u> that Allah spoke to <u>directly</u>, rather than through the angel <u>Jibril</u> (Gabriel). He's <u>important</u> as he kept trying to guide people to believing in <u>one god</u>, even when they worshipped <u>others</u>.

3) <u>Dawud</u> is known for <u>killing Jalut</u> (Goliath) during a battle between <u>Jalut</u>'s <u>large</u> army and <u>Talut</u>'s (Saul's) <u>smaller</u> one. <u>Dawud</u> later succeeded Talut as <u>king</u>. As well as his bravery, he's known for his <u>wisdom</u> and his <u>loyalty</u> to Allah — he would <u>pray</u> for a <u>third</u> of each night.

4) Allah sent <u>Isa</u> when he thought people had <u>strayed</u> from <u>Musa's</u> teachings. <u>Muslims</u> believe Isa <u>wasn't</u> <u>crucified</u> (Allah wouldn't let that happen) but after 3 years' teaching Allah brought him up into <u>heaven</u>.

5) Muslims believe all these <u>prophets</u> paved the way for <u>Muhammad</u>:

### Muhammad

- <u>Muhammad</u> was born about <u>570 CE</u> in <u>Makkah</u> (Mecca).
  One day, while Muhammad was <u>meditating</u>, Allah sent the <u>angel Jibril</u> to him with a message.

- Muhammad was <u>scared</u> at first, but as <u>Jibril</u> gradually revealed more and more of the message from Allah, Muhammad began <u>preaching</u> this message to <u>others</u>.

- The <u>early</u> messages said people should worship <u>one god</u>, <u>Allah</u>, and that people would be <u>judged</u> on their behaviour. Later on, the <u>revelations</u> gave more <u>detail</u> on <u>how</u> Muslims should live their lives.

- Eventually, this message from Allah was written down as the <u>Qur'an</u>.
  The <u>Qur'an</u> is seen by Muslims as a <u>miracle</u> — the <u>final revelation</u> from Allah.

- <u>Muhammad</u> is often called the 'seal of the prophets' — most Muslims believe he was the <u>last</u> prophet that there will be. He is believed to have been a <u>wise leader</u>, who settled disputes and brought different communities <u>together</u>. He performed several <u>miracles</u>.

- As <u>Muhammad</u> was Allah's last prophet, Muslims pay <u>particular attention</u> to his words and actions. They use them to work out how to live their lives (p.27), as they see him as a <u>role model</u>.

## Islam shares some of its prophets with Christianity and Judaism

When you're naming the prophets in your exam you can use the Muslim names or the Christian/Jewish names — just make sure you're consistent and stick with one way or the other.

# Key Beliefs in Islam

The Qur'an was revealed to Muhammad by the angel Jibril and is the literal word of Allah. It's really important.

## The Qur'an is the Word of Allah

Qur'an is sometimes spelt 'Koran' in English.

1) Muslims think the Qur'an is the most important holy book. They believe it's a complete and accurate record of Allah's exact words to Muhammad, as Qur'an 53:10-11 describes: "he revealed to His Servant what he revealed. The heart did not lie [about] what it saw." The Qur'an allows humans to know Allah.

2) In the Qur'an, Allah tells Muslims what they need to know and how to lead their lives to please him. Muslims try to live according to its guidance. This helps them be rewarded by Allah and get to Paradise.

3) Many Muslims learn the Qur'an by heart. The Qur'an was revealed in Arabic — if it's written in another language the meaning might change, so Muslims learn Arabic to ensure they're reading the true Qur'an.

4) There's often dispute over how to interpret the Qur'an though, e.g. in relation to jihad (p.34). It can be difficult to apply its teachings to modern life, because so much has changed since it was revealed.

## The Qur'an is Divided into 114 Surahs

1) The Qur'an is organised into 114 surahs (chapters), each made up of ayahs (verses). The surahs are in order of length — longest first, shortest last (except surah 1, a short statement of Muslims' basic beliefs).

2) Because the Qur'an is so important, Muslims treat it with great respect. The Qur'an is often ornately decorated, inside and out. Many Muslims:

> 1) keep their Qur'an wrapped up to keep it clean
> 2) wash their hands before touching it
> 3) keep it on a higher shelf than all other books
> 4) place it on a special stand when they read it

3) The Qur'an is read during private and public prayers, so Muslims get to know it well.

## Angels are Allah's Messengers

1) The purpose of angels is to follow Allah's orders and communicate with humans, often via the prophets. In heaven, they praise him and guard his throne. They welcome humans into paradise.

"They exalt [Him] night and day [and] do not slacken." Qur'an 21:20

2) They're thought to be genderless, made of light and to have wings. They're immortal and don't have free will, as their role is to obey Allah — they're therefore incapable of sin. Allah created them before humans.

3) Some angels record people's good and bad deeds for the Day of Judgement — Qur'an 43:80 says "Our messengers are with them recording". Guardian angels protect people from danger and evil. Some think they're the same thing and recording angels act as guardians too.

4) Belief in angels is an article of faith for Sunnis, so it's important. The thought of a guardian angel can be comforting for Muslims. Having an angel recording their deeds can influence Muslims to do good things.

5) Jibril (who you might know as Gabriel) is an important angel. He revealed Allah's words (the Qur'an) to Muhammad. He also revealed messages to other prophets, so he's known as the angel of revelation. He told Maryam (Mary) she was pregnant with Isa (Jesus) — see Qur'an 19:16-22.

"Gabriel ... has brought the Qur'an down upon your heart, [O Muhammad], by permission of Allah." Qur'an 2:97

6) Mika'il (Michael) is also an important angel. He asks Allah to forgive people's sins.

7) Izrail (Azrael) is the angel of death (Qur'an 32:11). He takes souls from people's bodies when they die.

8) It's believed that Israfil (Raphael) will blow the trumpet on the Day of Judgement.

---

**EXAM TIP**

## Allah revealed the Qur'an to Muhammad through the angel Jibril

You need to refer to sacred texts in your answers for 5-mark questions to get top marks. The Qur'an is a great source for this — just make sure you know a selection of quotations from it.

# Key Beliefs in Islam

Allah revealed holy books to other prophets, as well as revealing the Qur'an to Muhammad.

## There are Other Holy Books in Islam

As well as the Qur'an, Muslims see the Suhuf Ibrahim, the Tawrat, the Zabur and the Injil as holy books.
But they believe they've been changed over time through editing, and only the Qur'an exists in its original form.

1) The first holy book is thought to have been given to Ibrahim.
Known as the Suhuf Ibrahim (scrolls of Ibrahim), it is now lost.
The Qur'an mentions it several times, for example in Qur'an 87:18-19.

2) The Tawrat (Torah) is the book given to Musa. It's the main Jewish holy book.
The Qur'an says it contains the "judgement of Allah" (Qur'an 5:43) so it's valued
by Muslims. It includes the Ten Commandments, basic rules for a religious life.

> "We sent down the Torah, in which was guidance and light." Qur'an 5:44

3) The Zabur (Psalms) was given to Dawud. It's thought to be linked to the
Psalms of David in the Christian Bible and the Jewish Tenakh, but many
Muslims believe the original has been corrupted, perhaps beyond recognition.

> "...to David We gave the book [of Psalms]." Qur'an 4:163

4) Muslims believe Allah gave the Injil (Gospels) to Isa — Qur'an 57:27 says "We sent ... Our messengers
and followed [them] with Jesus ... and gave him the Gospel". They think the Injil prophesies the
coming of Muhammad. Many Muslims believe the Christian New Testament contains the same ideas
as those given to Isa, but not his exact words. Others think the Injil was another book entirely.

## The Hadith and Sunnah Give Guidance to Muslims

1) Muslims also pay a lot of attention to the guidance and example they get from the following:

**Hadith**

The hadith are reports of Muhammad's words and actions, recorded by his
followers. They're not in the Qur'an — they weren't revealed by Allah.
Each one's been assessed as to how authentic it is. There are different collections
of them, e.g. Sahih al-Bukhari, Sahih Muslim and Sunan Abi Dawud.

**Sunnah**

The sunnah sets out Muhammad's way of life, as recorded in the hadith.

2) The hadith and the sunnah give valuable advice in addition to the Qur'an,
especially on issues concerning daily life — but some Muslims believe
it's best just to use the Qur'an, as the hadith might be unreliable.

3) Shi'a Muslims also follow the hadith (sayings) of the imams, especially those of Ali.

---

## Tawrat, Zabur, Injil, Suhuf Ibrahim...

...there are lots of names on this page — and you need to learn them all (as well as how to spell
them). Without looking at the book, see if you can write down the names of all the holy books,
and give a brief description of each one. These books can be a good source of quotations too.

# Life After Death

Islam teaches that people will be judged on their behaviour during their life by Allah.

## Al-Qadr means Predestination

1) Al-Qadr is the idea that Allah has decided everything that will happen. This idea appears in teachings such as Sahih al-Bukhari 78:685, in which Muhammad said vowing to do something "does not bring about ... anything [Allah] has not decreed" — humans can't choose to do something Allah hasn't chosen for them.

2) This might seem to be contradicted by the idea of the Day of Judgement (see below) when Allah will judge people on the basis of their actions. That suggests people have free will and can choose how they act — there'd be no point judging them on their actions if what they did had already been decided by Allah.

3) However, many Muslims believe in a mix of these two ideas:

| | |
|---|---|
| Sunnis tend to believe Allah knows everything that's going to happen — he's above normal laws of time, so knows what humans will choose before they've chosen it. It's believed humans choose their actions, but Allah has made it impossible that they'll choose anything other than what he's decided. Some think once someone's chosen to act, the act becomes 'theirs' so they can be judged for it. | Shi'as focus a bit more on free will. They often believe Allah has ultimate control and the power to change things in the world if he wants, but that people's lives are usually determined by their choices. Like Sunnis, they tend to believe Allah knows what's going to happen as he is outside 'human' time — but for Shi'as, what happens is what people choose for themselves. |

4) To some Muslims, the idea of al-Qadr is comforting — if something bad has happened, it's reassuring to feel it's part of Allah's plan. Some people like to feel that they're guided to do Allah's will by al-Qadr.

## Yawm ad-Din is the Day of Judgement

1) On Yawm ad-Din, Allah decides how people will spend the afterlife, based on their behaviour during their lives. It's then too late to beg forgiveness for any wrongdoing.

2) Allah will judge everyone — not just Muslims. On Yawm ad-Din, the dead will be resurrected. Everyone will receive a record of their good and bad deeds, on which they'll be judged.

> "We will call forth every people with their record [of deeds]." Qur'an 17:71

3) The idea of judgement is important as it encourages Muslims to live their lives in a good way. It can be comforting to think bad people will be punished. Other Muslims think it's best to concentrate on this life — they think people should do good things anyway, not just because they're focusing on their afterlife.

4) Intentions are also important — intending to do something good counts, but intending to do something bad but not doing it doesn't count against you (Sahih Muslim 1:233).

## Al-Akhirah Means the Afterlife

1) Belief in the afterlife — al-Akhirah — is a key part of Islam. The afterlife is where people go after the Day of Judgement.

2) The reward for good people will be entry into jannah (paradise) — this is a place of peace, happiness and beauty. The Qur'an refers to Paradise as "Gardens of Pleasure" (Qur'an 31:8).

> "...for one whose scales are heavy [with good deeds], He will be in a pleasant life. ...for one whose scales are light, His refuge will be an abyss." Qur'an 101:6-9

3) For those who have done bad deeds, the punishment is jahannam (hell). The Qur'an describes jahannam as a place of scorching fire and boiling water. Here, those who have ignored Allah's teaching and failed to act righteously will be punished. Allah is merciful though, so they may eventually be sent to paradise.

4) The Qur'an sometimes mentions a 'barrier' between this world and the next called barzakh, where people's souls stay from the time they die until Yawm ad-Din. Many Muslims focus more on jannah and jahannam than barzakh.

> "...behind them is a barrier until the Day they are resurrected." Qur'an 23:100

## Belief in an afterlife helps many Muslims to lead a good life

There's a lot to learn on this page and some tricky words to spell, so you should spend some time reading over it to make sure you know it all — and take time to practise those difficult spellings as well.

# Worked Exam Questions

Look over the completed exam questions on this page, then try the ones on the next page for yourself.

1 Which of the following is the belief in life after death?
Put a tick (✓) in the correct box.

A Nubuwwah ☐

B al-Akhirah ✓

C Imamah ☐

D Tawhid ☐

*[1 mark]*

2 Which of the following means that God is good?
Put a tick (✓) in the correct box.

A Just ☐

B Transcendent ☐

C Immanent ☐

D Benevolent ✓

*[1 mark]*

3 Give two beliefs about the imams in Shi'a Islam.

1) Imams are all descended from Muhammad.

2) Imams are infallible, incapable of being wrong.

*[2 marks]*

4 Explain two Muslim beliefs about holy books other than the Qur'an.
Your answer should refer to specific Muslim teachings or sacred texts.

There are four holy books aside from the Qur'an: the Tawrat (Torah), the Suhuf Ibrahim (scrolls of Ibrahim), the Zabur (Psalms) and the Injil (Gospels). All holy books are equally important, but none of the books apart from the Qur'an contain the perfectly recorded teachings of Allah.

The scrolls of Ibrahim are the earliest of the holy books but have been lost: "Indeed, this is the former scriptures, The scriptures of Abraham and Moses" (Qur'an 87:18-19). It is believed that Ibrahim received a number of teachings from Allah.

*[5 marks]*

# Exam Questions

**5** Which of the following is the belief in angels?
Put a tick (✓) in the correct box.

A    al-Qadr    ☐

B    Nubuwwah    ☐

C    Sunni    ☐

D    Malaikah    ☐

*[1 mark]*

**6** Give two Muslim beliefs about what will happen on the Day of Judgement.

1) ................................................................................................................................

................................................................................................................................

2) ................................................................................................................................

................................................................................................................................

*[2 marks]*

**7** Explain two ways in which belief in Tawhid might influence Muslims today.

................................................................................................................................

................................................................................................................................

................................................................................................................................

................................................................................................................................

................................................................................................................................

................................................................................................................................

*[4 marks]*

**8** 'Muhammad's main role was to communicate Allah's message in the Qur'an.'    SPaG MARKS

Evaluate this statement. Your answer should include the following:
• examples from Muslim teachings
• arguments that support the statement
• arguments that disagree with the statement
• a conclusion.

*Write your answer on a separate sheet of paper.*

*[12 marks]*

# Worship and Duties

There are key actions Muslims try to follow — the Five Pillars for Sunnis, and Ten Obligatory Acts for Shi'as.

## Sunni Muslims are Required to Follow the Five Pillars of Islam

### 1) Shahadah — declaration of faith

"There is no god but Allah, and Muhammad is his messenger." Muslims should say this several times a day. It's said at birth and death, as well as in the call to prayer (adhan) and prayers. People can convert to Islam by saying it. The exact words aren't in the Qur'an, but come from passages such as Qur'an 3:18 — "Allah witnesses that there is no deity except Him". It's essential to Shi'a Muslims too, though it's not one of their Ten Obligatory Acts (see below). They add "Ali is the helper of Allah", as Ali is significant to their faith (see p.23).

### 2) Salah — prayer five times a day

The second most important duty in Islam. Muslims should pray five times a day — at sunrise, around noon, late afternoon, after sunset, and late evening. See the next page for more detail.

### 3) Zakah — charitable giving

Each person decides where to donate their money. Zakah encourages generosity and compassion. See p.33 for more detail.

### 4) Sawm — obligation to fast during Ramadan

Ramadan is the ninth month of the Muslim calendar. Muslims are obliged to fast during it. This teaches self-discipline, which brings Muslims closer to Allah. See p.33 for more detail.

### 5) Hajj — pilgrimage to Makkah

Every Muslim should do hajj at least once. It's only obligatory if you can afford it and you're healthy enough to do it. See p.34 for more.

## Shi'a Muslims Follow the Ten Obligatory Acts

Twelver Shi'as follow these acts. Others follow different sets of acts.

Four of these — salah, sawm, zakah and hajj — are the same as the Five Pillars. There are six others:

### Khums — annual tax

Khums is a kind of tax Shi'as pay each year on any 'profit' (excess money) they earn, at a rate of 20%. It goes towards supporting Islamic education and anyone descended from Muhammad who's in need.

### Jihad — 'struggle'

The word means 'struggle' or 'striving'. There are two types of jihad — the 'greater' jihad is Muslims' personal struggle to live a good life, and the 'lesser' jihad is Muslims' struggle to defend Islam against its critics. See p.34 for more.

### Amr-bil-Maroof and Nahi Anil Munkar

These come as a pair. The phrase means "enjoin what is right and forbid what is wrong" (Qur'an 9:71) — it asks Muslims to encourage good deeds and avoid bad ones.

### Tawalla and Tabarra

These also come as a pair. They mean 'love' and 'aloofness' — Muslims should love those who follow Allah and they shouldn't associate themselves with anyone who's an 'enemy' of Allah or Muhammad.

## Not all Shi'a Muslims follow the Ten Obligatory Acts

The Five Pillars (for Sunni Muslims) and the Ten Obligatory Acts (for Twelver Shi'as) are fundamental parts of how they live their lives. That's why it's important you know them all, so get learning...

## Islam | **Worship and Duties**

Muslims are required to pray <u>five times a day</u> and must follow specific rituals <u>before and during</u> the prayers.

## **Salah** is Very Important

1) <u>Salah</u>, the five daily prayers, should ideally take place in a <u>mosque</u>, but they can be done anywhere. Sunnis only <u>combine</u> the prayers if they have a very <u>good reason</u> that <u>prevents</u> them praying at five separate times, e.g. if they're <u>travelling</u>. Shi'as <u>combine</u> some prayers, so they tend to pray <u>three</u> times a day rather than <u>five</u> — but they still say <u>all</u> the <u>same</u> prayers.

> In Muslim countries, the <u>muezzin</u> makes the call to prayer (<u>adhan</u>) from the <u>minaret</u> of a <u>mosque</u>.

2) Each <u>prayer cycle</u> (<u>rak'ah</u>, see below) includes saying '<u>Allahu akbar</u>' ('<u>God is great</u>') multiple times, as well as reciting the <u>first surah</u> of the Qur'an (known as the <u>Fatiha</u>) and <u>other verses</u> from the Qur'an.

3) Most men are obliged to go to <u>Friday</u> prayers (<u>Jummah</u>) at the mosque. Requirements <u>vary</u>, but a <u>certain number</u> of people should be present. The Friday prayers are <u>led</u> by an <u>imam</u>, who also gives two <u>sermons</u>.

4) Salah keeps Muslims in <u>close contact</u> with Allah and encourages moral and spiritual <u>discipline</u>. This keeps them from committing <u>shirk</u> (see p.24) and increases <u>taqwa</u> (reverence for Allah). It's an expression of <u>solidarity</u> — doing the same as other Muslims, which is a reminder that everyone's <u>equal</u>.

> "...prayer prohibits immorality and wrongdoing, and the remembrance of Allah is greater." Qur'an 29:45

## There are **Rituals** to **Follow** with **Salah**

1) <u>Wudu</u> (washing before prayer) is important — Muslims must be <u>pure</u> and <u>clean</u> when approaching Allah, both <u>physically</u> and <u>spiritually</u>. Muslims wash their face, arms, feet and part of the hair before prayers. A <u>prayer mat</u> is often used when <u>not</u> praying in a mosque, in order to ensure <u>cleanliness</u>.

2) Muslims should face <u>Makkah</u> in Saudi Arabia when praying. The direction of Makkah is called the <u>qiblah</u>.

3) The <u>rak'ah</u> is a set prayer ritual. It may be repeated <u>several</u> times at each prayer session. Each rak'ah involves <u>standing</u>, then <u>kneeling</u>, then putting your <u>forehead</u> to the ground as a sign of submission to Allah. If several Muslims are praying in one place, then the rak'ah is done <u>together</u> at the same time.

4) <u>Shi'a</u> prayers are a bit <u>different</u>. Shi'as touch their foreheads to a <u>clay</u> or wooden tablet during the <u>rak'ah</u> — they believe putting their forehead on something <u>natural</u> is what Muhammad advised. The tablet is often made of clay from <u>Karbala</u>, where <u>Husayn</u> was <u>killed</u> (p.35), to remind Shi'as of his <u>sacrifice</u>.

5) When at the mosque, women and men pray <u>separately</u> — so people concentrate on <u>Allah</u> rather than on the <u>opposite sex</u>. This has <u>changed</u> in some mosques though, where <u>mixed prayer</u> is <u>allowed</u>.

6) Many Muslims perform <u>salah</u> in the <u>home</u> rather than at the <u>mosque</u>, particularly <u>women</u>. It's seen as an important way for <u>children</u> to <u>learn</u> about <u>Islam</u>. Some Muslim families may have a <u>room</u> just for <u>salah</u>.

## The rak'ah is repeated several times whilst praying

Salah is one of the Five Pillars for Sunni Muslims and one of the Ten Obligatory Acts for Shi'a Muslims. Make sure you know the similarities and differences between how both groups treat their daily prayers.

# Worship and Duties

Zakah (giving to charity) and Sawm (fasting during Ramadan) are done by both Sunni and Shi'a Muslims.

## Zakah is Charitable Giving

1) Zakah involves redistributing wealth. Muslims think wealth is given by Allah, so should be used to serve him.

2) The amount is usually 2.5% of a person's wealth each year. Muslims can decide how much to give and who they want to donate it to. It's often used to help Muslims who are less well off, or given to charities or mosques — it is for the "poor and... needy" Qur'an 9:60.

3) It's a sign of concern for others and encourages generosity: "Zakah...[is] for bringing hearts together" Qur'an 9:60.

4) Some Shi'as pay khums (see p.31) in addition to zakah.

## Sawm is Fasting During **Ramadan**

1) Muslims must fast between sunrise and sunset during the month of Ramadan. The Muslim calendar is lunar (determined by the moon) so Ramadan isn't always at the same time of the solar (sun) year.

> "O you who have believed, decreed upon you is fasting ... that you may become righteous..." Qur'an 2:183

2) Muslims eat just before sunrise (suhur) and just after sunset (iftar). The fast is often broken slowly with dates, before a bigger meal later. Iftar is often eaten with family or friends, or sometimes at the mosque.

There are exceptions to the obligation to fast:

- Children don't have to fast until they're about 12 years old. Old people (there's no specific age) don't have to fast either.

- People can be excused for medical reasons. Women who are pregnant, breastfeeding or menstruating can also be excused. It's fine to take medicine which has to be regular, e.g. antibiotics. If you're on a journey, you can be excused too.

- If you've missed a few days of the fast, Qur'an 2:184 says that you should make up for it, either by fasting for the same number of days later on, or by giving food to someone who might need it.

3) Sawm doesn't just involve not eating or drinking, but also abstaining from other things such as listening to music, sex and smoking. Muslims should also try particularly hard to avoid bad thoughts or actions.

4) Ramadan is a time of both physical and moral self-discipline, and a time of obedience to Allah. It's supposed to help Muslims understand hunger, and so makes them more willing to help others.

5) It's also a time to show publicly that Allah matters more than any physical needs.

Laylat al-Qadr (the Night of Destiny or Power) falls during Ramadan. Muslims believe Muhammad received at least part of the Qur'an during this night. So Ramadan is also a time of thanksgiving for the Qur'an — during Ramadan it's read from beginning to end at the mosque. Laylat al-Qadr is the holiest night of the year — the Qur'an says it's "better than a thousand months" (Qur'an 97:3) and many Muslims spend the whole night at the mosque to celebrate it, praying and listening to readings of the Qur'an. It's important because many Muslims believe Allah will forgive their sins on this night.

## Muslims fast to bring themselves closer to Allah

Cover this page and write down what Laylat al-Qadr is, and why and how it is celebrated. Then explain why Muslims fast during Ramadan, giving as many reasons as possible.

# Worship and Duties

The hajj is an important action for a Muslim to do. Around 2 million Muslims go each year.

## The **Hajj** is the **Pilgrimage** to **Makkah**

"...proclaim to the people the Hajj..." Qur'an 22:27

1) Muslims must make the pilgrimage at least once in their lifetime, as long as they can afford it and they're healthy enough to cope with the journey. It has to happen in the Muslim month of Dhu'l-Hijja to count.

2) Adam, Ibrahim and Isma'il are all associated with Makkah and Muhammad lived there, so it's a holy place.

3) All pilgrims wear simple white clothing (ihram) so they're equal before Allah.

4) The Ka'aba is in Makkah — it's a giant stone cube covered with black cloth. Some Muslims think Ibrahim and Isma'il built it as a place of worship — Qur'an 2:127 suggests they did. Others think Adam built it. It's the holiest place in Islam. Muslims must do seven circuits anticlockwise of the Ka'aba, touching the stone if possible — this ritual is called the tawaf.

5) Next, a pilgrim must make seven journeys between the hills of Safa and Marwa (where Hajar, Ibrahim's wife and servant, searched for water for their son Isma'il). This part of the pilgrimage is called the sa'y. Pilgrims then draw water from the Zamzam Well, which Allah made for Hajar.

6) Then pilgrims go to Mount Arafat to stand and pray for Allah's forgiveness. This is where Muslims believe Adam was forgiven after being thrown out of Eden and also where the Day of Judgement will take place.

7) The pilgrims spend the night at Muzdalifa, a valley between Arafat and Mina, where they collect pebbles.

8) The pebbles are then thrown at three pillars in Mina, to symbolise driving the devil away — Ibrahim is believed to have once thrown stones at Shaytan (the devil). This happens on Id ul-Adha (see p.35).

9) The title 'hajji' is given to those who complete the hajj. Many find the hajj helps their faith and increases unity between Muslims. Some hadith say it cleanses the hajji of all sins, e.g. Sahih al-Bukhari 26:596: "he will return (after Hajj free from all sins) as if he were born anew".

## There are Two Kinds of **Jihad**

Jihad means 'striving' or 'struggle' and is often misunderstood by non-Muslims. It's one of the Ten Obligatory Acts for Shi'as (see p.31) but it's part of Sunni Islam too. Most Muslims believe there are two kinds:

### The Greater Jihad

1) This is every Muslim's struggle to obey Allah, follow his teachings and become a better Muslim.

2) It's the greater struggle because it's individual and personal. Qur'an 35:18 says "no bearer of burdens will bear the burden of another" (burdens mean sins), so you and you alone will be held responsible for your behaviour. If you're not a good Muslim, it's harder to help make the world better (lesser jihad).

### The Lesser Jihad

1) This is the struggle to make the world a better place. Part of this means struggling against wrongs such as poverty and injustice.

When Islam began, Muslims fought to survive as people of other religions persecuted them. The Qur'an reflects this struggle, which is why it refers to defending Islam against its enemies.

2) Part of it is the struggle to defend Islam against threats. It can be in peaceful ways, such as helping others be good Muslims.

3) The Qur'an and Islamic law say that actual fighting should only be in self-defence and not against people who aren't fighting (non-combatants) — "Permission [to fight] has been given to those who are being fought" (Qur'an 22:39). Qur'an 4:75 says Muslims should fight on behalf of people being oppressed.

4) Islamic terrorists claim the Qur'an supports violence to defend Islam against oppression, e.g. Qur'an 2:193 says "...if they cease, then there is to be no aggression except against the oppressors". The vast majority of Muslims condemn this and think that Islamic terrorists aren't true Muslims.

EXAM TIP

## And that's the last of the duties...

You might see some of the Arabic words spelled slightly differently, e.g. zakat rather than zakah or Eid al-Adha rather than Id ul-Adha. Make sure you always stick to one spelling in the exam.

# Festivals

There are several festivals throughout the year.  Id ul-Adha and Id ul-Fitr are important to Sunnis and Shi'as.

## Id ul-Adha Focuses on the **Importance** of **Obeying Allah**

1) Id ul-Adha is a festival celebrating complete obedience to Allah, as it commemorates the time when Ibrahim nearly sacrificed his own son, Isma'il.  It's a very important festival and it forms part of the hajj.

2) Ibrahim dreamt that Allah told him to sacrifice Isma'il.  He told Isma'il about it and Isma'il agreed it had to be done.  But at the last minute, Allah told Ibrahim to sacrifice a ram in place of Isma'il, so Isma'il survived.  It was a test of Ibrahim's loyalty to Allah.

> " '...my son, indeed I have seen in a dream that I [must] sacrifice you ...' He said, 'O my father, do as you are commanded.' "  Qur'an 37:102

3) Muslims should attend mosque on Id ul-Adha — the service includes communal prayers and a sermon focused on the importance of obedience to Allah and the lessons to be learnt from Ibrahim and Isma'il.

4) An animal is often sacrificed and divided up into three — a third is kept by the family, a third goes to relatives or neighbours and a third goes to the poor.

5) Id ul-Adha is a time of communal joy and festivity lasting up to four days.  Muslims dress up in their best clothes and spend time with family and friends.  Presents are often exchanged.

## Id ul-Fitr Marks the **End** of **Ramadan**

1) Id ul-Fitr is at the end of Ramadan (see p.33).  It's a day of thanksgiving to Allah for giving Muslims the strength to fast for a month.  It's a joyful festival which also celebrates the fact that Muslims have completed the fourth pillar of Islam by observing sawm, and therefore have become closer to Allah.

2) Muslims pay a special zakah for Id ul-Fitr.  Usually around £5, it helps Muslims who are less well off celebrate Id ul-Fitr as well.  It's often given out in the form of food by charities or mosques.

3) The festival involves a service with prayers and a sermon (at the mosque or outside), and a meal to break the fast.  Like Id ul-Adha, it's a time of celebration, when family and friends meet up, presents are exchanged and people wear their best clothes.

© David Grossman / Alamy Stock Photo

4) Thousands of people attend celebrations of both Ids in the UK — many Muslims find it important for community cohesion between Muslims and with those of other faiths.

## Ashura Commemorates the **Death** of **Husayn**

1) Id ul-Adha and Id ul-Fitr are important for both Sunnis and Shi'as, but Ashura is mostly a Shi'a festival.

2) Originally, Ashura was a compulsory day of fasting for all Muslims.  But when Muhammad said Muslims should observe sawm during Ramadan, fasting on Ashura became voluntary.

3) Sunnis now tend to think of it as a day of atonement.  Many Sunnis fast, but it's not compulsory.  It's believed that fasting may absolve people of their minor sins in the previous year.

4) Ashura is important for Shi'as because it was the day Husayn, Ali's son and Muhammad's grandson (see p.23), was killed in a battle.  The ten days up to and including Ashura (Ashura is the tenth day) are a period of mourning for Shi'as.  Mosques often provide free meals for people during the ten-day period.

5) On Ashura, Shi'as wear black as a sign of mourning.  There are often public processions (there's usually one in London) and 'passion plays', in which the story of Husayn is performed.  Poems or stories about Husayn are often read out.

6) Some Shi'as hurt themselves to commemorate Husayn's suffering.  This is banned in some countries.

7) For Shi'as, Ashura is a reminder of the suffering the Shi'a community has experienced — Shi'as have been persecuted as a minority.  The processions are sometimes used as protests against injustice.

REVISION TASK

## Ashura is especially important to Shi'a Muslims

For each of the three festivals on this page, write down their name, the reason for them and some common practices that happen during them.  Try to use some Islam-specific vocabulary too.

# Worked Exam Questions

The next two pages are full of questions just like the ones you'll get in the exam.
The first few have been done for you, then there are some for you to have a go at.

---

**1** Which of the following is the ritual washing before prayer?
Put a tick (✓) in the correct box.

    **A**    Zakah    ☐

    **B**    Hajj    ☐

    **C**    Rak'ah    ☐

    **D**    Wudu    ☑

*[1 mark]*

---

**2** Explain two contrasting ways of marking the festival of Ashura.

Some Shi'a Muslims harm themselves to share in the experience of Husayn's suffering.

This practice is controversial within Shi'a Islam and has been banned in some countries.

Sunni Muslims discourage the harming of the body to mark Ashura. This practice is believed

to conflict with teachings about preserving and respecting the body.

*[4 marks]*

---

**3** Explain two contrasting understandings of charity.

Charity (zakah) is one of the Five Pillars for Sunni Muslims and one of the Ten Obligatory Acts

for Shi'a Muslims. It involves giving away 2.5% of a person's wealth each year to charitable causes.

For Shi'a Muslims, charity may refer to khums, another of the Ten Obligatory Acts. It's a 20%

tax on all surplus earnings and wealth for the purposes of Islamic education and helping others.

*[4 marks]*

---

**4** Explain two reasons why Shahadah is important to Muslims.
Your answer should refer to specific Muslim religious teachings or sacred texts.

Shahadah is the first of the Five Pillars of Islam. While all the pillars are equally important,

Shahadah has a special place as the central pillar, as without this one the others would not be possible.

It is the Muslim declaration of faith. The declaration is not directly from a holy book but comes

from key passages in the Qur'an: "Allah witnesses that there is no deity except Him" (Qur'an 3:18).

*[5 marks]*

---

# Exam Questions

**5** Which of the following means the simple white clothing worn on Hajj?
Put a tick (✓) in the correct box.

- **A** Ka'aba ☐
- **B** Mina ☐
- **C** Sawm ☐
- **D** Ihram ☐

*[1 mark]*

**6** Which of the following is a prophet celebrated by Muslims during Id ul-Adha?
Put a tick (✓) in the correct box.

- **A** Isa ☐
- **B** Muhammad ☐
- **C** Musa ☐
- **D** Ibrahim ☐

*[1 mark]*

**7** Give two places that Muslims visit on the hajj journey.

1) ...................................................................................................................................

...................................................................................................................................

2) ...................................................................................................................................

...................................................................................................................................

*[2 marks]*

**8** Explain two ways in which sawm is important to Muslims.
Your answer should refer to specific Muslim teachings or sacred texts.

...................................................................................................................................

...................................................................................................................................

...................................................................................................................................

...................................................................................................................................

...................................................................................................................................

...................................................................................................................................

...................................................................................................................................

*[5 marks]*

38

# Revision Summary

Now you've made it to the end of the Islam section, it's time to see how much you've learnt.

- Try these questions and tick off each one when you get it right.
- When you've done all the questions for a topic and are completely happy with it, tick off the topic.

## Beliefs (p.23-28) ☑

1) Which group of Muslims followed Ali's descendents following his death?
2) Give an example of an article of faith which Sunni and Shi'a Muslims both share.
3) Give an example of an article of faith which Sunni Muslims hold but Shi'a Muslims do not.
4) What word is used to describe the concept of Allah being the one and only god?
5) What does the word 'Allah' mean in Arabic?
6) What is shirk?
7) Give and explain two characteristics of Allah.
8) Who do Muslims believe was the first prophet?
9) Which prophet did Allah speak to directly?
10) How did Allah communicate with Muhammad?
11) What is the Qur'an?
12) Why is it important for Muslims to learn Arabic?
13) Describe one way Muslims show respect for the Qur'an.
14) What is the role of angels?
15) Why is it impossible for an angel to sin?
16) What did the angel Jibril do?
17) Name another holy book, in addition to the Qur'an.
18) What are the hadith?
19) What is al-Qadr?
20) Why is the Day of Judgement important for Muslims?
21) What are the Muslim terms for heaven and hell?
22) What is the Muslim term for belief in the afterlife?

## Practices (p.31-35) ☑

23) What are the Five Pillars of Sunni Islam?
24) What do Shi'a Muslims follow rather than the Five Pillars?
25) Give a description of salah and explain its importance.
26) What is rak'ah?
27) Give one reason why Muslims believe it is important to donate some of their money to the needy.
28) Give one reason why a Muslim may not fast during Ramadan.
29) What occurred during the Laylat al-Qadr?
30) When does the hajj take place?
31) Describe one thing that Muslims must do whilst on pilgrimage in Makkah.
32) Describe the two kinds of jihad.
33) What does Id ul-Adha commemorate?
34) Which festival marks the end of Ramadan?
35) What does Ashura commemorate?

Beliefs, Teachings and Practices — Islam

## Introduction to Judaism — Judaism

There are different branches of <u>Judaism</u>, but all Jews believe in <u>one God</u> and follow the <u>Torah</u> as a sacred text.

## The **Tenakh** and the **Talmud** are the Jewish **Sacred Texts**

1)  The **TENAKH** is the main sacred Jewish text. It's basically the same as the Christian <u>Old Testament</u>, except it's in a <u>different order</u>. The word 'TeNaKh' will help you remember what's in it.

### T = Torah (Instructions / Law / Teachings)

The <u>Torah</u> is the <u>first five</u> books of the <u>Old Testament</u>. It's seen as the <u>holiest part</u> of the Tenakh — <u>God</u> gave it to Moses. It contains the <u>mitzvot</u> (commandments, see p.42) which Jews are meant to follow. 'Torah' can refer to all Jewish <u>teachings</u>, or to the whole <u>Tenakh</u>, as well as this <u>first part</u> of the <u>Tenakh</u>.

*The <u>Torah</u> is made up of Genesis, Exodus, Leviticus, Numbers and Deuteronomy.*

### N = Nevi'im (Prophets)

This is a <u>collection of books</u>, divided into <u>two parts</u>. The <u>Former Prophets</u> trace the history of the Israelites (ancestors of the Jews) after the death of Moses. The <u>Latter Prophets</u> contain the words of <u>15</u> prophets such as Isaiah, Jeremiah and Ezekiel. They encourage Jews to <u>obey God</u> and <u>follow the Torah</u>.

### K = Ketuvim (Writings)

Among other things, this contains the 'three Ps': <u>Psalms</u> (hymns), <u>Proverbs</u>, and <u>Philosophy</u>. This part of the Tenakh is <u>less authoritative</u> than the others.

*The <u>prophets</u> are believed to have been <u>inspired by God</u>.*

2)  The **TALMUD** is a <u>collection of teachings</u> and a record of originally <u>spoken</u> discussions between <u>Torah scholars</u>. It's made up of <u>two parts</u> — the <u>Mishnah</u>, which explains how the <u>mitzvot</u> in the <u>Torah</u> should be <u>applied</u>, and the <u>Gemara</u>, which <u>discusses</u> and <u>comments</u> on the <u>Mishnah</u>.

## There are **Different Branches** of Judaism

### Orthodox Judaism

1)  <u>Orthodox Jews</u> believe that the <u>Torah</u> and <u>Talmud</u> are of <u>divine origin</u> (they come from <u>God</u>). They should be followed <u>to the letter</u> — their <u>teachings</u> should <u>not</u> be <u>changed</u> to adapt to <u>life today</u>.

2)  They strictly observe <u>Shabbat</u> (<u>day of rest</u>, see p.48-49), and <u>kashrut</u> (<u>dietary laws</u>, see p.49).

### Progressive Judaism

1)  <u>Progressive Jews</u> believe the Torah and Talmud are people's <u>interpretation</u> of God's word. They see Judaism as a <u>developing</u> religion, so they apply the sacred texts to <u>modern life</u> in a more <u>flexible</u> way.

2)  They tend to follow the <u>mitzvot</u> about <u>morality</u> (see p.42). However, they believe the <u>ritual commandments</u>, e.g. <u>dietary laws</u>, can be <u>adapted</u> or <u>abandoned</u> in response to <u>changes in society</u>.

3)  There are <u>two</u> main movements of Progressive Jews:

**REFORM JUDAISM**

- This is a mix of <u>new</u> and <u>old</u> traditions, e.g. Reform Jews have a <u>Shabbat</u> service but at a <u>different time</u> to Orthodox Jews (p.48).
- A <u>key difference</u> from Orthodox Judaism is that women and men are completely <u>equal</u>. Men and women sit <u>together</u> in services and there are male and female <u>rabbis</u> (religious leaders).

**LIBERAL JUDAISM**

- Liberal Judaism <u>formed from</u> Reform Judaism — it's similar to but more <u>radical</u> than Reform. It has a similar <u>emphasis</u> on treating everyone <u>equally</u>.
- It teaches that observing any of the <u>mitzvot</u> is a matter of carefully considered <u>personal choice</u>.

<u>Masorti</u> (<u>Conservative</u>) Jews follow <u>Jewish law</u> like Orthodox Jews, but with a <u>more liberal</u> interpretation.

## Remember, the word 'Torah' can be used in different ways

Make sure it's clear which way you're using it in the exam, so the examiner doesn't get confused.

## Judaism | Key Beliefs in Judaism

Jews, Christians and Muslims all believe God has some of the <u>same characteristics</u>, but there are some <u>differences</u>.

## Jews Believe **God** has **Certain Characteristics**

Although there are <u>different strands</u> of Judaism (see p.39), <u>nearly all</u> Jews believe that God is...

> Some write '<u>G-d</u>' to stop the word 'God' being <u>accidentally erased</u> or <u>damaged</u>, which is <u>forbidden</u>.

1) **ONE** — Judaism is a <u>monotheistic</u> religion — Jews believe there's only <u>one God</u>. They believe God is <u>one entity</u> — they don't believe God has <u>different parts</u>, as most <u>Christians</u> do (p.2).

2) **ETERNAL** — Jews believe God has and always will exist.

3) **THE CREATOR** — He made <u>everything</u> in the universe. Jews believe that <u>creation</u> proves <u>God exists</u>.

4) **OMNIPOTENT** — God is <u>all-powerful</u> — although he still allows each person <u>free will</u>.

5) **OMNISCIENT** — God <u>knows everything</u>, even people's <u>thoughts</u>.

6) **OMNIBENEVOLENT** — God is <u>all-good</u> — he can do no evil.

> "The Lord is good to all; he has compassion on all he has made." Psalm 145:9 NIV

7) **OMNIPRESENT** — God is <u>everywhere</u> at <u>all times</u>. He's beyond time and space.

8) **THE LAWGIVER** — Jews believe they should <u>obey God's laws</u> as part of the <u>covenant</u> (see next page).

9) **THE JUDGE** — Jews believe their behaviour will be <u>judged</u> by God after they die (see p.43). However, they believe he is just and <u>merciful</u>. He will <u>save</u> his people from <u>sin</u> and <u>suffering</u>.

10) **TRANSCENDENT** — God is <u>beyond</u> this <u>world</u>. His existence doesn't rely on the <u>universe</u>.

11) **IMMANENT** — But God is <u>present</u> in the world and sustains it — see the concept of <u>Shekhinah</u> below.

## Shekhinah is God's **Presence on Earth**

1) The word <u>Shekhinah</u> is used to refer to <u>God</u> when he is <u>present</u> in a <u>particular place</u> on Earth.

2) The term is used to describe <u>God's presence</u> in the <u>tabernacle</u> (a portable place of worship used by Moses — p.41) and the <u>Temple</u> Jews built in Jerusalem. Many Jews pray at the <u>remaining part</u> of the <u>Temple</u> walls in <u>Jerusalem</u> (the <u>Western Wall</u>) as they believe that Shekhinah is still present there.

> "The glory of the Lord filled the tabernacle." Exodus 40:35 NIV

3) Some Jews believe that Shekhinah is present when they're <u>praying</u> together or discussing the <u>Torah</u>.

4) <u>Shekhinah</u> is often seen as <u>feminine</u>, and has 'feminine' characteristics, such as being <u>caring</u>.

5) The concept of Shekhinah can help Jews in times of <u>suffering</u>, as it means God is <u>there alongside</u> them.

---

## Make sure you learn how to spell the 'omni-' words correctly

Shut this book and see if you can write down the characteristics of God listed above, as well as what they mean — you'll only be able to use them correctly in the exam if you understand them.

# Key Beliefs in Judaism

God made <u>covenants</u> with Jews through Abraham and Moses — making the Jews his <u>chosen people</u>.

## Jews Believe in a **Covenant** Between **Them** and **God**

A <u>covenant</u> is a <u>formal agreement</u> between two or more people.
<u>God</u> made a covenant with the <u>Jews</u> which defines them as his <u>chosen people</u>.

1) The <u>first covenant</u> was between <u>God</u> and <u>Abraham</u>. Abraham was the <u>first</u> of the <u>founders</u> of Judaism. Jews call him <u>Avraham Avinu</u> ('our father Abraham').

2) God told Abraham to leave his home and go to <u>Canaan</u> (the '<u>Promised Land</u>').

> "The whole land of Canaan … I will give as an everlasting possession to you and your descendants … and I will be their God." Genesis 17:8 NIV

3) God promised to give Abraham and his wife <u>Sarah</u> a <u>child</u>, and to <u>protect</u> them and their <u>descendants</u> as his <u>chosen people</u>. In return, God asked Abraham and his descendants (known as the <u>Israelites</u>) to <u>obey</u> God and lead by <u>example</u>.

4) He asked for all of their <u>male</u> descendants to be <u>circumcised</u> as a sign of this <u>covenant</u> (see p.50).

> <u>Israel</u>, in the Middle East, is a <u>state</u> that was founded in 1948 in roughly the same area as <u>Canaan</u> had been. Many Jews see the state of <u>Israel</u> as the <u>fulfilment</u> of the promise of the Promised Land. However, some Orthodox Jews believe that Jews <u>shouldn't</u> have created the state themselves — they should have waited for <u>God's action</u>. Many <u>Progressive</u> Jews only became <u>supportive</u> of the formation of a Jewish state <u>after the Holocaust</u>, in which <u>6 million</u> Jews were killed by the Nazis.

## God also made a **Covenant** with **Moses**

1) <u>Moses</u> was also a <u>founder</u> of Judaism. He led the Jews back to <u>freedom</u> in <u>Canaan</u> after they'd been <u>slaves</u> in Egypt for 400 years (they'd had to leave Canaan due to a famine). This was called the <u>Exodus</u>.

2) On the way back, God made a <u>covenant</u> with Moses at <u>Mount Sinai</u>, setting out in detail what the Israelites had to <u>do</u> in <u>return</u> for being God's <u>chosen people</u>.

> "Now if you obey me fully and keep my covenant, then out of all nations you will be my treasured possession." Exodus 19:5 NIV

3) God gave the <u>Torah</u> to Moses. This included the mitzvot — the <u>Ten Commandments</u> plus many other laws. The Ten Commandments (the <u>Decalogue</u>) were written separately on <u>stone tablets</u>. Moses was also given an <u>explanation</u> of the <u>Torah</u>, known as the <u>oral Torah</u>, which was eventually <u>written down</u> in the <u>Mishnah</u> (p.39).

4) The Israelites <u>promised</u> to "do everything the Lord has said" (Exodus 19:8 NIV).

5) <u>Orthodox</u> Jews believe the <u>Torah</u> came directly from God, but <u>Progressive</u> Jews believe the Torah is people's <u>interpretation</u> of God's word — they think it was written by <u>people</u> rather than <u>God</u>.

## Moses led the Israelites out of Egypt to freedom

Cover the page and write down as many details as you can about the covenants God made with Abraham and Moses — see if you can include quotations from the Torah as well.

# Key Beliefs in Judaism

The <u>mitzvot</u> are <u>laws</u> telling Jewish people how they should live their lives.

## The **Mitzvot** are **Jewish Laws**

The singular form of mitzvot is <u>mitzvah</u>.
It's sometimes translated as a '<u>good deed</u>'.

1) The <u>613 mitzvot</u> cover a variety of issues, including <u>food</u>, how to <u>worship God</u> and how to help the <u>poor</u>.

2) They were taken from the Torah by scholars, who made slightly different lists of them. The <u>standard</u> list was compiled by <u>Maimonides</u> in his <u>Mishneh Torah</u>. The mitzvot can be <u>divided</u> up in different ways:

- <u>248</u> of the mitzvot are <u>positive</u>, telling Jews what they should do. They're called <u>mitzvot aseh</u> in Hebrew.
- <u>365</u> mitzvot are <u>negative</u>, telling Jews what they shouldn't do. They're known as <u>mitzvot ta'aseh</u>.

- <u>Ritual</u> mitzvot list things Jews must or must not do to avoid offending God — they are between <u>a person</u> and <u>God</u>.
- <u>Moral</u> (ethical) mitzvot are about a Jew's dealings with <u>other people</u> — they are between <u>one person</u> and <u>another</u>.

3) The <u>Ten Commandments</u> are <u>important</u> mitzvot. The <u>first</u> is the central belief of Judaism (see p.48).

1. I am the Lord your God.
2. You shall have no other gods before me. You shall not make for yourself an image... [or] bow down to them or worship them. ——→ <u>Don't worship idols</u> (objects or pictures of God).
3. You shall not misuse the name of the Lord your God.
4. Remember the Sabbath day by keeping it holy.
5. Honour your father and your mother.
6. You shall not murder.
7. You shall not commit adultery.
8. You shall not steal.
9. You shall not give false testimony against your neighbour.——→ This means <u>don't lie</u> about <u>other people</u>.
10. You shall not covet. ——→ This means <u>don't be jealous</u> of what <u>other people</u> have.

Exodus 20:2-17 NIV

4) Jews believe that humans have <u>free will</u>, so they're <u>responsible</u> for following the mitzvot. This means they can be <u>judged</u> on their actions by God. He will <u>forgive</u> someone who's <u>sorry</u> for their sins though.

5) Orthodox Jews <u>follow</u> the mitzvot <u>closely</u>. They try to go <u>further</u> than the mitzvot, so they don't <u>break one</u> by accident. Progressive Jews follow the mitzvot <u>less strictly</u> (see p.39). Some mitzvot can't be obeyed as they refer to the <u>Temple</u>, which no longer exists, but following as many as possible is a <u>key part</u> of many Jews' <u>relationship</u> with God. Doing so <u>unites</u> Jews and gives them an <u>identity</u> as <u>God's people</u>.

## There are Other **Important Principles**

1) <u>Pikuach nefesh</u> (saving a life) is <u>more important</u> than any mitzvot, except commandments 1, 2, 6 and 7. It follows the belief in the <u>sanctity of life</u> — life being holy. For example, a doctor can <u>break the Sabbath</u> to <u>save</u> someone's <u>life</u>. The person's life doesn't have to be in <u>immediate danger</u> (the action can be <u>preventative</u>). There's debate about whether it applies to <u>animals</u>.

"Every danger to human life suspends the [laws of the] Sabbath." Talmud Yoma 83a

2) Jews believe people are the Earth's <u>custodians</u> — they have a <u>responsibility</u> to <u>look after</u> the world. This includes the idea of <u>tikkun olam</u> ('mending the world') — acting <u>morally</u> to improve life on Earth.

3) <u>Justice</u>, <u>charity</u> and <u>kindness</u> are important morals included in some <u>mitzvot</u>. <u>Gemilut hasadim</u> (acts of loving kindness) is a central principle of Judaism. The concept of <u>tzedakah</u> (charity) is also important — it should be given to make the world more <u>just</u>, so it's an <u>obligation</u> rather than a <u>choice</u>.

## The mitzvot are important, but saving a life is often more valued

The most important mitzvot are the commandments about belief in God (commandments 1 and 2), the sanctity of human life (commandment 6), and the sanctity of marriage (commandment 7).

# Key Beliefs in Judaism

Judaism focuses on this life rather than the afterlife.  There are different ideas about what happens after death.

## Jews have **Different Beliefs** about the **Afterlife**

1) The Torah focuses more on life on Earth than on an afterlife — Jews are encouraged to lead good lives for the sake of life on Earth, rather than the hope of what's to come.

2) The Tenakh talks about Sheol, where the souls of the dead live as shadows for eternity.

3) But ideas about the afterlife gradually developed — beliefs are now largely based on ideas in the Talmud.

- Many Jews believe life after death is spent in Gan Eden ('Garden of Eden' or Paradise) and/or Gehinnom.

- Some see Gan Eden as a place of banquets and sunshine.  Others have a more spiritual view of it as a closeness to God.  Only if you've lived a blameless life will you be sent straight to Gan Eden when you die.

- Most souls go to Gehinnom before they reach Gan Eden.  Some see it as a place of torment, where people are punished.  Some see it as a place for purification, where people are shown the wrong they did in this life.  The truly wicked don't move on — some think they're tormented forever, others that their souls are destroyed.

4) God judges how good or evil people have been, to decide their fate in the afterlife.  Some Jews see this as a motivation for good behaviour in this life, others argue that you should do good things simply because they are good.

> "God will bring every deed into judgment ... whether it is good or evil."  Ecclesiastes 12:14 NIV

5) Some Progressive Jews don't believe in the afterlife, as it's not explicitly mentioned in the Torah.  Others believe we live on in how we've influenced others during our lives.

6) The term olam ha-ba (the world to come) is also used for the afterlife.  It's sometimes used to refer to the Messianic Age (see below), rather than where souls go straight after death.

7) Many Jews also believe they will eventually be physically resurrected — see below.  Belief in resurrection is important in Judaism.  Maimonides listed it as one of his 13 principles of faith.

## A **Messiah** will bring **Peace** on **Earth**

'Messiah' comes from the Hebrew 'mashiach' which means 'anointed one' — someone who is chosen to rule.

1) Many Jews believe that the Messiah, an inspirational leader, will bring an era of perfect peace and prosperity called the Messianic Age.  He'll establish God's kingdom on Earth and everyone will acknowledge God.  (Unlike Christians, Jews don't believe that Jesus was the Messiah.)

2) Jews believe that the Messiah will be human — not divine (god-like) as Jesus is for Christians (see p.2).  He'll be a male descendant of the Jewish king David and will himself be "a King who will reign wisely and do what is just and right" (Jeremiah 23:5 NIV).  He will spread God's laws throughout the world, reunite the Jewish people in Israel (the Promised Land) and rebuild the Temple there.

3) It is thought that the prophet Elijah will appear just before the Messiah comes.

4) It's believed that people will be judged by God and the Messiah on their actions.  Some Jews believe everyone will be resurrected so they can be judged.  Others think only the righteous will be resurrected to share in the Messianic Age.

> "Multitudes who sleep in the dust of the earth will awake: some to everlasting life, others to shame and everlasting contempt."  Daniel 12:2 NIV

- Orthodox Jews believe that the physical body will be resurrected, intact, in the Messianic Age.  Because of this, the body shouldn't be cut after death (autopsies are frowned upon) and cremation is forbidden.  A Jewish cemetery is called the 'House of Life' (Bet ha-Chaim), which reaffirms the view that the body will be resurrected.

- Progressive Jews believe that the body is simply a vessel for the soul (which they believe carries on without the body), and reject the idea of physical resurrection.  So Progressive Jews accept cremation and organ donation.

5) Not all Jews believe a Messiah will come though.  Many Progressive Jews believe instead that people themselves can bring about a peaceful and prosperous age on Earth through their own good actions.

# Worked Exam Questions

To test what you've learnt so far, and to give you an idea of what the questions in your exam will be like, there are some exam-style questions on the next couple of pages. The answers have been completed for you on this page.

**1**  Which of the following is a place where Jews believe God is present on the Earth today?
Put a tick (✓) in the correct box.

    **A**    Canaan    ☐

    **B**    Gan Eden    ☐

    **C**    The Western Wall    ✓

    **D**    Sheol    ☐

*[1 mark]*

**2**  Which of the following is the number of mitzvot generally accepted by Jews?
Put a tick (✓) in the correct box.

    **A**    3    ☐

    **B**    10    ☐

    **C**    365    ☐

    **D**    613    ✓

*[1 mark]*

**3**  Give two Jewish beliefs about life after death.

    **1)** The afterlife is spent in either Gan Eden or Gehinnom.

    **2)** Most souls leave Gehinnom although some remain forever (or are destroyed).

*[2 marks]*

**4**  Explain two ways in which belief in free will influences Jews today.

    The belief in free will means Jews may take responsibility for following and obeying the mitzvot themselves. It means that they will be judged by God in the afterlife according to their choices and actions on Earth.

    The belief in free will means Jews believe that human beings have a special place in creation. This may influence them to act as the custodians of the Earth and the life it contains.

*[4 marks]*

# Exam Questions

**5** Which of the following books contains the Ten Commandments?
Put a tick (✓) in the correct box.

    **A**    Genesis    ☐

    **B**    Exodus    ☐

    **C**    Leviticus    ☐

    **D**    Psalms    ☐

*[1 mark]*

**6** Explain two Jewish beliefs about the Covenant with Abraham.
Your answer should refer to specific Jewish teachings or sacred texts.

........................................................................................................................

........................................................................................................................

........................................................................................................................

........................................................................................................................

........................................................................................................................

........................................................................................................................

........................................................................................................................

........................................................................................................................

*[5 marks]*

**7** 'Only the Messiah can bring about peace and prosperity on Earth.'

    (SPaG MARKS)

Evaluate this statement. Your answer should include the following:
- examples from Jewish teachings
- arguments that support the statement
- arguments that disagree with the statement
- a conclusion.

*Write your answer on a separate sheet of paper.*

*[12 marks]*

## Judaism

# Worship

A Jewish place of worship is called a <u>synagogue</u>. The word means '<u>assembly</u>' or '<u>coming together</u>'. Jews sometimes call it a '<u>shul</u>' instead.

## All Synagogues have the Same Four Features

The <u>layout</u> of the <u>main (prayer) hall</u> commemorates some aspects of the <u>Temple</u> in <u>Jerusalem</u>, which was the <u>centre of Jewish worship</u> before it was <u>destroyed</u> in 70 CE. All synagogues have these <u>four</u> features:

There are <u>no rules</u> stating what a synagogue should look like on the <u>outside</u>.

### Aron Hakodesh (the Ark)

A large <u>cupboard</u> or <u>alcove</u> with <u>doors</u> or a <u>screen</u>, on the <u>wall facing Jerusalem</u>. It's the <u>centrepiece</u> of the synagogue — it holds the <u>Torah</u> (see p.39) and <u>symbolises</u> the <u>ark</u> (box) that held the tablets God gave to Moses. Often, a copy of the <u>10 commandments</u> is hung above the ark.

### Sefer Torah (Scroll of the Torah)

A parchment <u>scroll</u> kept <u>inside</u> the <u>ark</u>. It must be <u>handwritten</u> by a <u>sofer</u> (scribe). It's usually covered with a <u>mantle</u> (cloth), or sometimes by a <u>case</u>, which is <u>ornately decorated</u>.

### Ner Tamid (Perpetual Light)

A <u>light</u> above the ark which <u>never</u> goes out. It represents the <u>menorah</u> (see below) which was <u>always alight</u> in the Temple.

"...keep the lamps burning before the Lord..." Exodus 27:21 NIV

### Bimah or Almemar

A <u>raised platform</u> with a <u>reading desk</u>. <u>Orthodox</u> synagogues usually have it in the <u>centre</u>, while <u>Progressive</u> ones often have it <u>close</u> to the <u>ark</u>. It represents the <u>altar</u> in the Temple.

## Synagogues are Important to the Community

1) There are <u>no pictures</u> of <u>God</u> or <u>people</u> in a synagogue. This is because the <u>second</u> of the Ten Commandments (see p.42) forbids <u>idolatry</u> (worshipping pictures or objects).

2) Some synagogues also have a <u>menorah</u> — a <u>seven-branched</u> candlestick.

3) <u>Orthodox synagogues</u> have <u>separate sections</u> for <u>women</u>. <u>Progressive</u> synagogues have <u>mixed</u> seating.

4) Synagogues are not only used for <u>worship</u> but are <u>important centres</u> for the Jewish <u>community</u> — they are used as <u>meeting places</u> for <u>study groups</u> and <u>social clubs</u>.

REVISION TASK

## Learn the names of the four main synagogue features

Orthodox and Progressive synagogues share many of the same features with just a few differences. See if you can write down the main features you would expect to find in a synagogue and then explain the differences between an Orthodox synagogue and a Progressive synagogue.

# Worship

Orthodox services and Progressive services have some similarities but also some big differences.

## There are **Three Daily Services**

1) The Tenakh shows it's important to worship God together — for example, Psalm 116:14 NIV says "I will fulfil my vows to the Lord in the presence of all his people", i.e. in the presence of other Jews.

2) Attending synagogue can remind Jews of the importance of their faith and of their closeness to God. Some Jews believe God (Shekhinah, see p.40) is present when Jews worship together.

3) Orthodox synagogues hold services three times a day — shacharit (the morning service), minchah (afternoon) and ma'ariv (evening). Minchah is often just before sunset so that ma'ariv can follow straight afterwards (at sunset). Progressive synagogues tend not to have weekday services, although some do.

> Shacharit is the longest service (an hour), while minchah and ma'ariv last about half an hour each. They include blessings (thanks to God), songs of praise, prayers and sometimes a sermon from the rabbi. On Mondays, Thursdays, Shabbat and festivals, shacharit includes a Torah reading (sidrah) and a Nevi'im reading (haftarah).

## **Prayer** is a **Central Part** of the **Service**

1) The siddur (prayer book) is used during each service — it sets out the order of the daily prayers.

2) Ten people (known as a minyan) must be present for certain prayers to be said and the Torah to be read. In Orthodox Judaism these must all be men, but in Progressive Judaism they can be women too.

3) Services are often led by a rabbi — a religious leader responsible for teaching and advising the community. But any adult (male in Orthodox Judaism) with enough religious knowledge can do so. A hazzan (cantor — singer) leads the prayers, which are often sung or chanted. They might also lead the service.

4) The hazzan stands at the front of the hall. The hazzan prays in the same direction as everyone else in Orthodox services. If Progressive synagogues have a hazzan, they tend to face the congregation.

5) Progressive Jews pray in unison. Orthodox Jews pray at their own pace, often with varying movements.

6) Orthodox services are in Hebrew, except the sermon — Progressive ones are partly in the local language.

7) Progressive synagogues may have instruments or choirs to accompany singing, but Orthodox ones don't.

8) Jews face Jerusalem during prayer. There are times in prayer, e.g. during the Amidah (p.48), when Jews bend their knees and bow to show respect to God. Orthodox Jews often sway to help them concentrate.

## The **Torah** is Treated with **Great Respect**

The Torah can't be touched, so the reader uses a yad (pointer) to keep their place in the text.

1) Members of the congregation can be called to read from the Torah, which is an honour. It's known as aliyah (going up). There's a reader to do it for them if they don't know Hebrew well enough.

2) A Torah extract is read each week, so the whole Torah is read over 1 year (or 3 in Progressive Judaism).

3) During the service, the ark (see p.46) is opened and the Torah is carried through the congregation to the bimah. As it passes them, people will bow to, kiss or touch the Torah with their tallit (see next page).

---

**EXAM TIP**

## For Jews, worshipping as a group helps strengthen their faith

For 4-mark questions in your exam you can be asked to give two contrasting beliefs or practices, so make sure you're paying special attention to contrasting ideas between different groups.

# Worship

Prayer is an important part of Jewish life, both at the synagogue and at home.

## Prayer is Very Important

1) Prayer is a central part of Jews' relationship with God — they believe God listens to their prayers. Prayers can include giving thanks or praise, confessing to sins, or asking God for something.

2) Many Jews pray three times a day even if they don't attend synagogue — it's a mitzvah to do so. They say the same prayers as in the services, but in a reduced form. This includes the Shema and Amidah.

> "Evening, morning and noon I cry out in distress, and he hears my voice." Psalm 55:17 NIV

- The Shema is a declaration of faith in only one God. It's in three parts, taken from the Torah (Deuteronomy 6:4-9 and 11:13-21 and Numbers 15:37-41). Jews should say it morning and night. The first sentence of the Shema is said when the Torah's taken from the ark.

> "Hear, O Israel: the Lord our God, the Lord is one." Deuteronomy 6:4 NIV

- Many Jews have a copy of the first two parts of the Shema on every doorpost in their house (except the bathroom). It's written on a tiny parchment scroll called a mezuzah.

The Amidah ('standing prayer') is a set of 19 blessings. It begins by praising God, then asks for things such as justice, and ends with thanksgiving and asking for peace. It's said at weekday services — a short version is used for Shabbat and other festivals.

3) Women are traditionally seen as exempt from the mitzvah concerning services and prayer, but as a minimum it's thought they should say the Amidah twice a day. They often pray at home.

4) Full concentration on prayer is vital — it's known as 'kavanah', and without it prayers don't count.

5) Jews can pray spontaneously (make up their own prayers when they want) — this should be in addition to set prayers, which provide a structure for daily prayer. Many Jews say blessings before and after meals.

6) Jewish men often wear special clothing for prayer and worship. Tefillin are two boxes containing Torah passages, worn during shacharit (except on Shabbat and festivals). One is strapped to the upper arm and one to the head, reminding them to serve God with head and heart. A tallit (prayer shawl) is also worn during shacharit — it has fringes (tzitzit) tied in a special way, to remind Jews of the mitzvot.

7) Many men wear a cap called a kippah (yarmulke) as a sign of respect to God. Orthodox men wear them all day — Progressive and Conservative Jews tend to wear them only if praying or at the synagogue.

## Shabbat (Sabbath) is Celebrated in the Synagogue

> Observing Shabbat is one of the 10 Commandments.

Shabbat is a day of rest to commemorate the seventh day of creation, when God rested after creating the universe. It begins at sunset on Friday and lasts until Saturday evening. It's a time for reflection and worship, away from the stress of daily life. It's also a chance for the community to get together — Shabbat services are well-attended family occasions. The services are similar to the weekday ones, with some additions:

| Friday Evening | Saturday Morning | Saturday Afternoon/Evening |
|---|---|---|
| Progressive synagogues tend to have this at a set time rather than at sunset. The kiddush (see p.49) is said. Shabbat is welcomed with a set of hymns, psalms and prayers called Kabbalat Shabbat (Welcoming the Sabbath). | The main service of the week. There are Torah and Nevi'im readings, and hymns and prayers about the importance of the Torah. Orthodox Jews have an additional service called musaf afterwards. | The afternoon service includes a reading from the Torah, as well as prayers. It's followed by ma'ariv, which finishes with the havdalah (see p.49) to end Shabbat. |

## Prayer has to be focused and sincere

Shut the book, and write down as much as you can about the Shema and Amidah. Just testing...

# Family Life

The <u>home</u> is also an important place of <u>worship</u> and <u>ritual</u> for Jews — Judaism is a <u>family-focused</u> religion.

## Shabbat is Celebrated in the Home

1) The house is <u>cleaned</u> and <u>tidied</u> before Shabbat. Any <u>food</u> to be eaten on Shabbat is cooked <u>in advance</u>, because no 'work' can be done on Shabbat. 'Work' includes things like <u>cooking</u> or <u>gardening</u>. The <u>Torah</u> lists what 'work' is <u>forbidden</u>, but rabbis have updated it to <u>today's world</u>, e.g. to include <u>driving</u>.

2) A <u>family member</u> (usually <u>female</u>) lights two <u>candles</u> to mark the start of Shabbat. They say a blessing while <u>covering</u> their eyes. They may pass their hands over the candles to <u>welcome</u> Shabbat to the home.

3) At the <u>start</u> of the Shabbat meal, <u>kiddush</u> is said to set the Shabbat apart as <u>holy</u>. It includes reciting Genesis 2:1-3 (in which God rests after creation) and saying a blessing over <u>wine</u> which is then drunk.

4) After kiddush, Jews <u>wash their hands</u> in a set way. <u>Challot</u> are eaten — these are <u>two plaited loaves</u> to commemorate the double portion of '<u>manna</u>' (miraculous food) provided by God the day before each Shabbat during the <u>Exodus</u> (see p.41). A blessing is said over them before they're cut and dipped in salt.

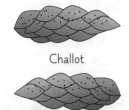

Challot

5) <u>Parents</u> (traditionally the <u>father</u>) often <u>bless</u> their <u>children</u>. Shabbat is a key way they <u>learn</u> about Judaism.

6) The <u>havdalah</u> ('division') ceremony marks the <u>end</u> of Shabbat, separating it from the six days ahead. Blessings are said over sweet-smelling <u>spices</u>, a cup of <u>wine</u> and a <u>plaited candle</u> with several wicks.

## Many Jews Follow Strict Dietary Laws

1) The set of <u>food laws</u> written in the Torah is known as <u>kashrut</u> — have a look at Leviticus 11 and Deuteronomy 14:2-21. Permitted food is called <u>kosher</u> — everything else is <u>trefah</u> ('torn').

*You might come across '<u>treif</u>', which is <u>Yiddish</u> for '<u>trefah</u>'.*

2) To be <u>kosher</u>, a mammal must have both <u>cloven</u> (split) hooves and <u>chew cud</u>. Sea creatures with both <u>fins</u> and <u>scales</u> are kosher, but <u>no</u> other seafood is. All <u>poultry</u> is <u>kosher</u>, but some other birds aren't.

3) Animals must be killed by a specially-trained person, with <u>a cut across the throat</u> using a sharp blade. <u>Blood</u> can't be eaten, so it must be drained from meat. <u>Meat</u> and <u>dairy</u> products can't be eaten <u>together</u>.

4) Some foods <u>can't</u> be eaten if they've been cooked only by someone who isn't <u>Jewish</u>.

5) <u>Orthodox</u> Jews keep <u>kashrut</u>. <u>Progressive</u> Judaism leaves it up to the <u>individual</u> — some <u>Progressive</u> Jews only observe <u>some</u> of the laws, or keep kashrut at <u>home</u> but eat <u>non-kosher food</u> elsewhere.

6) Keeping <u>kashrut</u> shows <u>self-control</u> and <u>obedience</u> to God — it's a religious <u>ritual</u> and part of the <u>mitzvot</u>. However, because of <u>pikuach nefesh</u> (p.42), kashrut can be <u>broken</u> if necessary for <u>medical</u> reasons.

## Kosher food relates to what is allowed and how it should be prepared

Kosher meat, for example, doesn't just relate to what kind of animal the meat comes from, but how it was killed, processed and prepared. Some Jews follow these dietary laws more strictly than others — make sure you know the differences in opinions between different branches of Judaism.

# Family Life

Jewish children go through rituals when they are born and to celebrate when they come of age.

## Judaism has **Rituals** to **Mark** Different **Life Stages**

There are Jewish rituals to mark different life stages. These tend to vary between different strands of Judaism. This begins from birth, with the brit milah (circumcision) for boys or simchat bat (naming ceremony) for girls.

### Brit milah — circumcision

1) Nearly all boys are circumcised (have their foreskin removed), regardless of which strand of Judaism they're born into. Boys don't have to be circumcised to be Jewish, but many people worry that their son will be alienated if he isn't circumcised.

2) It's a sign they belong to the Jewish faith and it's part of the covenant God made with Abraham (p.41) — God asked that "every male among you shall be circumcised" (Genesis 17:10 NIV).

3) It's usually done at home, 7 days after the baby's born (even if it's Shabbat). If the boy's not healthy enough, it happens later.

4) The circumcision is performed by a mohel (a Jewish person trained to do the procedure). The mohel and the father each say a blessing before it starts.

5) The brit milah is followed by saying the kiddush and giving the boy his Hebrew name. Then there's a celebratory meal.

### Simchat bat — naming ceremony

1) This can also be known as the brit bat or the zeved habat (bat means daughter).

2) This developed recently so that there was an equivalent ceremony in the home to welcome the birth of a girl.

3) The ceremonies vary a lot, but they often involve songs of thanks, blessings, a ritual to welcome the girl into the covenant (e.g. lighting candles), an explanation of the choice of names, and the kiddush.

4) Orthodox Jews are less likely to do this. Instead, the girl is given her Hebrew name during a synagogue service. Her father will give a Torah reading.

## The **Bar** or **Bat Mitzvah** is a **Coming of Age** Ceremony

In Progressive Judaism it's 13 for both genders.

1) At 13 a Jewish boy becomes bar mitzvah and at 12 a girl becomes bat mitzvah — a son or daughter of the commandments. It means they have to fulfil the mitzvot — they're responsible for living in a religious way.

2) They don't have to do anything to become bar or bat mitzvah — it's defined by their age — but there's often a ceremony to celebrate. The ceremony is also known as a bar or bat mitzvah.

3) The ceremony forms part of a synagogue service (often on Shabbat). The young person might lead some of the prayers, read from the Tenakh, give a speech or read some of the blessings. If they give a reading, they prepare for it beforehand by studying the relevant portion and learning to read it in Hebrew.

- In Orthodox Judaism, most girls don't have a bat mitzvah ceremony, as they don't have the same responsibilities towards worship as men (see p.48). There is continuing debate about whether this should change so they're treated equally.

- Instead, Orthodox girls have a bat hayil (daughter of valour) ceremony. It's held after one of the services, and all girls who have turned 12 in the previous year recite a religious passage or give a speech in front of family and friends.

- Nearly all Progressive Jews have a bar/bat mitzvah — as do Conservative Jews. They tend to be the same for boys and girls.

## Ceremonies for girls differ between Orthodox and Progressive Jews

The brit milah and bar mitzvah are treated in similar ways for Orthodox and Progressive Jews, but the ceremonies for girls are treated differently. Make sure you know the possible ceremonies for girls and boys.

# Family Life | Judaism

Marriage is central to the idea of family in Judaism. The importance of family is also seen in Jewish mourning rituals — there are set rules that Jews follow when mourning family members, particularly when a parent dies.

## Marriage is Very Important in Judaism

1) Marriage is important in Judaism, because much of Judaism is focused on family and the home.

2) Marriage ceremonies are in two parts, called the kiddushin (the betrothal) and the nisuin (the wedding).

3) The wedding usually happens in a synagogue. It takes place under a huppah (canopy), which can be a simple tallit (p.48) or more elaborate. The huppah symbolises the home the couple will build together.

4) Firstly, blessings are said over a cup of wine, which the couple drinks, symbolising the life they will share.

5) The groom gives the bride a ring and says the wedding vow — this completes the kiddushin. At Progressive Jewish weddings, both the bride and the groom exchange rings and say the vow.

6) The ketubah (marriage contract) is read out. The traditional ketubah states the bride's right to be cared for by her husband and her entitlements in case of divorce or death (a bit like a prenuptial agreement). Progressive Jews have rewritten the ketubah to be a mutual statement of love and commitment.

7) The nisuin starts with seven blessings (sheva b'rakhot) said over wine, in which God is praised for creating the universe and humanity, and for the gift of children. There are also blessings for Israel and Jerusalem.

8) Finally, a glass is broken by stepping on it. There are various interpretations of this — it's thought to symbolise the destruction of the Temple (see p.46) or emphasise that love needs to be protected.

## Jewish Mourning Rituals Allow People Time to Grieve

1) Mourning family members perform kriah — they make a tear in clothing or a ribbon, as a symbol of grief.
2) The funeral service often includes prayers, psalms and a eulogy (a speech praising the dead person).
3) The Kaddish, a prayer praising God, is said so people focus on God at a time they may feel far from him.
4) The seven days following the burial are known as shiva. Close family mourn during this time. Orthodox Jews (and some Progressive) don't leave the house, attend synagogue or work during shiva. Other mourners visit their house to comfort them and to form a minyan (see p.47) for the Kaddish.
5) The loss of a parent is particularly significant in Judaism. If someone has lost a parent they remain in mourning for a whole year — this is known as avelut. During this time, there are some restrictions, e.g. they won't go to parties. They also say the Kaddish every day for 11 months. For other relatives, Jews mourn for a month after the funeral — this is called sheloshim (thirty).
6) The Kaddish is also said on each Yahrzeit (anniversary of the death). On the eve of the Yahrzeit, many light a candle for 24 hours. It's a day of remembrance, during which some people fast.

**EXAM TIP**

## There are a fair few Hebrew words on this page...

...so make sure you learn to spell them correctly — it could get you marks for SPaG (see p.169-171). Make a list of any words you struggle to spell, so you can try extra hard to learn them.

# Festivals

Rosh Hashanah, Yom Kippur and Pesach (Passover) are important holy days in the Jewish year.

## Rosh Hashanah and Yom Kippur focus on Atoning for Sins

These festivals are two stages in the process of judgement and atonement (making amends for wrongdoing).

**ROSH HASHANAH** is the Jewish New Year — it falls in September or October. It's a time for Jews to consider any wrongdoing in the past year and what they intend to do better in the next, in preparation for Yom Kippur.

1) During the last month of the old year and on the day itself, a shofar (ram's horn) is blown. The shofar is a call for repentance (being sorry for the things you've done wrong) and spiritual reawakening.

2) As on Shabbat, no work is done and Jews spend most of the day in the synagogue. Prayers describing God's judgement and his role as 'king' are said, as well as ones hoping for forgiveness. The Torah is read.

3) Bread and apples dipped in honey are eaten, to symbolise the hope for a 'sweet' (pleasant) year to come.

4) It's thought God writes people's names in certain books on Rosh Hashanah. The truly good go straight into the 'Book of Life', but most go in the 'intermediate' book (there's a 'Book of Death' for the truly evil).

5) Those in the intermediate book can affect whether they'll end up in the Book of Life during the days of awe (the 10 days until Yom Kippur). The decision can be influenced by repentance — also known as teshuva, meaning 'turning' back to God. Prayer and good deeds (tzedakah) can also help.

6) The tashlich ('casting away') ceremony takes place — a prayer is said to ask God to remove the sins of his people. The ceremony is carried out next to water, e.g. a river or the sea.

**YOM KIPPUR** is a day of atonement. It's the holiest day of the year, so no work is done during it. It gives Jews the chance to ask God to forgive the sins they've committed over the past year.

1) It involves fasting for 25 hours — this helps Jews focus on spiritual rather than physical matters. Washing, bathing, using cosmetics, wearing leather shoes and having sex are all forbidden on Yom Kippur.

2) Worship in the synagogue is central to Yom Kippur. It's a mitzvah to attend all the services:

> • On Yom Kippur eve, the Kol Nidre ('all vows') prayer is said. It cancels all vows between a person and God in the coming year. It releases Jews from a focus on vows they might not keep, so they can concentrate on their true relationship with God.
>
> • The next day is spent in the synagogue, with readings from the Torah and prayers to confess any sins and show repentance.
>
> • The day ends with a service called the Neilah ('closing of the gates'), symbolising a final chance to repent as the gates of heaven are about to close and the Book of Life will be sealed. The shofar is then blown to mark the end of Yom Kippur.

## Pesach (Passover) Commemorates the Exodus
Pesach is in March or April.

1) Pesach commemorates the events leading up to the Israelites' escape from slavery in Egypt, as well as the Exodus itself (see p.41). Pesach means 'to spare' or 'to pass over', referring to the night when the angel of death killed the Egyptians' first-born sons, but 'passed over' the Israelites without harming them.

2) It lasts 7 or 8 days. On the first night or first two nights, it's celebrated with seder — a service and meal.

3) Each food symbolises a part of the Exodus story, which is retold by the head of the family during seder using a book of ritual called the Haggadah. Exodus 12:3-8 states what food to include in seder.

> • Karpas — a vegetable dipped in salt water, to remind Jews of the pain and tears caused by slavery.
>
> • Matzah (unleavened bread) — bread made from flour, water and no yeast, which Jews made for the Exodus. Anything made from grain and water that has 'risen' (fermented) is called 'chametz' and can't be eaten during Pesach.
>
> • Maror (bitter herbs) — a bitter vegetable, usually raw horseradish, is eaten to remind Jews of the bitterness of slavery.
>
> • Baytsah (egg) — the egg's hard-boiled and roasted. It symbolises the sacrifices once offered in the Temple.
>
> • Z'roah (lamb bone) — this isn't eaten (neither is the egg) but it symbolises the lamb sacrificed on the night of the Exodus.

# Worked Exam Questions

On the next couple of pages there are some questions similar to the ones you'll get in your exam.
On this page, the answers have been filled in for you, but on the next page you'll have to fill them in yourself.

1  How long does Passover (Pesach) last?
Put a tick (✓) in the correct box.

A    6-7 days        ☐

B    7-8 days        ✓

C    9-10 days       ☐

D    12 days         ☐

*[1 mark]*

2  Which of the following is the Jewish declaration of faith in one God?
Put a tick (✓) in the correct box.

A    Mitzvot         ☐

B    Menorah         ☐

C    Tallit          ☐

D    Shema           ✓

*[1 mark]*

3  Give two ways in which the Torah is treated with respect.

1) The Torah is kept in the Ark (Aron Hakodesh).

2) It must not be touched directly. Those reading from the Torah use a pointer (yad).

*[2 marks]*

4  Explain two Jewish beliefs about circumcision (brit milah).
Your answer should refer to specific Jewish teachings or sacred texts.

Jewish boys should be circumcised at birth as a mark of faithfulness to God and the covenant.

Circumcision was a part of the covenant between God and Abraham in the Torah: "every male

among you shall be circumcised" (Genesis 17:10 NIV).

Circumcision should be accompanied by a blessing, the naming of the boy with his Hebrew name

and a celebratory meal.

*[5 marks]*

# Exam Questions

**5** Which of the following refers to the meaning behind the Jewish festival of Yom Kippur? Put a tick (✓) in the correct box.

A   Atonement ☐

B   Judgement ☐

C   Exile ☐

D   Confession ☐

*[1 mark]*

**6** Give two examples of Jewish marriage rituals.

1) ...................................................................................................................................

...................................................................................................................................

2) ...................................................................................................................................

...................................................................................................................................

*[2 marks]*

**7** Give two contrasting ways in which mourning rituals are carried out.

...................................................................................................................................

...................................................................................................................................

...................................................................................................................................

...................................................................................................................................

...................................................................................................................................

...................................................................................................................................

...................................................................................................................................

*[4 marks]*

**8** 'The Tenakh contains everything Jews need to know to live their daily lives well.'

Evaluate this statement. Your answer should include the following:
• examples from Jewish teachings
• arguments that support the statement
• arguments that disagree with the statement
• a conclusion.

*Write your answer on a separate sheet of paper.*

*[12 marks]*

# Revision Summary

Now that Judaism is all wrapped up, it's time to test how much you've learnt.

- Try these questions and <u>tick off each one</u> when you <u>get it right</u>.
- When you've done <u>all the questions</u> for a topic and are <u>completely happy</u> with it, tick off the topic.

## Beliefs (p.39-43) ☑

1) What is the Tanakh? ☑
2) What is contained in each of the two parts of the Nevi'im? ☑
3) Explain how Orthodox and Progressive Jews view the Torah and Talmud differently. ☑
4) What are the two main movements of Progressive Jews? ☑
5) Name and describe two characteristics of God. ☑
6) What is Shekhinah? ☑
7) What did God promise to Abraham? ☑
8) What did God ask of Abraham and his descendants? ☑
9) What was the Exodus? ☑
10) What did God give to Moses? ☑
11) What are the mitzvot? ☑
12) What are the mitzvot ta'aseh? ☑
13) What is the difference between ritual and moral mitzvot? ☑
14) Why is pikuach nefesh more important than many of the mitzvot? ☑
15) What is Sheol? ☑
16) Where do some Jews believe souls will go after they die to be purified? ☑
17) What do many Jews believe the Messiah will do when he comes? ☑
18) Why is cremation forbidden for Orthodox Jews? ☑

## Practices (p.46-52) ☑

19) What are the four features found in all synagogues? ☑
20) What is a menorah? ☑
21) What are the Jewish terms used to describe the three daily services at Orthodox synagogues? ☑
22) What is a yad? ☑
23) What is the Shema? ☑
24) What is kavanah and why is it important? ☑
25) When is the Shabbat? ☑
26) Why is food cooked in advance of the Shabbat? ☑
27) What is kashrut? ☑
28) What meat is kosher? ☑
29) Why is the brit milah important? ☑
30) Why might some Jewish girls not have a bat mitzvah? ☑
31) What does the huppah symbolise? ☑
32) Give one explanation for why a glass is broken at a Jewish wedding. ☑
33) What is shiva? ☑
34) What happens on the eve and on the day of Yahrzeit? ☑
35) What is Yom Kippur? ☑
36) Give an example of a food eaten at Pesach and explain its symbolism. ☑

## All religions | Sexuality and Sexual Relationships

For this whole section, you must be aware of religious and non-religious views in Britain, and be able to give two or more contrasting religious views on homosexuality, contraception and sex before marriage, at least one being Christian.

## Islam, Christianity and Judaism have Similar Attitudes to Sex

1) Traditionally, all three religions teach that the only correct context for sexual activity is within marriage.

2) Sex outside of marriage is seen as a sin. This means cohabitation (living together unmarried) isn't approved of. These ideas are backed up by sacred texts and teachings in Christianity, Judaism and Islam:

> Qur'an 23:7 states that "whoever seeks beyond [marriage] then those are the transgressors".

> The Catechism of the Catholic Church says "Sexuality is ordered to the conjugal love of man and woman" (2360). 'Conjugal' means 'within marriage'. It also says that sex is 'unitive' and 'procreative' — to bring married couples together as one and for having children.

> In Judaism, Maimonides' list of mitzvot says sexual relationships shouldn't happen without a ketubah and kiddushin (p.51) — see Sefer Hamitzvot no. 355.

3) Christians, Muslims and Jews are urged to keep sex within marriage for positive reasons as well — marriage is believed to make sex more special. All three religions stress the importance of enjoying sex. The Song of Songs in the Bible and Ketuvim contains poems celebrating sexual desire and relationships.

> "Let him kiss me with kisses of his mouth — for your love is more delightful than wine."
> Song of Songs 1:2 NIV

> "I belong to my beloved, and his desire is for me. Come my beloved, let us go to the countryside, let us spend the night in the villages"
> Song of Songs 7:10-11 NIV

4) 'Strict' members of all three faiths think the principle of only having sex within marriage still applies. More liberal members might see this as outdated, although they still tend to see marriage as the ideal.

## Others in Society Have Very Different Views

- Promiscuity (having multiple sexual partners) is often seen as wrong in all three religions. But many British people think it's acceptable, especially now contraception (see p.58) is widely available — though a large number of sexual partners is seen more negatively.

- Atheists and humanists tend to accept sex outside of marriage. Humanists accept it as long as it causes no harm to anyone. Generally, sex outside of marriage is considered normal in British society.

## You'll be asked to refer to sacred texts in the exam

In some questions you'll be asked to support a view by referring to a sacred text. Make a list of quotes for the religions you're studying while you're revising, so you can look back over them later.

# Sexuality and Sexual Relationships

Homosexuality is attraction to members of the same sex. Heterosexuality is attraction to the opposite sex.

## Homosexuality is a Disputed Topic

1) Many people in British society consider both heterosexuality and homosexuality to be natural and normal.

2) The Christian, Muslim and Jewish scriptures seem to say that homosexual sex is wrong — though the relevant bits are interpreted differently by some. They only condemn sex between men, not between women, which is hardly mentioned. (Though it's often frowned upon because male homosexuality is.)

> The story of Sodom (see Genesis 19:3-25) is used by Christianity, Islam and Judaism to argue against homosexuality. The city's destroyed after the men in Sodom demand sex with two male angels God sent, which some people use to show that homosexuality's wrong. The angels say God sent them to destroy the city because of sin, so others say he was going to destroy it anyway and it wasn't because the men wanted sex with them.

3) The texts don't condemn people who have homosexual feelings but don't act upon them. This means some people who are homosexual and religious opt for celibacy (they don't have sexual relationships).

4) Some argue that as the scriptures were written in a different cultural context from ours, we can't apply their standards today. Generally, the religions condemn homophobia and they're becoming more accepting of homosexuality, but it isn't seen as ideal and many see homosexual sex as a sin.

## There are Different Opinions Within Religions

There are different points of view about homosexuality — even within the same religion. For example:

> The Anglican Church is split on the topic. There are some openly gay clergy in the Church of England, but conservative members don't approve of homosexuality. 1 Corinthians 6:9-10 suggests it's a sin.

> The Catechism of the Catholic Church says "Under no circumstances can [homosexual acts] be approved" (2357). It urges homosexual people to stay celibate but says they shouldn't face any discrimination.

> Many Muslims think the Qur'an bans homosexuality, due to the Sodom story (e.g. Qur'an 7:81 "you approach men with desire, instead of women ... you are a transgressing people"). Some Muslims disagree and argue that these teachings should be reinterpreted.

> Progressive Jews usually accept homosexuality. Homosexual people can become Progressive rabbis. Orthodox Jews tend to be against it — homosexual sex is forbidden in Leviticus 18:22 NIV, which calls it 'detestable'.

The first same-sex marriages in the UK took place in 2014 — see p.59-62 for different religions' views.

---

 **EXAM TIP** Traditionally the religions had quite similar views on these topics...

...but remember there are now different views within each religion, e.g. Orthodox and Progressive Jews. You often have to give two views in the exam and you get marks for the level of detail.

# Contraception

For this topic, you need to learn one Christian view as well as at least one other contrasting religious view.

## Contraception Prevents a Woman Becoming Pregnant

*Using contraception is sometimes called 'family planning'.*

1) Contraception is also known as birth control and is used to stop a woman conceiving. It can be temporary (e.g. the contraceptive pill or condoms) or permanent (sterilisation).

2) Most atheists and humanists have no objection to contraception. They think it's better if people only have children if they really want them. Contraception allows people to choose when to have sex, by limiting the risk of pregnancy. Some types also reduce the risk of STIs (sexually transmitted infections).

3) Some Christians, Muslims and Jews object to forms of contraception that might destroy a fertilised egg, such as the morning after pill — this is because they see it as being the same as abortion (see p.80).

4) Many religious people don't believe in sterilisation, which prevents people ever having children.

## The Roman Catholic Church is Against Artificial Contraception

1) The Catholic Church says anything "deliberately contraceptive" is "intrinsically wrong" (Humanae Vitae 14). Married couples should "transmit human life" (Catechism of the Catholic Church 2367), i.e. have children.

2) Many individual Roman Catholics disagree with this stance, especially because of concerns about STIs.

3) The Church says contraception may lead to promiscuity (p.56) and sees some methods as abortion. It does allow natural contraception — only having sex at the less fertile times in a woman's menstrual cycle.

4) Other Christian Churches have different views. The Anglican, Methodist and Presbyterian Churches are in favour of contraception, suggesting that it lets parents plan their family in a responsible way.

5) Many Christians believe that contraception should be a question of individual conscience. They see it as positive that women can control when they get pregnant.

## Orthodox and Progressive Jews tend to have Differing Views

1) Judaism traditionally teaches that a child is a gift from God, and contraception interferes with God's plans to bless couples with children.

*"A man shall not abstain from [propagating] the race unless he already has children." Talmud Yevamot 61b*

2) Most Orthodox Jews only accept contraception for compassionate reasons, e.g. if pregnancy could be physically or psychologically harmful to the mother or an existing child.

3) Some find contraception within marriage acceptable if the couple do plan to have children later on.

4) Progressive Jews find contraception more acceptable and leave the decision to each individual.

5) Sex should be as natural as possible so hormonal contraceptives like the pill are generally preferred to barrier methods like condoms. But some agree with barrier methods as a means of preventing STIs.

## There are Different Attitudes to Contraception within Islam

1) Some Muslims see contraception as wrong — they might refer to the hadith Sahih al-Bukhari 34:432, which says conception is Allah's will and suggests people shouldn't try to avoid it. Other Muslims believe that another hadith, Sahih al-Bukhari 62:136, supports the use of contraception.

2) It's the right of both husband and wife to try for children, so both partners must agree to contraception.

3) Reasons for using contraception are usually focused on whether another child may cause harm to the mother, any existing children or to the potential child, e.g. if the family can't afford to feed another child.

4) Only 'reversible' methods are allowed, though — sterilisation and vasectomies are usually not accepted.

## Remember that religious views focus on marital sex

Views on contraception focus mainly on its use within marriage to help married couples plan their families. 'Strict' members of some religions think that contraception might also encourage sex outside of marriage.

# Marriage and Divorce

Marriage is becoming less common in modern British society, but is still highly valued in religion.

## Marriage in the UK — Things have Changed

1) The number of marriages taking place in the UK each year has been decreasing over the last 40 years. People are also tending to get married later in life, and many people have children without being married.

2) Same-sex marriages are now legal in the UK. Many people see this as a good thing because it creates equality.

3) Although many non-religious people still see marriage as important, others see it as unnecessary. It's now more common (and acceptable) for people to cohabit (live together) — either before marrying or instead of getting married. Cohabiting couples don't have the same legal rights as married ones though.

4) Divorce is also far more common. Non-religious people often see it as sensible if the couple don't get on, as they'll be happier if they divorce. Some argue parents fighting can harm children more than divorce. However, many religious people see marriage as very important, and try to avoid divorce if at all possible.

## Christians think Marriage is Important and Holy

1) The Christian faith values marriage very highly — marriage reflects the union of Jesus with his followers. In the book 'Not Just Good, but Beautiful', Pope Francis said marriage is 'indispensable' to society.

2) Marriage is a covenant (contract) between two people to offer love, support and commitment, and to have children. Nearly all Christians see polygamy (marriage to multiple people) as wrong.

3) Many accept cohabitation, especially as preparation for marriage. Some don't — they disagree with sex outside marriage. The Catholic Church tends to be against it, but Pope Francis has recognised it can be hard for people to marry, e.g. for financial reasons — but they should be encouraged to marry eventually.

4) Faithfulness in marriage is important — adultery is forbidden in the Ten Commandments (Exodus 20:14).

## Christians are Divided over Same-Sex Marriage

1) The decision to legalise same-sex marriage in the UK was criticised by the Catholic Church and the Church of England. Many members of the clergy are against it.

> "The Church of England affirms, according to our Lord's teaching, that marriage is ... a union... of one man with one woman."  Canon B30

2) But some Church of England clergy will say thanksgiving prayers with same-sex couples after they marry in civil (non-religious) ceremonies.

3) It's splitting the Anglican Church. Supporters of same-sex marriage say Christians should be loving to all and should support anyone who wants to marry. Those against it say it's a sin. They also think it's wrong because one of the main purposes of marriage is having children.

4) The Catholic Church is more strongly against homosexual relationships and same-sex marriage.

5) Members of the congregation (particularly younger people) within the Catholic Church and the Church of England tend to be more likely to be in favour of same-sex marriage than their church leaders.

---

## Opinions on marriage differ within Christianity

Try comparing the views of the various branches of Christianity with others in modern British society.

# Marriage and Divorce

Christians use religious teachings to guide their opinions on divorce.

## Different Christian Churches have Varying Attitudes to Divorce

1) There are different views as to whether divorce is permissible, or even possible.

- The Roman Catholic Church says it's impossible to divorce (Catechism of the Catholic Church 2382). Marriage is a sacrament — God made the couple one flesh, which can't be undone. However, a marriage can be annulled (declared void) if the couple never had sex or if a partner didn't consent to or understand the marriage, or refused to have children.

- The Church of England says divorce is possible and accepts that some marriages fail. Divorcees can re-marry in church if they find a minister willing to marry them. Some Church members disagree with this.

- Nonconformist Churches (e.g. Baptists and Methodists) will usually re-marry divorcees, but an individual minister can refuse to do so if it goes against their conscience.

2) Jesus himself was anti-divorce:

> "A man [and] his wife ... will become one flesh. ... what God has joined together, let no one separate."  Mark 10:7-9 NIV

> "I tell you that anyone who divorces his wife, except for sexual immorality, and marries another woman commits adultery"  Matthew 19:9 NIV

3) Jesus was also forgiving of someone who had broken their marriage vows, but encouraged them to change their ways. In John 8:2-11, Jesus forgives a woman who's committed adultery — but he tells her, "Go now and leave your life of sin" (NIV).

4) Some Christians view an unhappy marriage as a waste of two lives, and so see divorce as preferable.

## Marriage is Strongly Recommended in Islam

1) Marriage provides companionship, love and stability. Muslims believe marriage is Allah's will — it says in Qur'an 24:32 "marry the unmarried among you" and 30:21 "He created for you ... mates that you may find tranquillity in them; and He placed between you affection...".

2) Islam is family-oriented, so marriage is important. It's a secure environment for having children (procreation). Cohabitation often isn't accepted as it tends to involve sex outside of marriage.

3) According to a hadith, Muhammad said that marriage was half of a Muslim's faith.

4) Qur'an 4:1-24 clearly sets out rules for who people can marry and how much different people inherit.

5) Nikah is the name for marriage under shari'ah — Islamic law. To have the marriage recognised as legal in Britain, couples must also have a civil wedding ceremony.

6) Some Muslims have arranged marriages. This is where the parents will choose a marriage partner for their child. However, both potential partners have the right to say no to marrying their parents' choice.

7) Polygamy is criticised by many Muslims, but others believe the Qur'an allows it. A man should only take multiple wives if he can treat them equally. Some criticise the fact it's only allowed for men. Polygamy is illegal in the UK, but polygamous marriages are accepted if they took place elsewhere.

8) Adultery is a sin — the Qur'an calls it "evil" (Qur'an 17:32). Some Muslim countries punish it severely.

# Marriage and Divorce

<u>Muslims</u> have different opinions on <u>same-sex marriage</u> — some support it but some are against it.

## Same-Sex Marriage is a **Controversial Topic** in Islam

1) Many Muslims are <u>against</u> same-sex marriage as they believe <u>homosexual sex</u> is <u>forbidden</u> by the Qur'an (see p.57). The <u>Muslim Council of Britain</u> spoke against the law <u>legalising</u> same-sex marriage in the UK, arguing it was <u>unnecessary</u> because <u>civil partnerships</u> gave same-sex couples <u>equal rights</u> anyway and that same-sex marriage <u>undermined</u> the definition of marriage as between a man and a woman.

2) Some Muslims see it as <u>wrong</u> because marriage is partly for having <u>children</u>.

3) However, some Muslims do <u>support</u> same-sex marriage. They argue that homosexuality is <u>normal</u> and that it's <u>good</u> for same-sex couples to have the chance to be married, as <u>marriage</u> is <u>important</u> in Islam.

4) Others have argued that, since Muslims are a <u>minority</u> in <u>Britain</u>, they should help out another minority by <u>supporting</u> same-sex marriage, regardless of their <u>individual</u> views on homosexuality.

## Divorce is the **Last Resort** in Islam, but it's **Accepted**

*"Of all the lawful acts the most detestable to Allah is divorce."* Sunan Abi Dawud 12:2173

1) <u>Divorce</u> is <u>permitted</u>, but only as a last resort. If things aren't going well, an <u>arbiter</u> from <u>each family</u> should be appointed to try to sort things out.

2) Muslims see <u>reconciliation</u> as particularly important when the couple have <u>children</u>.

3) Qur'an 2:226-241 lays out the <u>conditions</u> under which divorce can happen. It's possible for a <u>man</u> to divorce his <u>wife</u> by saying 'I divorce you' <u>three times</u>. However, it's often recommended that it should be said <u>once</u> on three <u>separate</u> occasions and that there's a three-month <u>waiting period</u>, to allow time for <u>reflection</u>. The waiting period also ensures the woman is not <u>pregnant</u>.

4) A woman can divorce a man in this way (divorce '<u>by talaq</u>') if it was written into her <u>marriage contract</u>. Otherwise she has to apply to a <u>shari'ah court</u> for a divorce '<u>by khul</u>' (if her husband agrees to divorce) or a <u>tafreeq</u> divorce (if the husband doesn't agree).

5) As Islamic law <u>isn't</u> part of <u>British law</u>, these kinds of divorce dissolve the <u>nikah</u>, but don't count as a <u>legal divorce</u> if the couple also had a <u>civil marriage</u> — they would have to get a <u>civil divorce</u> too.

6) After divorce, both men and women are <u>free</u> to <u>re-marry</u>.

## Marriage is **Important** in Judaism

1) To Jews, <u>marriage</u> is an <u>emotional</u>, <u>intellectual</u> and <u>spiritual</u> union. Many see it as the proper context for <u>sex</u> (seen as natural and God-given) and <u>having children</u> (procreation), but it is also for <u>companionship</u>.

2) Marriage is seen as a <u>sacred</u> thing — the word for the first part of the wedding ceremony, <u>kiddushin</u>, means <u>sanctification</u>. God <u>recommends</u> marriage — in Genesis 2:18 he says "It is not good for the man to be alone" (NIV) and then creates Eve to accompany Adam.

*"He who finds a wife finds what is good and receives favour from the Lord."* Proverbs 18:22 NIV

3) <u>Adultery</u> is seen as <u>sinful</u>, as it goes <u>against</u> the <u>7th commandment</u> (Exodus 20:14).

4) Marriage and children <u>continue</u> the Jewish <u>faith</u>, as it's passed on through the <u>family</u>.

5) This means there's often some <u>anxiety</u> over '<u>marrying out</u>' — marrying someone who <u>isn't Jewish</u>. Jews who have '<u>intermarried</u>' are <u>less likely</u> to carry on Jewish <u>customs</u> and <u>practices</u>. '<u>Intermarriage</u>' is more <u>accepted</u> than it used to be though.

## There are lots of different reasons for marriage

Close up this book and see if you can write down all the reasons given for why people get married.

## Judaism | Marriage and Divorce

Views on alternatives to traditional marriage vary widely within Judaism — with some groups backing same-sex marriage before it was legal, and others still strongly against it.

## There are **Different Views** on **Alternatives** to **Traditional Marriage**

1) Orthodox Jews don't tend to cohabit because sex outside of marriage is seen as wrong. Progressive Jews see cohabitation in a more positive light, but ideally the relationship should be stable and long-term.

2) Technically, the Torah allows polygamy for men — Abraham had two wives, for example. But almost no Jews today are in polygamous marriages.

3) Same-sex marriage is a divisive topic in Judaism:

> **Jewish views on same-sex marriage**
>
> - Liberal and Reform Judaism both backed same-sex marriage before it became legal in the UK, and both hold same-sex weddings in their synagogues now that it's legal.
>
> - Jews who support same-sex marriage refer to Genesis 1:27, "God created mankind in his own image" (NIV) — they say being homosexual can't be wrong, as people have been created homosexual.
>
> - Many Masorti Jews support same-sex marriage. They have created a shutafut (partnership) ceremony for same-sex marriages or civil partnerships — this is different from the traditional kiddushin.
>
> - Individual rabbis in all three movements can choose not to hold same-sex weddings if they want to though.
>
> - Orthodox Jews don't tend to support same-sex marriage, believing it goes against the teachings of the Torah on homosexual sex. There's a growing recognition though among some Orthodox Jews that homosexual Jews need to be welcomed in synagogues and supported.

## **Divorce** is **Allowed**, but it's the **Last Resort**

1) Jews accept that some marriages don't work out, and that it's better for a couple to divorce than to stay together and be unhappy. But divorce is a last resort after all attempts at reconciliation have failed.

2) The Torah teaches that a husband and wife become one entity when they marry, so divorce is difficult and shouldn't be entered into lightly. However, Maimonides' Mishneh Torah does set out conditions for when divorce should happen, e.g. if a man knows his wife has committed adultery.

> "...a man leaves his father and mother and is united to his wife, and they become one flesh." Genesis 2:24 NIV

3) Traditionally, a woman cannot initiate divorce. This has caused an issue for Orthodox women who can't get their husband to agree to a divorce, as they can't remarry in a Jewish ceremony without a get (divorce certificate issued by Jewish courts). Women in this situation are known as agunot (chained women). Wives can also refuse consent for a divorce, but this happens less often.

4) Reform synagogues recognise civil divorces, but people may want a religious divorce too. A Reform Jewish court can issue a get even if the husband won't agree. Reform Jews don't need a get to remarry.

---

## Some Jewish and Christian views come from the same texts...

...so try comparing their views and the different sources they use. This will help you in the exam if you're asked to give similar or contrasting beliefs about marriage and divorce.

# Worked Exam Questions

The next two pages have some exam-style questions on what you've learnt so far.
The first few have been filled in already, so you can see how to go about answering the rest.

1    Which of the following is the term for having multiple sexual partners?
     Put a tick (✓) in the correct box.

     A    Monogamy            ☐

     B    Promiscuity         ✓

     C    Heterosexuality     ☐

     D    Celibacy            ☐

*[1 mark]*

2    Give two religious beliefs about same-sex marriage.

   **1)**  Orthodox Jews tend to reject same-sex marriage due to teachings from the Torah on same-sex
           relationships.

   **2)**  Some Church of England clergy believe we are all accepted by God and will say thanksgiving
           prayers with a same-sex couple following a civil (non-religious) marriage ceremony.

*[2 marks]*

3    Explain two religious beliefs about the purpose of marriage.
     Your answer should refer to specific religious teachings or sacred texts.

       Christians believe that one of the purposes of marriage is companionship.  They believe marriage
     was part of God's intention when he created Eve as a companion for Adam.  Genesis 2:18 says Eve
     was created because "It is not good for the man to be alone".
       Muslims believe that marriage is very important because it provides the right environment for
     having children.  Families are a key feature in Islamic culture and marriage is viewed as an essential
     part of developing the faith.

*[5 marks]*

# Exam Questions

**4** Which of the following is the term for being unfaithful to your marriage partner? Put a tick (✓) in the correct box.

A  Cohabitation ☐

B  Divorce ☐

C  Adultery ☐

D  Annulment ☐

*[1 mark]*

**5** Give two religious beliefs about divorce.

1) ...........................................................................................................................................

...........................................................................................................................................

2) ...........................................................................................................................................

...........................................................................................................................................

*[2 marks]*

**6** Explain two similar religious beliefs in British society today about homosexuality. You must refer to the main religious tradition in the UK and at least one other religious viewpoint.

...........................................................................................................................................

...........................................................................................................................................

...........................................................................................................................................

...........................................................................................................................................

...........................................................................................................................................

...........................................................................................................................................

...........................................................................................................................................

...........................................................................................................................................

*[4 marks]*

# Families

Family life is seen as important in all three religions for the protection and religious education of children.

## Family is Important to Christians, Jews and Muslims

1) Ideally, a stable family can give a child a sense of identity and a feeling of security. They'll learn how to behave, how to give and receive love, and about right and wrong.

2) Many Christians, Jews and Muslims think it's best for a child to have a father and a mother present (ideally the child's biological parents), so that they grow up with one role model of each sex. Ideally, the couple would be married, as it's believed this provides more stability.

3) For religious people, family life can be a way of introducing their children to their faith.

### Christianity and Catholic Christianity

- Family life is important for most Christians. It's seen as a way to build a stable society.

  "family is 'the first and vital cell of society'." Pope John Paul II, Familiaris Consortio 42 (Catholic teachings on family)

- Many Christians believe it's important to have children and educate them in the faith — see for example Catechism of the Catholic Church 2226 and this quote. →

  "bring [your children] up in the training and instruction of the Lord." Ephesians 6:4 NIV

- This might include activities at home such as reading the child Bible stories, or teaching them about prayer by saying grace (giving thanks) before meals.

- Children become part of the faith at baptism, and this develops as they attend church and prepare for confirmation (see p.12). Many churches offer help in raising children, through Sunday schools. These schools aim to teach Christian morals and ideals through the study of Bible stories.

- Festivals such as Christmas and Easter have a strong emphasis on celebration within the family.

- Children are asked to honour their parents — to look after and respect them (Exodus 20:12).

### Judaism

- Family life is also very important to Jews, as it's through the family that the Jewish religion and customs are passed on. Children are seen as a divine gift — Psalm 127:3 NIV says "Children are a heritage from the Lord". Orthodox Jews consider anyone whose mother is Jewish to be Jewish — Progressive Jews say the father can 'pass on' Jewishness as well.

- Children should look after their parents — honouring your parents is a mitzvah (Exodus 20:12).

- Many Jewish rituals happen in the home, such as celebrating Shabbat or keeping kashrut (see p.49), so family life is important for educating children about the Jewish faith.

- Children often attend classes at a heder (a religious school run by the synagogue) to learn Hebrew, and study the Torah and Talmud. This helps them be able to participate in prayers and services.

- Rituals like brit milah (male circumcision) and simchat bat (a girl's naming ceremony) connect the child to the faith. Their bar/bat mitzvah ceremony (p.50) requires them to learn about Judaism.

### Islam

- Many Muslims think family life teaches people to be kind, considerate and affectionate. Strong family ties help strengthen the Muslim community — the ummah.

- The Qur'an asks people to care for their parents — "We have enjoined upon man, to his parents, good treatment" (Qur'an 46:15). Muslims place importance on the extended family too.

- Rituals such as aqiqah (a naming ritual) and the bismillah ceremony, which marks the start of the child's religious education, help connect the child to the faith.

- Following Muslim food laws by having halal food in the home helps introduce the child to Islam.

- Mosques often have schools (madrasahs) to teach children about Islam. They learn Arabic so they can read the Qur'an and say prayers. They're also taught from the hadith and sunnah (see p.27).

**All religions**

# Families

Views on contemporary family issues are changing — but they still differ widely within and between religions.

## Family Life in the UK has Changed

1) For a long time, the nuclear family was seen in Britain as the ideal family model. Traditionally, a nuclear family was a married man and woman and their children. Religious families are more likely than the UK average to follow this model.

2) Today, the term may include same-sex parents, unmarried couples, and reconstituted (or blended) families (where divorcees with children find new partners). Single-parent families are more common too.

3) Some people worry it's bad for children to grow up with same-sex parents, because they will only have role models from one gender. However, many people believe same-sex couples can provide a stable, loving home, which is what's important.

4) An extended family includes grandparents, cousins and so on. An extended family might live together, which has become more common as people live longer, house prices rise and both parents work. For example, parents and children might share a home with grandparents to save money on houses. The grandparents can then be looked after by the parents but also help look after the children.

## Christians Try to Welcome Different Families

1) Some Christians' views on divorce and homosexuality make it difficult for them to accept certain types of family. But whatever their opinions, many Christians focus on making sure reconstituted families and single or same-sex parents feel welcome in church. They consider it important that the family remains connected to the church, particularly so that any children will still be brought up in a Christian way.

2) For example, Pope John Paul II said Catholics should take "solicitous care to make sure that [divorcees] do not consider themselves as separated from the Church" (Familiaris Consortio 84). However, divorced Catholics aren't allowed to take communion (see p.11), which could mean they feel unwelcome in church.

3) The Catholic Church is more strongly against same-sex parenting than many other denominations. Catholics believe homosexuality is wrong and God created men and women to form a family.

## Jewish Views Tend to Vary

1) Single parents aren't considered the ideal but many Jews try to make them feel welcome in the community. It can be harder for single parents to have time and money to take a full part in synagogue and Jewish life.

2) It can sometimes be more difficult for divorced parents within the Orthodox (and especially the ultra-Orthodox) community. Family is such an important part of Judaism that divorcees can be seen as going against the faith. Women without a get (see p.62) who have a new relationship can be seen as committing adultery, and their children are considered illegitimate.

3) Progressive and Conservative Jews tend to be more accepting of divorcees, reconstituted families and same-sex parents. They focus on each individual being happy.

## Muslim Views are Changing

1) Some Muslims are accepting of divorced people and reconstituted families, while others are less so.

2) Many Muslims would frown upon same-sex parents because they see homosexuality as wrong. Other Muslims believe that, whatever their personal opinion, they should be accepting of same-sex parents because no one is without sin, so they shouldn't judge. Others are in favour of same-sex parents.

3) The extended family is also important in Islam, particularly for offering love and support.

---

## There are a variety of opinions on modern family life

Make sure you know similar and contrasting views on issues such as divorcees and same-sex parents. Jot down some viewpoints — from both within a religion and from different religions.

# Gender Equality

Gender equality is a big topic that affects people in and outside the home...

## Discrimination Based on Gender is Widespread

1) Gender discrimination is a problem in British society, although the situation's gradually improving.

2) Fixed ideas about men's and women's roles are slowly giving way to an acceptance that you shouldn't define people by gender, and that the idea of certain roles is unnecessary and bad for both genders:

- Gender stereotypes — e.g. women being more emotional or men being more confident — are now seen by many people as false and damaging to both genders. For example, many people think it's bad that men might feel less able to show or express their emotions because it's thought not to be 'manly' to do so.

- Some people argue there is still a long way to go before women are treated equally to men, e.g. well below half of MPs are women. Others think the genders are treated more or less equally.

- There have been shifts in gender balance in some areas, e.g. women are now more likely than men to go to university.

- Religious views on gender roles have shifted over time as well — see p.68-69.

## Men and Women Often Have Different Roles in the Home

1) Taking care of the family and home has often been seen as the 'woman's role', with the man's role being to earn money to support the family. Having different roles doesn't necessarily mean either are unequal, but these fixed ideas make it hard for either gender to do the opposite role.

2) These traditional roles were, and often still are, supported by Christianity, Islam and Judaism (p.68-69).

3) Some of the key issues that affect men and women today are given below:

- Traditionally, family care is seen as a 'woman's role'. This can disadvantage both parents though — for women, it may mean they have to sacrifice their career or other parts of their life to raise children, while for men, working as the 'breadwinner' may mean that they can't spend as much time as they'd like with their family. This is slowly changing — shared parental leave (SPL), introduced in the UK in 2015, gives parents the option to share the time off work to look after their child in its first year.

- However, if the parents don't choose to take shared parental leave, which involves the woman giving up part of her maternity leave, men are only entitled to 2 weeks' paid paternity leave. Women are entitled to 52 weeks' maternity leave, with 39 weeks being paid. This reflects the fact that women give birth and many women breastfeed, but some men feel 2 weeks is too little. Very few men have taken SPL so far.

- Women may encounter problems in the workplace after taking time off to have children — many find their male colleagues have been promoted in the meantime, or struggle to afford childcare to allow them to return to work. Many women still do more housework than men, even if they're working.

## Gender equality means treating men and women equally

This page gives some general opinions on gender equality and roles — religious opinions are covered on the next couple of pages. Make sure you know Christian views, and views from one other religion.

**General & Christianity**

# Gender Equality

Men and women are often <u>treated differently</u> in the <u>workplace</u>, although there are laws in place to help <u>promote</u> gender equality. The views within religious groups can be <u>varied</u> and <u>don't</u> always support gender equality.

## There are **Problems** with **Equality** in the **Workplace**

1) <u>Contrary</u> to what many people believe, women have <u>always worked</u>. However, in the past women were <u>prevented</u> from doing many jobs, <u>by law</u> or <u>by other people</u>. Some had to stop work when they <u>married</u>.

2) <u>Women</u> were often <u>paid less</u> than <u>men</u> for the <u>same job</u>, or only offered jobs with <u>less responsibility</u> and <u>lower pay</u>. This is <u>still the case</u>, although it's <u>less common</u> now in the UK because it's been made <u>illegal</u>.

> • The <u>Equal Pay Act 1970</u> and the <u>Sex Discrimination Act 1975</u> made gender discrimination <u>illegal</u>, e.g. by saying <u>both genders</u> had to be <u>paid</u> the <u>same amount</u> and have the <u>same working conditions</u> for the <u>same job</u>.
>
> • The <u>Equality Act 2010</u> brought all the legislation together in <u>one act</u>. It also made <u>positive action</u> legal. <u>Positive action</u> is action to help a group who's <u>underrepresented</u> in a <u>profession</u> or <u>organisation</u>. For example, if a <u>male-dominated</u> company has two <u>equally-qualified</u> candidates for a job, it's <u>legal</u> for them to pick the <u>female</u> candidate to help <u>women</u> become <u>better represented</u> in the <u>company</u>.
>
> • The Act allows for '<u>occupational requirements</u>'. This means it's <u>legal</u> to only offer a job to a <u>certain group</u> if there's an <u>objective reason</u> why they're <u>best</u> for it, e.g. only offering a <u>male role</u> in a <u>play</u> to <u>male actors</u>.

3) <u>Despite</u> these laws, there are professions in which <u>one gender</u> is <u>underrepresented</u>. <u>Nursing</u> or <u>midwifery</u> are seen as <u>women's jobs</u>, while <u>building</u> or <u>firefighting</u> are seen as <u>men's</u>. This is <u>difficult</u> to <u>change</u>.

4) <u>Women</u> are <u>underrepresented</u> in <u>positions of authority</u>, e.g. as <u>politicians</u> or <u>company directors</u>.

5) Many women still face <u>discrimination</u> at work, such as <u>not</u> being considered for <u>promotion</u> or being <u>sexually harassed</u>, although it's <u>illegal</u>. It can be <u>hard</u> to <u>prove</u> it happened because of their <u>gender</u> — or even to <u>find out</u> it's happening. E.g., it's <u>hard to tell</u> if you're being <u>paid less</u> than someone else in the <u>same job</u>.

## The Bible is a bit **Unclear** on the Status of **Women**

1) The <u>Bible</u> gives different messages on the subject of <u>gender discrimination</u>. Some of Jesus's followers were women, e.g. Mary and Martha (Luke 10:38-42), and he treated them <u>equally</u>.

2) Galatians 3:28 says "There is neither ... male [nor] female, for you are all one in Christ Jesus" (NIV). But 1 Timothy 2:12 says: "I do not permit a woman to teach or to assume authority over a man; she must be quiet" (NIV), which suggests that men and women <u>aren't equal</u>.

> For <u>most</u> of Christian history, women <u>weren't</u> allowed to be <u>priests</u>. This is no longer the case — women can now be <u>ministers</u> in most <u>Protestant</u> denominations, and <u>Anglican priests</u> and <u>bishops</u>. But they can't be <u>Roman Catholic</u> or <u>Orthodox</u> priests.

3) The Bible also says wives should do as their husbands <u>tell them</u>. But many Christians say this reflects the <u>ideas</u> of <u>society</u> at the time, and doesn't correspond with <u>Jesus's attitude</u> towards women.

> "Wives, submit ... to your own husbands as you do to the Lord. For the husband is the head of the wife as Christ is the head of the church..." Ephesians 5:22-23 NIV

4) Many Christians now believe men and women should be <u>equal</u>. The Catechism of the Catholic Church 1938 mentions "sinful inequalities" and says Catholics <u>fight against this</u>.

5) <u>Pope John Paul II</u> said "society should create and develop conditions favouring work in the home" for women (Familiaris Consortio 23). Other <u>denominations</u> are less focused on <u>traditional</u> gender roles.

**REVISION TASK**

## Gender equality in the workplace is a tricky issue

Learn some specific examples of careers where men and women are underrepresented.

# Gender Equality

In Judaism and Islam, men and women are <u>generally</u> considered <u>equal</u> but have <u>different roles</u> within the family.

## Jewish Men and Women are Often Seen as 'Separate but Equal'

1) The book of Genesis is often used to support the idea that men and women are seen as <u>equals</u> before God, although <u>different</u>, and with different <u>responsibilities</u>.

> "So God created mankind in his own image...
> male and female he created them" Genesis 1:27 NIV

2) Judaism doesn't suggest that women should <u>not</u> be able to follow their chosen career. However, there is still a belief that motherhood is a <u>privilege</u>, and women should devote some of their life to it.

3) Views vary between the <u>different branches</u> of Judaism:

- <u>Orthodox Jews</u> aim to uphold Jewish <u>tradition</u>, so are more likely to suggest women stay at home as <u>wives</u> and <u>mothers</u>. Women play an important role in celebrating <u>Shabbat</u> and teaching <u>children</u> about the <u>faith</u>.
- Many <u>ultra-Orthodox women</u> work at least <u>part-time</u> though, so their husbands can <u>study</u> the Torah.
- <u>Reform</u> and <u>Liberal Judaism</u> are committed to <u>full gender equality</u>, e.g. they have female <u>rabbis</u> (p.39).

## In Islam, Men and Women are Equal but have Different Roles

1) Men and women have an <u>equal</u> <u>obligation</u> to Allah in terms of <u>prayer</u>, <u>fasting</u>, <u>pilgrimage</u> and <u>charity</u>.

> "Indeed, the Muslim men and Muslim women, the believing men and believing women, the obedient men and obedient women ... the charitable men and charitable women, the fasting men and fasting women... and the men who remember Allah often and the women who do so — for them Allah has prepared forgiveness and a great reward." Qur'an 33:35

2) Some teachings might suggest men are <u>superior</u>. But they're usually taken to mean that men and women just have <u>different roles</u> within the community — men are <u>responsible</u> for <u>providing</u> for the <u>family</u>, and women are <u>responsible</u> for the <u>home</u>.

> "Men are in charge of women by [right of] what Allah has given one over the other and what they spend [for maintenance] from their wealth" (Qur'an 4:34).

3) There are a <u>variety</u> of views on some issues:

- Many Muslims believe it's OK for women to <u>work</u>. However, some believe women should only work if <u>essential</u> or to fill jobs they see as more <u>suited</u> to women, e.g. midwifery. Some Muslims see work as a <u>distraction</u> from women's primary role of looking after the <u>family</u> and <u>home</u>.
- Wearing <u>modest clothing</u>, often including a <u>head covering</u>, is an important part of Islam for many Muslim women. Many others <u>don't</u> consider it part of their faith. Some people see it as a way of <u>oppressing</u> women and believe Muslim women are <u>forced</u> to wear it. Many Muslim women argue it's their <u>choice</u>, and that any <u>ban</u> on head coverings would be just as <u>oppressive</u>, as it <u>takes away</u> that choice.

## Sacred texts can seem to contain conflicting points of view

Try comparing the different views on gender equality within the religions you're studying. Think about what passages from sacred texts you could use to back up these views in the exam.

# Worked Exam Question

It's time to have another go at answering some exam questions based on the things you've just read.
This page has a question that's already completed — so take a look at it before you give the others a go yourself.

---

1    'Men and women are equal and should have equal status within the family.'

Evaluate this statement.  Your answer should include the following:
• religious arguments that support the statement
• religious arguments that disagree with the statement
• a conclusion.
You can also include non-religious points of view in your answer.

> You don't need to include views from all three religions in the exam — just write about the ones you've been studying.

    Most modern Christians believe that men are equal to women.  They use Paul's teachings in

Galatians 3:28 which says "nor is there male and female, for you are all one in Christ Jesus" (NIV)

to support their views.  In Judaism, the weekly celebration of Shabbat indicates that both parents

have equal status whilst maintaining different roles.  For example, the mother will begin the ceremony

by lighting two candles and the father will usually bless the children at the end.  In Islam, the woman

is traditionally the homemaker whilst the man is the breadwinner.  It can be argued that this doesn't

indicate that one gender has higher status than the other — the roles are simply different.

    Alternatively, some people might believe that these different roles for men and women mean that

they do not have equal status in the family.  Some teachings in the Qur'an may even imply that men

are superior to women: "Men are in charge of women..." (Qur'an 4:34).  Therefore this could suggest

that women have to be obedient to men.  Similarly, some Christians and Jews interpret Genesis as

evidence that men are superior to women, because God makes a woman out of the rib of Adam to

be his helper.

    In the UK, men and women are equal in law.  Shared parental leave was introduced to allow

parents to share the time taken off work during the first year of their child's life.  However, few

couples choose to take shared parental leave, suggesting that society views women as being the main

carers for children.

    In conclusion, I think that although men and women have equal status in law, they are still not

treated equally by all.  Religious teaching sometimes encourages women to have more of a role in

caring for the home and family.  Although it can still be argued that the genders have equal worth,

just different roles, I think there's a danger of this leading to women being seen as inferior.

*[12 marks]*

---

# Exam Questions

**2** Which of the following terms implies that men and women might not be viewed as equals in British society? Put a tick (✓) in the correct box.

A    Transgender    ☐

B    Gender inequality    ☐

C    Matriarchy    ☐

D    Harassment    ☐

*[1 mark]*

**3** Explain two contrasting beliefs about same-sex parenting.
You must refer to the views of at least one religious group.

.............................................................................................................................

.............................................................................................................................

.............................................................................................................................

.............................................................................................................................

.............................................................................................................................

.............................................................................................................................

*[4 marks]*

**4** Explain two religious beliefs about educating children in a religious family.
Your answer should refer to specific religious teachings or sacred texts.

.............................................................................................................................

.............................................................................................................................

.............................................................................................................................

.............................................................................................................................

.............................................................................................................................

.............................................................................................................................

.............................................................................................................................

*[5 marks]*

# Revision Summary

Well, that's <u>Relationships and Families</u> taken care of — time to see <u>how much</u> you can remember.
- Try these questions and <u>tick off each one</u> when you <u>get it right</u>.
- When you've done <u>all the questions</u> for a topic and are <u>completely happy</u> with it, tick off the topic.

If a question asks about a religion you <u>haven't</u> studied, just <u>skip it</u> and move on to the next question.

## Sexuality and Sexual Relationships (p.56-58) ☑

1) What term is used to describe an unmarried couple living together?
2) Describe two views in British society about promiscuity.
3) Give two contrasting beliefs about sex outside of marriage.
4) Explain what the scriptures of two religions suggest about homosexuality.
5) What is the Roman Catholic Church's view on homosexuality?
6) Give one situation in which contraception would be allowed by Orthodox Jews.
7) Which methods of contraception are not usually accepted within Islam?
8) Explain the views of one Christian Church on the use of contraception.

## Marriage and Divorce (p.59-62) ☑

9) Give two reasons why couples get married.
10) What is meant by the term 'polygamy'?
11) How was the legalisation of same-sex marriage received by Christians?
12) What did Jesus say about divorce?
13) What did Muhammad say marriage is "half of"?
14) Why do some Muslims believe same-sex marriage is wrong?
15) How can a Muslim man initiate divorce from his wife?
16) What reason do some Jews give for supporting same-sex marriage?
17) What document must a Jewish woman obtain in order to remarry?

## Families (p.65-66) ☑

18) Describe the traditional family model.
19) Give one way in which Christians might introduce children to their faith.
20) Orthodox Jews believe 'Jewishness' is passed on by the father. True or false?
21) What is the purpose of attending classes at a 'heder' for Jewish children?
22) Why are Muslim children taught Arabic?
23) What is meant by the term 'extended family'?
24) In the Catholic Church, which part of mass are divorcees not allowed to take part in?
25) Why is it often harder for single parents to take part in Jewish community life?

## Gender Equality (p.67-69) ☑

26) Describe the traditional roles of men and women in the home.
27) What problems can women encounter when returning to work after childbirth?
28) Paying a woman less for doing the same job as a man is illegal in the UK. True or false?
29) Give two contrasting views on gender equality in Christianity.
30) Why might ultra-Orthodox Jewish women work part-time?
31) Give a reason why many Muslims believe men and women should be treated as equals.

## The Origins of the Universe                    All religions

No one saw exactly how the Earth came to be like it is... but science and religion both have their theories.

## Scientific Arguments — There are **Two** Main Types

### Cosmological Theories — How the Universe Began

Chief amongst these is the Big Bang theory. It says that the Universe began in an explosion of matter and energy. Matter from this explosion eventually formed stars, planets and everything else. The Universe still seems to be expanding — important evidence for this theory.

### Evolutionary Theories — How Living Things Changed

Charles Darwin argued that life on Earth originated from simple cells. Life evolved (gradually changed) over millions of years into a huge variety of forms, and those best adapted survived — 'survival of the fittest'. According to this theory, people evolved from apes, not Adam and Eve.

Non-religious people look to science for answers. They believe that the universe and human life came about by chance. They say that since people evolved from apes, they can't have been created by God.

## **Religions** have their own **Ideas** about all this...

Some religious people believe only in the stories written in scriptures. Others believe that science tells them how the world was created, but religion explains why. They believe that God caused the Big Bang, and evolution is the way he made humans.

### Christian Ideas

- Genesis chapter 1 says God created everything over six days. On the seventh day he rested. Genesis chapters 1 and 2 describe how God created people in his image, and made woman from man (see p.3).
- Some believe the Bible gives a literal account of what happened. People who disagree with evolution claim there's a lack of proof backing up the theory — fossils don't show the full process of evolution.
- However, lots of Christians view the creation story as symbolic and also believe in scientific theories. The Big Bang theory was actually first put forward by a Roman Catholic priest, Georges Lemaître, so religion and science don't have to be completely separate.
- In fact, many believe that science and religious ideas can exist in harmony. Both the Church of England and the Roman Catholic Church have recognised the benefits of the two working together.

"Collaboration between religion and science is mutually beneficial..." General Synod of the Church of England, 2010

"Evolution in nature does not conflict with the notion of Creation..." Pope Francis, Pontifical Academy of Sciences, October 27 2014

### Jewish Ideas

- The Jewish creation story is in Genesis and is the same as the Christian one. ——→ "So God created mankind in his own image..." Genesis 1:27 NIV
- Jews interpret this story in different ways. Ultra-Orthodox Jews believe it is literally true, and would find it difficult to accept scientific arguments.
- Others would argue that the Torah account is a metaphor, and are open to scientific evidence.

### Islamic Ideas

- The Muslim creation story is similar to that in Genesis: "It is Allah who created the heavens and the earth and whatever is between them in six days" (Qur'an 32:4).
- The Qur'an says Allah "began the creation of man from clay" (Qur'an 32:7) and breathed life and a soul into the first man, Adam — and all humans descend from him.
- Some see the descriptions of creation in the Qur'an as agreeing with science. E.g. the Qur'an says: "Have those who disbelieved not considered that the heavens and the earth were a joined entity, and We separated them..." (Qur'an 21:30) — this could be understood to support the Big Bang theory.

## General   The Environment and Stewardship

Religious believers think people should <u>look after</u> the environment because it was created by God.

## The **World** is a Way for God to **Reveal** His **Presence**

1) Many believers <u>appreciate</u> the world and what's in it because it is <u>God's creation</u>.
2) They feel that he reveals himself constantly in the world through <u>experiences</u> that inspire <u>awe</u> and <u>wonder</u>, where someone can <u>feel God's presence</u> — e.g. a <u>beautiful sunset</u>, a <u>wild sea</u> or a <u>butterfly's wing</u> might convince someone there must be a creator.
3) But people <u>don't</u> always take good <u>care</u> of the world we live in...

## Humans have **Damaged** the Environment

### Global Warming

- Certain <u>gases</u> in the atmosphere, known as 'greenhouse gases', help keep the Earth <u>warm</u>.
- Over the past century, the amount of greenhouse gas in the atmosphere has <u>increased</u>, and measurements show that the Earth has <u>got hotter</u>.  This is called <u>global warming</u>.
- Higher temperatures make <u>ice melt</u>, which causes <u>sea levels</u> to <u>rise</u>.  This could lead to <u>flooding</u> in low-lying areas.
- It is mainly caused by the <u>fuels</u> used to generate energy, like <u>oil</u>, <u>coal</u> and <u>gas</u>.

### Natural Resources

- A <u>natural resource</u> is anything found naturally that's <u>useful</u> to humans.
- The Earth's population is <u>increasing</u> and people use more <u>raw materials</u> and more <u>energy</u> every year.  If people carry on like this, many <u>natural resources</u> will eventually <u>run out</u>.
- <u>Fertile land</u> for growing crops is also rapidly <u>declining</u>. Each year, activities such as <u>overgrazing</u> and <u>irresponsible farming methods</u> turn more fertile land into unusable <u>desert</u>.

### Pollution

- Pollution from chemicals can <u>contaminate</u> the environment.
- <u>Sewage</u> and <u>chemicals</u> can pollute lakes, rivers and seas.  These pollutants <u>harm</u> the plants and animals that live in and around the water, including humans.
- People use <u>toxic chemicals</u> for farming.  They also bury <u>nuclear waste</u> underground, and dump a lot of <u>household</u> and <u>industrial waste</u> in landfill sites.  The toxic chemicals can <u>kill</u> plants and animals, and cause <u>cancer</u> in humans.
- <u>Smoke</u> and <u>gases</u> from vehicles and industry can pollute the <u>air</u>, cause <u>health problems</u> in humans and damage the <u>ozone layer</u>.

# The Environment and Stewardship

Many religious people believe they have an <u>obligation</u> or <u>responsibility</u> to help <u>look after</u> the environment...

## There are Many Ways to **Tackle** these **Environmental Problems**

1) Many people, both religious and non-religious, work to <u>reduce</u> and <u>repair</u> the harm caused to the <u>environment</u>. They think that it's <u>important</u> to look after the planet for <u>future generations</u>.

2) Many religious believers feel it's their <u>duty</u> to <u>look after</u> the environment. God <u>gave</u> people the Earth, but expects them to <u>care</u> for it — this idea is called <u>stewardship</u>. There's more on different religious beliefs below, and on the next page.

3) Lots of people try to be environmentally friendly by <u>recycling</u> things like <u>paper</u> and <u>plastic</u>. They may also take <u>public transport</u> or <u>walk</u> to cut down on pollution caused by vehicle fumes.

4) There's a <u>limit</u> to the <u>Earth's resources</u>, so many people believe it's <u>important</u> to be able to <u>manage</u> the resources currently available and to find alternative, <u>sustainable</u> options too.

5) Some also <u>campaign</u> to better inform others about the <u>damage</u> being done to the environment.

## **Christians** Believe in **Looking After** the Environment

1) In Genesis 1:26, God said humans could "rule over the fish in the sea and the birds in the sky, over the livestock and all the wild animals..." (NIV). This power is known as <u>dominion</u>. Some people think it means humans can use the environment <u>however</u> they want.

2) However, many Christians believe that God made them <u>stewards</u> of the <u>environment</u>. They have no right to <u>abuse</u> God's creation, and they have a <u>responsibility</u> to protect it.

> "humanity's dominion cannot be understood as licence to abuse, spoil, squander or destroy what God has made..." Christian Declaration on Nature, Assisi 1986

> "The Lord God took the man and put him in the Garden of Eden to work it and take care of it." Genesis 2:15 NIV

3) Some Christians believe that everything is <u>interdependent</u> (i.e. everything depends on everything else), so driving species of animal or plant to <u>extinction</u>, or harming the <u>planet</u>, eventually ends up harming <u>people</u>.

4) The <u>damage</u> humans do to the environment <u>clashes</u> with their role as <u>stewards</u>. Christian organisations such as <u>CAFOD</u>, <u>Christian Aid</u> and <u>Tearfund</u>® are concerned with putting this responsibility into <u>practice</u>. They put pressure on <u>governments</u> and <u>industry</u> to think more about how people are <u>abusing</u> the <u>planet</u>.

---

## Don't rush straight into writing your answer in the exam

You've probably been told this before, but always read the questions carefully. The 4-mark questions will ask you about similar or different views within each theme, so pay close attention.

# The Environment and Stewardship

The idea of <u>stewardship</u> of the Earth is also <u>important</u> in Judaism and Islam — with many members of these religions believing God or Allah gave them a <u>special responsibility</u> to take care of the <u>environment</u>.

## Judaism also Teaches **Stewardship**

1) Jews <u>value</u> the world because it is <u>God's</u> and he created it.

> "The earth is the Lord's, and everything in it, the world, and all who live in it;
> for he founded it on the seas and established it on the waters" (Psalm 24:1-2 NIV).

2) Like Christians, Jews believe in the concept of <u>stewardship</u>. Concern for the <u>natural world</u> is often seen as being at the <u>heart</u> of Jewish teaching.

3) God's creations should <u>remain</u> as he intended, and humans have <u>no right</u> to abuse them.

> "humanity was given dominion over nature, but was commanded to behave towards the rest of creation with justice and compassion". Jewish Declaration on Nature, Assisi 1986

> "...it is our Jewish responsibility to put the defence of the whole of nature at the very centre of our concern." Jewish Declaration on Nature, Assisi 1986

4) Some Jews think everything is <u>interdependent</u>, with <u>trees</u> being particularly <u>important</u>. Since the creation of <u>Israel</u> in 1948, <u>millions</u> of trees have been <u>planted</u> to aid the <u>reclamation</u> of the desert and help <u>rebuild</u> the <u>nation</u>.

5) Jews also believe that as <u>custodians</u>, they're responsible for making the world <u>better</u> — this is called <u>tikkun olam</u> ('mending the world').

6) Tikkun olam isn't <u>just</u> about the environment — it's a general <u>ideal</u> that includes helping the <u>poor</u>, and behaving <u>morally</u>.

## **Muslims** are **Khalifah** of the Earth

1) The Earth is seen as being a <u>product</u> of the <u>love of Allah</u>, so Muslims should treat it with <u>love</u>.

2) Muslims believe they have been appointed <u>khalifah</u> (vice-regents or trustees) of the Earth. This is the idea that while they're on Earth they should take <u>responsibility</u> for the world (<u>stewardship</u>), and make it the sort of place Allah wants it to be.

3) This means Muslims have an <u>obligation</u> to protect the environment. Muslims might carry out their duty as khalifah by being <u>careful</u> with the <u>resources</u> they use, and <u>encouraging others</u> to take care of the environment too.

4) The <u>Prophet Muhammad</u> (called Allah's Apostle here) said that planting a tree is a <u>good</u>, <u>charitable deed</u>:

> "Allah's Apostle said, 'There is none amongst the Muslims who plants a tree or sows seeds, and then a bird, or a person or an animal eats from it, but is regarded as a charitable gift for him.' " Sahih al-Bukhari 39:513

5) At the <u>Day of Judgement</u>, Muslims believe <u>questions</u> will be asked of them. They will be required to <u>answer</u> for any <u>ill-treatment</u> of the planet and its resources.

## Members of the three religions believe they are stewards

Have a go at defining what stewardship is in your own words, then write a few points about how religious people might go about carrying it out. Don't forget to include any religion-specific terms.

# Animal Rights All religions

You need to know about <u>views</u> on animal experimentation in <u>Christianity</u> and <u>one other religious tradition</u>.

## Animal Experimentation and Vegetarianism are Key Issues

1) Animals are sometimes used to <u>test products</u> used by humans or for <u>medical experiments</u>. Some people see this as <u>cruel</u>. Others look at the issue in a utilitarian way — <u>utilitarianism</u> is the idea that <u>decisions</u> should be made based on what has the <u>best balance</u> of <u>good</u> and <u>bad outcomes</u>. This can be used to argue that <u>animal testing</u> is <u>acceptable</u> if it could <u>help</u> many people, even if animals <u>suffer</u>.

2) Animals are also used for <u>food</u>. Some say that humans are <u>built</u> to <u>consume meat</u>. Other people argue that <u>hurting</u> animals is <u>wrong</u>, so it's better to be <u>vegetarian</u> or <u>vegan</u>.

## Christians believe Animals should be Treated Well

1) Some people might argue that <u>dominion</u> gives humans the right to do what they want with animals, but others say <u>stewardship</u> means caring for God's creatures. Christianity teaches that animals should be treated with <u>kindness</u>, but that they can be used to <u>benefit</u> mankind (as long as their <u>suffering</u> is considered): "The righteous care for the needs of their animals" (Proverbs 12:10 NIV). Many would say <u>only human life</u> is <u>sacred</u>, as only humans were created in the <u>image of God</u>.

2) The <u>Catholic</u> Church tolerates <u>animal testing</u>, but only if it <u>benefits</u> mankind (e.g. if the experiments lead to the development of life-saving medicines).

> "Medical and scientific experimentation on animals is a morally acceptable practice if it remains within reasonable limits and contributes to caring for or saving human lives. It is contrary to human dignity to cause animals to suffer or die needlessly." Catechism of the Catholic Church, 2417-2418

3) Some Christians think it's always <u>wrong</u> to cause <u>suffering</u> to animals to <u>increase</u> our <u>scientific knowledge</u>, particularly since medicines <u>don't</u> always have the same <u>effect</u> on <u>humans</u> as they do on animals. Some denominations, e.g. the <u>Society of Friends</u> (<u>Quakers</u>), are <u>against</u> any <u>ill-treatment</u> of animals.

4) Unlike some other religions, Christianity has no specific <u>food laws</u>. So <u>vegetarianism</u> (not eating meat) and <u>veganism</u> (not eating or using any animal products) are matters for <u>individuals</u> to decide about. The <u>Bible</u> talks about eating meat, so many Christians believe it's <u>fine</u>.

## Judaism has Laws about Eating Meat

1) The <u>Noahide Laws</u>, a set of <u>rules</u> Jews believe people should follow, <u>forbid cruelty</u> to animals. The <u>Torah</u> contains specific food laws — only certain <u>animals</u> can be eaten, and the ones that are allowed must be <u>slaughtered</u> in a <u>humane</u> fashion. Foods that are allowed are called <u>kosher</u> (see p.49).

2) The Torah teaches people to treat animals in a <u>sustainable</u> way. Deuteronomy 22:6-7 NIV says that a person can take <u>young birds</u> from a nest, but should <u>not</u> take the mother.

3) <u>Experiments</u> on animals may be <u>tolerated</u> if they result in a <u>benefit</u> for mankind, but only as a <u>last resort</u>. Jews believe in <u>pikuach nefesh</u> — the idea that human <u>life</u> must be <u>saved</u>, even if that means going against other <u>Jewish laws</u> (see p.42). This can be used to argue in <u>favour</u> of animal testing.

## Islam Teaches that Animals Should Never be Mistreated

1) The idea of <u>khalifah</u> affects how Muslims treat animals (see p.76). Animals are part of <u>Allah's creation</u>, which Muslims are entrusted to <u>look after</u>.

> "It is Allah who made for you the grazing animals... you eat." Qur'an 40:79

2) Cruelty to animals is <u>forbidden</u>, as is their use simply for <u>pleasure</u>.

3) Muslims believe in showing <u>compassion</u> for all creatures — animals must be slaughtered <u>humanely</u> for the meat to be <u>halal</u> (Arabic for 'allowed').

> "Allah's Apostle said, 'Whoever keeps a dog, one Qirat of the reward of his good deeds is deducted daily, unless the dog is used for guarding a farm or cattle.'" Sahih al-Bukhari 39:515

4) Muslims will generally only allow animal testing if it is done to produce <u>genuine medical advances</u> for humans. The animals should be treated humanely, and <u>no unnecessary pain</u> should be inflicted on them.

# Worked Exam Question

Now let's take a look at how these topics might be covered in the exam. There's a question that's already been filled in on this page and then some more for you to have a go at yourself on the next page.

1  'Performing experiments on animals is always wrong.'

Evaluate this statement. Your answer should include the following:
- religious arguments that support the statement
- religious arguments that disagree with the statement
- a conclusion.
You can also include non-religious points of view in your answer.

You don't need to include views from all three religions in the exam — just write about the ones you've been studying.

Some religious people think performing experiments on animals is always wrong.

Many Christians believe that animals should be treated with kindness. The Bible says that

"The righteous care for the needs of their animals" (Proverbs 12:10 NIV), so some Christians would

agree that experimenting on animals is always wrong. Similarly, Jews follow the Noahide Laws,

which forbid cruelty to animals. This means that many Jews believe that animal experimentation,

especially when it does not save human lives, is wrong. Muslims believe they are khalifah of the

Earth, meaning God has given them the responsibility to care for it, so some would argue that

animal experimentation is wrong because it causes suffering to animals that they should

be protecting.

On the other hand, some religious people think that experimenting on animals can be justified.

Catholicism teaches that experiments on animals can be acceptable, but only if they will benefit

mankind, such as testing medicine. Similarly, some Muslims argue that human life is so valuable

that in special cases, animal experimentation is not wrong. However, even in these cases, the

animals must be treated humanely and they should not suffer any unnecessary pain.

Some Jews also believe that almost all Jewish laws can be set aside in order to save human life.

In the Mishnah it says that "anyone who saves a life is as if he saved an entire world" (Mishnah

Sanhedrin 4:5). This means that they also believe that caring for animals can be set aside if the

result is saving human lives. Likewise, utilitarians believe the right thing to do is the one that brings

most good, so animal experimentation can be justified if a lot of people are helped by it.

In conclusion, I believe that although allowing animals to suffer is wrong, if the experiments could

benefit humanity then they should be allowed. However, the experiments must have great benefits,

such as medical or scientific advances, and should not be for non-essential products (e.g. cosmetics).

*[12 marks]*

# Exam Questions

**2** Which of the following is a scientific theory about the origins of the Universe?
Put a tick (✓) in the correct box.

   **A**    The Big Bang theory    ☐

   **B**    The theory of gravity    ☐

   **C**    Genesis    ☐

   **D**    The story of creation    ☐

*[1 mark]*

**3** Which of the following is an argument used to justify eating meat?
Put a tick (✓) in the correct box.

   **A**    Animals bred for meat often suffer.    ☐

   **B**    Humans don't need meat to survive.    ☐

   **C**    Eating meat is good for the environment.    ☐

   **D**    Only human life is sacred.    ☐

*[1 mark]*

**4** Give two religious beliefs about the creation of the Universe.

**1)** ................................................................................................................

........................................................................................................................

**2)** ................................................................................................................

........................................................................................................................

*[2 marks]*

**5** Explain two similar religious beliefs about the environment.
You must refer to the views of at least one religious group.

........................................................................................................................

........................................................................................................................

........................................................................................................................

........................................................................................................................

........................................................................................................................

........................................................................................................................

*[4 marks]*

## General & Christianity

# Abortion and Euthanasia

Make sure you know what <u>Christianity</u> and <u>another religious tradition</u> teach about abortion and euthanasia.

## Abortion and Euthanasia are **Controversial Issues**

Abortion is when a <u>foetus</u> is removed <u>prematurely</u> from the womb <u>before</u> it can <u>survive</u>. It's <u>legal</u> in England, Scotland and Wales and can take place until the <u>24th week</u> of pregnancy. Abortions can take place <u>after</u> this time if there's a <u>danger</u> to the <u>health</u> of the mother or foetus.

<u>Euthanasia</u> is killing someone to <u>relieve suffering</u>, often from an incurable illness. <u>Active</u> euthanasia is when a patient <u>requests</u> help to die, often using <u>drugs</u> — it is <u>illegal</u> in the <u>UK</u>, but legal in some countries, e.g. <u>Belgium</u>. In <u>passive</u> euthanasia, medical treatment that might extend someone's life is <u>withdrawn</u> — they might <u>refuse</u> further treatment, or a <u>life-support machine</u> might be turned off if there is no hope of recovery. This is <u>legal</u> in the <u>UK</u>.

1) Christianity, Islam and Judaism teach that <u>all life</u> is created by <u>God</u>. As God's creation, all life <u>belongs</u> to God and is therefore <u>holy</u>. This is the '<u>sanctity of life</u>' argument.

2) Based on this, many religious people believe that people <u>don't</u> have the <u>right</u> to <u>interfere</u> with when life <u>ends</u>, or to <u>prevent</u> the beginning of a <u>new life</u>.

3) Other people take into consideration a person's <u>quality of life</u> (how <u>able</u> they are to live a <u>normal</u> life).

## **Many** Christians see Abortion as **Undesirable**

1) Abortion is a very <u>complicated</u> and <u>emotional</u> issue, but generally speaking, Christianity teaches that abortion is <u>undesirable</u> as God "created mankind in his own image" (Genesis 1:27 NIV).

2) However, the <u>Roman Catholic Church</u> goes so far as to say that abortion is <u>murder</u>, as it teaches that human life <u>starts</u> as soon as the egg is fertilised at <u>conception</u>. ➝

   "...all direct abortion... [is] to be absolutely excluded as lawful means of regulating the number of children." Humanae Vitae, section 14

3) Many argue abortion is wrong because God <u>cares</u> a lot about <u>children</u>. Jesus said "Let the little children come to me, and do not hinder them, for the kingdom of God belongs to such as these" (Luke 18:16 NIV).

4) Not all Churches see it in such black and white terms. The Church of England believes that abortion is <u>permissible</u> in <u>certain circumstances</u>, such as when the pregnancy puts the <u>mother's life</u> at <u>risk</u>. The Society of Friends (the <u>Quakers</u>) argues that the <u>life</u> of the unborn child <u>cannot</u> be valued <u>above</u> that of the woman. Many Christians argue that allowing a woman to <u>choose</u> is a way of showing <u>Christian compassion</u> — whether they agree with the choice made or not.

5) The Bible <u>doesn't</u> actually mention abortion, but it connects <u>life</u> with <u>breath</u>, e.g. in the creation of Adam — so it could be argued that the foetus is only <u>alive</u> when it breathes <u>independently</u>. Other Christian writings (e.g. the <u>Didache</u>, a 2nd century manual of Christian teaching) are quite specifically <u>against</u> it.

## Some Christians are Strongly **Against Euthanasia**

1) <u>Roman Catholics</u> are the most <u>strongly opposed</u> to euthanasia. They believe that anything that intentionally causes death is <u>wrong</u>. So even those who are <u>unlikely</u> to recover consciousness should be kept <u>alive</u>. ➝

   "...an act or omission which... causes death in order to eliminate suffering constitutes a murder gravely contrary to the dignity of the human person and to the respect due to the living God, his Creator." Catechism of the Catholic Church, 2277

2) Some Christians view euthanasia as going against the commandment "You shall not murder". Some might argue that only <u>God</u> should <u>decide</u> when a person's life <u>ends</u>, as he gave them life in the first place.

3) Many Christians believe suffering is <u>part of life</u>. Job was made to <u>suffer</u> by Satan, but <u>refused</u> to <u>end</u> his life: "Shall we accept good from God, and not trouble?" (Job 2:10 NIV).

4) Euthanasia could be seen to <u>ruin</u> the natural course of death, when a <u>soul</u> starts to make its way to God.

5) Many Christians feel they must <u>care</u> for sick people, and euthanasia <u>goes against</u> this. Local churches often have links with <u>hospices</u> — a hospice is a place where <u>terminally ill</u> people can be well <u>cared for</u>. Christians would argue this allows a person to feel <u>valued</u> as they reach the end of their life.

© Isabelle Plasschaert / Alamy Stock Photo

# Abortion and Euthanasia

## Some Christians **Support Passive Euthanasia**

1) Some Christians suggest that the use of 'extraordinary treatment' (e.g. life-support machines which are keeping someone alive artificially) is not always the best approach — they suggest the easing of suffering through passive euthanasia is a way of demonstrating Christian compassion.

2) However, many only agree with euthanasia if the dying person chooses it for themselves.

3) Anglican denominations are against active euthanasia. However, they agree that terrible distress should not be suffered at all costs, and that death may be considered a blessing rather than continuing life-extending treatment. They argue that a person's quality of life must also be considered.

## Judaism Allows **Abortion** in Some Cases

1) As a general rule, Judaism is opposed to abortion that is carried out for non-medical reasons. Human life is part of the universe that God created, and he "created mankind in his own image" (Genesis 1:27 NIV). An unborn child is part of that creation.

> "For you created my inmost being; you knit me together in my mother's womb." Psalm 139:13 NIV

2) Some Jews might argue that it is up to God to decide when life starts and ends (see below).

3) However, Judaism does not teach that the life of an unborn child is more valuable than that of the mother — the foetus isn't seen as a human until birth. Many Jews accept that, in certain cases, abortion should be allowed. Most rabbis allow abortion if pregnancy becomes physically or mentally dangerous for the woman concerned, or if the child is likely to be severely disabled and unable to lead a full life. But it cannot be carried out simply for convenience.

> "...anyone who saves a life is as if he saved an entire world." Mishnah Sanhedrin 4:5

## Judaism Teaches That Only **God** Can **Decide** When People **Die**

1) Jewish teaching is generally opposed to the practice of euthanasia. There are some rabbis who have come out in support of it, but most Jews see life as a sacred gift from God. They believe people do not have the right to decide when a life should end.

2) Many see euthanasia as going against pikuach nefesh (see p.42) — Jews should do all they can to save human life, not bring about its end.

(see p.42)

3) The relief of pain and suffering is a key part of Jewish teaching. So although euthanasia is seen as wrong if it involves actively doing something to cause someone's death, it may be possible to withhold treatment, if this treatment would cause further distress. Reform Jews would agree with this idea, but ultra-Orthodox Jews are strongly against stopping treatment.

4) The words of Rabbi Moses Isserles are sometimes used to argue that it may be reasonable to switch off a life-support machine that's keeping someone alive: "If there is anything which causes a hindrance to the departure of the soul... then it is permissible to remove it."

5) The Jewish sacred text, the Nevi'im, contains an example of euthanasia. Abimelek is hit by a stone:

> "...a woman dropped an upper millstone on his head and cracked his skull. Hurriedly he called to his armour-bearer, 'Draw your sword and kill me, so that they can't say, "A woman killed him." ' So his servant ran him through, and he died." Judges 9:53-54 NIV

To avoid being killed by a woman, which would have been seen as embarrassing, he gets a man to kill him instead. This could be seen as supporting the right to die in a dignified way, but the text doesn't condone or condemn the action, and most don't see it as giving support for euthanasia.

---

## There are a lot of terms you need to know for this section

Write down a list of any new words you've come across in this section (e.g conception and sanctity of life) and then try to write a definition for each. Practise until you get them spot on.

# Abortion and Euthanasia

## Islam Allows Abortion **Before Ensoulment** in some Circumstances

Muslims believe that people's lives are <u>sacred</u> (see p.80).  The Qur'an teaches that "whoever kills a soul...
it is as if he had slain mankind entirely" (Qur'an 5:32).  This means that abortion is <u>generally</u> seen as wrong.

1) The passage on the right sums up Islamic teaching on <u>abortion</u>.
   But there are circumstances in which it is <u>permissible</u>.

> "And do not kill your children... We provide for them and for you.  Indeed, their killing is ever a great sin." Qur'an 17:31

2) When the <u>mother's</u> life is in <u>danger</u>, abortion is <u>lawful</u>.  The <u>potential</u>
   life in the womb is <u>not</u> as <u>important</u> as the <u>actual</u> life of the mother.

3) When a <u>foetus</u> gets its <u>soul</u>, this is called <u>ensoulment</u>.  Islam teaches that this happens
   <u>after 120 days</u>, when 'the soul is breathed into his body' (Sahih al-Bukhari 55:549).

4) This means that within the <u>first 120 days</u>, abortion can be allowed if the mother's life is
   <u>at risk</u>, or if the baby would be born with a serious <u>defect</u>, though not all Muslims agree
   with this.  After 120 days, abortion is <u>only</u> allowed to save the <u>life</u> of the mother.

5) Some Muslim women argue that they should be <u>free</u> to <u>choose</u> what happens to their <u>bodies</u>,
   so it should be <u>their choice</u> whether or not they can have an abortion.

## Muslims are Usually **Against Euthanasia**

1) Euthanasia is seen as <u>wrong</u> by most Muslims, because their lives are <u>Allah's</u>.

2) Muslims believe that Allah has a <u>plan</u> for every living person — he has decided <u>how long</u>
   each person will live on this Earth, and they do not have the right to <u>interfere</u> with that plan.

3) Islam teaches that <u>life on Earth</u> is a <u>test</u>.  Allah knows <u>why</u> people <u>suffer</u>, and
   they do <u>not</u> have good reason to <u>end</u> their <u>own lives</u>, no matter how bad that
   suffering is.  Instead, those who are suffering should turn to <u>Allah</u>, <u>pray</u> and
   <u>wait</u> — Allah is <u>merciful</u>, and all will be revealed on the <u>Day of Judgement</u>.

> "O you who have believed, seek help through patience and prayer.  Indeed, Allah is with the patient." Qur'an 2:153

4) As a result, Muslims support <u>hospices</u>, but often they try to look
   after the ill person <u>at home</u> — this allows them to be surrounded
   and taken <u>care</u> of by their <u>family</u>, <u>friends</u> and <u>neighbours</u>.

5) However, when a patient has a terminal illness with <u>no hope</u> of
   <u>improvement</u>, Islam allows doctors to stop 'unnecessary' treatment.

> "...when disaster strikes them, [they] say, 'Indeed we belong to Allah, and indeed to Him we will return.'  Those are the ones upon whom are blessings from their Lord and mercy." Qur'an 2:156-157

## There are Many **Non-Religious Views** on Abortion and Euthanasia

1) Many atheists support abortion as it gives women <u>control</u> over what happens to their <u>bodies</u>.
   Humanists <u>prioritise</u> quality of life over sustaining life, and look at the <u>impact</u> on the <u>woman</u> first.

2) There is some <u>debate</u> surrounding the <u>time limit</u> on abortions.  Since some babies born <u>prematurely</u>
   at 24 weeks or less are <u>surviving</u>, some feel that the <u>timeframe</u> for abortions should be <u>shortened</u>.
   Others feel that there <u>shouldn't</u> be a time limit on abortions at all.

3) There is more of a <u>divide</u> in opinions when it comes to <u>euthanasia</u>.  Some support it when
   a person will <u>die</u> from an illness or where they are suffering from an <u>incurable</u> illness.
   They feel that ending someone's <u>suffering</u> through euthanasia is the <u>kindest</u> thing to do.

4) However, some people fear that <u>legalising</u> euthanasia would potentially lead to people feeling
   <u>pressured</u> into it.  Some also feel that <u>doctors</u> should work to <u>protect</u> lives, not the opposite.

5) With abortion and euthanasia, many people look at the factors of each particular case —
   this is known as <u>situation ethics</u>.  They think <u>decisions</u> should be made based on what is best
   in <u>each situation</u>, not by following <u>rules</u> that should apply to <u>every instance</u>.

**EXAM TIP**

## The last few pages have covered a lot of information...

...so go back over them if you need to.  You need to be able to talk about views on abortion and
euthanasia in Christianity and at least one other religion, so make sure you can compare them.

# The Afterlife

Every religion in the world has something to say about <u>death</u> — and what comes <u>after</u> it.

## Most Religions Teach that there is an **Afterlife**

1) Many people believe that, although your <u>body</u> may die and decay, your <u>soul</u> can live on — in other words, you move on to a different kind of <u>existence</u>. This is the basic idea of <u>life after death</u>.

2) Most religions teach that something happens to the soul <u>after death</u>. Some religions teach that the soul is <u>rewarded</u> or <u>punished</u> for the <u>actions</u> of the person on Earth. Others believe the soul is <u>reincarnated</u>.

3) Christians, Muslims and Jews believe that life on Earth isn't <u>everything</u> — a <u>better</u> <u>life</u> awaits them. It's still <u>important</u> though, and is <u>preparation</u> for the afterlife.

## A Person's **Actions** in **Life** Can Determine their **Afterlife**

### Christian views

<u>Christianity</u> teaches that people go to <u>heaven</u> or <u>hell</u>, depending on how God <u>judges</u> their actions — trying to live life according to Christian <u>teachings</u> and believing in <u>Jesus</u> will allow them to receive <u>God's grace</u> and go to <u>heaven</u>. Catholics believe that some go to <u>Purgatory</u> — a place where <u>sins</u> are <u>paid for</u> before going to heaven (see p.5).

"And God raised us up with Christ and seated us with him in the heavenly realms in Christ Jesus... For it is by grace you have been saved..." Ephesians 2:6-8 NIV

### Muslim views

<u>Muslims</u> believe the afterlife means going to <u>jannah</u> (paradise) or <u>jahannam</u> (hell). After a person dies, their soul goes to <u>barzakh</u> to <u>await judgement</u> (see p.28).
On <u>Yawm ad-Din</u> (the Day of Judgement), everyone's actions will be judged. Muslims believe Allah "...will assemble you for the Day of Resurrection..." (Qur'an 45:26). Those who Allah deems <u>good</u> go to <u>jannah</u>, and the <u>bad</u> to <u>jahannam</u>.

"...one who had repented, believed, and done righteousness, it is promised by Allah that he will be among the successful." Qur'an 28:67

### Jewish views

Lots of <u>Jews</u> believe in <u>Gan Eden</u> (paradise) and <u>Gehinnom</u>, a place where people are <u>punished</u> for bad things they've done (see p.43). Most people will <u>move</u> from Gehinnom to Gan Eden, but <u>evil</u> people will stay for <u>eternity</u>. Some believe they'll eventually be <u>resurrected</u>, when God "will swallow up death for ever" (Isaiah 25:8 NIV). This is part of <u>Maimonides</u>' 13 principles of faith. However, Jews tend to <u>concentrate</u> on <u>this life</u>, rather than what might happen after death.

---

**REVISION TASK**

## Pay attention to the smaller details

Have a go at comparing the different ideas on life after death held by members of the three religions to help you learn all the details (e.g. the different names for paradise and hell).

## General | The Afterlife

In contemporary British society, there are many contrasting opinions on the existence of <u>life after death</u>...

## Some People **Believe** There's **Evidence** for Life After Death

There are many <u>arguments</u> used by both <u>religious</u> and <u>non-religious</u> people to <u>support</u> life after death:

- Some people claim to have evidence of <u>reincarnation</u> (they lived a previous life, died, and were reborn in a new body). Lots of research has been carried out with young <u>children</u> who claim to remember <u>past lives</u>.

- The <u>paranormal</u> (things science can't explain, which are thought to have a spiritual cause, e.g. <u>ghosts</u>) is sometimes used as evidence. Some people (<u>mediums</u>) claim they can <u>talk</u> to the <u>dead</u>.

- People say they've had a <u>near-death</u> or <u>out-of-body experience</u> where they've spoken to long-dead <u>family members</u>.

- Some believe there must be <u>more</u> after <u>life on Earth</u>. They might see going to heaven or paradise as a <u>reward</u> for people who've been <u>good</u> all their lives — it must exist to <u>compensate</u> for the <u>unfairness</u> of life on Earth.

## Some People **Don't Believe** in Life After Death

1) Many people believe that when you die, that's it — you <u>cease to exist</u>. They might argue that there isn't any <u>concrete evidence</u> that there is life after death, so the <u>logical</u> answer is that it <u>doesn't exist</u>. They think people's <u>memories</u> of previous lives <u>aren't real</u> — they could've been <u>suggested</u> to the person.

2) They might say that believing in an afterlife is just a way of <u>helping</u> people deal with <u>death</u> — the idea provides <u>comfort</u>.

3) They could also argue that the idea of an afterlife is used by religions to put <u>pressure</u> on people to <u>follow</u> their teachings and <u>live</u> their lives in a certain way.

4) Believers would <u>disagree</u> with these arguments, since their own beliefs come from <u>sacred texts</u>.

5) Christians might argue that Jesus's <u>resurrection</u> shows that there's life after death: "He was put to death in the body but made alive in the Spirit" (1 Peter 3:18 NIV). However, <u>non-believers</u> may say that the stories of Jesus's resurrection are <u>made up</u>.

---

## In the exam you might have to summarise this information...

...or you might be asked a 12-mark question on it requiring lots of detail. Use the previous two pages to compile a list of the arguments for and against the existence of life after death.

# Worked Exam Questions

After all that, it's time to face some more exam-style questions. The first lot have already been completed so you can get an idea of how to answer them, then it's up to you to finish off the rest — good luck...

**1**   Which of the following is the meaning of the word 'abortion'?
Put a tick (✓) in the correct box.

   **A**   When a foetus is removed from the womb before it can survive.   ☑

   **B**   Helping someone die to relieve their suffering.   ☐

   **C**   When a foetus cannot survive after birth so it is removed from the womb.   ☐

   **D**   Helping someone die because they have a terminal illness.   ☐

   *[1 mark]*

**2**   Which of the following is the word for being reborn after death into a new body?
Put a tick (✓) in the correct box.

   **A**   Judgement   ☐

   **B**   Purgatory   ☐

   **C**   Reincarnation   ☑

   **D**   Resurrection   ☐

   *[1 mark]*

**3**   Explain two religious beliefs about euthanasia.
Your answer should refer to specific religious teachings or sacred texts.

   Catholic Christians believe euthanasia is always wrong. They believe that life is so sacred that it is a form of murder even to withdraw treatment from someone. The Catechism of the Catholic Church says "an act or omission which... causes death in order to eliminate suffering constitutes a murder" (Catechism 2277).

   Some Anglican Christians believe that they must have compassion for people when they are suffering, especially when their quality of life is poor. Treatment can be withdrawn from patients who are dying in very painful ways, or who have incurable illnesses.

   *[5 marks]*

# Exam Questions

**4** Which of the following is a country where euthanasia is legal?
Put a tick (✓) in the correct box.

A   UK   ☐

B   Belgium   ☐

C   Russia   ☐

D   France   ☐

*[1 mark]*

**5** Which of the following is **not** an argument for the existence of the afterlife?
Put a tick (✓) in the correct box.

A   Young children sometimes describe memories of past lives.   ☐

B   Some people claim to have seen the ghost of people who have died.   ☐

C   Believing in the afterlife is a comfort to people when someone dies.   ☐

D   Many sacred texts describe an afterlife.   ☐

*[1 mark]*

**6** Give two situations when abortion is allowed according
to UK law (excluding Northern Ireland).

1) ......................................................................................................................................

..........................................................................................................................................

2) ......................................................................................................................................

..........................................................................................................................................

*[2 marks]*

**7** 'The afterlife is more important than life on Earth.'

SPaG MARKS

Evaluate this statement. Your answer should include the following:
• religious arguments that support the statement
• religious arguments that disagree with the statement
• a conclusion.
You can also include non-religious points of view in your answer.

*Write your answer on a separate sheet of paper.*

*[12 marks]*

# Revision Summary

And there you have it, you've fully covered <u>Religion and Life</u> — time to test out <u>how much</u> you can remember.

- Try these questions and <u>tick off each one</u> when you <u>get it right</u>.
- When you've done <u>all the questions</u> for a topic and are <u>completely happy</u> with it, tick off the topic.

If a question asks about a religion you <u>haven't</u> studied, just <u>skip it</u> and move on to the next question.

## Origins of Life and the Universe (p.73) ☐

1) What evidence is there to support the 'Big Bang' theory?
2) What is 'evolution'?
3) In Genesis, how many days did God take to create everything?
4) Give two examples of Christian churches that believe that science and religion can coexist.
5) How do ultra-Orthodox Jews interpret the story of creation in Genesis?
6) According to the Qur'an, who are all human beings descended from?

## The Environment, Stewardship and Animal Rights (p.74-77) ☑

7) Give three ways in which humans cause damage to the environment.
8) What is meant by the terms 'stewardship' and 'dominion'?
9) Give two ways people might try to tackle environmental problems.
10) In which book of the Bible are Christians told:
    "the Lord God took the man and put him in the Garden of Eden to work it and take care of it"?
11) What word is used to describe the belief that everything depends on everything else?
12) What Jewish term means 'mending the world'?
13) What word is used in Islam to describe how Muslims are trustees of the planet?
14) When do Muslims believe they will be judged on their treatment of the environment?
15) Give an example of a group which believes animal experimentation is always wrong.
16) Why do some Christians believe that only human life is sacred?
17) In Judaism, Kosher is a set of rules that forbids cruelty to animals. True or false?
18) What word describes food that is allowed in Islam?

## Abortion, Euthanasia and Life After Death (p.80-84) ☑

19) Until what week of pregnancy can abortion take place legally in England, Scotland and Wales?
20) What is the difference between 'active' and 'passive' euthanasia?
21) Name a Christian church that teaches that abortion is murder, and explain why it holds this belief.
22) According to the Bible, who was made to suffer by Satan but refused to end their life?
23) In Judaism, give a reason why a rabbi might allow an abortion.
24) In Judaism, how might the words of Rabbi Moses Isserles support passive euthanasia?
25) In Islam, what is 'ensoulment'?
26) What does Islam teach people should do in response to suffering?
27) Why do some people fear legalising euthanasia even if they don't have religious objections to it?
28) Give the names used for paradise in the teachings of two religions.
29) What part of a person is said to survive after the body dies and decays?
30) What is 'reincarnation'?
31) What do some non-religious people accuse religions of hoping
    to achieve through teaching the existence of an afterlife?

**All religions**    # Design and Causation

The belief that God created the world is an important part of many religions, and often strengthens faith.

## Different People Believe for Different Reasons

1) About 84% of the global population belongs to a religion (source Pew Research Center). The rest don't have specific religious beliefs, or have no spiritual beliefs. There are many reasons for being religious:

   - People want to find out why life is as it is. Some people are convinced the 'design' or 'causation' arguments explain this.
   - Some are drawn to the purpose, structure and comfort religion provides, or simply by the desire to have something to believe. Some people's faith is strengthened by the feelings they experience during worship and as part of a religious community.
   - People brought up by religious parents or in a religious community are more likely to believe in a god.

2) There are various reasons why people might reject religion: they believe there's no proof there's a god, or that religion causes too much strife between people, or that the evil in the world shows there's no god.

3) Atheists reject the idea of a divine being. Agnostics believe it's impossible to know either way for certain.

## The Design Argument: 'The Universe Must Have Had a Designer'

1) Belief that God created the universe is a central part of belief in God — not only does the universe's existence prove God's existence, but believers think it shows some of his characteristics, e.g. his power.

2) Many Christians, Muslims and Jews believe a god exists because of 'design' arguments. The idea is that the intricate workings of the universe can't have come about by chance. There must have been some kind of designer — a god. The Bible, the Qur'an and the Torah support this argument:

   The Qur'an says aspects of nature are evidence Allah is the creator. "In the creation of the heavens and earth, and the alternation of the night and the day ... and ... the winds and the clouds ... are signs for a people who use reason." (Qur'an 2:164)

   The Bible's argument is similar. Romans 1:20 says "since the creation of the world God's invisible qualities — his eternal power and divine nature — have been clearly seen, being understood from what has been made" (NIV).

   "God created the heavens and the earth" Genesis 1:1 NIV — Torah/Bible.

3) Some think aspects of nature support this idea. For example, snowflakes form complex shapes that are unique to each individual snowflake. The distribution of petals and seeds on many plants and the spiral shape of some shells follow mathematical rules.

4) William Paley's watchmaker argument says that if you came across an intricate watch, you wouldn't think it was made by chance — you would assume it had been designed. The same must be true of complex structures in nature. A common example people give is the human eye, which is made up of many parts — it's so sophisticated, they believe that it must have had a designer.

5) Scientists say the conditions that led to the creation of the universe and life were extremely specific. The fine-tuning argument says this shows there was a designer — they couldn't have occurred by chance.

---

## The Design argument is used to support the existence of God

Some religious people believe theories like the watchmaker and fine-tuning arguments provide evidence for the existence of god. They also point to what is written in their sacred texts as proof that there was a creator.

# Design and Causation

The story of creation is told in the sacred texts of the three religions, but not everyone believes these accounts should be interpreted literally. Some see them as metaphors whilst others don't believe them at all.

## Some People **Aren't Convinced** by Design Arguments

1) Charles Darwin explained how species developed by adapting themselves to the conditions around them through 'survival of the fittest':

> Species or individuals that have characteristics that are beneficial for survival are more likely to live, while those that aren't well-adapted are more likely to die out. This helps to explain how species have developed their characteristics through time — known as evolution.

2) In 2009, a survey found 37% of people in Britain thought evolution was 'beyond reasonable doubt'.

3) Some Christians, Muslims and Jews believe evolution doesn't contradict the design argument — God or Allah must have 'designed' evolution. Darwin didn't see it as conclusive proof against God's existence.

4) Believers may struggle most to reconcile evolution with the belief that God created humans in his own image — it may seem unlikely he would have done so by slowly evolving humans from apes.

5) Scientists can explain things such as why plants and shells often have spiral patterns — shells have evolved to do so because it means the animal inside a shell can keep living in it as it grows.

6) Some people believe God created the universe but has not had any further involvement with it. Some believe that there's no evidence the 'designer' and creator still exists.

## Sacred Texts are Used as **Evidence** that **God Created the World**

1) Christian and Jewish teachings on creation are taken from Genesis 1, which says God created everything. The process took 6 days, and people didn't evolve from apes, but descended from Adam and Eve.

2) The Qur'an says that Allah created the world. It says Allah made Adam from clay and breathed life and a soul into him — and that all humans descend from Adam.

> "Allah constructed it"
> Qur'an 79:27

3) Descriptions in the sacred texts can be interpreted differently:

- Some believers take the descriptions in the sacred texts literally, e.g. some Christians and ultra-Orthodox Jews accept the account given in Genesis.

- Others see the accounts as symbolic, and some look to science to explain how it all happened — though they still believe God is the creator.

## Learn the arguments for both sides of the debate

It's very important to have a good knowledge of non-religious views on the design argument too (e.g. how evolution can explain how species developed). You can write about these arguments in your answer — as long as you mention the views of at least one religion as well.

# Design and Causation

Ideas about causation have been used over the centuries as evidence that a divine being exists.

## Causation: 'There Must Have Been a First Cause'

1) The First Cause argument, also known as the cosmological argument, is founded on a chain of logic.

2) Everything that happens is caused by something else. An event now was caused by an earlier event, that was caused by an even earlier event, etc. If you trace this chain back in time, there are two possibilities:

- The chain goes back forever — i.e. the universe has always existed, it's eternal.
- You eventually reach a starting point — an uncaused cause or 'First Cause'.

3) Some think the 'First Cause' was God, as only he is eternal and has enough power to create the universe.

## Religious Figures Have Theorised About the First Cause

1) The Muslim theologian al-Ghazali wrote in his book al-Iqtisad fil'Itiqad that everything that starts to exist was caused to exist. The universe started to exist, so it had a cause — Allah. The focus on the universe having started to exist (i.e. not being infinite) is a key part of the theory, known as the kalam cosmological argument. Al-Ghazali believed the universe was made up of chains of events that Allah had predetermined.

2) Thomas Aquinas, a 13th century monk, developed Five Ways to prove God exists. They've been influential in Christianity. Three of them have a similar logic to the 'First Cause' theory:

| Movement | Contingency | Causation |
|---|---|---|
| • Nothing can move by itself. <br> • This means the first thing that ever moved needed something to move it. <br> • This first mover is God. | • Contingent beings are beings that are caused to exist. <br> • It's necessary for there to be a being which has created contingent beings. <br> • This necessary being must be God. | • Nothing can create itself. <br> • There can't be a chain of creation that's been happening forever. <br> • So there must have been a first cause — God. |

3) The Jewish theologian Maimonides wasn't sure whether the universe was eternal or created — "the world cannot but be either eternal or created in time. If it is created in time, it undoubtedly has a creator". Maimonides came up with some versions of the first cause argument as well.

## There are Differing Opinions on the First Cause Argument

1) Some people question its logic. They argue that the argument contradicts itself — it says everything has to have a cause, but then says there must be an event that didn't have a cause — the first cause.

2) There's no evidence that if there is a first cause, it has to be a divine being — a god.

3) Some say that even if a god was the first cause, it doesn't mean they still exist now. It also doesn't give any indication that the god has the characteristics of the Christian, Jewish or Muslim god.

4) However, many Christians, Muslims and Jews use the first cause argument as evidence there is a god. It's often used in combination with accounts from the scriptures and the design argument.

## There are lots of different ideas to take in here

It might be best to read these three pages again — they're pretty complicated, and it's easy to get the different arguments mixed up. Write down the key ideas from each one to get them in your head.

# Miracles All religions

The sacred texts contain accounts of miracles that are used in religious teachings, but these are often interpreted differently by different people. Make sure you can remember specific examples of miracles for the exam.

## Many Believe Miracles Prove There is a God

1) Miracles are seemingly inexplicable events, such as people with apparently incurable illnesses being healed.

2) Christianity, Islam and Judaism all involve some belief in miracles, though to differing extents. These include events in their scriptures, though some people believe miracles also happen nowadays. Others argue that the miracles in religious texts should be interpreted symbolically rather than literally.

3) People believe miracles offer proof there is a god because they go against the laws of nature — only God would have the power to do so.

4) They also show God's benevolence, as many miracles are beneficial, e.g. healing someone who is ill. Healing people also shows that God can decide who lives or dies.

## Christians Read Stories of Miracles in the New Testament

1) Jesus performed miracles to show he had the power of God, and to show the importance of faith. Examples include the feeding of the 5000 and healing a blind man — see p.143 for more detail.

2) Christians believe the birth and resurrection of Jesus were miracles in their own right (see p.6-7).

## Miracles are Important in Judaism

1) Many miraculous events are described in the Torah. A well-known example is God sending down manna (miraculous food) from heaven so the Israelites could eat while they were in the desert — see Exodus 16.

2) Some Progressive Jews say the stories simply send a spiritual message — they don't have to be taken literally. More orthodox believers might believe the events happened as described in scripture.

3) The word 'nes' is used for 'miracle' in Hebrew — it means 'sign' or 'marker', as miracles are signs of God. But the Torah warns Jews not to be influenced by miracles alone — it's more important to focus on God.

"If a prophet ... announces to you a sign or wonder, and if the sign or wonder ... takes place, and the prophet says, '... follow other gods ...,' you must not listen to the words of that prophet ... It is the Lord your God you must follow." Deuteronomy 13:1-4 NIV

4) Many Jews prefer to focus on God, the Torah and the wonder of creation as a miracle in itself.

## Muslims Believe the Qur'an is a Miracle in Itself

1) Muslims believe the Qur'an is a miracle — the direct word of Allah, with a style that's impossible to copy. Qur'an 17:88 says "If mankind ... gathered ... to produce the like of this Qur'an, they could not".

2) Some believe the Qur'an contains 'scientific miracles' — it describes facts discovered centuries later, such as an account of how the human embryo develops (Qur'an 23:13-14) or a reference to the Big Bang (Qur'an 21:30). Others disagree, saying the descriptions aren't detailed enough to be certain.

3) Many Muslims think that the prophets performed miracles in order to show they had been sent by God.

## Some People Don't Believe in Miracles

1) Some believers prefer to focus on God and living their life in a moral way rather than on miracles.

2) Atheists and humanists don't believe in miracles. They believe they can either be explained scientifically, or are fakes or misunderstandings. For example, they might explain someone being cured of a terminal disease by saying they must have been misdiagnosed, or the hope of a religious figure healing them had stimulated their recovery — called the placebo effect, this also happens when people are given fake pills.

3) It can be a matter of perspective — a religious person might seek a miraculous explanation for something atheists and humanists would call a coincidence, e.g. something happening soon after you prayed for it.

# Revelation

For <u>nature as revelation</u> and <u>visions</u>, you need to be able to compare <u>Christian</u> and <u>non-religious</u> views.

## Revelation is How God's **Presence** is **Revealed**

1) It's <u>difficult</u> to <u>conclusively prove</u> God <u>exists</u>. So Christians, Muslims and Jews look for <u>evidence</u> to reveal God's <u>presence</u>. They believe he is <u>revealed</u> in <u>different</u> ways, including through the <u>scriptures</u>, the <u>world</u> around us and <u>religious experiences</u>.

2) Revelation doesn't just involve knowing God <u>exists</u>, but also what he's <u>like</u> and what he <u>expects</u> of people. Revelations can <u>give rise to</u> or <u>strengthen</u> people's <u>belief</u> in a god. There are <u>two</u> main types of <u>revelation</u>:

### General Revelation

- <u>General revelations</u> are revelations <u>available</u> to <u>everyone</u>. They're more <u>indirect</u> and therefore have to be <u>interpreted</u>.

- Many think the <u>world</u> is an <u>example</u> of <u>general revelation</u>. <u>Believers</u> think God <u>created</u> the world, so it <u>proves</u> he exists.

- Many think our <u>conscience</u> proves God exists, as people all over the world have <u>similar</u> <u>morals</u>, e.g. that <u>killing</u> is wrong. God must have <u>created</u> this within <u>every person</u>.

### Special Revelation

- <u>Special revelations</u> are revelations to <u>specific</u> people, e.g. <u>Allah's</u> revelation of the <u>Qur'an</u> to <u>Muhammad</u>.

- They include revelations through <u>prophethood</u> (written down as <u>scriptures</u>), <u>visions</u> and <u>miracles</u> (see p.91).

- They're <u>direct</u> and <u>personal</u>, so they can be <u>powerful</u> experiences. However, they're hard to <u>prove</u>.

- Some think they <u>still</u> occur today, while others <u>disagree</u>.

## The **Scriptures** are **Important Revelations**

1) Christians, Muslims and Jews believe God's <u>nature</u> and <u>will</u> are revealed in their <u>holy books</u>. Many believe they were either <u>inspired</u> by <u>God</u> or came <u>directly</u> from him. They contain <u>knowledge</u> of <u>God</u> and the <u>faith</u>.

2) Most religious people believe that <u>all</u> or <u>parts</u> of them were <u>special revelations</u>, as they were revealed to <u>specific prophets</u>. In their <u>written</u> form, they also have some <u>features</u> of <u>general revelation</u> — they are <u>available</u> to <u>everyone</u>, all the <u>time</u>, and they need to be <u>interpreted</u> to be <u>understood</u>.

### The Bible

The Bible is a <u>collection</u> of books written by <u>various</u> authors. Some Christians think the authors were <u>inspired</u> and <u>guided</u> by God as they <u>wrote</u>, but he didn't <u>directly</u> reveal it to them. The <u>New Testament</u> describes Jesus's <u>life</u> — Jesus is seen as the <u>completion</u> of God's <u>revelation</u> to people. Hebrews 1:1-2 says "God spoke to our ancestors through the prophets at many times and in various ways, but in these last days he has spoken to us by his Son" (NIV). <u>Jesus</u> is seen as the '<u>new covenant</u>' — he <u>died</u> for people's <u>sins</u>, but in return <u>people</u> should <u>worship</u> God.

### The Torah

<u>Orthodox</u> Jews believe the <u>five</u> books of the <u>Torah</u> were <u>directly</u> revealed to <u>Moses</u> by God. <u>Progressive</u> Jews tend to believe it contains God's <u>message</u> but the text was <u>written</u> by <u>people</u>.

### The Qur'an

Muslims believe <u>Allah</u> revealed the <u>Qur'an directly</u> to Muhammad. It's a <u>fully accurate</u> record of Allah's <u>final</u> revelation to <u>humankind</u>. Muslims believe he gave <u>earlier</u> revelations to prophets such as <u>Musa</u> (Moses) and <u>Isa</u> (Jesus) but the texts have been <u>altered</u>.

3) Many <u>atheists</u> and <u>humanists</u> think the scriptures just depict their authors' <u>ideas</u> about <u>God</u>, and that many of the events in them <u>didn't occur</u>. They may see these ancient texts as largely <u>irrelevant</u> to <u>life today</u>.

## Revelations come in two different forms — general and special

Try comparing general and special revelation and come up with some examples of each.

# Revelation

Some religious people believe that <u>nature</u> reveals some of <u>God's characteristics</u> through its beauty and complexity.

## Revelations Show God's **Nature**

1) <u>Christians</u>, <u>Muslims</u> and <u>Jews</u> have <u>similar</u> beliefs about many of God's <u>characteristics</u>.  He is:

- <u>omniscient</u> — all-knowing
- <u>infinite</u> — he has no limits
- <u>omnipotent</u> — all-powerful
- <u>transcendent</u> — beyond this world
- <u>immanent</u> — involved in the world
- <u>eternal</u> — he has always existed and always will
- the <u>creator</u> and <u>sustainer</u> of the universe — he made it and keeps it going
- <u>all-loving</u> — infinite in his mercy and compassion and completely <u>good</u>
- <u>personal</u> — many believe they can have a <u>relationship</u> with God, e.g. through <u>prayer</u>
- <u>impersonal</u> — others see him as <u>distant</u> from people as he <u>rarely</u> acts in the world

2) The scriptures can show God's <u>characteristics</u>, e.g. Qur'an 57:4 says "He is with you wherever you are", while Psalm 139:1 says "Lord ... you know me" (NIV).  This suggests to believers that God is <u>personal</u>.

*For more about the <u>nature</u> of God, see p.1 for <u>Christianity</u> or p.40 for <u>Judaism</u>.  For more on <u>Allah</u>, see p.24.*

3) Believers think God shows his <u>compassion</u> through his <u>intervention</u> in the world — e.g. showing people how to live a <u>better life</u> through the <u>prophets</u> in all three faiths, and through <u>Jesus</u> as Messiah in Christian belief.

## Some See **Nature** as **Revelation**

1) Christians, Muslims and Jews believe <u>God</u> created the <u>world</u>, so it <u>shows</u> God <u>exists</u>.

2) Many believers feel that nature provides <u>numinous</u> (<u>spiritual</u>) experiences.  These are events that inspire <u>awe</u> and <u>wonder</u>, where someone can feel God's <u>presence</u>, e.g. a beautiful <u>sunset</u> might convince them there is a <u>creator</u>.  <u>Interventions</u> in <u>nature</u>, e.g. <u>miracles</u>, show God's <u>immanence</u>.

3) Nature may show God's <u>transcendence</u> — he <u>created</u> it but isn't <u>present</u> in it — as well as other <u>aspects</u>:

| | |
|---|---|
| Many <u>Christians</u> believe <u>characteristics</u> such as God's <u>intelligence</u> are revealed through the <u>complexity</u> of nature.  The Catechism of the Catholic Church says "The beauty of creation reflects the infinite beauty of the Creator" (341).<br><br>Nature is often <u>cruel</u>, which can be hard to explain.  Some believe nature became <u>cruel</u> after the <u>Fall</u> — when Adam and Eve <u>sinned</u>.  So nature no longer fully shows what God is <u>like</u>. | Many <u>Jews</u> see the universe's <u>existence</u> as <u>proof</u> enough that God exists — <u>no more proof</u> is needed.  The <u>wonders</u> of creation may <u>deepen</u> their <u>relationship</u> with God — Jews may offer <u>blessings</u> to God if they see something <u>beautiful</u> in nature.<br><br>Jews believe <u>all</u> of nature comes from God, even the <u>negative</u> parts — Isaiah 45:7 says "I bring prosperity and create disaster" (NIV).  Jews have a <u>responsibility</u> to <u>look after</u> his <u>creation</u>. |

*"The heavens declare the glory of God; the skies proclaim the work of his hands." Psalm 19:1 NIV*

<u>Muslims</u> believe Allah created the universe — all <u>beauty</u> comes from him as a gift, and can move people to <u>faith</u> in its creator.  One of the 99 names of Allah is <u>Al-Musawwir</u> — The <u>Shaper</u> of <u>Beauty</u>.  The beauty of the <u>world</u> shows the beauty of <u>Allah</u>.

4) <u>Atheists</u> and <u>humanists</u> don't believe that <u>nature</u> reveals <u>God</u>.  They argue that even aspects of <u>nature</u> we don't fully understand, e.g. how animals <u>navigate</u> as they <u>migrate</u>, will one day be <u>explained</u> by <u>science</u>.

# Revelation

Religious experiences, such as visions, can confirm the existence of God to some people and change their lives. Examples of visions are found in Christianity, Judaism and Islam — read the next two pages to find out more.

## God can be Revealed Through Religious Experiences

1) Religious experiences are personal experiences of God — they're a form of special revelation.

2) They can take many forms — a vision, a dream, hearing a voice, a feeling of ecstasy or peace, or feelings of being loved, forgiven or guided. They can take place during prayer or worship, or at other times. They can be so powerful they change the life of the person, or they might be more gentle experiences.

3) Other religious believers may take inspiration from someone who's had such an experience. Some people who have had religious experiences become well known — see below and the next page.

## Visions are a Dramatic Form of Religious Experience

1) A vision is a religious experience in which a person sees something sacred — such as an angel. Visions usually tell the receiver about God and his will, or about the receiver's own life.

2) Visions are direct and powerful forms of religious experience. They often change how believers live their lives — they can strengthen people's faith or even induce them to believe in something they didn't believe in before. They can convince people that God exists — only he could have made them happen.

## There are Many Examples of Visions in Christianity

1) Some visions are reported in the Bible, which gives them authority, as they're part of the scripture. For example:

- The disciples saw a vision of Moses and Elijah with Jesus, who was covered in light — see Matthew 17:1-13 and p.144.
- St Paul was originally named Saul. He persecuted Christians. One day he saw a light, and heard Jesus asking why Saul was persecuting him. This transformed Saul's life — he became a Christian and spent the rest of his life preaching the gospel.

2) Other visions of Mary or angels appeared to people later. The Churches confirm if they think they're authentic. Belief in this type of vision is more significant in Catholicism than in Protestant Christianity.

- Joan of Arc was a French peasant. She had visions of the archangel Michael, among others. These encouraged her to lead France against England in the Hundred Years' War. She was captured and killed by English allies. The Catholic Church declared her a saint — Catholics think her visions were genuine.
- Many Catholics report visions of Mary. One example is Bernadette Soubirous, who claimed she saw Mary several times in 1858 near Lourdes (France). Lourdes is now a popular pilgrimage site — many think people can be healed by visiting it.

## Branches of the same faith may have different views...

...so make sure you revise different opinions, as you might be asked to give two contrasting beliefs in the exam. Keep in mind similarities within different branches of the same religion, as well as similarities and differences between religions (see the next page for visions in Judaism and Islam).

# Revelation

## Judaism was Founded by Men who had Visions of God

1) Many visions are recorded in the Torah, and elsewhere in the Tenakh.

2) Abraham and his wife were old and childless. God's word came to him in a vision, promising him a son and countless descendants. He believed God — and what God promised happened.

> "...the word of the Lord came to Abram in a vision" Genesis 15:1 NIV

3) Jacob had a vision of a ladder with angels on it reaching from Earth to Heaven — see Genesis 28:10-22.

4) God first spoke to Moses from within a burning bush — see Exodus 3. This is an indirect or veiled revelation — another example is God appearing as a pillar of cloud in Deuteronomy 31:15.

5) Moses is the only person to have seen God — he spoke to "Moses face to face, as one speaks to a friend" (Exodus 33:11 NIV). These were direct revelations — a direct experience of God.

6) Many Jews believe in the visions of God in the Tenakh, but some Progressive Jews may see them as metaphorical stories. Visions in more recent times aren't really a key part of Judaism.

## The Qur'an Mentions Stories of People who had Visions

1) The Qur'an includes the story of the angel Jibril (Gabriel) appearing to Maryam (Mary), the mother of Isa (Jesus) — see Qur'an 19:16-22. Jibril told her she would bear a son, even though she was a virgin.

2) The angel Jibril appeared to Muhammad while he was meditating in a cave outside Makkah. Muhammad recited the verses Jibril gave to him — these were the first verses of the Qur'an to be revealed.

3) Sufi Muslims are Muslim mystics who seek to be filled with knowledge and love of Allah through direct experience of him, which can include visions. This affects them spiritually at a deep level.

4) Sufis can be Sunni or Shi'a, but many Muslims are sceptical of the Sufis' religious experiences.

5) There are other examples of seemingly miraculous events or visions in Islam. Qur'an 2:118 says "We have shown clearly the signs to a people who are certain [in faith]", showing how Allah reveals himself.

## Many People Don't Believe in Religious Experiences

Religious experiences are private, so it's impossible to show proof of them to someone else. Atheists and humanists don't believe in God, so think religious experiences can be explained in other ways:

1) Some may happen because of wish fulfilment — the person wants the experience so much that their subconscious makes it happen. Religious people tend to have visions consistent with their own religious beliefs, and not of figures or ideas from another religion, which casts doubt on them.

2) The person involved may be lying about their experience, perhaps because they might profit from being believed.

3) Some religious experiences may result from things which affect the brain, such as mental illness, or physical illness such as brain tumours, or drugs. An example is the 12th century nun Hildegard of Bingen, who saw visions all her life, but some people think she was actually suffering from migraines.

4) The person might have misinterpreted their experience, or chosen to interpret it in a religious way. For example, if you were ill and dreamt you would be cured the next day, and the next day you felt much better, you might decide God was involved — or you might just think it a coincidence.

Some believers may not believe in these experiences either, particularly ones not written in their sacred text. They might prefer to focus on God and living a good life instead of events which may or may not be true.

1) Religious experiences can bring up contradictions in the ideas people have about God. It's hard to understand why, if God is capable of acting in the world, he doesn't do it more often.

2) Miracles (see p.91) show God's power as they break the laws of nature, but this doesn't explain why he doesn't use his power to prevent suffering (see p.96).

# All religions — Arguments Against the Existence of God

## Atheists and Humanists Argue There's No Evidence

1) Many atheists and humanists don't believe in God because they don't think there's any evidence he exists.

2) They say visions and miracles have scientific or straightforward explanations, and aren't proof of a divine being. Many such experiences happened a long time ago, before science could explain them. For example, some scientists believe that the 10 plagues in Egypt before the Exodus could be explained by the eruption of a volcano in the Mediterranean, which contradicts the belief that God sent the plagues.

3) Atheists and humanists argue that science provides sufficient explanation for the origins of the universe.

## Many Think the Big Bang Theory Explains Creation

1) The theory says that the universe suddenly expanded from an initial state of very high density and temperature — this event is known as the 'Big Bang'. Matter from this explosion eventually formed stars, planets and everything else. There's quite a lot of evidence to back up this theory.

2) However, we don't know what caused the Big Bang — so many Christians, Jews and Muslims argue that it was God or Allah who caused it, which seems to fit with the 'First Cause' argument. Some Muslims think the Qur'an mentions Allah creating the Big Bang:

> "...the heavens and the earth were a joined entity ... We separated them and made from water every living thing." Qur'an 21:30

## Evil and Suffering Make People Doubt There is a God

1) Christians, Jews and Muslims all believe in a God who is omniscient (all-knowing), omnipotent (all-powerful), and benevolent (kind). So they believe he knows what happens in the world, doesn't want people to suffer, and is powerful enough to do something about it.

2) However, there's a lot of suffering in the world, which seems to contradict these ideas. Some people find it hard to see how God could allow it to happen, and therefore doubt he exists.

3) In the scriptures, suffering is often described as punishment for people's sins, e.g. in all three faiths' sacred texts, God destroyed a town of people he considered sinful, while sparing a few who weren't.

4) However, suffering is widespread and affects everyone, so atheists and humanists might argue that justifying suffering as punishment doesn't make sense. They might also argue that it doesn't seem to add up because animals suffer too, even though they can't be being punished for their sins.

5) Believers might explain it by saying that humans need to be able to choose between good and evil as a test of their character — that's why they have free will. Without bad things happening, good can't exist.

Christians believe the concept of original sin can explain suffering (see p.4). God gave people free will — they choose to create suffering or good. St Augustine said suffering was the price people pay for free will. St Irenaeus thought people were created with faults because they had to develop into being children of God — so they needed evil and suffering to exist, else they'd have no concept of what's right. Christians try to follow God's example of goodness — Psalm 119 asks for his help to do so. Isaiah 45:7 says "I bring prosperity and create disaster" (NIV), which suggests God isn't only responsible for good — he creates suffering as a punishment.

Muslims believe suffering can be a test from Allah. Everything is part of Allah's plan and there are good reasons for it, even if we can't see them. Evil gives people the chance to do good and help those in need. If we ourselves are suffering, Muslims believe we must bear it with patience and faith. Qur'an 2:155-156 says: "good tidings to the patient, Who, when disaster strikes them, say, 'Indeed we belong to Allah' ".

Jews believe suffering is a test from God. In the Torah, Job endures many hardships, but despite this, he decides suffering must be accepted as we can't understand God's plan. A lot of Jewish thought doesn't try explaining evil, and the Holocaust makes it particularly hard to do so. Many Jews struggle to understand why God let it happen, especially as Psalm 103:17-18 says "the Lord's love is with those ... who keep his covenant" (NIV). Many believe evil needs a response, not an explanation — e.g. helping those who are suffering.

# Worked Exam Questions

Now you've read through everything for Theme C, it's time to have a go at some exam questions.
The questions on this first page are already filled in for you — then it's your turn to answer the rest.

**1** Which of the following is the name for someone who does not believe in God?
Put a tick (✓) in the correct box.

    **A**    Atheist    ✓

    **B**    Agnostic    ☐

    **C**    Theist    ☐

    **D**    Monotheist    ☐

*[1 mark]*

**2** Give two strengths of the Design argument.

    **1)** Complicated things like the human eye seem to have been designed.

    **2)** The argument is supported by the Torah, the Qur'an and the Bible.

*[2 marks]*

**3** Explain two similar religious beliefs about miracles.

    Jews believe that miracles took place in the Torah. They are signs from God, and they show

    his power.

    Similarly, Muslims believe that the prophets performed miracles. This showed their power,

    and the fact that they had been sent by God.

*[4 marks]*

**4** Explain two religious beliefs about how nature shows the existence of God.
Your answer should refer to specific religious teachings or sacred texts.

    Jews believe that the beauty and complexity of nature prove the existence of God: "The heavens

    declare the glory of God" (Psalm 19:1 NIV). Beauty in the world can inspire feelings of awe and

    strengthen someone's belief in God.

    Christians also believe that nature can show God's existence by demonstrating his qualities.

    Some believe the cruelty of nature came after the Fall, and so this does not reflect the nature of God.

*[5 marks]*

# Exam Questions

**5** Which of the following is the scientist who is famous for developing the theory of evolution?
Put a tick (✓) in the correct box.

A    Maimonides ☐

B    Charles Darwin ☐

C    Al-Ghazali ☐

D    Thomas Aquinas ☐

*[1 mark]*

**6** Which of the following is a form of special revelation?
Put a tick (✓) in the correct box.

A    Nature ☐

B    Morality ☐

C    Visions ☐

D    Philosophy ☐

*[1 mark]*

**7** Give two scientific arguments against the existence of God.

1) ......................................................................................................................................

......................................................................................................................................

2) ......................................................................................................................................

......................................................................................................................................

*[2 marks]*

**8** Explain two contrasting beliefs in British society today about general revelation.
You must refer to the main religious tradition in the UK and non-religious viewpoints.

......................................................................................................................................

......................................................................................................................................

......................................................................................................................................

......................................................................................................................................

......................................................................................................................................

......................................................................................................................................

*[4 marks]*

# Exam Questions

**9**  Which of the following is **not** a reason why religious scriptures are important? Put a tick (✓) in the correct box.

    **A**    They were written centuries ago   ☐

    **B**    They reveal God's will   ☐

    **C**    They show us God's nature   ☐

    **D**    They come directly from God or were inspired by him   ☐

*[1 mark]*

**10**  Which of the following is a reason why non-religious people might dismiss miracles as proof of God's existence?  Put a tick (✓) in the correct box.

    **A**    There isn't enough scientific evidence that they happened.   ☐

    **B**    Miracles are only ever witnessed by one person.   ☐

    **C**    It is completely impossible for reports of these things to survive.   ☐

    **D**    There aren't enough examples of miracles to offer proof.   ☐

*[1 mark]*

**11**  Give two reasons why people might not believe that religious experiences prove God's existence.

    **1)** ...................................................................................................................................

    .............................................................................................................................................

    **2)** ...................................................................................................................................

    .............................................................................................................................................

*[2 marks]*

**12**  'Visions prove that God exists.'

    (SPaG MARKS)

    Evaluate this statement.  Your answer should include the following:
    • religious arguments that support the statement
    • religious arguments that disagree with the statement
    • a conclusion.
    You can also include non-religious points of view in your answer.

    *Write your answer on a separate sheet of paper.*

*[12 marks]*

# Revision Summary

Now you've explored the <u>Existence of God and Revelation</u>, have a go at these questions to recap what you've learnt.

- Try these questions and <u>tick off each one</u> when you <u>get it right</u>.
- When you've done <u>all the questions</u> for a topic and are <u>completely happy</u> with it, tick off the topic.

If a question asks about a religion you <u>haven't</u> studied, just <u>skip it</u> and move on to the next question.

## <u>Design and Causation (p.88-90)</u> ☐

1) What percentage of the world's population belong to a religion?
2) Give two reasons why people might reject religion.
3) Describe the 'Design' argument.
4) What object did William Paley use to argue for the existence of a creator?
5) According to the theory of evolution, how did species develop?
6) Which book of the Bible tells the story of creation?
7) What does the Qur'an say Adam was made from?
8) Give the two possibilities that are implied by the First Cause theory.
9) What did the Muslim theologian al-Ghazali believe was the First Cause?
10) Which three of the Five Ways relate to the First Cause theory?
11) Name the Jewish theologian who came up with ideas about the First Cause argument.
12) Why do some people believe the First Cause argument contradicts itself?

## <u>Miracles and Revelation (p.91-95)</u> ☐

13) What is a miracle?
14) Give one example of a miracle performed by Jesus.
15) How do Progressive Jews interpret miracles in their holy scriptures?
16) Give one example of a 'scientific miracle' the Qur'an is believed to describe.
17) How do atheists and humanists view miracles?
18) Describe the difference between general and special revelation.
19) What events do the New Testament of the Bible focus upon?
20) Name a Muslim prophet other than Muhammad who received revelations.
21) Give three characteristics of God's nature.
22) How do believers think God reveals compassion to the world?
23) Explain beliefs from two different religions about nature.
24) What do visions usually communicate to the receiver?
25) Which branch of Christianity believes most strongly in visions?
26) Give an example of a vision that is recorded in the Tenakh.
27) Name the angel who visited both Maryam and Muhammad according to the Qur'an.
28) Give one possible scientific explanation for religious experiences such as visions.

## <u>Arguments Against the Existence of God (p.96)</u> ☐

29) What do scientists suggest might have caused the ten plagues of Egypt?
30) Why do some believe the Big Bang theory does not exclude the existence of a god?
31) Why do believers think people have free will?
32) According to St Irenaeus, why are people born with faults?
33) Why did Job believe that suffering must be accepted?
34) How do Muslims view suffering?

## Peace and Conflict

World peace — a pretty tall order, but there are a lot of people striving for it...

## Peace is the **Absence** of **Conflict** and **Violence**

1) Peace means that everyone in the world lives in harmony, and there is no conflict.

2) Many organisations, such as the United Nations (UN), work to find peaceful solutions to disputes and to end all wars, all over the world.

3) Christianity, Islam and Judaism all encourage believers to work towards achieving peace in the world.

### Pacifism

- A pacifist is someone who has strongly held beliefs that war and physical violence are wrong. Pacifists believe that all disputes should be settled peacefully.

- There were pacifists in Britain who refused to fight in the world wars. Many of these 'conscientious objectors' went to prison rather than go against their beliefs — they were prisoners of conscience. They suffered humiliation in prison, and after they'd been released.

- There are different degrees of pacifism — some people are against violence under any circumstances, whereas others may disagree with violence, but understand that sometimes violence is the least horrible option.

## **Violence** Has Many **Different Forms**

1) Crime is a source of a lot of violence, e.g. assault or murder.

2) Terrorism is when a person or group deliberately seeks to cause fear and inflict suffering on other people through violence, sometimes for political reasons. The attack on the World Trade Center by the terrorist organisation al-Qaeda in New York in September 2001 was the worst terrorist attack in history.

3) War is when two or more groups or countries fight one another. It's usually decided by governments.

4) War and terrorism have caused many deaths. Lots of religious people believe in the sanctity of life argument, that life is given by God and is sacred, so war and terrorism are in direct conflict with this.

5) Violence can occur during protests — a protest is when a group of people join together to campaign for a cause they support. While many protests occur peacefully, some protests become violent if protesters don't feel their views are being heard, or if protesters clash with people with opposing views.

## Wars Can Have **Many Causes**

Most wars have causes that are a combination of lots of different factors:

1) RELIGION — this has been the cause of many conflicts in the past and the present (see p.102-105).

2) SELF-DEFENCE — wars started to combat a threat from another country or to stop them from attacking first, e.g. a pre-emptive strike.

3) TRIBALISM — this tends to trigger wars where a group of people fight for their own independent state.

4) HONOUR — wars fought to defend the honour and dignity of a country, or to save face.

5) GREED/ECONOMICS — acts of aggression (attacking without provocation) are condemned by the UN, so purely economic wars driven by greed (e.g. raids and invasions to gain territory or goods) are few and far between. Economic factors still have an impact though — poverty and economic imbalances can make wars more likely.

6) RETALIATION — a war might be started in revenge for something, e.g. World War One started after Franz Ferdinand, Archduke of Austria, was assassinated.

## 140 million people died in wars in the 20th century

In this section, you have to know how Christians and believers from another religious tradition view violence, weapons of mass destruction and pacifism, so make sure you know what's what.

# Peace and Conflict

Some wars are seen as necessary and 'just'. Others are sometimes seen as being fought for God.

## Many People Think There Can Be 'Just Wars'

1) Although most people see peace as being ideal, many do recognise that sometimes a war will have to be fought. Just War theory is a philosophical theory that explains the conditions that must be met for a war to be classed as necessary:

- There must be a good reason for the war, e.g. self-defence or to help innocent people under threat.
- All other options have been attempted to avoid war.
- It must be started by a proper authority — such as an elected government or president.
- A war must have a reasonable chance of success.
  Fighting an unwinnable war is considered a waste of lives.
- Any harm caused by fighting the war mustn't be as bad as the harm it's trying to prevent.

There are also conditions for fighting a war justly. These are:

- Discrimination: war should discriminate between combatants and civilians — it's not seen as 'just' to deliberately target civilians.
- Proportionality: the military advantage gained by an attack must outweigh any harm to civilians.

2) Religious and non-religious people might turn to situation ethics to decide if a war is 'just'. They'd look at all the factors surrounding the case, and choose what they think would most likely bring about peace.

## People Who Fight in Holy Wars Believe They're Supported by God

1) A holy war is one where people believe that God is 'on their side'. Wars are mentioned in both the Old Testament and the Tenakh, and in the Qur'an.

2) In the past, holy wars have been fought over territory or to convert people, e.g. the crusades in the 11th to 13th centuries. However, holy wars can be declared for different reasons, such as to protect a religion.

3) Religion has been a factor in modern wars too (though often not the only factor). Although the civil war in Syria didn't start over religion, Sunni and Shi'a Muslims have fought on opposite sides. Jews and Muslims are on opposing sides in the conflict in Palestine.

4) Atheists and humanists, who don't believe in God, have criticised religion for causing conflict and wouldn't support starting a war over religion — but neither would many religious people. Some atheists and humanists also identify as pacifists, and don't agree with conflict being used at all.

## Christians Believe People Should Be Peaceful

1) Many of Jesus's teachings show that peace is the ultimate goal for all human beings.

2) Isaiah 9:6 referred to the Messiah as the "Prince of Peace" (NIV) — Christians believe Jesus was the Messiah and God wanted him to create peace on Earth.

3) For Christians, Jesus's command to "Love your enemies" (Luke 6:27 NIV) is very important in the way they live their lives. He said that people shouldn't follow the Old Testament teachings about retaliation:

> "You have heard that it was said, 'Eye for eye, and tooth for tooth.' But I tell you... If anyone slaps you on the right cheek, turn to them the other cheek also." Matthew 5:38-39 NIV

This implies that Christians shouldn't meet violence with violence.

4) This is evident in Matthew 26:47-56. Even though Judas had betrayed him, Jesus didn't condone anyone being violent. Jesus said "all who draw the sword will die by the sword" (Matthew 26:52 NIV), suggesting that people who engage in conflict will die because of it.

5) In his Sermon on the Mount, Jesus said "Blessed are the peacemakers" (Matthew 5:9 NIV). He also told his followers "Peace I leave with you; my peace I give you" (John 14:27 NIV).

# Peace and Conflict — Christianity Christianity

## Many Christians Follow **Jesus's Teachings** and **Work for Peace**

1) Some Christians put Jesus's teachings into action and work to put an end to violence in the world.

> Dorothy Day was a Catholic activist who followed Jesus's pacifist teachings. She protested against the Spanish Civil War, WW2, violence and nuclear weapons in the USA (see p.106). She co-founded 'The Catholic Worker', a newspaper which was firmly anti-war and eventually evolved into a pacifist group of campaigners.

> Archbishop Oscar Romero worked for peace during turbulent times in 1970s El Salvador. He raised awareness of the suffering and violence people were being subjected to by the military and the police. He helped those affected by the cruelty, fought for their rights and promoted peace between opposing groups. He was killed for his beliefs in 1980.

2) Some, such as Dorothy Day, believe that Jesus's teachings mean Christians should be pacifists. The Society of Friends (Quakers) is opposed to war under all circumstances.

3) Because of their belief in peace, Christians tend to use passive resistance against injustice — campaigning without violence.

> Dr Martin Luther King was a Baptist minister who dedicated his life to trying to change the way black people were treated in the USA. He organised peaceful marches, rallies and boycotts, and in 1965 blacks were given equal voting rights with whites.

> Thomas Merton was a Catholic monk and a famous pacifist. In the 1960s, his writings influenced many in the civil rights movement for racial equality and he was against the violence of the Vietnam War.

4) Most Christians wouldn't support violent protests, but some might think it's sometimes justified — when Jesus saw that some people were exploiting the temple, he "overturned the tables of the money changers and the benches of those selling doves" (Matthew 21:12 NIV) in protest at what they were doing.

## Some Christians Recognise **Just Wars**

1) Although war goes against the teachings of Jesus, most Christian denominations accept that there can be such a thing as a 'just war'. They would agree with the conditions of the Just War theory (see p.102). It doesn't mean that the war is right — it's just not the worst option.

2) Some interpret this verse as meaning the government has the right to use violence to ensure peace:

> "...if you do wrong, be afraid, for rulers do not bear the sword for no reason. They are God's servants, agents of wrath to bring punishment on the wrongdoer." Romans 13:4 NIV

Some believe that sometimes war is the only way to find peace, e.g. against an evil regime. Christians are taught to "Love your neighbour" (Mark 12:31 NIV) — this could involve defending people in war.

3) The Catechism of the Catholic Church (2265) says that "Legitimate defence can be not only a right but a grave duty for one who is responsible for the lives of others". However, due to the advanced weaponry used in modern-day wars (see p.106) and the horrendous impact that war has had in Syria, the Catholic Church is reconsidering its stance on just war.

4) Christians are strongly against the indiscriminate killing involved in terrorism.

## Holy Wars are Now **Rejected** by Nearly All Christians

1) In the 11th, 12th and 13th centuries, Christians went on crusades to 'free' the Christian holy places in Palestine. The wars caused a lot of devastation.

2) In the past, holy wars were fought to convert other people to Christianity. Jesus told his disciples: "Do not suppose that I have come to bring peace to the earth. I did not come to bring peace, but a sword" (Matthew 10:34 NIV). Many think Jesus wasn't actually talking about violence here — he meant that spreading the Christian message would cause divisions between believers and non-believers.

3) The vast majority of Christians don't believe in the idea of a holy war any more. Although it's for different reasons, their stance on holy war would be the same as an atheist's (see p.102).

# Peace and Conflict — Islam

## Islam Teaches People to be Peaceful

1) Islam promotes living a peaceful existence — the Qur'an teaches that people should be kind to others, even if they don't treat them well. Muslims believe Allah sees everything and will judge people.

> "And the servants of the Most Merciful are those who walk upon the earth easily, and when the ignorant address them [harshly], they say [words of] peace." Qur'an 25:63

> "If you should raise your hand against me to kill me - I shall not raise my hand against you to kill you. Indeed, I fear Allah, Lord of the worlds." Qur'an 5:28

2) Muslims believe they should play their part to bring about peace. They can do this through prayer, campaigns or by working with people from other religions to create peace in the community.

3) The majority of Muslims disagree with pacifism, as war is sometimes justified in the Qur'an: "Fight in the way of Allah those who fight you but do not transgress. Indeed. Allah does not like transgressors" (Qur'an 2:190). It means they can fight in self-defence, but should only do what's absolutely necessary.

4) Some are against all war and violence as they believe peaceful action is always best, and is key to Islam.

5) The Arab Spring in 2011 saw many Muslims in countries such as Egypt demanding more political power for ordinary people. Many demonstrations were carried out peacefully, with a focus on passive resistance. Islam teaches people to protest against injustice, but not in violent ways.

## In Islam, a Just War is Known as Military Jihad

1) Jihad means 'striving' or 'struggle', and the concept is often misunderstood. There are two types of jihad — greater and lesser jihad (see p.34). Lesser jihad is the 'struggle' to improve the world, and war is an example of it, but it must be fought only as a last resort. The Qur'an teaches that people can fight: "Allah will punish them by your hands and will disgrace them and give you victory over them..." (Qur'an 9:14).

2) The part of jihad involving military action is known as Harb al-Maqadis (holy war). It's a war considered to be justified by God to protect Muslims and their religion. Some believe the Qur'an says that war is an acceptable option to defend Islam: "Those who believe fight in the cause of Allah" (Qur'an 4:76).

3) Sunni and Shi'a Muslims have similar views on jihad nowadays. Both consider it a key part of their religion as it's covered in the Qur'an — in Shi'a Islam it's also formally recorded as one of the Ten Obligatory Acts (see p.31). In the past, Twelver Shi'a Muslims believed that jihad could only be declared when the last Imam came out of hiding (see p.23), but jihad for defensive purposes was still allowed.

4) Military jihad has very strict rules — these are the conditions in Islam for a just war. There are many similarities with Just War theory:

- It is justified to bring about freedom from tyranny, restore peace, combat oppression, or right injustice.
- Jihad must be in the name of Allah, and according to his will. It must be declared by a religious leader.
- If an Islamic country has been assaulted, then war is justified.
- In the past, jihad was used to spread Islam and gain more land. However, now many Muslims believe jihad must not be used to colonise, suppress or impose Islam on non-believers.
- The hadith Muwatta Malik 21:10 also sets out some conditions for battle: "Do not kill women or children or an aged, infirm person. Do not cut down fruit-bearing trees. Do not destroy an inhabited place".
- If the opposition wants to end the war, then Muslims must accept it: "And if they incline to peace, then incline to it [also]..." (Qur'an 8:61).

5) Some believe that if they do fight for Allah, they'll be rewarded in the afterlife "And he who fights in the cause of Allah and is killed or achieves victory — We will bestow upon him a great reward" (Qur'an 4:74).

6) Some Muslims believe that just wars can no longer exist because of, e.g., the use of WMDs (see p.107).

7) The term 'jihad' is sometimes used by Islamic terrorists to justify their acts of terror. However, nearly all Muslims are strongly against this — they don't consider the terrorists to be real Muslims.

---

### Learn all the conditions for a just war in Islam
Close the book and see how many Muslim beliefs about conflict you can remember.

# Peace and Conflict — Judaism

## Judaism Teaches that **Peace** is **Very Important**

1) The universal greeting among Jews is 'shalom' (peace). Jews don't support war unless it's deemed essential — the Torah teaches that peace should be the first approach, and war shouldn't be started without good reason.

2) Trying to bring about peace is very important in Judaism, and it features in many Jewish prayers. Peace is believed to be given by God.

3) Jews expect that a Messiah will come and bring peace to Earth (see p.43). Micah 4:3 prophesies that when this happens, weapons will be unnecessary and will be turned into ploughshares (the blade of a plough): "They will beat their swords into ploughshares and their spears into pruning hooks" (NIV). Isaiah 2:4 demonstrates how Jews hope that war will end: "Nation will not take up sword against nation, nor will they train for war any more" (NIV).

4) Jews are against terrorism, and hope God will defend the weak from terrorists: "defending the fatherless and the oppressed, so that mere earthly mortals will never again strike terror" (Psalm 10:18 NIV).

5) Most Jews aren't pacifists, but non-violence is seen as a good choice if it's the only way to survive, or if using violence would be pointless. This is why Jews generally don't respond violently to anti-Semitism. Only non-violent protest against injustice would be encouraged.

> Emanuel Ringelblum provided food and tried to improve conditions in the ghettos of Warsaw (under German control at the start of WWII). He collected accounts of the atrocities that happened and hid them underground — some information eventually reached other countries in Europe. He defied the Germans without resorting to violence.

## **Violence** is Sometimes **Allowed**

1) Pikuach nefesh (the duty to save life) means Jews must try to save someone who's in danger of being murdered — even if they must kill the murderer. However, they should use the minimal necessary force.

2) According to the Talmud and the Torah, a person can kill someone else in self-defence if their own life is under threat: "Whoever sheds human blood, by humans shall their blood be shed" (Genesis 9:6 NIV).

3) These ideas can apply to war, and many Jews believe that sometimes war is needed to bring about peace.

## There are Two Types of **War** — **Obligatory** and **Optional**

1) War is split into two types — milchemet mitzvah (obligatory war) and milchemet reshut (optional war).

2) Milchemet mitzvah are thought to be commanded by God, so could be thought of as holy war. In the Old Testament, God supported the Israelites in war — King David praised God for his help: "The Lord... shot his arrows and scattered the enemy" (2 Samuel 22:14-15 NIV). Milchemet mitzvah might be:

> - a war fought in self-defence, or a pre-emptive strike in order to avoid being attacked.
> - a war to help neighbouring countries — so that your own country is not invaded.

These conditions are similar to Just War theory.

3) In recent times, wars have been fought by the state of Israel. Many Jews see these as milchemet mitzvah. Some see them as defending the Promised Land that was given to Abraham by God.

4) Milchemet reshut refers to wars described in the Tenakh to expand Israel's territory. Maimonides said they could only be fought while the Temple existed — many think they can't be fought today.

5) There were conditions on milchemet reshut, e.g. in Deuteronomy 20. One condition was peace must be offered first: "When you march up to attack a city, make its people an offer of peace" (Deuteronomy 20:10 NIV). It includes rules about the treatment of women and children, and cutting down trees too.

6) Although some of these aren't in line with Just War theory, they've been developed into modern ideas about just war, such as protecting non-combatants and not causing unnecessary destruction.

## Make sure you know the difference between mitzvah and reshut

For 12-mark questions, both religious and non-religious opinions will get you closer to top marks.

## General Weapons of Mass Destruction

Weapons of mass destruction can be quite a controversial topic to religious believers and non-believers alike. This page covers some general arguments for and against them.

## Weapons of Mass Destruction Cause a Huge Amount of Damage

1) Some wars have used weapons of mass destruction (WMDs). These are weapons that can destroy large areas of land and/or lots of people all at once, e.g. chemical, biological and nuclear weapons. They're indiscriminate — they harm soldiers and civilians alike.

2) Chemical and biological weapons are banned by international law — using them is considered a war crime. There are many arguments for and against possessing nuclear weapons — some key points are given below.

### Arguments For Weapons of Mass Destruction

- Nuclear weapons serve as a deterrent to ensure peace — a country might not attack another if that country has nuclear weapons. Many countries give this as the reason for keeping nuclear weapons. In the 1900s, several conflicts were settled or sidestepped because nuclear weapons posed too big a risk.

- Some have a utilitarian perspective — the best course of action is the one that brings about the best balance of positive and negative results. The USA bombed Hiroshima and Nagasaki in Japan in WW2 as they thought that using nuclear weapons would save the most lives overall, and end the war faster.

- Nuclear weapons could be used by a country in order to defend itself if under attack.

### Arguments Against Weapons of Mass Destruction

- Many religious and non-religious people oppose nuclear weapons because of the huge loss of life, long-term health issues and environmental damage they can cause.

- Nuclear weapons are costly. Many people argue that funds could be better spent, e.g. on healthcare.

- Many religions believe in the sanctity of life — life was given to humans by God and should be respected. Widespread suffering caused by nuclear weapons completely goes against this.

- Believers who agree with Just War theory might argue that the indiscriminate nature of nuclear weapons (they would kill innocent people) could never be classed as just.

- Earth is God's creation — using nuclear weapons would destroy what God trusted humans to take care of.

## Make sure you know arguments for and against WMDs

Most of the arguments on this page aren't specific to any particular religion — they're general points that could be made by any believers or non-believers. Christian, Muslim and Jewish viewpoints are covered on the next page. It's important to know all opinions on this topic, not just religious views.

# Weapons of Mass Destruction All religions

Make sure you know what <u>Christians</u> and <u>another religious tradition</u> think about weapons of mass destruction — you'll need to know <u>both sides</u> of the argument for each religion.

## Many Religious Believers are **Against WMDs**

### Christian views

- Some Christians use <u>Jesus's teachings</u> about <u>peace</u> to argue against nuclear weapons. <u>All</u> Christian denominations are <u>against</u> using them.
- However, some think nuclear weapons help to <u>keep the peace</u> as countries are afraid of starting a nuclear war.

### Muslim views

- Many Muslims are against WMDs as they don't follow the conditions of <u>lesser jihad</u> (see p.104) — <u>innocent people</u> would get hurt or killed.
- <u>Pakistan</u> has nuclear weapons, but many other Muslim countries have come out <u>against</u> possessing WMDs.

"...whoever kills a soul... it is as if he had slain mankind entirely." Qur'an 5:32

### Jewish views

- The Talmud says that if something will inflict harm on over a <u>sixth</u> of the population, then it's <u>not allowed</u>.
- Many Jews believe that although actually using WMDs <u>can't</u> be <u>justified</u> because of the scale of damage they cause, a country could <u>say</u> that they'll use nuclear weapons, <u>without</u> ever intending to <u>use</u> them, to <u>stop</u> something <u>bad</u> happening. They might support this idea with the <u>sanctity of life</u> argument. Israel has <u>never</u> revealed <u>whether</u> it has nuclear weapons.

Both <u>Christians</u> and <u>Jews</u> might turn to Deuteronomy 20. It suggests that <u>women</u> and <u>children</u> should be <u>spared</u>, and <u>unnecessary damage</u> shouldn't be caused: "When you lay siege to a city for a long time... do not destroy its trees by putting an axe to them, because you can eat their fruit" (Deuteronomy 20:19 NIV). The <u>total destruction</u> that WMDs would cause goes <u>against</u> this.

## **Atheists** and **Humanists** have a Variety of Views

1) Some <u>atheists</u> are in favour of WMDs to <u>deter</u> an opponent and to potentially <u>use</u> — they don't believe their <u>actions</u> will be <u>judged</u>.
2) Other atheists are strongly <u>anti-WMDs</u> as they believe people only live <u>one life</u> on Earth.
3) <u>Humanists</u> have <u>opposed</u> the use of WMDs due to the <u>huge number</u> of people that would <u>suffer</u>.

## Learn the quotations from the religious texts

The quotation from Deuteronomy on this page is really helpful, as it can be used to support both Christian and Jewish arguments against WMDs. The Qu'ran quotation is a useful one as well, as it can be applied to lots of different situations. Learning some key quotations will help you get that extra mark in 5-mark questions.

**All religions** | # Peacemaking

Finding peace and resolving conflicts is important to Christians, Jews and Muslims.

## Justice, Forgiveness and Reconciliation are Key to Peacemaking

1) Justice is the idea of each person getting what they deserve, and maintaining what's right. Believers think that God is just — he treats and judges people fairly as he created everyone equally. Justice leads to a fairer society — if people feel they're treated equally, there's more chance of peace.

2) Forgiveness is when a person stops feeling hurt by something another person has done to them. Another of God's characteristics is that he is merciful — he forgives people for the things they've done wrong. As God is merciful towards them, believers feel that they should forgive other people, and that forgiveness is the only way true peace can be achieved.

3) Reconciliation is bringing people together that previously were in conflict to make peace.

## Christians Believe That God is Fair and Forgiving

1) Christians believe that justice is very important, since people are equal in the eyes of God. Christians have a duty to look after other people, and try to guide them to do what's right and repent of their sins.

2) They believe they should follow God's example and be just to others: "...what does the Lord require of you? To act justly and to love mercy and to walk humbly with your God" (Micah 6:8 NIV). The parable of the sheep and goats shows God treats people well if they've done the same to others.

3) Forgiveness is important to Christians — read p.117 to learn more about it. They believe they should seek God's forgiveness and forgive people who've hurt them.

> "Blessed are the merciful, for they will be shown mercy." Matthew 5:7 NIV

4) If they repent, and put their faith in God, God forgives people and they are reconciled with him. Christians believe the same sort of reconciliation is needed between people to create peace.

## Muslims Try to Forgive and Reconcile as Muhammad Did

1) Muslims believe strongly in justice and that they should treat all people fairly and equally. They consider maintaining justice to be part of their role as 'khalifah' — vice-regents of Allah's creation.

2) Islam teaches that Allah and the Prophet Muhammad are forgiving — have a read of p.117.

3) Muslims are encouraged to work to restore peace. They believe it's important to reconcile fractured relationships — this is something that the Prophet Muhammad did.

> "And not equal are the good deed and the bad. Repel [evil] by that [deed] which is better; and thereupon the one whom between you and him is enmity [will become] as though he was a devoted friend." Qur'an 41:34

## Jews Must Work for Justice and Ask for Forgiveness

1) Justice is a major part of Judaism — Jews believe in fairness. Pirkei Avot 1:18 (part of the Talmud) says that "By three things is the world sustained: law, truth and peace."

2) Many Jews believe that true peace can only happen when everyone is treated fairly and any people in conflict are reconciled.

> "Learn to do right; seek justice. Defend the oppressed." Isaiah 1:17 NIV

3) Seeking forgiveness from God and people you've wronged is very important in Judaism. In conflict situations, asking for forgiveness and forgiving others is an important step to reconciliation. Turn to p.117 to find out more about forgiveness in Judaism.

---

## Learn all the different beliefs on these topics

Draw a grid on a piece of paper. Down one side, write 'Christianity', 'Islam' and 'Judaism'. Along the top, write 'Justice', 'Forgiveness' and 'Reconciliation'. Fill it in with what you've learned.

# Peacemaking All religions

Many religious organisations work towards peace and help people in countries devastated by war.

## Religious Believers Can Work for Peace Directly and Indirectly

1) Many religious believers feel they must act to create peace — see p.103-105 for some examples. Some might be directly involved in peacemaking by working for organisations which offer relief to war-torn areas.

2) Some religious charities campaign for help for groups in conflict to rebuild their relationship. For example, Christian Aid has urged governments to find a compromise in the Israel/Palestine conflict.

3) Religious people can also help to create peace indirectly, e.g. by donating money to charitable causes and by holding protests and demonstrations against conflicts. Some may work to ensure that people have equal human rights, which could help to avoid conflict.

## Christian Charities Work for Peace and Help Victims of War

In the Sermon on the Mount, Jesus says "Blessed are the peacemakers, for they will be called children of God" (Matthew 5:9 NIV). Many feel that it's important to help people caught up in conflict zones and to try to bring peace to the area.

Tearfund® helps people who are refugees from war-torn areas. They help people in the short term by giving them some food and somewhere to stay. However, they also help people to get back on their feet permanently by teaching them valuable skills they can use to support themselves.

Pax Christi is a Catholic organisation that works for peaceful conflict resolution. Read more about it on p.17.

## Muslims Can Give Money to Support Peacemaking

1) Muslims believe it's important to try to create a peaceful world. They believe that this is part of their role as khalifah.

2) Individuals can help to make the world more equal through zakah — 2.5% of their yearly savings should be given to the needy, no matter how rich or poor they are. Zakah could be donated to a number of different charities which are involved in peacemaking and supporting victims of war.

- The Muslim Peace Fellowship is a group of Muslims who want to promote peace, justice and non-violence.
- It strives to do good through Islam — the group promotes peace through faith, and works to bring about changes that make society fair and compassionate to everyone. They do this by raising awareness through events, prayer and working with other faiths.

- Islamic Relief UK is a group inspired by their faith to try to help as many people as possible.
- They help people affected by war — in Syria they've given people essentials such as food and healthcare. They also help people in neighbouring countries who've fled their homes because of the conflict.

## Many Jews Work for Peace in Israel

1) Jews believe that peace is something that God gives the world. Many Jews protest for peace and try to create a fairer world, since they believe that peace is only really possible when everyone is treated justly.

2) Charity through financial aid is called tzedakah. Everyone is expected to contribute 10% of their wealth — this money can help people affected by war and help to create equality to avoid war.

The Jewish Peace Fellowship is a pacifist organisation, founded to help conscientious objectors in WWII. The organisation believes that military action never solves conflicts, and that active non-violence (e.g. negotiations, promoting social justice) is the only way to settle disputes. They're helping to resolve the conflict in Israel and reconcile the people there.

Natal (Israel Trauma Center for Victims of Terror and War) helps people in Israel who've been affected by the conflict there. It aims to care for and treat people suffering from health problems related to war, e.g. post traumatic stress disorder.

# Worked Exam Questions

Time to check your exam skills with some questions — the ones on this page have been done for you, then there are some for you to have a go at for yourself.

**1** Which of the following is **not** a religious group which works towards peacemaking?
Put a tick (✓) in the correct box.

| | | |
|---|---|---|
| **A** | Muslim Peace Fellowship | ☐ |
| **B** | Tearfund® | ☐ |
| **C** | Campaign for Nuclear Disarmament | ✓ |
| **D** | Jewish Peace Fellowship | ☐ |

*[1 mark]*

**2** Explain two contrasting beliefs in British society today about the possession of nuclear weapons. You must refer to the main religious tradition in the UK and at least one other religious viewpoint.

Some Christians and Jews believe that the possession of nuclear weapons is justified in order to preserve peace. The principle of mutually assured destruction means that just having nuclear weapons can be enough to stop countries starting a war.

However, most Islamic countries do not agree with possessing nuclear weapons because of their destructive and indiscriminate nature. Where military defence is necessary, as governed under the rules of the lesser jihad, it is preferable to possess conventional military weapons which can be directed more specifically.

*[4 marks]*

**3** Explain two religious beliefs about reconciliation.
Your answer should refer to specific religious teachings or sacred texts.

In Islam, working towards reconciliation between groups in conflict is encouraged.

Muhammad taught that people should try to resolve conflicts between groups of Muslims.

Reconciliation is a central theme of the Jewish festival of Yom Kippur. Jews ask to be reconciled with God and should seek forgiveness from those they have hurt in their lives: "...for with the Lord is unfailing love and with him is full redemption" (Psalm 130:7 NIV).

*[5 marks]*

# Exam Questions

**4** Which of the following describes no longer feeling angry because of something another person has done?  Put a tick (✓) in the correct box.

A    Repentance    ☐

B    Pacifism    ☐

C    Retaliation    ☐

D    Forgiveness    ☐

*[1 mark]*

**5** Which of the following is a term used to describe weapons which cause harm to civilians and soldiers alike?  Put a tick (✓) in the correct box.

A    Non-lethal    ☐

B    Reconciliation    ☐

C    Retribution    ☐

D    Indiscriminate    ☐

*[1 mark]*

**6** Give two criteria for a just war.

1) ................................................................................................................................

................................................................................................................................

2) ................................................................................................................................

................................................................................................................................

*[2 marks]*

**7** 'Religious people should focus on their own relationship with God before resolving conflicts between others.'

Evaluate this statement.  Your answer should include the following:
• religious arguments that support the statement
• religious arguments that disagree with the statement
• a conclusion.
You can also include non-religious points of view in your answer.

(SPaG MARKS)

*Write your answer on a separate sheet of paper.*

*[12 marks]*

# Revision Summary

That's the end of Religion, Peace and Conflict — time to see how much you can remember.

- Try these questions and <u>tick off each one</u> when you <u>get it right</u>.
- When you've done <u>all the questions</u> for a topic and are <u>completely happy</u> with it, tick off the topic.

If a question asks about a religion you <u>haven't</u> studied, just <u>skip it</u> and move on to the next question.

## <u>Peace and Conflict (p.101-105)</u> ☑

1) What is peace?
2) Explain what pacifism is.
3) Give a brief description of: a) terrorism,   b) war.
4) Write down three possible causes of wars.
5) What are the conditions of Just War theory?
6) What is a holy war?
7) Explain Christian teachings on peace.
8) Name one Christian who used passive resistance to campaign against injustice.
9) Describe Muslim views on pacifism.
10) What is the Muslim concept of lesser jihad?
11) What is the Muslim name for a holy war?
12) What does the Jewish greeting 'shalom' mean?
13) Explain the difference between the Jewish ideas of milchemet mitzvah and milchemet reshut.

## <u>Weapons of Mass Destruction (p.106-107)</u> ☑

14) Explain what weapons of mass destruction are.
15) Give two arguments in favour of weapons of mass destruction.
16) Give two arguments against weapons of mass destruction.
17) Explain the views of any two religions on weapons of mass destruction.
18) Why do Humanists oppose weapons of mass destruction?

## <u>Peacemaking (p.108-109)</u> ☑

19) Give a brief definition of justice, forgiveness and reconciliation.
20) Explain the views of any two religions on:  a) forgiveness,
                                                 b) justice,
                                                 c) reconciliation.
21) Give one way religious believers can indirectly help to create peace.
22) Describe the work of the Christian charity Tearfund®.
23) What is the Muslim concept of zakah?
24) Name one Muslim charitable organisation that works towards peace.
25) What is the Jewish practice of tzedakah?
26) Describe the work of the Jewish organisation Natal.

# Religion and the Law

Religious beliefs about <u>good</u> and <u>evil</u> influence how people act.

## People Should **Do Good** and **Avoid Evil**

Christianity, Islam and Judaism all teach people to live <u>good lives</u>. This includes <u>following</u> religious <u>teachings</u>, e.g. by helping other people. The good things that people do will <u>please God/Allah</u>. People should <u>avoid</u> sin and evil, as their actions will be <u>judged</u> when they die.

### Christians Believe **Everyone** is Capable of Evil

- In <u>Christianity</u>, the <u>sheep</u> and <u>goats</u> parable (Matthew 25:31-46) says that everyone will be <u>judged</u> and <u>separated</u> into the <u>good</u> (the sheep) and the <u>bad</u> (the goats).

- Jesus said that <u>helping</u> another person is like helping <u>him</u>. If you <u>ignore</u> someone in need of help, it's like <u>ignoring him</u>: "...whatever you did not do for one of the least of these, you did not do for me" (Matthew 25:45 NIV).

- Many Christians believe that <u>evil</u> is caused by humans <u>misusing</u> their <u>free will</u> — they believe that the <u>original sin</u> people are born with makes them <u>capable</u> of sin (see p.4). Some say <u>Satan</u> tempts people to sin.

### Muslims Believe Allah **Judges** Their Deeds

- <u>Islam</u> teaches that Allah is <u>merciful</u> and those who have done <u>good things</u> will be <u>rewarded</u>, but he will come down <u>harshly</u> on people who do <u>bad things</u>.

> "He admits whom He wills into His mercy; but the wrongdoers - He has prepared for them a painful punishment." Qur'an 76:31

- If people <u>intend</u> to do something <u>good</u>, that will <u>help</u> them on the <u>Day of Judgement</u>, but if they intend to do something <u>bad</u>, it <u>won't</u> count against them (see p.28).

- Many Muslims believe that the <u>devil</u>, <u>Iblis</u>, tries to make humans turn to <u>evil</u>.

### Jews Believe God Will **Forgive** Sinners

- The <u>Jewish</u> sacred texts explain how to <u>behave</u> in a <u>good</u> way.
- Jews believe that <u>evil</u> is the result of humans <u>taking advantage</u> of the <u>free will</u> they were allowed by God.
- But God will <u>forgive</u> people if they commit <u>sin</u>: "I will have mercy on whom I will have mercy, and I will have compassion on whom I will have compassion" (Exodus 33:19 NIV).

## Learn the quotations about good and evil

Judgement and free will are key themes when thinking about good and evil. It's all linked to the idea of the afterlife as well — where people are judged on their thoughts and actions during their life. Forgiveness is an important idea here as well — it's covered in more detail on p.117.

# Religion and the Law

Most religions teach people to <u>follow</u> the <u>law</u>, but some people think that religious law should take <u>priority</u>.

## Law is **Essential** to Most Societies

1) The <u>laws of the state</u> define what's <u>right</u> and <u>wrong</u>, though this can <u>differ</u> from <u>religious ideas</u>.

2) Most nations believe that the <u>rule of law</u> is the best way of <u>protecting</u> people in society. Without law there's the risk of <u>chaos</u>. With it, people know what they <u>can</u> and <u>cannot</u> do.

3) In the UK, <u>laws</u> are rules made by Parliament and <u>enforced</u> by the courts.

4) Christianity, Islam and Judaism all teach that <u>God</u> has commanded people to follow law. But some religious believers think that <u>religious law</u> is more important than the <u>laws of the land</u>.

5) Where religious law and state law <u>disagree</u> some believers think it's better to commit a <u>crime</u> if it means they avoid committing a <u>sin</u> (see p.115-116).

## Christians Believe **Sins** and **Crimes** are **Different**

For <u>Christians</u>, there's a difference between a <u>sin</u> and a <u>crime</u>:

- A <u>sin</u> is when <u>religious</u> law is broken, i.e. when God's teaching is disobeyed.

- A <u>crime</u> is when the <u>state</u> laws are broken.

They have a <u>duty</u> to look after <u>other people</u>, and try to <u>guide</u> them to do what's right and <u>repent</u> of their sins.

## **Muslims'** Religious Law is called **Shari'ah Law**

- <u>Muslims</u> have a clear and detailed religious law (<u>shari'ah</u>), and this is often the <u>basis</u> for <u>state law</u> in Islamic countries. <u>Saudi Arabia</u>, for example, is run according to this religious law.

- Shari'ah <u>councils</u> in <u>Britain</u> make rulings according to shari'ah law, but UK law takes <u>precedence</u>.

## **Jews** Must Follow the **Law** and the **Mitzvot**

- <u>Judaism</u> teaches that Jews should <u>obey</u> the <u>laws</u> of the <u>land</u> that they live in, as well as following the <u>613 mitzvot</u> (religious commandments) in the <u>Torah</u> (see p.42).

- <u>Rabbinical courts</u> (<u>Bet Din</u>) exist in many countries to sort out Jewish disputes. There are some in the UK, but <u>UK law</u> has <u>greater authority</u>.

- The Torah is filled with details of <u>laws</u>, <u>rewards</u> and <u>punishments</u>. But for many modern Jews the punishments listed in the Torah are considered <u>too extreme</u> (see p.118).

## Christians, Muslims and Jews All Believe in **Justice**

<u>Justice</u> is the idea of each person getting what they <u>deserve</u> (including <u>punishing</u> the <u>guilty</u>), and maintaining what's <u>right</u> (see p.108). It's <u>important</u> to all three religions.

**REVISION TASK**

## Learn about the law — and that's an order

Write a short summary about what each religion teaches about the law.

# Crime

Crime happens on a <u>daily</u> basis for many reasons. Many <u>religious organisations</u> work to put an <u>end</u> to it.

## Many Crimes **Break Religious Laws** and **Teachings**

1) There are many <u>different types</u> of crime, including <u>murder</u>, <u>theft</u> and <u>hate crimes</u>.

2) Christianity, Islam and Judaism are against these as they break <u>religious moral laws</u>.

3) <u>Christians</u> and <u>Jews</u> are strongly against <u>murder</u> and <u>theft</u> as they <u>break</u> two of the <u>Ten Commandments</u>. In <u>Islam</u>, the Qur'an also <u>condemns</u> murder and theft.

4) Murder, often seen as the <u>worst</u> crime, goes against the idea of <u>sanctity of life</u> (the belief that life is <u>sacred</u>) held by <u>all</u> three religions.

5) <u>Theft</u> and <u>hate crimes</u> disregard religious teachings that people should be treated <u>equally</u>, as the offender shows <u>no concern</u> for the victim.

A hate crime is any type of crime committed against someone because of their ethnicity, religion etc.

## Crime is **Caused** by Lots of **Different Factors**

Most religious believers would agree that if someone does something <u>illegal</u>, they <u>deserve</u> to be <u>punished</u>. But the cause of crime <u>isn't</u> as simple as someone just being <u>bad</u> — there are many different <u>reasons</u> why a person might <u>commit</u> a <u>crime</u>:

1) **POVERTY** — People who are poor might turn to <u>crime</u> out of <u>desperation</u>. They might <u>steal food</u> or <u>money</u>, or earn <u>money</u> illegally, e.g. selling stolen goods.

2) **UPBRINGING** — Some people might become criminals if they've had a <u>troubled</u> <u>childhood</u>, or if they've <u>grown up</u> around crime and it's become <u>normal</u> to them.

3) **MENTAL ILLNESS** — This can lead people to commit crimes because, e.g., they may not fully <u>understand</u> the <u>difference</u> between what's <u>legal</u> and <u>illegal</u>. Others may be easily <u>persuaded</u> into committing a crime.

4) **ADDICTION** — Being dependent on something such as <u>drugs</u> or <u>alcohol</u> can lead to people doing illegal things to <u>fund</u> their <u>addiction</u>.

5) **GREED** — Someone might <u>steal</u> or <u>earn</u> money <u>illegally</u> to get something they <u>want</u> but can't afford.

6) **HATE** — A person might do something illegal because someone else has <u>treated</u> them <u>badly</u>, or because they're driven by <u>prejudice</u>, e.g. racism.

7) **OPPOSITION TO UNJUST LAW** — A law might be <u>broken</u> as a <u>protest</u> if it's seen as unfair. In the 1950s and 60s many people, such as <u>Rosa Parks</u>, broke laws that treated black people <u>unfairly</u> in the <u>USA</u>.

> Many feel that the <u>reason</u> behind the crime should be taken into <u>consideration</u>, and many religious people would want to <u>help</u> the <u>individual</u> as well as tackle the <u>bigger issues</u> that cause crime. However, certain causes would be more likely to get <u>sympathy</u> than others, e.g. <u>poverty</u> would be seen as more <u>reasonable</u> than <u>greed</u>. Many think that breaking a law that is <u>unfair</u> or that goes <u>against</u> religious law is <u>acceptable</u>.

## **Christians** Work to **Prevent** Crimes

1) Christians are <u>strongly against</u> crime — they're told to <u>care</u> for others: "Love your neighbour as yourself" (Mark 12:31 NIV). Committing a crime such as <u>theft</u> or a <u>hate crime</u> doesn't treat the victim as an <u>equal</u>. Murder is seen as <u>destroying</u> something <u>created</u> by God.

2) Christians have <u>defied laws</u> to fight for what's <u>right</u>, e.g. Martin Luther King (see p.103). In this case, Christians may <u>support</u> breaking laws: "We must obey God rather than human beings!" (Acts 5:29 NIV).

3) Some people might be driven to crime by <u>poverty</u>. Christians may <u>take actions</u> to reduce poverty to try to prevent this — for example, they might donate to <u>charity</u> or help out in <u>food banks</u>.

4) <u>Christian groups</u> also play their part to try to <u>prevent</u> crime. <u>Street Pastors</u>, who help people out at night (see p.17), have helped to <u>lower</u> crime rates and <u>prevent violence</u>.

> The <u>Prison Fellowship</u> is a Christian organisation in England and Wales that helps prisoners by <u>praying</u> for them and through <u>group activities</u> and maintaining <u>contact</u> with their <u>families</u>. They try to make prisoners see how they have <u>affected victims</u> of their crimes and <u>stop</u> them from <u>committing crime</u> again when they leave prison, e.g. through <u>restorative justice</u> (see p.117).

**Islam & Judaism**

# Crime

Elements of both Islam and Judaism help to <u>prevent</u> crime.

## Muslims Believe Crime Interrupts the Relationship with Allah

1) Muslims believe that on <u>Yawn ad-Din</u> (the Day of Judgement — see p.28), those who've committed crimes might <u>not</u> be sent to <u>jannah</u>.

> "Allah orders justice and good conduct and giving to relatives and forbids immorality and bad conduct and oppression." Qur'an 16:90

2) Many Muslims also believe that a life of crime <u>doesn't</u> allow believers to <u>focus</u> on what really <u>matters</u> — their <u>faith</u> and connection with <u>Allah</u>.

3) <u>Murder</u> is seen as one of the <u>worst</u> crimes: "whoever kills a soul... it is as if he had slain mankind entirely" (Qur'an 5:32). <u>Theft</u> and <u>hate crimes</u> defy Islamic <u>teachings</u> about people being <u>equal</u>.

4) Muslims hope that <u>key elements</u> of their religion help to <u>reduce</u> the likelihood of <u>crime</u>. For example, <u>compulsory</u> charitable donations (<u>zakah</u> — see p.33) help to tackle poverty. Alcohol, drugs and gambling are <u>banned</u>, reducing the chance of <u>addiction</u>. Parents are taught to follow <u>teachings</u> in the Qur'an to give their child the best possible <u>upbringing</u>, which should <u>prevent</u> them from turning to crime. Some <u>mosques</u> offer help for families too.

5) Islam teaches Muslims to <u>speak out</u> against <u>unjust laws</u> that go against Allah's teachings, so many would <u>understand</u> someone breaking an unjust law in <u>protest</u> against it.

6) In <u>shari'ah courts</u>, the <u>circumstances</u> surrounding the crime are looked into <u>thoroughly</u>, so the defendant is punished <u>accordingly</u>.

7) Some Muslims work to try to <u>reduce</u> crime by <u>helping prisoners</u> and <u>ex-offenders</u>:

> The <u>Muslim Chaplains Association</u> offers <u>religious guidance</u> in <u>prisons</u> in the UK. It aims to <u>reform</u> prisoners and <u>stop</u> them from committing crimes after they are <u>released</u>, e.g. by helping them to <u>reintegrate</u> into society again. It also tries to keep ex-offenders <u>connected</u> to <u>chaplaincies</u> in their local <u>community</u> so they continue to receive <u>support</u> after prison.

> <u>Mosaic</u> is a charity that pairs <u>young people</u> approaching the <u>end</u> of their prison sentence with a <u>mentor</u>. As they adjust to life outside of prison, the mentor will <u>help</u> them with things like finding a <u>job</u> and somewhere to <u>live</u> — with the aim that this should <u>prevent</u> them from returning to a life of <u>crime</u>.

## Judaism Forbids Murder and Theft in the Noahide Laws

1) The <u>Noahide Laws</u>, which Jews believe that <u>everyone</u> in the world should follow, state that <u>murder</u> and <u>theft</u> are <u>forbidden</u>. <u>Hate crimes</u> go against Jewish teachings on <u>equality</u>.

> "...the Lord's anger will burn against you, and he will shut the heavens so that it will not rain and the ground will yield no produce, and you will soon perish..." Deuteronomy 11:17 NIV

2) Crime goes against <u>God's teachings</u> — Judaism teaches that people who <u>disobey</u> God will be <u>punished</u> by him.

3) Some <u>aspects</u> of Judaism work to <u>reduce</u> the chances of crime. For example, Jewish <u>financial aid</u> (<u>tzedakah</u>) is donated to charity and helps to combat <u>poverty</u>. Jewish parents are told to <u>guide</u> their <u>children</u> and to make sure they know what's <u>right</u> and <u>wrong</u>.

4) Many Jews would <u>protest</u> against <u>unjust laws</u>, and perhaps <u>break</u> them, as there are <u>examples</u> in the <u>Torah</u> of defying the law for what is right. In Exodus 1:16-17, two <u>midwives</u> were told by the king to <u>kill</u> Hebrew baby boys, but they <u>didn't</u> follow his instructions.

5) Some <u>rabbis</u> work with the <u>Jewish Prison Chaplaincy</u> in order to provide support for Jewish prisoners. The <u>support</u> offenders receive can help them to <u>turn their backs</u> on crime when they leave prison.

## There's lots to learn here, so have another read if you need

Make sure you know different religions' opinions on crime. It's a good idea to learn how religious believers go about tackling the causes of crime, plus their attitudes towards prisoners, and what they do to help them.

# Forgiveness

You need to know views from <u>Christianity</u> and at least one other <u>religious tradition</u> about forgiveness.

## Forgiveness can **Reunite People** and **Prevent Reoffending**

1) Forgiveness means stopping being <u>angry</u> with someone who's done something <u>wrong</u>. It is very important for many religious believers. They believe God is <u>merciful</u> towards people who <u>genuinely</u> seek his <u>mercy</u> and that they should <u>reflect</u> God's forgiving nature in their <u>own behaviour</u>.

2) Many believe it's important to <u>forgive</u> criminals so they can be <u>reconciled</u> with the <u>community</u>. If they leave prison <u>isolated</u> from others, with <u>no job</u> and <u>little prospects</u>, <u>reoffending</u> might seem like the <u>only option</u>. Forgiveness allows <u>both</u> victims and perpetrators to <u>move on</u>. However, most religious people believe that <u>criminals</u> should still be <u>punished</u> for what they've done.

3) Forgiveness can be <u>shown</u> in many ways. <u>Lesser offences</u> no longer stay on people's <u>records</u> <u>permanently</u>, and there are <u>schemes</u> that give ex-offenders <u>skills</u> and a <u>job</u> when they're released.

4) <u>Restorative justice</u> is where an offender might <u>meet</u> people who've <u>suffered</u> because of the crime they committed. Actually meeting the people they've hurt can help offenders to <u>realise</u> the extent of the <u>damage</u> they've done, try to <u>make up for</u> their actions and <u>discourage</u> them from <u>reoffending</u>. It helps the <u>victim</u> to work towards <u>forgiving</u> the offender.

## **Christianity** Teaches that **Forgiveness** Comes from **Love**

1) Jesus taught that <u>God</u> is always ready to <u>forgive</u> and that Christians must <u>accept</u> that forgiveness, and forgive <u>others</u> in turn. The <u>Lord's Prayer</u> includes a verse about forgiveness (Matthew 6:12).

2) Jesus told people to seek <u>reconciliation</u> in any disagreements <u>before</u> offering a <u>gift</u> to God at the temple: "First go and be reconciled to them; then come and offer your gift" (Matthew 5:24 NIV). He also taught people to forgive "not seven times, but seventy-seven times" (Matthew 18:22 NIV).

3) Forgiveness is closely related to <u>repentance</u>. Christians believe that God's forgiveness can only come when they <u>repent</u> of their sins (i.e. say sorry, and turn their backs on them).

## **Islam** Teaches that **Allah** is **Forgiving**

1) Muslims can seek <u>retribution</u> (see p.118) for injuries, but they're encouraged to <u>forgive</u> instead. Whenever the <u>Qur'an</u> describes <u>punishment</u>, it talks about <u>forgiveness</u> too.

2) Muslims believe that they must be <u>merciful</u> so that <u>Allah</u> will do the <u>same</u> to them on <u>Yawm ad-Din</u> (the Day of Judgement).

> "But if you pardon and overlook and forgive - then indeed, Allah is Forgiving and Merciful." Qur'an 64:14

3) They believe that wrongdoing should be forgiven if the offender is <u>sorry</u> and tries to <u>make amends</u>.

4) The <u>Prophet Muhammad</u> was forgiving, as told in the Hadith — Muslims believe in <u>following</u> his <u>example</u>.

5) But some <u>crimes</u> are seen as so <u>awful</u> that forgiveness isn't an option, e.g. <u>shirk</u> (see p.24).

## **Jews** Should Follow **God's Example** and Be **Forgiving**

1) Jews believe that <u>God</u> is <u>forgiving</u> and <u>merciful</u>, so they <u>must</u> forgive other people too: "...for with the Lord is unfailing love and with him is full redemption" (Psalm 130:7 NIV).

2) For the festival of <u>Yom Kippur</u>, Jews ask for <u>forgiveness</u>, both from <u>people</u> they've hurt and from <u>God</u> (see p.52). Jews believe that you can only be forgiven by the <u>one</u> you've <u>hurt</u>, so God can only forgive a sin against God, <u>not</u> another person.

3) Jews should allow criminals to <u>repent</u> for what they've done and <u>seek forgiveness</u>:

> "Let the wicked forsake their ways and the unrighteous their thoughts. Let them turn to the Lord, and he will have mercy on them, and to our God, for he will freely pardon." Isaiah 55:7 NIV

## People can forgive, and so can God or Allah

Find a couple of quotations about forgiveness for each religion, write them down and learn them.

## All religions — Punishment

Punishment can be used to 'get back' at someone for committing a crime, or to prevent crime in the future.

## Punishment can have **Various Aims**

Punishment is needed in society so that people follow the law. Criminals should face the consequences for their actions and victims should get justice. Punishment has many purposes:

### Retribution

Some people think of punishment as a way of taking revenge on a criminal, of making them 'pay' for what they've done. Critics of this way of thinking argue that revenge doesn't put right the wrong — that it's better to look for a more constructive solution.

### Protection

If a criminal is considered dangerous, this is the idea that their punishment should protect the rest of society, e.g. imprisonment. Not many people would disagree with this, but some would argue that you protect society best by reforming offenders.

### Reformation

Punishment should aim to change criminals so they won't reoffend again — the idea being that nobody is inherently bad. Many religious people feel this allows offenders to repent and seek forgiveness from God for their actions. Programmes to reform criminals include counselling and giving them work in the community.

### Deterrence

The idea that if a punishment is sufficiently bad in some way (e.g. expensive, embarrassing, restricting, painful) it will put people off committing the crime — they understand the consequences. Critics argue that people don't stop to think about punishment before they commit a crime, especially if they've taken drugs or alcohol, so deterrence doesn't work.

## There are **Various Christian Views** on the Aims of Punishment

1) Christians think that criminals should be punished for what they've done in a just way. Some think punishment should be "eye for eye" (Leviticus 24:20 NIV), so focus on retribution. Others believe they should "turn... the other cheek" (Matthew 5:39 NIV), and so look more towards reformation.

2) Jesus told people to look at their own behaviour before criticising others. In John 8, a woman who was accused of adultery was saved by Jesus when he said: "Let any one of you who is without sin be the first to throw a stone at her" (John 8:7 NIV). No one did, and it reminds Christians that everyone sins.

3) Being merciful is important in Christianity, and Christians believe reformation is important: "...if someone is caught in a sin, you who live by the Spirit should restore that person gently" (Galatians 6:1 NIV).

4) Christians also value deterrence and protection — these help make communities less dangerous.

## **Islamic** Punishments Held **Publicly Deter** People

1) Many Muslims believe in reformation, and punishment should give criminals the opportunity to see the error of their ways. ⟶

> "Allah wants to make clear to you [the lawful from the unlawful] and guide you to the [good] practices of those before you and to accept your repentance." Qur'an 4:26

2) The Qur'an mentions punishments such as whipping that are carried out publicly — the aim of this is to deter the criminal, but some believe this form of punishment can reform offenders too, and offers retribution. See p.119 for how this is applied today.

3) The Qur'an also says that the punishment should fit the crime: "...an eye for an eye..." (Qur'an 5:45). But Qur'an 2:178 explains that the offender can sometimes compensate the victim financially.

## Many **Jews** Disagree with the **Punishments** in the **Torah**

1) The Torah teaches that the punishment should match the crime: "Anyone who injures their neighbour is to be injured in the same manner: fracture for fracture, eye for eye, tooth for tooth" (Leviticus 24:19-20 NIV). The Torah also explains that "Whoever sheds human blood, by humans shall their blood be shed" (Genesis 9:6 NIV). But many Jews think the punishments set out in the Torah are too harsh.

2) However, Jewish people do believe that punishment is important. They value punishment in terms of deterrence, protection and retribution: "When justice is done, it brings joy to the righteous but terror to evildoers" (Proverbs 21:15 NIV). But the majority of Jews also believe that punishment should give offenders the chance to reform.

# Punishment
**All religions**

Punishments <u>vary</u> according to the crime, and religious believers hold <u>different views</u> on these punishments.

## There are Many Different **Types** of **Punishment**

1) Depending on the <u>severity</u> of the <u>crime</u> committed, criminals can be given <u>various sentences</u>, including <u>prison</u>, <u>community service</u> and (in countries where it's legal) <u>corporal punishment</u>.

2) <u>Corporal punishment</u> is when the criminal is punished through <u>physical pain</u> delivered by e.g. <u>beating</u> or <u>flogging</u> them. It's <u>not</u> used in <u>Europe</u>, but it is used <u>elsewhere</u> in the world.

3) Prisoners have <u>human rights</u> — many argue corporal punishment goes <u>against</u> this and promotes <u>violence</u>.

4) Others might argue that corporal punishment and the <u>suffering</u> it causes would put people off <u>reoffending</u>.

5) Religious people are often in <u>favour</u> of <u>community service</u>. They believe it allows the offender to <u>repay</u> their <u>debt</u> to society yet still lead a <u>normal life</u>, which should help to <u>ensure</u> they don't <u>reoffend</u>.

## **Christians** are **Mostly Against** Corporal Punishment

1) Christians believe that prisoners have the <u>right</u> to be treated <u>fairly</u> — many want <u>better conditions</u> in prison and visit <u>offenders</u> in prison.

> "Speak up and judge fairly; defend the rights of the poor and needy." Proverbs 31:9 NIV

2) But some think that life in <u>prison</u> should be <u>difficult</u> in order to make offenders <u>think twice</u> about <u>crime</u>.

3) The <u>majority</u> of Christians are <u>strongly against</u> corporal punishment — Jesus was against violence, saying "all who draw the sword will die by the sword" (Matthew 26:52 NIV). The Bible says that "Whoever spares the rod hates their children" (Proverbs 13:24 NIV), suggesting that <u>disciplining</u> children through <u>corporal punishment</u> is <u>allowed</u>, but many would <u>disagree</u> as it goes against idea of Christian <u>compassion</u>.

4) However, there are <u>examples</u> in the <u>Bible</u> of corporal punishment being used on criminals (Deuteronomy 25:2), so these might be used to argue that it's <u>acceptable</u> in some situations.

## **Islamic** Laws **Permit** Corporal Punishment

1) The Qur'an teaches that <u>prisoners</u> should be treated <u>fairly</u>.

2) However, some argue that treating prisoners <u>harshly</u> can be <u>more effective</u> in <u>reforming</u> them.

> "And they give food in spite of love for it to the needy, the orphan, and the captive" Qur'an 76:8

3) Under <u>shari'ah law</u>, corporal punishment is <u>permissible</u> for certain crimes, such as drinking <u>alcohol</u> and <u>stealing</u>. The Qur'an says that "[As for] the thief... amputate their hands in recompense for what they committed as a deterrent [punishment] from Allah" (Qur'an 5:38).

4) However, there are <u>rigorous rules</u> about the <u>evidence</u> needed before using corporal punishment, and many Muslim countries <u>don't</u> actually <u>use</u> them. Some Muslims believe corporal punishments are <u>too severe</u>, and don't respect the offender's <u>human rights</u>.

5) Some Muslims are <u>against community service</u> as they believe it's <u>too easy</u> and doesn't stop reoffending.

## Many **Jews** are **Against** Corporal Punishment

1) Judaism teaches that <u>offenders</u> should be treated <u>fairly</u>, and lots of Jews are concerned about the <u>condition</u> of <u>prisons</u> and prisoners' <u>wellbeing</u>.

2) The <u>Torah</u> includes examples of when <u>corporal punishment</u> is appropriate, but <u>many</u> Jews are <u>against</u> it: "If the guilty person deserves to be beaten, the judge shall... have them flogged... with the number of lashes the crime deserves" (Deuteronomy 25:2 NIV).

3) Although the Torah teaches an "eye for eye" (Exodus 21:24 NIV), most Jews understand this as meaning that the severity of the <u>sentence</u> given to the offender should be <u>appropriate</u> for the <u>crime</u> committed.

**EXAM TIP** ## Corporal punishment causes pain
Learn views from Christianity and at least one other religious tradition on corporal punishment.

**All religions**

# The Death Penalty

The death penalty is <u>killing</u> someone as punishment for a crime — it's also called <u>capital punishment</u>.

## The **Death Penalty** Isn't Used Much Nowadays

1) Capital punishment has been <u>abolished</u> in many countries, including most of Europe and South America. Elsewhere, it only tends to be used for <u>very serious</u> crimes, e.g. <u>murder</u>, <u>espionage</u> (spying) and <u>treason</u>.

2) <u>Religious</u> and <u>non-religious</u> people might make some of these <u>arguments</u> for and against the death penalty:

| **For the Death Penalty** | **Against the Death Penalty** |
|---|---|
| • The risk of death might act as a <u>better deterrent</u> to violent criminals than a prison sentence. <br><br> • If you execute a murderer, it's <u>impossible</u> for them to <u>kill again</u>. Imprisoned murderers have been known to <u>order</u> killings from jail, or to <u>reoffend</u> when released on parole. In cases like these, the <u>suffering</u> of the criminal could potentially <u>protect</u> many people. <br><br> • <u>Utilitarianism</u> (or the <u>principle of utility</u>) is the idea that the <u>best</u> course of action creates the best <u>balance</u> of <u>good</u> and <u>bad</u> results, e.g. it could be used to argue that killing criminals, although bad for them, would be good for the <u>majority</u> of society. | • Killing as punishment is <u>just as bad</u> as murder — many <u>religious people</u> and <u>humanists</u> are against <u>any</u> form of killing. <br><br> • It doesn't give the offender the chance to <u>reform</u>. <br><br> • There have been cases where someone has been proved <u>innocent after</u> having been executed. <br><br> • Life is <u>special</u> and should be <u>preserved</u> — many religious people believe in the <u>sanctity of life</u>. <br><br> • Many religious believers think <u>God alone</u> can decide when to <u>end</u> someone's <u>life</u>. |

3) <u>Christians</u> and <u>Jews</u> might be against the death penalty because the <u>Ten Commandments</u> forbid killing.

4) Some people might use <u>situation ethics</u> to decide on a <u>case-by-case</u> basis if the death penalty should be applied. This could lead to people being <u>for</u> the death penalty in <u>some</u> cases, but <u>against</u> it in <u>others</u>, depending on, e.g., the <u>severity</u> of the crime and the <u>background</u> to the case.

## **Christians** have **Mixed Views** on Capital Punishment

1) Many <u>Christians</u> are opposed to <u>capital punishment</u>, as it doesn't allow for <u>reform</u>, or show <u>mercy</u>. <u>Jesus</u> said to set aside "eye for eye" (Matthew 5:38 NIV) and told people to "love your enemies" (Matthew 5:44 NIV). Many are against the <u>violent nature</u> of the death penalty.

2) However, some Christians in the <u>United States</u> (where capital punishment is <u>legal</u>) believe that the death penalty is a <u>good</u> thing. They say it <u>protects</u> the innocent. They might refer to <u>biblical texts</u> such as "Whoever sheds human blood, by humans shall their blood be shed" (Genesis 9:6 NIV) and "Anyone who strikes a person with a fatal blow is to be put to death" (Exodus 21:12 NIV).

## **Islamic** Law **Allows** the Death Penalty

1) The Qur'an outlines crimes punishable by <u>death</u>, but <u>encourages</u> victims' families to take <u>compensation</u>.

2) Muhammad said that death could be a punishment in <u>three</u> cases: "the married adulterer, a life for life, and the deserter of his Din (Islam)" (Sahih Muslim 16:4152). This is reflected in <u>shari'ah law</u>.

3) However, some Muslims believe that <u>Allah</u>, not humans, should decide when <u>life ends</u> — they <u>don't</u> agree with capital punishment.

## Many **Jews** are **Against** Capital Punishment

1) Exodus 21:12-17 outlines crimes <u>punishable</u> by death, such as <u>kidnapping</u>. Someone who "schemes and kills someone deliberately" (Exodus 21:14 NIV) could face the <u>death penalty</u>. Many Jews <u>disagree</u> with this — people can <u>pay</u> for their <u>actions</u> and seek <u>forgiveness</u>. The death penalty is an option in <u>Israel</u>, but is <u>hardly</u> used.

2) Mishnah Makkot 1:10 suggests that the death penalty should be <u>avoided</u>. A court "that would execute somebody once in seven years would be considered destructive". The <u>Talmud</u> put many <u>restrictions</u> on using the death penalty so it was nearly <u>unusable</u>.

# Worked Exam Questions

The questions on the next few pages are just like the ones you'll get in the exam.
The ones on this page have the answers written in for you, but the rest are for you to do yourself.

1   Which term refers to the principle of creating the best balance of good and bad results?
    Put a tick (✓) in the correct box.

    **A**    Sanctity    ☐

    **B**    Utility    ✓

    **C**    Counselling    ☐

    **D**    Severity    ☐

*[1 mark]*

2   Which of the following refers to a person's aim or purpose when they act?
    Put a tick (✓) in the correct box.

    **A**    Sanctity of life    ☐

    **B**    Duty    ☐

    **C**    Chaos    ☐

    **D**    Intention    ✓

*[1 mark]*

3   Give two examples of serious crimes.

    **1)** Murder .......................................................

    **2)** Rape .......................................................

*[2 marks]*

4   Explain two similar religious beliefs in British society today about the use
    of the death penalty. You must refer to the main religious tradition in the UK
    and at least one other religious viewpoint.

    Many Christians oppose the death penalty as it does not show mercy or allow for the criminal

    to be reformed or rehabilitated. The Sermon on the Mount places an emphasis on loving one's

    enemy, even where this is very difficult.

    The Talmud, whilst acknowledging the legitimate use of the death penalty, places many

    restrictions on its use, making it nearly unusable. Some Jews argue that the reference to the death

    penalty in the Torah is a way of expressing the seriousness of some crimes.

*[4 marks]*

# Exam Questions

**5**  Which of the following is often considered a reason for crime in society?
Put a tick (✓) in the correct box.

    **A**    Wealth    ☐

    **B**    Compassion    ☐

    **C**    Poverty    ☐

    **D**    Justice    ☐

*[1 mark]*

**6**  Explain two religious beliefs about obeying the law.
Your answer should refer to specific religious teachings or sacred texts.

..............................................................................................................................

..............................................................................................................................

..............................................................................................................................

..............................................................................................................................

..............................................................................................................................

..............................................................................................................................

..............................................................................................................................

..............................................................................................................................

*[5 marks]*

**7**  'Prison should not be a positive experience.'

SPaG MARKS

Evaluate this statement. Your answer should include the following:
• religious arguments that support the statement
• religious arguments that disagree with the statement
• a conclusion.
You can also include non-religious points of view in your answer.

*Write your answer on a separate sheet of paper.*

*[12 marks]*

# Revision Summary

That's the end of Religion, Crime and Punishment — time to see how much you can remember.

- Try these questions and <u>tick off each one</u> when you <u>get it right</u>.
- When you've done <u>all the questions</u> for a topic and are <u>completely happy</u> with it, tick off the topic.

If a question asks about a religion you <u>haven't</u> studied, just <u>skip it</u> and move on to the next question,

## Religion, the Law and Crime (p.113-116) ☑

1) Which Christian parable teaches that good and bad people will be judged and separated?
2) What is the Muslim name for the devil?
3) What do Jews and Christians believe that evil is the result of?
4) Explain the difference between a crime and a sin according to Christians.
5) What is the name of the Islamic religious law?
6) Name one country that follows Islamic religious law.
7) What is the Jewish word for a rabbinical court?
8) Give a brief definition of justice.
9) What is a hate crime?
10) Which crime is often considered to be the worst type of crime?
11) Give three reasons why someone might commit a crime.
12) Give the names of two religious organisations that aim to help prisoners.
13) Describe two ways in which religious believers might try to help prevent or reduce crime.
14) Explain one situation in which religious believers think it would be acceptable to break a law.

## Forgiveness (p.117) ☑

15) Explain what is meant by forgiveness.
16) What is restorative justice?
17) Which Christian prayer asks for forgiveness of sins?
18) Which crime do Muslims view as unforgiveable?
19) In which festival do Jews ask for forgiveness?

## Punishment and the Death Penalty (p.118-120) ☑

20) Name and describe three different purposes of punishment.
21) Give one quotation from the Bible that talks about punishment.
22) Explain why Islamic punishments are sometimes held publicly.
23) Describe the Torah's teachings on punishment.
24) Explain what corporal punishment is.
25) Describe the views of any two religions on corporal punishment.
26) Give two crimes that might be punished by the death penalty.
27) Explain two arguments in favour of the death penalty and two arguments against the death penalty.
28) How are situation ethics used with regard to the death penalty?
29) Describe the views of any two religions on the death penalty.

**General & Christianity**

# Attitudes to Equality

You need to be aware of different views in British society for this whole section. You need to be able to give Christian views on the status of women in religion, as well as views on this from one other religious tradition.

## Prejudice and Discrimination Prevent Equality

*Difference in wealth is another form of inequality — see p.133-136.*

1) Prejudice and discrimination are two different things:

> **PREJUDICE** is judging something or someone for no good reason, or without full knowledge of a situation.

> **DISCRIMINATION** is treating someone unjustly or differently, often because of prejudice.

2) Prejudice comes in different forms. Sexism is the belief one gender is inferior to the other. Racism is prejudice against people of other races. Homophobia is prejudice against people who are homosexual.

3) In the UK, people are protected against discrimination by law:

> The Equality Act 2010 says it's illegal to discriminate on the grounds of 'protected characteristics', which include race, gender, age and sexual orientation. The Act aims to ensure everyone is treated equally.

4) Positive discrimination is when someone in a group that often suffers discrimination is given an advantage. This often relates to job applications — it's only legal if they're as well qualified as the other applicants.

## Christianity Teaches Equality

1) 'Do to others what you would have them do to you' is a fundamental part of Christian teaching, often called the 'Golden Rule'. Many Christians think everyone was created equal, so try to avoid discrimination.

2) In many parts of the Bible, Jesus preached about loving others and avoiding discrimination:

- Jesus said "A new command I give you: love one another" (John 1 3:34 NIV) — i.e. don't mistreat others.

- Jesus said the second most important commandment, after loving God, is "Love your neighbour as yourself" (Mark 12:31 NIV).

- Through the Good Samaritan parable (Luke 10:25-37 NIV), Jesus gave an important teaching on prejudice. Two holy men ignore a man who's been beaten and robbed. The man is then helped by a Samaritan, a group who were despised at the time. The story shows how prejudices can be wrong.

3) The Catechism of the Catholic Church 1935 says "...discrimination ... on the grounds of sex, race, colour, social conditions, language, or religion must be ... eradicated as incompatible with God's design".

## Christian Attitudes to Gender Equality have Shifted

1) Traditionally, Christians believed women's roles were to look after the home and children, while men earned money and led the family. Some still believe this, but most now think both genders can do either role. For more on this, see p.68.

2) Women traditionally had less authority in religion — there were no female church leaders for centuries. There are now female ministers in most Protestant denominations, though not Catholic or Orthodox ones.

---

**You need to know different religious opinions on equality**

You'll also be expected to recall facts, such as definitions of certain terms (e.g. homophobia or positive discrimination), to answer the 1-mark multiple choice questions in the exam.

# Attitudes to Equality

Like Christianity, Judaism teaches that God created all people equal, but views on equality vary between the different branches of both religions. Homosexuality is a particularly divisive topic for many people.

## Christian Teaching on Racism is Clear

1) Christianity teaches that racism is unacceptable, and God made everyone equal:

> "From one man he made all the nations" Acts 17:26 NIV

> "...you are all one in Christ Jesus" Galatians 3:28 NIV

This means many Christians believe it's their duty to fight racism.

2) This can be done by an individual, e.g. by welcoming someone of another ethnicity to the community, or at an institutional level, e.g. a church asking its members to treat everyone equally. The Church of England recommends that people make "neighbours out of strangers" in its report Faithful Cities.

3) Racial equality can be difficult to achieve. The Church of England has been criticised for not having enough ethnic minority people among its clergy — it's now making efforts to increase diversity.

4) A good example of a Christian figure working against racism is Desmond Tutu:

> Desmond Tutu was an Anglican archbishop who fought against apartheid in South Africa, in which the white minority population oppressed everyone else. After apartheid ended, he led the Truth and Reconciliation Commission, which investigated the crimes of the apartheid era and focused on unity between everyone.

## There's a lot of Debate on Homosexuality in the Christian Churches

1) Homosexuality is a divisive topic in Christianity. The idea of loving your neighbour seems to contradict the Bible teachings forbidding homosexuality, such as 1 Corinthians 6:9-10.

2) Many Christians focus on loving your neighbour and therefore accept homosexuality. Others focus on the fact it's seen as a sin. For more, see p.57 and 59.

> The Anglican Church is split on the issue. Church of England bishops issued a report in 2017 saying they wouldn't change the Church's definition of marriage as being between one man and one woman (Canon B30), but many members of the Church disagree with this.

> The Catholic Church is in a similar position — its Catechism says homosexual acts are "contrary to the natural law" (2357) but many individual Catholics accept homosexuality.

## Different Jewish Traditions Have Different Views on Gender Roles

1) Jews believe that men and women are equal, based on Genesis 1:27, which says "So God created mankind in his own image ... male and female he created them" (NIV).

2) Men and women tend to have different roles in Orthodox Judaism — but they're still seen as equal in God's eyes. Men are obliged to pray three times a day, but women aren't (but they should say the Amidah twice daily — see p.48). Only men can read the Torah in synagogue and make up a minyan (the group of at least 10 people needed for some prayers). Traditionally, only men can be rabbis, but this is changing.

3) Women are exempt from such duties as it's expected they'll be looking after the home and children. They have religious duties in the home, such as lighting the Shabbat candles while saying a blessing. Traditionally, 'Jewishness' is passed on via the mother — a child with a non-Jewish mother isn't a Jew.

4) In Liberal, Reform and Masorti Judaism, religious duties can be carried out by women too. All three have male and female rabbis. Liberal, Reform and some Masortis have developed gender-neutral liturgy, e.g. avoiding calling God 'Father' or 'King'. They have equivalent rites of passage for boys and girls (p.50).

## Sacred texts are used to support arguments on both sides

Different branches of the same religion can have contrasting views on subjects such as equality, but often use the same sacred texts to support their arguments. This is because these texts contain lots of passages, many of which either expressly say different things or can be interpreted in a variety of different ways.

| Judaism & Islam | # Attitudes to Equality |
|---|---|

Many Jews believe that people of all races should be treated equally, but views on homosexuality vary. Muslim opinions on homosexuality differ as well.

## The Torah Preaches Racial Equality

1) Genesis says all of humanity comes from the same source and is, therefore, equal before God. The Torah makes it clear that people of different ethnicities should be treated the same as each other:

> "When a foreigner resides among you in your land, do not ill-treat them. The foreigner residing among you must be treated as your native-born. Love them as yourself, for you were foreigners in Egypt." Leviticus 19:33-34 NIV

2) Most Jews believe that Jewish people are God's chosen people. This doesn't mean they think they're better than anyone else — just that God gave them extra responsibilities in the covenants (see p.41).

3) Jews have often been persecuted throughout history, particularly during the Holocaust, when 6 million Jews were killed. This means many Jews are vocal about racism and make efforts to try to reduce it.

4) Ahavat ha-beriot means loving all of God's creations. It's a mitzvah (commandment) to do so, so it's important. This encourages Jews to accept everyone, regardless of their ethnicity.

5) The Jewish Council for Racial Equality (JCORE) works for racial equality, focusing especially on attitudes to asylum seekers and refugees. It campaigns against negative attitudes to immigrants in the UK.

## Views on Homosexuality Also Vary Between Jewish Traditions

1) Orthodox Jews tend not to approve of homosexuality. They're against homophobia, but tend to see being in homosexual relationships as a sin. Sex between men is forbidden in Leviticus 18:22 (so it's assumed sex between women is banned too). Orthodox synagogues don't hold same-sex weddings.

2) Attitudes are beginning to change within the Orthodox community though. Efforts are being made to welcome and support homosexual Orthodox Jews in the community.

3) Progressive Jews accept homosexuality and welcome homosexual people into their communities. They argue that as God created everyone in his image (Genesis 1:27), homosexuality can't be wrong.

4) Both Liberal and Reform Judaism campaigned for the legalisation of same-sex marriage in the UK, and hold same-sex weddings now they're legal. Homosexual people can become Liberal and Reform rabbis.

5) Many Masortis accept homosexuality. They have a shutafut (partnership) ceremony for same-sex marriages or civil partnerships, different from the traditional kiddushin.

## Homosexuality is Controversial in Islam

1) Many Muslims believe that the Qur'an forbids homosexuality — for example, Qur'an 7:81 says "you approach men with desire, instead of women ... you are a transgressing people" (the quote is addressed to men). This means they're against the legalisation of same-sex marriage (see p.61).

2) Some Muslims disagree, arguing that as Allah created all people, homosexuality is part of his creation.

3) Muslims often speak against homophobia, as Muslims should be tolerant towards others.

4) Some Muslim organisations state that they are against homosexual acts but believe homosexual people should be respected. Others, such as Imaan, support homosexual Muslims and campaign for their rights.

---

## Homosexuality is often a divisive topic in religion

Have a go at comparing the different views on homosexuality within the religions you are studying — and then compare the opinions of one religion to another. Look for similarities and differences.

# Attitudes to Equality  Islam

Islam teaches that Allah <u>created</u> everyone to be <u>equal</u>, even though people are <u>different</u> from each other.

## Islam says People are Created Equal, but not Identical

1) Islam teaches that <u>all people</u> were created by <u>Allah</u>, and were created <u>equal</u> (although <u>not</u> the <u>same</u>). He intended humanity to be created with <u>differences</u>. But this just means we're all <u>individuals</u>.

2) Muslims all over the world are united by the <u>ummah</u> — the <u>community</u> of Islam. The ummah consists of <u>all Muslims</u>, regardless of <u>nationality</u>, <u>tradition</u> (i.e. Sunni or Shi'a) and so on. This helps promote <u>racial</u> and <u>social harmony</u>, as in theory no one's <u>excluded</u> or <u>discriminated</u> against.

3) Muslims follow the <u>teachings of Muhammad</u> on racial equality:

> The final sermon of Muhammad is clear that <u>no race</u> is <u>superior</u> to another: "you are all descended from Adam and none is higher than the other except in obedience to Allah. No Arab is superior to a non-Arab. Between Muslims there are no races and no tribes." The only <u>important</u> thing is whether someone's a <u>good Muslim</u> or not.

4) People on <u>hajj</u> all wear <u>simple white clothes</u>, showing everyone's <u>equal</u> — race, gender etc. <u>don't matter</u>.

5) Sahih al-Bukhari 56:681 says everyone should be <u>treated</u> the <u>same</u> way, regardless of <u>who</u> they are.

6) A good <u>example</u> of a Muslim figure <u>working against racism</u> is <u>Malcolm X</u>:

> Malcolm X was a <u>prominent figure</u> in the struggle for <u>civil rights</u> for <u>African Americans</u> in the <u>US</u>. He initially advocated <u>black supremacy</u> and <u>separatism</u>, but later supported <u>interethnic dialogue</u>. He inspired many with his campaigning for <u>human rights</u>.

## Men and Women have Different Roles within Islam

1) The <u>Qur'an</u> makes it <u>clear</u> that men and women are <u>equal</u> when it comes to their <u>religious obligations</u>, e.g. prayer, fasting, hajj and charity — have a look at Qur'an 33:35 on p.69, which also has more information on <u>gender equality</u>. All that counts is how good a <u>Muslim</u> they are, not their <u>gender</u>:

> "O mankind, indeed We have created you from male and female and made you peoples and tribes that you may know one another. Indeed, the most noble of you in the sight of Allah is the most righteous of you." Qur'an 49:13

2) Women don't <u>have</u> to attend mosque for <u>prayer</u>, but it is <u>permitted</u>. If women do go to the mosque, they must pray in a <u>separate</u> group — behind (or otherwise out of sight of) the men. Like in <u>Judaism</u>, this is because it's thought it might be <u>distracting</u> for both genders to pray in a mixed group.

3) Women can't lead prayers in <u>mixed groups</u>, but they can lead prayers being said by groups of <u>women</u>.

4) There is a growing movement working for women to have a more <u>prominent role</u> in Islam. Several women have led <u>mixed-gender</u> prayers across the world. Their actions have been <u>condemned</u> by some Muslims as not following the teachings of Islam. There are plans for a <u>mosque</u> run by women in Bradford.

5) Some say it's <u>part of Islam</u> for Muslim women to wear <u>modest clothing</u> — Qur'an 24:31 says "tell the believing women ... to wrap [a portion of] their headcovers over their chests and not expose their adornment". Others argue it doesn't say they have to cover up <u>completely</u> and that their <u>faith</u> and <u>piety</u> are more <u>important</u> than clothing — Qur'an 7:26 says "the clothing of righteousness — that is best".

## Remember, there are usually different opinions

You'll often be asked to discuss contrasting beliefs in the exam, so make sure you learn both sides of the argument. You'll lose marks in the 12-mark questions if you only give one opinion.

**All religions** | # Human Rights

Human rights are <u>moral</u>, <u>legal</u> and <u>political</u> rights that should give people <u>freedom</u> and <u>protection</u> worldwide.

## The **United Nations** Defined **Human Rights**

1) In 1948, the <u>United Nations</u> (UN) published the <u>Universal Declaration of Human Rights</u>. The aim was to lay down minimum <u>rights</u> for <u>every person</u>, in <u>every country</u>.

2) It states that all human beings are born <u>free</u> and <u>equal</u> in dignity and rights. It also lists specific rights, e.g. the right to <u>life</u>, freedom from <u>slavery</u>, freedom from <u>imprisonment</u> or <u>exile</u> without <u>good reason</u>, freedom of <u>opinion</u> and <u>expression</u>, the right to have an <u>education</u> and to seek <u>work</u>.

3) The Universal Declaration of Human Rights <u>stated</u> how things <u>should</u> be, but meant <u>nothing</u> in a court of law. So in 1953, the Council of Europe brought into effect the <u>European Convention on Human Rights</u>, which is a <u>similar</u> list of rights to the UN declaration. It's enforced by the European <u>Court</u> of Human Rights (ECHR). These rights became part of the UK's <u>domestic law</u> in 1998, with the <u>Human Rights Act</u>.

4) Most religious believers agree that all human beings should be treated <u>fairly</u> and with <u>respect</u>. This is based on a belief in <u>human dignity</u> — all human life is <u>valuable</u>, because people are created in the <u>image of God</u> — and a belief in <u>justice</u>, the idea everyone should be treated <u>fairly</u>. Everyone should be <u>free</u> to <u>think</u> and to <u>choose</u> how to act (though hopefully they'll live a good <u>moral</u> life).

## Many **Christians** Support **Human Rights**

1) The <u>Catholic Church</u> highlights the role of the <u>individual</u> as well as the <u>state</u> in <u>protecting</u> human rights. It says human rights aren't just defined by <u>states</u> putting them into <u>law</u>, but "Every member of the community has a duty ... in order that the rights of others can be satisfied and their freedoms respected" (The Common Good and the Catholic Church's Social Teaching: 37).

> "So God created mankind in his own image, in the image of God he created them; male and female he created them." Genesis 1:27 NIV

> "You ... were called to be free. But do not use your freedom to indulge the flesh; rather, serve one another humbly in love." Galatians 5:13 NIV

2) <u>Christians</u> may find their views <u>contradict</u> others' ideas about rights. E.g. many think <u>women</u> should have the right to <u>abortion</u>, but some Christians <u>disagree</u>, believing the <u>foetus</u>'s right to <u>life</u> is more <u>important</u>.

## **Human Rights** are **Important** for Most **Jews**

1) Most Jews <u>support</u> human rights — Deuteronomy 16:20 asks Jews to "Follow justice and justice alone" (NIV). <u>Teachings</u> such as the two below ask Jews to <u>protect</u> the rights of <u>specific people</u>:

> "Whoever oppresses the poor shows contempt for their Maker, but whoever is kind to the needy honours God." Proverbs 14:31 NIV

> "When a foreigner resides among you in your land, do not ill-treat them ... Love them as yourself" Leviticus 19:33-34 NIV

2) However, Jews may sometimes find that their <u>beliefs</u> conflict with other people's ideas about <u>human rights</u>. For example, some <u>Orthodox Jews</u> think homosexuality is wrong, which may lead them to oppose the legalisation of <u>same-sex marriage</u>.

## The **Qur'an** says **Justice** is Very **Important**

1) Most Muslims are supportive of human rights. The <u>Qur'an</u> frequently emphasises the <u>importance</u> of <u>justice</u>, saying for example "O you who have believed, be persistently standing firm for Allah, witnesses in justice ... Be just; that is nearer to righteousness" (Qur'an 5:8).

> "Indeed, Allah orders justice and good conduct and giving to relatives and forbids immorality and bad conduct and oppression. He admonishes you that perhaps you will be reminded." Qur'an 16:90

2) Some Muslims argue that <u>Islamic law</u> sometimes <u>undermines</u> Muslim <u>women's</u> rights, e.g. they don't have <u>equal rights</u> in <u>divorce</u> to men.

---

### Human rights give everybody a free and equal status

Shut the book and have a go at writing down as many human rights as you can remember.

---

# Freedom of Belief

You need to be able to give contrasting views on this topic from Christianity and one other religious viewpoint.

## The UK is a Diverse, Multi-Faith Society

*About half of the population say they have no religious belief.*

1) Freedom of religion and belief is a legal right in the UK — it gives the freedom to follow any or no religion.

2) People are protected from being discriminated against because of their beliefs. The beliefs they hold as part of their religion are protected, e.g. religions can choose not to hold same-sex marriages in their places of worship if it doesn't fit with their beliefs. Freedom of belief is sometimes a tricky area though.

- Some people feel there isn't enough recognition of those who don't hold religious beliefs, e.g. in schools.

- There can be a fine line between educating people about a faith and influencing them too much. Some may think that e.g. religious charities have too much influence, while the charities would argue they're not trying to convert people, just help them.

- Some people, including religious believers, object to the Church of England being the state church. For example, 26 bishops are peers in the House of Lords, which many see as unfair now that the country is more religiously diverse and many people don't have a religion at all. Others say the UK is a Christian country so it's acceptable — it's part of the culture.

- A religious person saying homosexuality is sinful clashes with homosexual people's right not to be discriminated against and could be seen as hate speech (a crime) — but stopping people from expressing their views undermines their freedom of belief.

3) Most religious believers happily live alongside others in the UK and enjoy the different perspectives it gives them. The Inter Faith Network for the UK promotes mutual understanding and combats prejudice.

4) Living in a multi-faith society can make it harder for some believers to practise their faith — e.g. some Christian festivals are UK bank holidays while other faiths' festivals aren't, making it harder to celebrate.

## Religions Are Generally Accepting of Other Faiths

### Christian views

- Though many Christians think Christianity's the true religion, they think people have the right to practise any faith. It's "an inalienable requirement of the dignity of man" (Catechism of the Catholic Church 1747).
- Some Christians think the only way to reach heaven is by being Christian, so they try to convert people.

### Jewish views

- Jews are a people as well as a religious group. Jews don't try to convert people, although people can convert if they want after a period of study. Once they've converted, they're seen as Jewish for ever.
- Freedom of belief is important to Jews as they have often been persecuted, most horrifyingly during the Holocaust, when six million Jews were killed. They're often inspired by the Torah story of Esther, who saved the Jewish people from being killed by Haman. Esther risked her life to beg for mercy. The story shows the importance of allowing everyone to live without persecution, and having faith in the face of it.

### Muslim views

- The Qur'an says "There shall be no compulsion in [acceptance of] the religion" (Qur'an 2:256) — people are free to choose. Muslims believe that Islam is the only true faith — but they also believe that all righteous people will be favoured by Allah. Most Muslims don't try to convert others to Islam.
- However, Muslims' freedom of belief is often restricted by the common belief that converting to another religion from Islam or becoming an atheist is unacceptable in Islam — it's known as apostasy. Some hadiths say it deserves the death penalty.
- Some Muslims disagree, as the Qur'an leaves judgement up to Allah — Qur'an 3:85 says "whoever desires other than Islam ... he, in the Hereafter, will be among the losers". It can be hard for ex-Muslims — they're often cut off from their family.
- Muslims call Muslims, Christians and Jews 'people of the book', as they're linked by a shared religious heritage. They all believe in prophets such as Ibrahim (Abraham) and many Muslims believe the Torah and New Testament contain important messages. Qur'an 29:46 says "our God and your God is one".

# Worked Exam Questions

The next two pages contain some exam-style questions on the things you've just learnt. To show how it's done, the ones on this page have been done for you already, and then there are some more for you to try for yourself.

1   Which of the following is the belief that one gender is inferior to another?
Put a tick (✓) in the correct box.

A   Sexism        ✓

B   Racism        ☐

C   Homophobia    ☐

D   Maternity     ☐

*[1 mark]*

2   Which of the following terms describes when someone who belongs to a group that's often discriminated against is given an advantage?
Put a tick (✓) in the correct box.

A   Racism                    ☐

B   Prejudice                 ☐

C   Negative discrimination   ☐

D   Positive discrimination   ✓

*[1 mark]*

3   Explain two religious beliefs about racism.
Your answer should refer to specific religious teachings or sacred texts.

Christians and Jews believe that racism is wrong and that all races should be treated equally.

The first chapter of Genesis says that man was created in the image of God, which suggests that all

people are a likeness of God, regardless of their race.

Similarly, Muslims believe in racial equality. They follow the teaching in the final sermon of

Muhammad, which makes it clear that racism is wrong. He said "Between Muslims there are no

races and no tribes".

*[5 marks]*

# Exam Questions

**4** Which act from 2010 makes it illegal to discriminate against people based on certain protected characteristics? Put a tick (✓) in the correct box.

    **A**    The Inequality Act   ☐

    **B**    The Freedom of Speech Act   ☐

    **C**    The Equality Act   ☐

    **D**    The Disability Act   ☐

*[1 mark]*

**5** Which of the following can describe changing from one faith to another? Put a tick (✓) in the correct box.

    **A**    Confession   ☐

    **B**    Transformation   ☐

    **C**    Conversion   ☐

    **D**    Agnosticism   ☐

*[1 mark]*

**6** Name two of the 'protected characteristics' that it is illegal to discriminate against in the UK.

1) ......................................................................................................................................

......................................................................................................................................

2) ......................................................................................................................................

......................................................................................................................................

*[2 marks]*

**7** 'Everyone should be free to make their own choices about the religious beliefs they hold.'

SPaG MARKS

Evaluate this statement. Your answer should include the following:
• religious arguments that support the statement
• religious arguments that disagree with the statement
• a conclusion.
You can also include non-religious points of view in your answer.

*Write your answer on a separate sheet of paper.*

*[12 marks]*

# Social Justice

Social justice is the idea that everyone should have equal rights and opportunities.

## Social Justice is the Idea that Everyone should be Treated Fairly

1) Social justice is putting into practice the principles of human rights. Working for social justice includes:

- Trying to ensure different groups of people aren't discriminated against or more disadvantaged than others. This includes discrimination on the grounds of race, gender, religion, social class, poverty, age or disability.
- Trying to redistribute wealth so everyone can afford to live comfortably. Some members of society are very wealthy while others struggle to meet their basic needs for food, shelter, warmth, etc.

2) Social justice efforts often focus on wealth, as a lack of it can deprive people of other opportunities and rights. Higher taxes for people on high incomes and free healthcare and education are ways to help.

3) Many people try to work for social justice. It's an important part of Christianity, Islam and Judaism.

## Christianity Teaches that People Should Help Those in Need

1) Christians follow Jesus's teaching to "Love your neighbour as yourself" (Mark 12:31 NIV). The parable of the sheep and goats is often used to teach about social justice — see p.19 for more.

Jesus was known for helping poor people and for healing the sick. In Luke 16:19-31, he teaches that people who don't help others when they're able to will be punished — the story is about a rich man who repeatedly ignores a poor man, and ends up in hell for not helping him. Jesus healed a man with leprosy by touching him, at a time when lepers were outcasts from society. Christians should therefore follow Jesus's example — by helping those who need it, they can express God's love.

2) The Catholic Church emphasises the importance of human dignity in social justice. It says people should be allowed "to obtain what is their due, according to their nature and their vocation" (Catechism 1928) — people should be given opportunities to make the most of their lives and their abilities.

3) Catechism 1928 also says social justice is better for everyone — it's for "the common good".

## Islam Encourages Helping Others

1) Muslims should work for social justice as part of their faith. Qur'an 76:8-9 says the righteous "give food in spite of love for it to the needy, the orphan, and the captive, [Saying] ... We wish not from you reward or gratitude". This means people should give help without expecting anything in return.

2) Zakah, charitable giving to redistribute wealth, is central to Islam — it's one of the five pillars (see p.33). The Qur'an says those who "give zakah ... will be the successful" (Qur'an 7:156-157).

3) It promises that those who have wealth to spare and give it away will be rewarded.

"Those who spend their wealth [in Allah's way] ... — they will have their reward with their Lord." Qur'an 2:274

## Jewish Teachings say Jews Should be Generous to Others

1) Many Jewish teachings support working for social justice. According to Deuteronomy 15:11, God told Jews "to be open-handed towards your fellow Israelites who are poor and needy in your land" (NIV). Jews should give generously and willingly, "without a grudging heart" (Deuteronomy 15:10 NIV).

2) Jewish ideas of charity (tzedakah) focus on justice — it's not only kind to give to charity, but it's righting a wrong. Amos 5:24 NIV says "let justice roll on like a river, righteousness like a never-failing stream!".

3) The concept of tikkun olam — repairing the world — is linked to this. Jews should be active in improving things that are wrong in the world. This doesn't only mean personally giving to charity and helping others, but also campaigning on a political level to make sure that society is fair and just for everyone.

4) If Jews oppress those who are disadvantaged, God "will certainly hear their cry" (Exodus 22:23 NIV).

# Wealth and Poverty

How <u>wealth</u> is <u>used</u>, and how it's <u>distributed</u> among people, is a <u>big issue</u> today.  For the <u>exam</u>, you need to be able to give <u>Christian</u> opinions on the <u>uses of wealth</u>, as well as views from <u>one other religious</u> tradition.

## Wealth Inequality is a Big Problem Today

1) The <u>gap</u> between the <u>poorest</u> and <u>richest</u> people is <u>huge</u>, and <u>growing</u>.  In 2017, <u>Oxfam</u> estimated that the richest <u>8</u> people in the world had <u>more wealth</u> than the poorest <u>half</u> of the world (<u>3.6 billion</u> people).

2) In the <u>UK</u>, the poorest <u>50%</u> of people own <u>8.7%</u> of wealth, while the richest <u>10%</u> own <u>45%</u>.

3) <u>Poverty</u> is not having <u>enough resources</u> (money, etc.) to meet your <u>basic needs</u>, e.g. <u>food</u> or <u>heating</u>.

4) Poverty has many <u>causes</u>.  In the UK, these causes often include <u>low wages</u>, <u>high costs</u> (e.g. renting a house or paying for childcare), a <u>lack of skills</u> so people can't get better-paid jobs, and <u>unemployment</u>.

   - <u>Fair pay</u> is an issue.  Many in <u>poverty</u> have <u>low-paid</u> jobs, so they work <u>long hours</u> to try to earn enough to live on.  In some <u>areas</u>, <u>well-paid</u> jobs <u>aren't</u> available.  <u>Part-time</u> work is often low-paid.

   - By law, people have to be paid the <u>National Minimum Wage</u>, but many people think it <u>isn't</u> enough.  Over-25s must be paid the <u>National Living Wage</u>, which is a bit <u>higher</u> than the minimum wage.  However, many say it still isn't <u>enough</u> to <u>live on</u> — it's not a <u>true</u> living wage.

   - <u>Businesses</u> are often <u>reluctant</u> to pay people <u>more</u> as it's <u>expensive</u> for them to do so — some try to <u>avoid</u> paying even the minimum wage.  Some say <u>increasing</u> wages will mean they <u>can't afford</u> to <u>pay</u> people so they would have to <u>cut</u> the number of jobs, which wouldn't help.

5) <u>Worldwide</u>, poverty is also caused by things such as <u>war</u>, <u>rapid population growth</u>, <u>natural disasters</u> and <u>exploitation</u>.  The <u>Fairtrade Foundation</u> works to ensure people in <u>developing countries</u> are paid a <u>fair price</u> for the products they <u>sell</u> and that they have <u>decent working conditions</u>.

## Finding a Solution is Difficult

1) Helping poverty caused by <u>disasters</u> (e.g. <u>war</u>) often involves <u>emergency relief</u> during the <u>disaster</u> and <u>long-term</u> help afterwards, e.g. rebuilding houses.  It can take <u>years</u> before things get back to <u>normal</u>.

2) In other situations, some people think giving <u>money</u> (e.g. benefits or donations) to people in poverty makes them too <u>reliant</u> on that money — they don't <u>help themselves</u> get out of poverty as they prefer to keep <u>receiving</u> the money.  Others argue that this <u>isn't</u> the case, and that people living in poverty need <u>financial help</u>, because <u>not</u> giving it to them means they might not be able to <u>eat</u> or <u>heat</u> their home.

3) Some say it's people's <u>own responsibility</u> to get out of poverty — they should work <u>harder</u> and use money more <u>responsibly</u>.  Others say that poverty is a result of <u>many factors</u> and that many do <u>work hard</u> — in 2016, <u>1 in 8</u> people employed in the UK were living <u>in poverty</u> (source Joseph Rowntree Foundation, 2016).

4) They say society should help those who face <u>many issues</u> such as <u>illness</u>, or a <u>lack of skills</u> or <u>opportunities</u>.  <u>Charities</u> often try to help people learn <u>new skills</u> on top of giving them <u>money</u> or <u>food</u>.

<u>Utilitarian ethics</u> say the <u>correct</u> course of action is the one which has the <u>largest</u> balance of <u>good</u> against <u>bad</u> outcomes for those involved.  Utilitarians often think people with <u>excess wealth</u> should give to people with <u>less wealth</u>.  But if the money could be spent on <u>another</u> cause that would have a <u>greater benefit</u> (e.g. preventing more climate change), then giving the money to people <u>in poverty</u> would be <u>wrong</u>.

## There are many different causes of poverty...

...so try writing down as many as you can remember, as well as some ways it can be reduced.

**General & Christianity**

# Wealth and Poverty

Poverty can be <u>linked</u> to <u>other problems</u> in society — and helping those <u>in need</u> is an <u>important</u> aspect of <u>religion</u>.

## There are **Other Problems** Often **Linked** with **Poverty**

### Excessive Interest on Loans

- People sometimes need <u>extra money</u>, e.g. to pay for something <u>unexpected</u>, or just to afford <u>food</u> until the <u>next payday</u>. One way of covering this is take out a <u>loan</u>. A quick and seemingly easy way to do so is to borrow from a <u>money lender</u>, but money lenders often lend money at <u>rates</u> that go up to <u>thousands</u> of percent of <u>interest</u> (called <u>usury</u>). People might take out <u>small</u> loans, but they soon become so <u>big</u> that they <u>can't repay</u> them.

- This was a <u>big</u> problem in the UK, so the <u>government</u> introduced some <u>regulations</u> to <u>limit</u> how much people have to <u>repay</u>. Now, people don't have to repay more than <u>twice</u> what they borrowed.

### People-trafficking

- People living in poverty are often more <u>vulnerable</u> to <u>people-trafficking</u>. People are forced to work for <u>little</u> or <u>no</u> money, after they've been transferred to a <u>new</u> place (often <u>abroad</u>) by the <u>traffickers</u>.

- People are often persuaded to move <u>willingly</u> by the promise of a <u>better life</u> elsewhere, but once they get there the traffickers <u>force</u> them to work to pay back the money they <u>owe</u> for the <u>move</u>.

## **Christians** Believe It's What You **Do** with Your **Money** that **Counts**

1) Christians believe it's important not to be <u>fixated</u> on wealth — Matthew 6:24 says "You cannot serve both God and Money" (NIV). People with <u>lots</u> of wealth should use it to <u>help</u> others who are <u>less well off</u>.

2) Many Christians think money should only be earned in <u>moral ways</u>, not in ways that might <u>harm</u> others, such as working for <u>arms manufacturers</u> or running a business that pays people <u>unfair wages</u>.

3) They also try to avoid <u>using</u> their money in a way that <u>harms</u> others, which includes <u>usury</u>.

> The Church of England has launched an <u>initiative</u> to combat lenders who charge <u>lots of interest</u>. The Church is offering <u>workshops</u> to <u>educate</u> people about <u>money matters</u>, as well as promoting <u>credit unions</u>, which lend money at <u>low rates</u> of interest.
>
> The Church <u>campaigned</u> for the introduction of the <u>Modern Slavery Act</u>, which helps <u>protect</u> victims of <u>people-trafficking</u>.

## **Charity** is **Important** to **Christians**

1) Giving to <u>charity</u> and <u>helping</u> others is <u>important</u> to many <u>Christians</u>, following the teaching to "Love your neighbour" (Mark 12:31 NIV). It's important to give in a way that helps people to help <u>themselves</u> — the <u>parable</u> of the <u>talents</u> (Matthew 25:14-30) says those who make <u>most</u> of what they <u>have</u> are <u>rewarded</u>.

2) Christians should give to <u>charity</u> as part of their <u>faith</u>. There are many <u>Christian</u> charities — see p.19.

> "If anyone has material possessions and sees a brother or sister in need but has no pity on them, how can the love of God be in that person?" 1 John 3:17 NIV

3) It's best to give donations <u>quietly</u> and <u>without boasting</u> about it — Matthew 6:2 tells Christians that "when you give to the needy, do not announce it with trumpets" (NIV).

4) <u>How much</u> you give <u>isn't</u> important — what's important is giving as <u>much</u> as you <u>can</u>. Jesus taught that a <u>poor woman</u> giving a <u>small</u> amount of money she couldn't <u>afford to lose</u> was <u>more</u> important than <u>rich</u> people giving <u>large</u> sums they could <u>easily</u> do <u>without</u>. For more teachings on wealth, see p.154 and 159.

5) Over <u>7500</u> churches are involved with the <u>Fairtrade</u> movement. For more on <u>Christian charities</u>, see p.19.

**REVISION TASK**

# Christians think that money should not be used in harmful ways

Close the book and write down as much as you can about Christian beliefs on wealth and charity.

# Wealth and Poverty

Charity and the redistribution of wealth is very important in Islam — they form one of the Five Pillars.

## Charity is One of the Five Pillars of Islam

1) Charity plays an important role in Islam — zakah (financial aid) is one of the five pillars of Islam, which every Muslim has to follow. Qur'an 2:177 says "righteousness is [in] one who ... gives zakah".

2) With zakah, 2.5% of your yearly wealth should be given as charity, unless your wealth is below a minimum threshold. It's usually given to charities or mosques, or to Muslims who are less well off.

3) Muslims think wealth is given to people by Allah, so they should use it to help others. Being wealthy or poor is Allah's test of people — they should try to help themselves or others, depending on the situation.

> "A man is not a believer who fills his stomach while his neighbour is hungry." Al-Adab al-Mufrad 6:112 (collection of hadith)

4) Sadaqah is another kind of charity. It includes a wide range of charitable acts, from simply smiling at someone to cheer them up, to giving money to help those in need. Sadaqah is seen as a duty, but it involves any amount of effort, time or money — it's up to the individual to decide how much they do.

5) There's a particular emphasis on 'ongoing charity' — actions that will have a long-term effect. It's seen as best to help people become able to support themselves, rather than relying on donations. This means the benefits of sadaqah are long-lasting and help the community — known as sustainable development.

6) There are Islamic charities that help people globally and in the UK, including Muslim Aid and Islamic Aid.

### Muslim Aid

- Muslim Aid provides disaster relief and development aid around the world. The charity works in over 70 countries.
- It provides not only initial emergency aid after a war or natural disaster, but ongoing help. This help includes building new housing, sanitation and schools, and offering interest-free loans to help start-up businesses.

### Islamic Aid

- Islamic Aid is an international organisation dedicated to reducing poverty and deprivation.
- It focuses on a long-term approach to helping communities and employs people from the communities it works in.

## How Money is Used is Important in Islam

1) Muslims shouldn't use money in ways that harm people — Islamic law says Muslims shouldn't harm others.

2) Islam forbids alcohol, so it's seen as immoral to make money from it. Islam is often focused on sexual modesty, so profiting from sex is forbidden (either directly or indirectly, e.g. sexually suggestive adverts).

3) Qur'an 2:275 says "Allah ... has forbidden interest" and that those who charge it will go to jahannam (hell). In Islam, money doesn't have a value in itself, so it shouldn't be used to make more money. This stops richer people profiting from poorer people, and ensures wealth is spread more fairly.

4) Muslims use Islamic bank accounts and run businesses that don't involve charging interest.

## There are many religious charitable organisations

Try writing about how the charitable work of religious organisations relates to the beliefs and the sacred texts of the religions they represent. Include any religion-specific technical terms.

# Wealth and Poverty

In Judaism, wealth is not usually seen as a bad thing, but using it to help others in need is still important.

## Jews Should Use Their Wealth to Help Others

1) Judaism teaches that there's nothing wrong in being wealthy, so long as you're not obsessed by it, and you give money to others. Wealth is seen as a gift from God. Jews should try to avoid being dependent on others if at all possible — although if they are really in need there's no shame in receiving charity.

2) Unfairness and dishonesty in business are condemned — you're answerable to God for any wrongdoing. All money should be earned morally, so any job that's harmful in any way is forbidden. Jews particularly frown on work that is damaging to God's creation (e.g. unsustainable tree felling).

3) Jews shouldn't charge interest on loans to other Jews (Leviticus 25:37). This doesn't apply to loans made to non-Jews: "You may charge a foreigner interest, but not a fellow Israelite" (Deuteronomy 23:20 NIV).

4) Jews try to avoid talking about or handling money on Shabbat — the day of rest.

## Charity is Important in Judaism

1) This passage from the Torah sums up Jewish teaching on charity:

> "If anyone is poor among your fellow Israelites in any of the towns of the land ... do not be hard-hearted or tight-fisted towards them. Rather, be open-handed and freely lend them whatever they need." Deuteronomy 15:7-8 NIV

2) The Jewish scholar Maimonides said the best way to give was to do so in a way that meant the recipient could help themselves. He also said giving anonymously was recommended, so the charity is given for the good of it alone, and not so the giver can be rewarded — they shouldn't expect anything in return.

3) There are two important charitable principles in Judaism — tzedakah and gemilut hasadim:

- Tzedakah: tzedakah means charity, but with a sense of justice — it's not just generous to give tzedakah, it's right as it makes society fairer. Everyone, even those in need, is expected to contribute 10% of their wealth. Deuteronomy 14:29 says people should donate some of their produce so "the foreigners, the fatherless and the widows who live in your towns may come and eat" (NIV), showing the importance of helping those in need.
- Gemilut hasadim: this means 'acts of loving kindness' — it refers to any compassionate actions towards others.

4) Many Jewish homes have collection boxes (called pushkes) in which money for charity can be placed.

5) Donating clothing and food to people who need them or visiting someone who's sick are considered gemilut hasadim (acts of loving kindness). There are Jewish charities that help people, including Tzedek:

> 1) Tzedek is a Jewish charity in the UK that seeks to get the Jewish community involved in helping to reduce poverty worldwide.
> 2) Their focus is on helping local projects, that improve a community's ability to get itself out of poverty.

## All Three Faiths Work to End People-Trafficking

1) Leaders of Islam, Christianity and Judaism have got together to combat people-trafficking worldwide. They've created the Global Freedom Network, an organisation which aims to end slavery.

2) It works with governments to get them to pass laws to combat slavery and people-trafficking.

---

## I hope you feel richer (in knowledge) after these pages

Learning the technical terms for the different kinds of charitable acts, such as tzedakah, will help you to improve the quality of your answers in the exam. Write out a quick list now to help you to remember them.

# Worked Exam Question

Here are some more exam-style questions for you to have a go at. As usual, the question on this page has been completed already, then there are some for you to do for yourself on the next page. Good luck.

---

1    'Money is not evil in itself.'

Evaluate this statement. Your answer should include the following:
• religious arguments that support the statement
• religious arguments that disagree with the statement
• a conclusion.
You can also include non-religious points of view in your answer.

> You don't need to include views from all three religions in the exam — just write about the ones you've been studying.

In Christian teaching, it is the love of money, rather than money itself, which is condemned. 1 Timothy 6:10 says, "the love of money is a root of all kinds of evil" (NIV). Those with wealth should be willing to give their money away to help others. Similarly, Jews teach that wealth is a gift from God and that it is perfectly acceptable to be wealthy, but they should use their wealth wisely and help others. Islamic teaching also focuses on the idea that money is a gift from Allah and therefore it should be used to help others. Some people might argue that it is their right to receive money and use it how they wish if they have worked hard — money isn't evil if it is their just reward for their work.

Jesus said, "It is easier for a camel to go through the eye of a needle than for someone who is rich to enter the kingdom of God" (Mark 10:25 NIV). This suggests that even if someone is generous with their wealth, they are going against God's ways if they possess lots of money, and so money must be evil. Islam says people shouldn't use money to make a profit from others, as the Qur'an states: "Allah... has forbidden interest" (Qur'an 2:275). It is also seen as wrong to make money from alcohol or sex. Jews also see some ways of earning money as immoral, such as any work that damages God's creation (e.g. felling trees in an unsustainable way). So certain ways of making money are seen as evil.

In conclusion, I do not believe that money is evil in itself, as long as it is earned and used in the right ways. If acquired or used in the wrong way, it can cause harm, but it is not the money itself that is evil.

*[12 marks]*

---

# Exam Questions

**2** Which of the following is **not** an organisation that focuses on poverty in developing countries? Put a tick (✓) in the correct box.

    **A**      Amnesty International      ☐

    **B**      The Fairtrade Foundation      ☐

    **C**      Tearfund®      ☐

    **D**      Muslim Aid      ☐

*[1 mark]*

**3** Which phrase describes the amount workers should be paid to give them an acceptable standard of living? Put a tick (✓) in the correct box.

    **A**      Universal credit      ☐

    **B**      National living wage      ☐

    **C**      Salary      ☐

    **D**      National minimum wage      ☐

*[1 mark]*

**4** Give two causes of poverty that religious believers might try to combat.

1) ......................................................................................................................

......................................................................................................................

2) ......................................................................................................................

......................................................................................................................

*[2 marks]*

**5** Give two similar religious beliefs about people-trafficking. You must refer to the views of at least one religious group.

......................................................................................................................

......................................................................................................................

......................................................................................................................

......................................................................................................................

......................................................................................................................

......................................................................................................................

*[4 marks]*

# Revision Summary

Now you've tackled <u>Religion, Human Rights and Social Justice</u>, it's time to test yourself on what you've learnt.

*   Try these questions and <u>tick off each one</u> when you <u>get it right</u>.
*   When you've done <u>all the questions</u> for a topic and are <u>completely happy</u> with it, tick off the topic.

If a question asks about a religion you <u>haven't</u> studied, just <u>skip it</u> and move on to the next question.

## <u>Attitudes to Equality (p.124-127)</u> ☑

1)  What is discrimination? ☑
2)  Give two forms of prejudice. ☑
3)  Positive discrimination is illegal in the UK under all circumstances. True or false? ☑
4)  What is the 'Golden Rule' of Christianity? ☑
5)  Describe the traditional Christian attitude towards the role of women. ☑
6)  Which Anglican archbishop fought against apartheid in South Africa? ☑
7)  Give two contrasting beliefs about homosexuality in Christianity. ☑
8)  Give a branch of Judaism in which women can become rabbis. ☑
9)  Give a quote from the Torah that promotes gender equality. ☑
10) What does the mitzvah ahavat ha-beriot mean? ☑
11) Describe the opinions on same-sex marriage from different branches of Judaism. ☑
12) What reason is given by some Muslims for why men and women must pray separately? ☑
13) How does the idea of 'ummah' support equality? ☑
14) Explain why plain, white clothes are worn by Muslims during hajj. ☑
15) Give two contrasting Muslim views on homosexuality. ☑

## <u>Human Rights and Freedom of Belief (p.128-129)</u> ☑

16) What was the aim of the UN's Universal Declaration of Human Rights in 1948? ☑
17) Give the name of the governmental body that enforces human rights in Europe. ☑
18) Give one view from a religion you are studying that might contradict human rights. ☑
19) Define the term 'freedom of belief'. ☑
20) What is seen as the only way to reach heaven by many Christians? ☑
21) How can a person convert to Judaism? ☑
22) What do Muslims call Muslims, Christians and Jews collectively? ☑

## <u>Social Justice, Wealth & Poverty (p.132-136)</u> ☑

23) Give one way of working for social justice. ☑
24) What parable is used in Christianity to teach about social justice? ☑
25) What name is given to the charitable redistribution of wealth in Islam? ☑
26) In Deuteronomy 15:11 NIV, how did God tell Jews to act towards their "fellow Israelites"? ☑
27) What is poverty? ☑
28) Why might some businesses be reluctant to pay their workers more than the minimum wage? ☑
29) Describe the principle of utilitarian ethics. ☑
30) In Christianity, giving as much as you can is more important than the amount given. True or false? ☑
31) In Islam, what is 'sadaqah'? ☑
32) What rules on loan interest are given to Jews in Leviticus and Deuteronomy? ☑
33) What is the purpose of the Global Freedom Network? ☑

# The Start of Jesus's Ministry

In this section, the <u>numbers</u> in the <u>subheadings</u> give the <u>reference</u> for the Gospel extract you need to study.

## John the Baptist Baptised People in the **River Jordan (1:1-8)**

1) Mark <u>doesn't</u> have any stories about <u>Jesus's birth</u> — he starts with the story of <u>John the Baptist</u>.

2) Mark quotes from the Old Testament, where God says he will send a messenger to "Prepare the way for the Lord" (Mark 1:3 NIV). Mark says that <u>John</u> was this messenger, preparing for the coming Messiah.

3) John baptised people in the <u>River Jordan</u> by <u>total immersion</u>. The water symbolises being <u>cleansed</u> of their sins — they had <u>repented</u> and now wanted to live <u>good</u> lives. The River Jordan was also <u>symbolic</u> to these people — in the Old Testament, the <u>Israelites</u> crossed the River Jordan to enter the <u>Promised Land</u>. The people baptised in the river by John entered the new 'Promised Land' of <u>God's kingdom</u>.

4) John predicted someone <u>greater</u> would come to <u>baptise</u> people, this time with the Holy Spirit.

> "After me comes the one more powerful than I, the straps of whose sandals I am not worthy to stoop down and untie. I baptise you with water, but he will baptise you with the Holy Spirit." Mark 1:7-8 NIV

5) The Old Testament prophet <u>Joel</u> had predicted the <u>Holy Spirit</u> would be present on <u>Earth</u> when the <u>Messiah</u> came (Joel 2). So John was saying the <u>Messiah</u> was coming — this Messiah was <u>Jesus</u>.

## Jesus was **Baptised** by John and **Tempted** by Satan **(1:9-13)**

1) <u>Jesus</u> was <u>baptised</u> in the River Jordan by John — this marked the <u>beginning</u> of Jesus's <u>ministry</u>. The <u>Holy Spirit</u> appeared as Jesus was being baptised.

> "...he saw heaven being torn open and the Spirit descending on him like a dove." Mark 1:10 NIV

2) He heard a <u>voice</u> from <u>heaven</u> saying "You are my Son, whom I love; with you I am well pleased" (Mark 1:11 NIV). God's words show how <u>important</u> Jesus is to him — this was God giving Jesus his <u>mission</u>.

3) Baptism is still <u>important</u> to Christians <u>today</u> — it's how people are <u>welcomed</u> into the <u>Church</u> (see p.12).

4) Then the Holy Spirit made Jesus go out into the <u>desert</u>:

> "...he was in the wilderness for forty days, being tempted by Satan... angels attended him." Mark 1:13 NIV

5) Jesus was being <u>tested</u> — Satan, God's <u>archenemy</u>, was trying to make Jesus <u>sin</u> and <u>go against</u> God. But Jesus didn't <u>give in</u> to Satan, which shows his <u>power</u>. God's love for Jesus is demonstrated by the way he sent his <u>messengers</u>, the <u>angels</u>, to <u>care</u> for him.

6) Christians believe they also will be <u>tested</u> and <u>tempted</u>. But with <u>God's help</u>, they can <u>get through</u> it just like Jesus did. Christians remember Jesus's struggle during <u>Lent</u> (see p.16) — a period which tests their ability to <u>overcome temptation</u>.

## Jesus's **Titles** Show How **Important** He Is

1) Mark calls Jesus "the Messiah, the Son of God" (Mark 1:1 NIV). Titles such as these explain his <u>role</u>.

2) By calling Jesus the '<u>Son of God</u>', Mark means Jesus is God's <u>special one</u> — he has a unique <u>relationship</u> to God, and God gave him a unique <u>mission</u>. The title would have stressed Jesus's importance to <u>1st century Jews</u> — it was used in the Old Testament for <u>kings</u>, and also for the whole <u>nation</u> of <u>Israel</u>.

3) <u>Messiah</u> means '<u>anointed one</u>' in Hebrew (Mark also uses '<u>Christ</u>', which is the <u>Greek</u> translation). It also used to be given to the <u>kings</u> of Israel. It later came to mean a <u>heavenly figure</u> who would come to <u>save</u> the <u>Jews</u> from their enemies — Mark believed <u>Jesus</u> was this saviour. The Messiah was often expected as a <u>military figure</u>, but since Jesus wasn't, he didn't <u>specifically</u> use it for <u>himself</u> (see p.144).

---

**EXAM TIP**

### Don't mix up John the Baptist and John the disciple

This section covers the Gospel of Mark in depth, and for the exam you'll need to know the key passages like the back of your hand. So sit down and have a read through them all.

# Jesus's Miracles

At the start of Jesus's ministry, he performed many miracles as he travelled around teaching. You need to be able to recall these miracles as told in St Mark's Gospel and know how they are interpreted by Christians.

## Jesus **Forgave** and **Healed** a Paralysed Man **(2:1-12)**

1) When Jesus was teaching in a crowded house, some men carried a paralysed man to him. Because there were so many people, there was no way in, so they had to find an alternative:

> "...they made an opening in the roof above Jesus... and then lowered the mat the man was lying on. When Jesus saw their faith, he said to the paralysed man, 'Son, your sins are forgiven'. " Mark 2:4-5 NIV

2) Jesus was impressed by their strong faith, but didn't immediately heal the man — he first forgave his sins.
3) There were people there who were shocked by what Jesus did:

> "Why does this fellow talk like that? He's blaspheming! Who can forgive sins but God alone?" Mark 2:7 NIV

4) They believed that only God could forgive sins — Jesus was falsely claiming God's authority.
5) Jesus then healed the man, who was able to walk out of the room. By demonstrating his power through healing, Jesus showed he also must be powerful enough to forgive sins. But to him, forgiving sins was more important.

> "But I want you to know that the Son of Man has authority on earth to forgive sins." Mark 2:10 NIV

6) The people "praised God, saying, 'We have never seen anything like this!' " (Mark 2:12 NIV). They realised that Jesus's power must have come from God. The story shows modern Christians that they must put their faith in Jesus's power.
7) This story can be interpreted in different ways:

- Some people see this story as something that really happened.
- Others interpret it as a metaphor that shows how Jesus is powerful enough to heal people spiritually, freeing them from their sins.
- Some believe that modern faith healers can sometimes cure people who have a strong enough faith.

## Jesus Uses the Title **'Son of Man'** in this Passage

1) The 'Son of Man' is a title that Jesus often uses when referring to himself.
2) There are various interpretations of what the title means:

- Some people believed it shows Jesus's humanity.
- Some believe that in Jesus's language, Aramaic, it was the normal way of talking about yourself, like using 'I'.
- Daniel 7:13-14 talks about the Son of Man as a powerful, heavenly figure.

## Not all Christians believe the same thing about Jesus's miracles

Like other stories in the Bible (e.g. Genesis), the miracles of Jesus are subject to different interpretations. Even Christians that don't believe the miracles occurred exactly as they are written in St Mark's Gospel do believe that they show Jesus was powerful enough to forgive people's sins, and that he was the son of God.

# Jesus's Miracles

Despite performing miracles on his <u>travels</u> and being <u>sought out</u> by <u>people in need</u>, Jesus was <u>rejected</u> in his hometown of <u>Nazareth</u> when he returned.  The people's <u>lack of faith</u> meant he <u>could not</u> perform any miracles there.

## Jesus Brought a Girl **Back to Life** (**5:21-24** and **5:35-43**)

1) <u>Jairus</u>, a synagogue leader, <u>begged</u> Jesus to help his <u>dying daughter</u>:

> "My little daughter is dying.  Please come and put your hands on her so that she will be healed and live" Mark 5:23 NIV

2) But the girl <u>died</u> while Jesus was on his way.  However, Jesus told Jairus to have <u>faith</u>. He'd <u>already</u> shown his faith by going to Jesus, but Jesus <u>encouraged</u> even <u>greater faith</u>.

3) When he saw the girl, "He took her by the hand and said to her... 'Little girl, I say to you, get up!' " (Mark 5:41 NIV).  The girl was brought <u>back to life</u>, and began to <u>move</u> around.  The words 'little girl' are translated from a phrase in Aramaic which literally means '<u>little lamb</u>', showing Jesus's <u>care</u> for the <u>child</u>.

4) Jesus tells them <u>not</u> to mention what had happened.

## Jesus was **Rejected** in his **Hometown** (**6:1-6**)

1) After being away from his hometown of <u>Nazareth</u>, Jesus <u>returned</u> in his new role and started <u>teaching</u> in the synagogue.

2) But the people there knew him as their <u>carpenter</u>, the <u>son of Mary</u>. They <u>didn't believe</u> he could be God's <u>chosen one</u>. ⟶

> "He could not do any miracles there, except lay his hands on a few people who were ill and heal them.  He was amazed at their lack of faith." Mark 6:5-6 NIV

3) Jesus said "A prophet is not without honour except in his own town, among his relatives and in his own home" (Mark 6:4 NIV).

4) Jesus previously said the <u>disciples</u> were his <u>true relatives</u>.  Many Christians were (and sometimes still are) <u>misunderstood</u> and <u>rejected</u> by their <u>families</u>.  They can <u>take heart</u> from the fact it happened to <u>Jesus</u> too.

## Jesus Miraculously **Fed 5000 People** (**6:30-44**)

1) A <u>large crowd</u> followed Jesus to an isolated place, so he decided to <u>teach</u> them. As it got late, Jesus instructed his <u>disciples</u> to <u>feed</u> the people, but they only had <u>five loaves</u> of bread and <u>two fish</u>.

2) Jesus managed to make the little food they have feed <u>everyone</u> — there were at least <u>5000 people</u> there but there was still lots <u>left over</u>.

> "Taking the five loaves and the two fish and looking up to heaven, he gave thanks and broke the loaves.  Then he gave them to his disciples to distribute to the people.  He also divided the two fish among them all." Mark 6:41 NIV

### The **Feeding of the 5000** is **Important** for **Many Reasons**

1) It would have reminded <u>1st century Jews</u> of the Old Testament story where God fed the <u>Israelites</u> on miraculous <u>manna</u> (bread) while they were with <u>Moses</u> in the <u>wilderness</u>.

2) For Christians today, it's a <u>reminder</u> of how Jesus also broke bread at the <u>Last Supper</u> — Christians are <u>fed spiritually</u> by Jesus when they remember this at the <u>Eucharist</u> (see p.146).

3) It also reminds them to have <u>faith</u> that God will <u>look after</u> them.  He can deal with <u>big problems</u> and do great things with the <u>small offerings</u> that they make in their lives.

4) The story appears in <u>all four Gospels</u> — Christians think this makes it likely that it's <u>true</u>.

**EXAM TIP** | **Learn the names of the people and places in these stories**
It's important to be able to recall them, as 1-mark multiple choice questions might ask about them.

# Jesus's Miracles

In St Mark's Gospel, Jesus performed one <u>last miracle</u> before his crucifixion in Jerusalem.

## Jesus **Restored Sight** to a Blind Man **(10:46-52)**

1) <u>Jesus</u> and his <u>followers</u> came across <u>Bartimaeus</u>, a blind man, <u>begging</u> at the side of the road.

2) He called out "Jesus, Son of David, have mercy on me!" (Mark 10:47 NIV) and told Jesus he wanted to be able to <u>see</u>. Jesus <u>healed</u> him:

> " 'Go... your faith has healed you.' Immediately he received his sight and followed Jesus along the road" Mark 10:52 NIV

3) Bartimaeus <u>threw away</u> his <u>cloak</u> before going to Jesus. He would have used it to <u>catch coins</u> that people tossed to him, so he <u>abandoned</u> his means of <u>livelihood</u> to <u>follow</u> Jesus, just like the <u>other disciples</u>. This reminds Christians today that they should <u>focus</u> more on their <u>faith</u> than on worldly goods.

4) Many Christians interpret this story as meaning that they're <u>spiritually blind</u> without Jesus, but if they have <u>faith</u> and <u>follow</u> him, their <u>eyes</u> will be <u>opened</u> to how they should <u>live</u> their lives.

### The Title **'Son of David'** is Used in this Passage

The title '<u>Son of David</u>' has multiple meanings:

- David was the greatest of the <u>kings</u> of Israel in the <u>Old Testament</u>, so people who used this title saw Jesus as a new king who would <u>rule justly</u>, like David did.
- Also, the <u>Messiah</u> was <u>prophesied</u> to be David's <u>descendant</u>, so by using this title, people <u>acknowledge</u> Jesus as the Messiah.

### The **Miracle Stories** Tell Us a Lot **About Jesus**

1) The <u>miracles</u> in Mark's Gospel show how Jesus had <u>God's power</u>. They also show his <u>compassion</u> for people who were suffering or in need.

2) Although Mark focuses on <u>Jesus's actions</u> in these stories, they also show Jesus as a <u>popular teacher</u>. Mark portrays how Jesus <u>travelled</u> around teaching, usually attracting <u>huge crowds</u>.

3) The miracle stories can be interpreted in different ways:

- Some Christians believe Jesus's miracles <u>actually happened</u>. Others think they're <u>metaphors</u> that <u>symbolise</u> a <u>spiritual truth</u>.
- Some Christians accept <u>both</u> meanings.
- Non-religious people would say they just <u>didn't happen</u>, or that there are ways to <u>explain</u> the events <u>rationally</u> using <u>science</u>.

## Learn this and you won't need a miracle to pass the exam

These stories show Christians how they should follow Jesus and have faith in their everyday lives. Jot down a quick summary of each miracle, and why they're important for modern-day Christians. Don't forget to include the names of the people and places involved in each of the miracles.

# The Later Ministry of Jesus

It's not until the second half of Mark's Gospel that Jesus is recognised as the Messiah.

## Jesus was Declared the Messiah and Predicted his Death (8:27-33)

1) This is an important turning point in Mark's Gospel. Jesus's ministry in Galilee had finished, and he was starting to move towards Jerusalem, where he knew he would die.

2) Jesus and his disciples were travelling near the town Caesarea Philippi when he asked them, "Who do people say I am?". They told him: "Some say John the Baptist; others say Elijah; and still others, one of the prophets" (Mark 8:27-28 NIV). John the Baptist had been executed, so some people thought he'd come back from the dead in Jesus.

3) So far, no one had said that Jesus was the Messiah. But when Jesus asked his disciples who he was, Peter replied: "You are the Messiah" (Mark 8:29 NIV).

4) But Peter had misunderstood Jesus's real mission — he may have thought the Messiah would be a political or military figure (see p.140).

5) Jesus then tells them about how he would suffer and die ➝ — but would come back to life.

> "...the Son of Man must suffer many things and be rejected by the elders, the chief priests and the teachers of the law... he must be killed and after three days rise again." Mark 8:31 NIV

6) Peter told him off. He thought it was impossible for the Messiah to die, so Jesus must be wrong.

7) Jesus replied: " 'Get behind me, Satan! ... You do not have in mind the concerns of God, but merely human concerns' " (Mark 8:33 NIV). Jesus was criticising Peter for trying to tempt him away from his true mission from God, just as Satan had tempted Jesus in the wilderness. However, God's plan for salvation involved Jesus being crucified.

## Jesus's True Nature was Shown to the Disciples (9:2-9)

1) Jesus went up a mountain with Peter, James and John — the three disciples he was closest to. Then, his appearance changed:

> "His clothes became dazzling white... And there appeared before them Elijah and Moses, who were talking with Jesus." Mark 9:3-4 NIV

2) This is called 'the transfiguration'. The disciples were shown the true divine nature behind Jesus's normal appearance.

3) Elijah and Moses were two of the greatest figures of the Old Testament. Moses gave Jews the Law and Elijah was the greatest of the Prophets. The way that they appeared with Jesus showed he was the Messiah in the Old Testament prophecies.

4) God spoke: "...a cloud appeared and covered them, and a voice came from the cloud: 'This is my son, whom I love. Listen to him!' " (Mark 9:7 NIV). This demonstrates how important Jesus's words were.

5) On the way down, Jesus forbade them to speak about it until he had come back from the dead.

6) The story reveals just how important Jesus was, and the power that God had given him.

## The Messianic Secret is a Big Part of Mark's Gospel

1) Jesus told his disciples not to tell anyone that he was the Messiah. The real nature of Jesus's messiahship is only truly understood after the resurrection — this is the Messianic Secret in Mark.

2) This has many parts. For example, Jesus told people not to talk about the miracles he performed, and his teachings in the form of parables could be difficult to understand (see p.153-154).

3) He may have wanted to keep his messiahship a secret in case it was misunderstood.

---

## Jesus predicted his own suffering, death and resurrection

Try to come up with two reasons why Peter was angry when Jesus told the disciples he would die.

# The Later Ministry of Jesus

Although Jesus tried to keep it a <u>secret</u>, by the time he got to <u>Jerusalem</u>, people were calling him the <u>Messiah</u>.

## Jesus Predicted his **Death** and **Resurrection Again** (10:32-34)

1) While going to <u>Jerusalem</u>, Jesus <u>again</u> told the disciples he would be <u>killed</u>, but would <u>rise</u> from the <u>grave</u>.

> "...the Son of Man will be delivered over to the chief priests and the teachers of the law. They will condemn him to death and will hand him over to the Gentiles, who will mock him and spit on him, flog him and kill him. Three days later he will rise." Mark 10:33-34 NIV

This was one of his 'passion predictions' — Jesus's suffering and death are called the 'passion'.

2) This was the <u>third time</u> he predicted his death — he gave <u>more detail</u> than before.

3) The <u>Gentiles</u> were the <u>Romans</u> — the Jews couldn't <u>execute</u> people because the Romans <u>ruled</u> over them, so they would have to <u>give</u> Jesus to the Romans.

4) The things Jesus predicted later <u>happened</u> (see p.146-148). Mark presents the events as the <u>fulfilment</u> of Jesus's <u>prophecy</u>, and as part of the <u>divine plan</u>.

5) The <u>crucifixion</u> came as a devastating <u>shock</u> to the disciples. But eventually they came to understand that it was an <u>essential</u> part of <u>God's plan</u>, not a defeat. Mark shows that Jesus <u>understood</u> this <u>in advance</u> and continued to Jerusalem despite <u>knowing</u> what awaited him.

## Jesus Told his Disciples about **Serving Others** (10:35-45)

1) <u>James</u> and <u>John</u> asked to sit on Jesus's <u>right</u> and <u>left sides</u> when he returned to <u>heaven</u> in <u>glory</u>. They wanted to be the <u>closest</u> to Jesus, and the <u>most important</u>.

2) Jesus asked if they would go through the <u>trials</u> he'd suffer: "Can you drink the cup I drink..." (Mark 10:38 NIV). They said yes. Jesus said they'd <u>suffer</u>, but the <u>places</u> by his side were <u>decided by God</u>.

3) The <u>other disciples</u> were <u>angry</u> that James and John wanted to be more important than them. Jesus said:

> "...whoever wants to become great among you must be your servant, and whoever wants to be first must be slave of all. For even the Son of Man did not come to be served, but to serve, and to give his life as a ransom for many." Mark 10:43-45 NIV

4) Only people who were <u>humble</u> and <u>served others</u> on Earth would be <u>rewarded</u> in <u>heaven</u>. Jesus would later serve <u>humanity</u> by dying so that they would be <u>reconciled</u> with God (see p.8).

5) Many Christians try to <u>serve</u> others, e.g. through their <u>job</u> or by <u>dedicating</u> themselves to the <u>Church</u>.

## Jesus Entered Jerusalem as a **New King** (11:1-11)

1) Jesus and his disciples were getting <u>near</u> to <u>Jerusalem</u> — the <u>holy city</u> where <u>David</u> and the other kings had reigned. Jesus told two disciples to bring him a young <u>donkey</u> (a colt), which Jesus rode.

2) In the Old Testament, the <u>Messiah</u> was predicted to enter Jerusalem on a <u>donkey</u> (Zechariah 9:9). Riding in on a donkey showed Jesus's <u>humility</u> and <u>peaceful</u> nature, something Christians should try to <u>follow</u>.

3) Some people laid <u>cloaks</u> and <u>branches</u> across Jesus's path, which showed how <u>respected</u> he was. As he rode into Jerusalem, they cried "Hosanna! Blessed is he who comes in the name of the Lord! Blessed is the coming kingdom of our father David!" (Mark 11:9-10 NIV). Hosanna means '<u>save now</u>' — the people of Jerusalem believed that Jesus was the <u>Messiah</u>, and was there to <u>help</u> them.

4) Jesus is celebrated as David's successor — the new <u>messianic king</u>. This follows straight after Bartimaeus called him 'Son of David' (see p.143).

5) Christians remember this event on <u>Palm Sunday</u>, named after the branches people used. They're reminded of how Jesus was <u>proclaimed</u> as the <u>saviour</u>, and also of his <u>humility</u>. But Christians today <u>know</u> how the crowd soon <u>turned against</u> Jesus. They must be <u>careful</u> to keep their <u>faith</u> in him.

### You'll need to know the order of these events
Summarise the events of the later stages of Jesus's ministry, and include references to Mark's Gospel.

# The Final Days in Jerusalem

Jesus had arrived in <u>Jerusalem</u>, and he knew that this was where he would be <u>betrayed</u> by one of his disciples.

## Jesus Ate with his Disciples at the **Last Supper** (14:12-26)

1) Jesus and the disciples ate the <u>Passover meal</u> (see p.52) together — this is known as the <u>Last Supper</u>. Passover is the Jewish festival that <u>remembers</u> the Jews' <u>escape</u> from <u>slavery</u> in Egypt. Christians believe that the death of Jesus also <u>rescues</u> people from sin and death.

2) At the meal, Jesus predicted that one of the disciples would <u>betray</u> him: "Truly I tell you, one of you will betray me — one who is eating with me" (Mark 14:18 NIV). They all denied it.

3) He <u>divided</u> up some <u>bread</u> and passed it to <u>everyone</u>, saying, "Take it; this is my body" (Mark 14:22 NIV). Then he <u>passed</u> around a cup of <u>wine</u>, saying "This is my blood of the covenant, which is poured out for many" (Mark 14:24 NIV). It <u>reflected</u> how Jesus's <u>body</u> would be broken, like the bread, and his <u>blood</u> shed at the <u>crucifixion</u>. 'Covenant' referred to the <u>agreement</u> God made with the <u>Jews</u> in the <u>Old Testament</u> (see p.41). Jesus was saying that his <u>life</u> and <u>death</u> created a <u>new relationship</u> with God.

4) Jesus's actions are still very important to Christians today — they re-enact them in the Eucharist. But there are different beliefs about what Jesus's words meant:

   - Some believe the <u>bread</u> and <u>wine</u> had <u>literally</u> become his <u>body</u> and <u>blood</u>.
   - Others think he meant that they just <u>represented</u> them.

   This is why the <u>Eucharist</u> is celebrated in different ways — read the <u>first section of p.14</u> for more about this.

5) Jesus also said, "...I will not drink again from the fruit of the vine until that day when I drink it new in the kingdom of God" (Mark 14:25 NIV). He knew that his <u>death</u> was <u>near</u>.

## Jesus was **Arrested** in the Garden of **Gethsemane** (14:32-52)

1) Jesus told the disciples to <u>keep watch</u> as he <u>prayed</u> in the <u>Garden of Gethsemane</u>, but they fell asleep.

2) Jesus asked <u>God</u> if he could <u>avoid</u> what was coming, but then he <u>submitted</u> to <u>God's will</u>.

> "Abba, Father... everything is possible for you. Take this cup from me. Yet not what I will, but what you will." Mark 14:36 NIV

   - Jesus was <u>afraid</u> to go through with the <u>suffering</u> ahead — this shows that he was a real <u>human being</u>. But his <u>obedience</u> to God is an <u>example</u> for Christians.
   - Early Christians followed his example in <u>trusting God</u>, even when <u>persecuted</u>.

3) Then <u>Judas</u> (one of the disciples) arrived with the chief priests' <u>armed men</u>. He <u>betrayed</u> Jesus with a <u>kiss</u>: "The one I kiss is the man; arrest him and lead him away under guard" (Mark 14:44 NIV). Jesus was placed under <u>arrest</u> by the men.

4) One of the <u>disciples</u> "drew his sword and struck the servant of the high priest, cutting off his ear" (Mark 14:47 NIV). Then, the disciples all <u>ran away</u>.

5) Jesus <u>questioned</u> why he was being <u>captured</u> — he asked if they thought he was leading a <u>rebellion</u>, which he <u>wasn't</u>. But he said, "the Scriptures must be fulfilled" (Mark 14:49 NIV).

---

REVISION TASK

## This was just the beginning of Jesus's suffering

Write a summary of the events that took place at the Last Supper and in the Garden of Gethsemane and explain why Jesus's actions leading up to his arrest are important for modern-day Christians.

# The Final Days in Jerusalem

Jesus was tried by the Jewish authorities who believed he had committed blasphemy by claiming to be God's son.

## Jesus was **Tried** by the **Jewish Authorities (14:53, 57-65)**

1) Jesus was tried before the Jewish high priest. The high priest asked him:

> "Are you the Messiah, the Son of the Blessed One?" Mark 14:61 NIV

2) Jesus replied:
> "I am... And you will see the Son of Man sitting at the right hand of the Mighty One and coming on the clouds of heaven" Mark 14:62 NIV

3) Witnesses gave false evidence against him, and their stories didn't agree. But Jesus was found guilty of blasphemy (because they believed he was falsely claiming to be divine) — a crime carrying the death penalty. He had to be handed to the Romans for his punishment.

## Jesus was Sentenced to **Death** by the **Roman Governor (15:1-15)**

1) Jesus was tried before the Roman governor, Pilate, the next day.
2) Blasphemy wasn't a crime to the Romans, but he could have been a political threat.
3) Pilate asked Jesus if he was the king of the Jews. He answered "You have said so" (Mark 15:2 NIV). He didn't defend himself — he submitted to God's plan.
4) Pilate realised Jesus wasn't really a threat — the priests had handed him over because they didn't like him. Since a prisoner was released every Passover, Pilate offered to release Jesus.
5) But the chief priests got the people to ask for Barabbas, a murderer, instead. When Pilate asked about Jesus they said "Crucify him!" (Mark 15:13 NIV). So Jesus was flogged and sent to be crucified.

## Jesus was **Crucified, Died** and was **Buried (15:21-47)**

1) Simon of Cyrene was made to carry Jesus's cross to Golgotha ('the place of the skull').

> Jesus was put on the cross at 9 am. A sign saying why he was being crucified said "The King of the Jews" (Mark 15:26 NIV).

> Jesus was mocked while on the cross: "Let this Messiah, this king of Israel, come down now from the cross, that we may see and believe" (Mark 15:32 NIV).

> It became dark at midday, showing the significance of Jesus's suffering. At 3 pm, Jesus shouted "My God, my God, why have you forsaken me?" (Mark 15:34 NIV) — he felt abandoned by God. He then died.

2) As Jesus died, the temple curtain ripped in two. This curtain hid the Holy of Holies — a special room inside the temple where God was believed to be present, and only the high priest could enter. This showed that everyone now had access to God.
3) The Roman soldier who saw Jesus die said "Surely this man was the Son of God!" (Mark 15:39 NIV). He recognised who Jesus was, but the Jewish leaders didn't.
4) Joseph of Arimathea was given Jesus's body by Pilate. He "bought some linen cloth, took down the body, wrapped it in the linen, and placed it in a tomb cut out of rock" (Mark 15:46 NIV).
5) Many Christians believe that Jesus's death saved mankind and repaired the relationship with God. But there are various views about the crucifixion — read the first section of p.8 for more detail.

# The Final Days in Jerusalem

Shortly after his death, Jesus's body <u>disappeared</u> from his <u>tomb</u> — Christians believe he was <u>resurrected</u> by God. This is a <u>very important</u> belief for Christians as it shows Jesus really was the <u>Son of God</u> and that he <u>conquered death</u>.

## Jesus's Tomb was Found Empty (16:1-8)

On the <u>Sunday morning</u> after Jesus's death:

1) <u>Mary Magdalene</u>, <u>Mary</u> (the mother of James) and <u>Salome</u> went to visit Jesus's tomb with "spices so that they might... anoint Jesus's body" (Mark 16:1 NIV), but they found the stone <u>rolled back</u> and the tomb <u>empty</u>.

2) There they saw a <u>man</u> in white (an <u>angel</u>). He told them: "He has risen! He is not here" (Mark 16:6 NIV).

3) The angel told them to tell the disciples that Jesus would meet them in <u>Galilee</u>. → "But go, tell his disciples... 'He is going ahead of you into Galilee. There you will see him, just as he told you.' " Mark 16:7 NIV

4) The women left the tomb, <u>frightened</u> and <u>confused</u> by what they saw, so they <u>didn't</u> tell anyone about it.

Some early Bibles <u>finish</u> the story <u>here</u> (at the end of verse 8), but later copies added <u>reports</u> of encounters Jesus's followers had with him after he'd been <u>resurrected</u>:

"When Jesus rose early on the first day of the week, he appeared first to Mary Magdalene" Mark 16:9 NIV

"Afterwards, Jesus appeared in a different form to two of them while they were walking in the country." Mark 16:12 NIV

"Later Jesus appeared to the Eleven as they were eating... He said to them, 'Go into all the world and preach the gospel to all creation.' " Mark 16:14-15 NIV

## Christians Believe in Jesus's Resurrection

1) The resurrection turned <u>despair</u> to <u>hope</u> for the disciples. Everything <u>hadn't</u> gone <u>wrong</u> — the crucifixion was part of <u>God's plan</u>.

2) The resurrection is <u>important</u> to Christians for many reasons — read the <u>first</u> section of p.7. It shows that <u>Jesus</u> really is <u>God's son</u>. It would also have given persecuted early Christians hope that there was something else beyond their suffering.

3) However, many people believe the resurrection is <u>scientifically impossible</u> — they explain the <u>empty tomb</u> in <u>other ways</u>. But those who <u>believe</u> in the resurrection have arguments <u>against</u> these explanations.

- Some say the women got the <u>wrong tomb</u>.
- But Mark 15:47 says Mary Magdalene <u>saw</u> the <u>tomb</u> where Joseph laid Jesus's body.

- Others say Jesus <u>wasn't</u> really <u>dead</u>.
- But at Pilate's request, a <u>soldier confirmed</u> he had died (Mark 15:44-45).

- Some think the disciples <u>stole</u> the <u>body</u>.
- But why would the <u>terrified</u> disciples <u>risk</u> their <u>lives</u> for a dead body?

## You need to know what happens in Jesus's final days

You also need to know what these events mean for different Christians. Some things, like what Jesus says and does at the Last Supper, are interpreted in various ways, so learn all these differences.

# Worked Exam Questions

That's all you need to know for Theme G, so now it's time to try out some exam-style questions.
Take a look at the questions that have already been completed on this page before having a go at the rest.

1   Which of the following is the person Jairus asked Jesus to heal?
    Put a tick (✓) in the correct box.

    A   His daughter   ✓

    B   His son   ☐

    C   His mother   ☐

    D   His wife   ☐

*[1 mark]*

2   Which of the following was **not** one of the replies given by the disciples when
    Jesus asked them who people said he was?  Put a tick (✓) in the correct box.

    A   Moses   ✓

    B   John the Baptist   ☐

    C   One of the prophets   ☐

    D   Elijah   ☐

*[1 mark]*

3   Give two things that happened at the Last Supper.

    1) Jesus predicted that one of the disciples would betray him.

    2) Jesus said that the bread is his body and the wine is his blood.

*[2 marks]*

4   Explain two reasons why the events in the Garden of Gethsemane are important for Christians.
    Your answer should refer to Mark's Gospel.

    While praying in the Garden of Gethsemane, Jesus asks God to "Take this cup from me"

    (Mark 14:36 NIV).  This brief weakness shows Jesus's humanity, and helps Christians who are

    suffering to remember that Jesus also suffered.

    Afterwards, Jesus submits to God's will — this teaches Christians that no matter what they

    are going through, they must trust in God's will.

*[5 marks]*

# Exam Questions

**5** Which of the following is the name of the man who baptised Jesus?
Put a tick (✓) in the correct box.

**A** John ☐

**B** Mark ☐

**C** Isaiah ☐

**D** Joel ☐

*[1 mark]*

**6** Which of the following is **not** one of the women who discovered Jesus's empty tomb?
Put a tick (✓) in the correct box.

**A** Salome ☐

**B** Mary Magdalene ☐

**C** Bethany ☐

**D** Mary, mother of James ☐

*[1 mark]*

**7** Give two things that Jesus predicted about his own future in Mark's Gospel.

**1)** ...................................................................................................................................

.........................................................................................................................................

**2)** ...................................................................................................................................

.........................................................................................................................................

*[2 marks]*

**8** Explain two ways in which the story of Jesus healing the paralysed man is
important to Christians today. Your answer should refer to Mark's Gospel.

.............................................................................................................................................

.............................................................................................................................................

.............................................................................................................................................

.............................................................................................................................................

.............................................................................................................................................

.............................................................................................................................................

.............................................................................................................................................

*[5 marks]*

# Exam Questions

**9** Which of the following happened just after Jesus died on the cross?
Put a tick (✓) in the correct box.

**A** Jesus rose from the dead ☐

**B** The temple curtain ripped ☐

**C** A Roman soldier mocked Jesus ☐

**D** Mary Magdalene began to weep ☐

*[1 mark]*

**10** Give two events that happened at the transfiguration.

**1)** ...........................................................................................................................

...........................................................................................................................

**2)** ...........................................................................................................................

...........................................................................................................................

*[2 marks]*

**11** Explain two contrasting Christian views about the significance of Jesus's crucifixion.

...........................................................................................................................

...........................................................................................................................

...........................................................................................................................

...........................................................................................................................

...........................................................................................................................

...........................................................................................................................

*[4 marks]*

**12** 'The story of Jesus's baptism is the most important story in Mark's Gospel.'    (SPaG MARKS)

Evaluate this statement. Your answer should include the following:
• references to Mark's Gospel
• arguments that support the statement
• arguments that disagree with the statement
• a conclusion.

*Write your answer on a separate sheet of paper.*

*[12 marks]*

# Revision Summary

Now you know all about <u>St Mark's Gospel: the Life of Jesus</u>, test your knowledge with the questions below.

- Try these questions and <u>tick off each one</u> when you <u>get it right</u>.
- When you've done <u>all the questions</u> for a topic and are <u>completely happy</u> with it, tick off the topic.

## The Start of Jesus's Ministry (p.140) ☑

1) What did the water of the River Jordan symbolise to the people who were baptised in it? ☑
2) Which Old Testament prophet predicted the Holy Spirit would come to Earth with the Messiah? ☑
3) For how many days did Jesus remain in the desert being tempted by Satan? ☑
4) Why was the title 'Son of God' special? ☑
5) What does the term 'Messiah' mean? ☑

## Jesus's Miracles (p.141-143) ☑

6) What impressed Jesus about those who brought the paralysed man to him? ☑
7) Before healing him, what did Jesus do for the paralysed man? ☑
8) Give two meanings of the title 'Son of Man'. ☑
9) After bringing the little girl back to life, Jesus told Jairus not to mention what had happened. True or false? ☑
10) What did Jesus do when he returned to his hometown of Nazareth? ☑
11) What Old Testament story did the feeding of the 5000 remind 1st century Jews of? ☑
12) What is often cited as evidence that the story of the feeding of the 5000 is true? ☑
13) What was the name of the blind man cured by Jesus? ☑
14) What does the throwing away of the blind man's coat after he was cured symbolise? ☑
15) Give one way in which the miracle stories are interpreted. ☑

## The Later Ministry of Jesus (p.144-145) ☑

16) Which disciple said that Jesus was the Messiah? ☑
17) Why did Jesus compare Peter to Satan? ☑
18) Describe the transfiguration of Jesus witnessed by Peter, James and John. ☑
19) Why might Jesus have wanted to keep his messiahship secret? ☑
20) Where were Jesus and his disciples when he predicted his death for the third time? ☑
21) Which two disciples asked to sit by Jesus's side when he returned to glory in heaven? ☑
22) Describe Jesus's entry into Jerusalem. ☑

## The Final Days in Jerusalem (p.146-148) ☑

23) What food and drink did Jesus pass round at the Last Supper? ☑
24) How did Judas identify Jesus to the guards that arrested him? ☑
25) Where was Jesus arrested? ☑
26) What crime was Jesus found guilty of by the Jewish high priest? ☑
27) What was the name of the Roman governor who sentenced Jesus to death? ☑
28) Why was Barabbas, the murderer, released instead of Jesus? ☑
29) What did the ripping of the temple curtain as Jesus died symbolise? ☑
30) Why did the three women visit Jesus's tomb? ☑
31) Why is the resurrection important to Christians? ☑
32) Give one alternative non-religious explanation for why Jesus's tomb was found empty. ☑

# The Kingdom of God

This section looks at Mark's Gospel and the kingdom of God, 1st century society, faith and discipleship.

## The **Kingdom of God** can have **Different Meanings**

1) The kingdom of God is the time and place where God rules.
   People will follow God's will and live according to it.

> The Lord's Prayer says "your kingdom come, your will be
> done, on earth as it is in heaven" (Matthew 6:10 NIV).

2) It was a central part of Jesus's preaching. He explained that:

> "The time has come... The kingdom of God has come near.
> Repent and believe the good news!" Mark 1:15 NIV

3) Kingdom of God' refers to different times and places in different passages of the Gospel.

4) The kingdom might exist as a state of being within the hearts and minds of individuals, or in the love and care shown within the community of believers. This applies both to Jesus's disciples and Christians now.

5) It can also refer to a physical kingdom in the future — God will establish a kingdom throughout the world, when Jesus returns in the Second Coming and the Last Judgement takes place (see p.5). Some think it may have already partly arrived in Jesus's healings and exorcisms (they show God's rule over sin and evil) but is still to arrive fully.

> Jesus explained what the kingdom of God is like by using parables — a parable
> is a story about everyday life which contains a message about spiritual truth.

## Parable of the **Sower** — People **React Differently (4:1-9, 14-20)**

1) Jesus told a story about a farmer who went to sow seeds in his field, and the seeds fell in different places. What happens to the seeds represents how people respond differently to Jesus's teaching.

> Some of the seed "fell along the path, and the birds came and ate it up"
> (Mark 4:4 NIV). The birds are a metaphor for Satan — it's easy for him to make
> people forget Jesus's teaching. These people hear the teaching, but don't act on it.

> Some fell where there was little soil. Although they quickly grew, they died from
> exposure to the hot sun: "they withered because they had no root" (Mark 4:6 NIV).
> This represents people who accept Jesus's message, but give up when things get difficult.

> Some "fell among thorns, which grew up and choked the plants, so that they
> did not bear grain" (Mark 4:7 NIV). These symbolise people who accept
> Jesus's message, but get distracted by other things, e.g. money and greed.

> Some seed "fell on good soil. It came up, grew and produced a crop..." (Mark 4:8 NIV).
> This group refers to people who understand Jesus's teaching, and try to live their lives by it.

2) Jesus told the disciples that "The secret of the kingdom of God has been given to you" (Mark 4:11 NIV). The parable shows that the kingdom of God is present through people who follow Jesus's teaching. It encourages Christians to spread Jesus's message, but to accept that people won't always respond.

## Parables are stories Jesus told to teach people moral lessons

The parable of the sower is about how different people respond to Jesus's message. It's an important parable, so make sure you spend some time reading over it to make sure you understand it fully.

# The Kingdom of God

Jesus taught people to <u>focus less</u> on <u>material things</u> so they could be a part of the kingdom of God.

## Parable of the **Growing Seed** — Symbol of the **Kingdom (4:26-29)**

1) Jesus told people that the <u>kingdom of God</u> was like a <u>farmer</u> who sows <u>seed</u> in a field.

> "Night and day... the seed sprouts and grows, though he does not know how. All by itself the soil produces corn — first the stalk, then the ear, then the full grain in the ear. As soon as the corn is ripe, he puts the sickle to it, because the harvest has come." Mark 4:27-29 NIV

2) The parable explains that the kingdom of God <u>grows</u> in a <u>mysterious way</u>. Christians might <u>not</u> understand <u>how</u> God is working, but they can be <u>confident</u> that he <u>is</u>.

3) The <u>harvest</u> represents <u>judgement</u> at the end of time — when the kingdom of God will be <u>fully established</u>. Those who've <u>followed</u> God's ways will be <u>harvested</u> to <u>live</u> in the kingdom of God.

## Parable of the **Mustard Seed** — the **Kingdom** would **Grow (4:30-32)**

1) Jesus explained that the <u>kingdom of God</u> "is like a mustard seed, which is the smallest of all seeds on earth. Yet when planted, it grows and becomes the largest of all garden plants... the birds can perch in its shade" (Mark 4:31-32 NIV).

2) Jesus was describing how the kingdom of God would <u>grow</u>. The parable portrays the kingdom as a <u>community</u>, rather than just <u>individuals</u> — it started with <u>Jesus</u>, but expanded to his <u>first followers</u> and then <u>thousands</u> of Christians.

3) <u>Early Christians</u> found this <u>encouraging</u>. Although there weren't many of them, it told them one day their <u>movement</u> would be <u>great</u>. <u>Birds</u> were a Jewish symbol for <u>Gentiles</u> (non-Jews), so it also encouraged them to look for <u>converts</u> in the Gentile world too.

4) Some <u>modern Christians</u> think the <u>big plant</u> refers to the <u>Church</u>. The Church is a large community which provides <u>care</u> and <u>protection</u> to anyone who needs it — like a large plant does to birds. Many believe it should work to <u>create</u> the kingdom of God on <u>Earth</u>.

## A Rich Man is **Unwilling** to **Give Up** his **Possessions (10:17-27)**

1) A <u>rich man</u> asked Jesus what he must do to get <u>eternal life</u>. Jesus reminded him of the <u>Ten Commandments</u>, but the man explained that he <u>already</u> followed them.

2) Jesus told him to "sell everything you have and give to the poor, and you will have treasure in heaven. Then come, follow me" (Mark 10:21 NIV). This may mean follow his <u>teachings</u> — or leave his home and join Jesus, <u>travelling</u> around spreading God's word.

3) The man left in <u>despair</u> because he <u>couldn't</u> bear to do that.

4) Jesus said to his disciples that it's very <u>difficult</u> for the <u>rich</u> to get into the <u>kingdom of God</u>:

> "It is easier for a camel to go through the eye of a needle than for someone who is rich to enter the kingdom of God." Mark 10:25 NIV

5) The 'eye' of a needle is the <u>small hole</u> which the <u>thread</u> is put through when sewing, so the saying means it's <u>almost impossible</u> for rich people to be <u>saved</u>. But Jesus does also say "all things are possible with God" (Mark 10:27 NIV).

6) 'The eye of the needle' may have been a <u>narrow gate</u> in <u>Jerusalem</u>. Camels loaded with goods needed to be <u>unloaded</u> to <u>pass</u> through. So <u>rich people</u> have to shed their <u>possessions</u> before they can enter the <u>kingdom of God</u>, like a camel had to shed its load to enter Jerusalem.

---

**EXAM TIP**

### Different Christians interpret Jesus's parables in different ways

For all parables in this section, make sure you understand the meaning behind each one, and what they meant for people back in the time of Jesus, and Christians in the present day.

---

Theme H — St Mark's Gospel as a Source of Religious, Moral and Spiritual Truths

# The Kingdom of God

Jesus's teachings on <u>wealth</u>, like many of his teachings, were <u>contrary</u> to what was generally believed <u>at the time</u>.

## Jesus's Teaching on **Wealth** was **Very Surprising**

Jesus's teaching on wealth surprised <u>1st century Jews</u>. They believed that <u>wealth</u> was a sign of <u>God's approval</u>. But Jesus saw wealth as an <u>obstacle</u> to <u>serving God</u> fully — his disciples <u>left</u> their <u>homes</u> and <u>possessions</u> behind to follow him.

<u>Modern Christians</u> interpret Jesus's teaching in a variety of ways:

- <u>Monks</u> and <u>nuns</u> take the teaching quite <u>literally</u> — they <u>give up</u> all their possessions and take a vow of <u>poverty</u>.

- Many think it means people shouldn't be too <u>attached</u> to <u>money</u> or <u>possessions</u>, but should <u>give generously</u> to those in need.

- Some think that Jesus's words about wealth <u>only</u> applied to <u>that man</u> — other people have <u>different problems</u> to overcome. The key point is that <u>God</u> must be <u>first</u> in your life — not money or anything else.

- Some say it only applied to the <u>time</u> when <u>Jesus lived</u>. Giving away all your money is <u>unrealistic</u> now when people need money to buy even the <u>basics</u>. In the <u>1st century</u>, people were more <u>self-sufficient</u>.

- Others suggest the teaching is just <u>wrong</u>. If everyone gave everything away, <u>society</u> would <u>collapse</u>. It also would mean <u>neglecting</u> your duty to your <u>family</u>.

## Jesus **Welcomes Young Children** Despite Opposition (**10:13-16**)

1) People took their <u>children</u> to see <u>Jesus</u> so he could <u>bless</u> them. The <u>disciples</u> tried to <u>stop</u> it, but Jesus <u>overruled</u> them, saying:

> "Let the little children come to me, and do not hinder them, for the kingdom of God belongs to such as these. Truly I tell you, anyone who will not receive the kingdom of God like a little child will never enter it." Mark 10:14-15 NIV

2) He meant that the <u>kingdom of God</u> was for people who accepted it with <u>childlike joy</u> — people who are completely <u>open</u> to embracing <u>new things</u>.

3) The kingdom here is a <u>present reality</u> in the <u>hearts</u> and <u>minds</u> of individuals who apply Jesus's teaching.

4) This encourages modern Christians to <u>accept</u> Jesus's <u>message</u> in this way, and to treat children with <u>love</u>.

## Christians each live by Jesus's teachings in their own way

There are a lot of different ways that Jesus's teachings can be interpreted, and various ways Christians choose to live by them. Cover the page and try to write down as many different ways that Christians use Jesus's teachings on wealth to help them live their lives as you can remember.

# The Kingdom of God

Jesus instructed his disciples to <u>love</u> other people.  Not just their friends — <u>everyone</u>.

## Love **God** and Love **Other People** (12:28-34)

1) The <u>Torah</u> (Jewish sacred text) contains hundreds of <u>commandments</u> (including the Ten Commandments).

2) A teacher of religion asked Jesus which was the <u>greatest commandment</u>.  He chose <u>two</u>:

> "the Lord our God, the Lord is one.  Love the Lord your God with all your heart and with all your soul and with all your mind and with all your strength." Mark 12:29-30 NIV

> "Love your neighbour as yourself." Mark 12:31 NIV

3) The teacher <u>approved</u> of Jesus's answer.  So Jesus said he was <u>close</u> to the <u>kingdom of God</u>, as he had <u>accepted</u> the key messages of the kingdom.

## The **First Rule** comes from **Deuteronomy**

The first rule Jesus chose was adapted from Deuteronomy 6:4-5.  Jesus meant that <u>God</u> should be the thing you <u>love</u> most in life — <u>nothing</u> should be more <u>important</u>.  This rule forms part of an important Jewish prayer (see p.48).

## The **Second Rule** is known as the **Golden Rule**

1) The second rule is from Leviticus 19:18.  Although Jesus used the <u>same</u> words, in Leviticus the rule <u>only</u> meant love your <u>own people</u> — fellow Jews.  Non-Jews <u>weren't</u> included.  Jesus <u>expanded</u> this rule to cover <u>all human beings</u>.

2) It is sometimes called the <u>Golden Rule</u>, and this part of the Gospel is still regarded as an <u>important</u> rule today.  It is <u>accepted</u> by most <u>secular</u> (non-religious) people.

3) Many <u>non-Christians</u> regard Jesus as an <u>important teacher</u>, and a <u>good man</u>.  Lots of modern people are <u>inspired</u> by his example of <u>selfless love</u> and <u>forgiveness</u> of <u>enemies</u>.

4) Many modern Christians agree that <u>loving God</u> and loving <u>other people</u> is the <u>essence</u> of Christianity.  Many Christians have <u>devoted</u> their lives to the <u>service</u> of <u>others</u> as a consequence, e.g. <u>Mother Teresa</u> of Calcutta.

## What if Jesus's Teaching **Contradicts** the **Law** or **Government?**

1) Christians believe that Jesus's <u>character</u> and <u>life</u> show what <u>God</u> is like.  They try to <u>obey</u> his teachings and to <u>live</u> in the <u>same way</u> that he did.

2) Most Christians believe they should keep the <u>laws</u> and <u>obey</u> the <u>government</u> of the country they live in.  But they believe it is <u>right</u> to <u>disobey</u> these if the laws or government are <u>wrong</u>.

3) For example, lots of Christians <u>refused</u> to obey the government in <u>Nazi Germany</u> — many <u>hid</u> Jews from the <u>government</u> so that they wouldn't be <u>killed</u>.

**REVISION TASK**

## Loving God and loving one another is important for Christians

Create a spider diagram all about the kingdom of God.  Include things like when and where people think it might happen, what it will be like and how to get to it, as well as Gospel references.

# People Disregarded by Society

Jesus made a point of <u>welcoming</u> and <u>helping</u> those who were <u>excluded</u> from normal society.
In doing this, he set an <u>example</u> for how Christians should <u>treat</u> those who are otherwise <u>disregarded by society</u>.

## Outcasts were Excluded from Society for Different Reasons

Many people were <u>outcasts</u> in 1st century Jewish society. Other people <u>didn't interact</u> with them,
and they were <u>excluded</u> from <u>worship</u> — so they were <u>cut off</u> from <u>God</u> as well as from other people.

### 1) Sinners

People who deliberately <u>broke</u> the <u>laws</u> which good Jews kept were outcasts. Jews considered
these laws to be <u>God-given</u>, and obeying them was <u>essential</u> to remain part of <u>God's people</u>.

### 2) The Ill and Disabled

These people were sometimes seen as being <u>punished</u> by God for their <u>sins</u>. Some diseases
were thought to be <u>spread</u> by <u>physical contact</u>, so sufferers were <u>isolated</u> to stop others from
getting <u>infected</u>. Some were thought to make the sufferer ritually <u>unclean</u>, so they couldn't
join in worship. Other people couldn't <u>touch</u> them, because that made them <u>unclean</u> too.

### 3) Gentiles

Parts of the <u>Old Testament</u> told Jews <u>not</u> to have any <u>contact</u> with non-Jews, and this was
taught by some <u>rabbis</u> at the time of Jesus. They weren't considered to be God's people.

### 4) The Poor

Very poor people <u>couldn't</u> afford to buy the <u>sacrifices</u> needed for worship at the Temple
in Jerusalem. These sacrifices were <u>needed</u> to <u>cleanse</u> their sins, so they remained <u>sinful</u>.

### 5) Tax Collectors

They worked for the occupying <u>Romans</u>, so they were considered <u>traitors</u>.
They often collected <u>more</u> than <u>necessary</u> and kept the rest for <u>themselves</u>.

## Jesus Welcomed Outcasts — So Christians Must Too

1) Jesus showed that <u>outcasts</u> were welcome in the kingdom of God. He also welcomed
   <u>women</u> and <u>children</u> — they were considered <u>less important</u> than <u>men</u> at the time.

2) Modern Christians are inspired by his <u>compassion</u> for outcasts, and so
   they welcome <u>all</u> types of people. They're encouraged to <u>accept</u> and
   <u>love everyone</u>, whatever their gender, race, religion or past behaviour.

3) This <u>attitude</u> has gradually been <u>built</u> into the <u>laws</u> of our society.
   <u>Discrimination</u> (treating people badly) because of their gender or race is now <u>illegal</u>.

**REVISION TASK**

## Jesus accepted everyone, even the most hated and excluded

During Jesus's time, a lot of people were cut off from the rest of society for many reasons.
Close the book and write out the different types of outcasts, explaining why they were
excluded from society in that period of history. Try to include as much detail as possible.

# People Disregarded by Society

Jesus healed and spoke with people who would otherwise be isolated, ignored and hated. He even chose an outcast to be one of his disciples.

## Jesus Healed a Leper and Helped Him Back into Society (1:40-45)

1) A leper (a person suffering from leprosy) asked Jesus for help. He said "If you are willing, you can make me clean" (Mark 1:40 NIV).

> Leprosy is a skin disease that can seriously harm or even kill people. People believed it was spread by touching, so lepers were driven out of their homes.

2) Jesus touched him (making himself 'unclean') and the leper was healed instantly. Jesus then told him to visit a priest and make the sacrifices needed to cleanse a leper and remove his impurity (only a priest could declare someone free of leprosy).

3) Jesus told the man to keep it a secret — but he told everyone.

4) Christians believe that they should follow Jesus's teachings and example. Early Christians cared for the sick during epidemics, and founded many of the first hospitals in Europe.

5) Many modern Christians also care for the sick, despite the risks. They believe compassion matters more than their own lives, and the best thing they can do is follow Jesus's teaching.

## Jesus Chooses an Outcast to be a Disciple (2:13-17)

1) Levi was a tax collector who became one of Jesus's disciples.

> "...he saw Levi... sitting at the tax collector's booth. 'Follow me,' Jesus told him, and Levi got up and followed him." Mark 2:14 NIV

2) Jesus later went to Levi's house to eat — other outcasts were also there. Visiting Levi's house and eating with him was a sign of acceptance of these outcasts.

3) Some people criticised Jesus for it, but he replied: "It is not the healthy who need a doctor, but those who are ill. I have not come to call the righteous, but sinners" (Mark 2:17 NIV).

4) Jesus showed that God values compassion and helping those in trouble above punishment for wrongdoing.

## Jesus Healed the Daughter of a Gentile Woman (7:24-30)

1) A Greek (sometimes called Syro-Phoenician) woman had a daughter who was possessed by a demon. The woman asked Jesus to heal her.

2) Jesus refused. He compared Jews and non-Jews to the children and dogs in a family: "...it is not right to take the children's bread and toss it to the dogs" (Mark 7:27 NIV). He was telling her that his mission was to help the Jews before any non-Jews.

3) The woman replied: "Lord... even the dogs under the table eat the children's crumbs" (Mark 7:28 NIV). Because of her humility and faith, Jesus healed her daughter.

4) Most Jews in Jesus's time had little to do with Gentiles, but there were several stories about Jesus helping Gentiles who approached him. Some Gentiles started becoming Christians soon after Jesus's death.

5) Jesus showed that people shouldn't be discriminated against because of their race or religion.

## You need to consider the historical context of what Jesus said and did

Interacting with the sick, or talking to tax collectors and non-Jews doesn't seem like a particularly radical act in the modern world. But in Jesus's time, it was — his actions would have seemed shocking to many.

# People Disregarded by Society

On this page are more stories from Jesus's life that give an insight into what Jesus considered important.

## Jesus Drove a **Demon** from a Boy **(9:14-29)**

1) A man's son was possessed by a spirit. It affected him physically:

> "...it throws him to the ground. He foams at the mouth, gnashes his teeth and becomes rigid" Mark 9:18 NIV

2) Jesus spoke harshly to everyone, calling them an "unbelieving generation" (Mark 9:19 NIV).
3) The man asked Jesus for help. Jesus said, "Everything is possible for one who believes" (Mark 9:23 NIV). But the man admitted his faith was weak: "I do believe; help me overcome my unbelief!" (Mark 9:24 NIV).
4) Jesus told the spirit to leave the boy and never return. It screamed, caused the boy to shake and then left. The boy lay still, as if he were dead. But Jesus held his hand and helped him up — he was cured.
5) Now people would recognise that the boy had epilepsy. But 1st century Jews — including Mark when he was reporting these events — didn't know the scientific explanation for epilepsy. Illnesses were often blamed on demon possession and sufferers were shunned.

## A Poor **Widow** Gave **All** She Had to the **Temple (12:41-44)**

1) People were giving money to the Temple. Some gave lots of money, but there was a poor widow who gave the little she had.
2) The rich donated only spare money, so Jesus said the widow's gift was more valuable:

> "They all gave out of their wealth; but she, out of her poverty, put in everything — all she had to live on" Mark 12:44 NIV

Widows were very vulnerable in Jesus's society. They had no one to protect them or provide for them — there was no help from the government.

3) The widow had faith that God would provide for her. This story helped early Christians believe that God would provide for them too if they had complete faith in him. It also shows that the poor are important to God — Christians should help them.

## A Woman **Anoints** Jesus with **Expensive Perfume (14:1-9)**

1) Jesus was with Simon the Leper when a woman tipped a jar of expensive perfume over Jesus's head.
2) People were angry with her — it was valuable perfume that could have been used to help the poor. But Jesus defended her. He said she had prepared his body for burial — this was just before his death.
3) He said, "The poor you will always have with you, and you can help them any time you want. But you will not always have me" (Mark 14:7 NIV).
4) As well as Jesus's appreciation of this woman's actions, the story also shows Jesus's respect for lepers.

## Don't disregard these stories — they're important

In many stories, Jesus doesn't act in the way you might expect — whether he's speaking harshly to someone or giving different responses from what you might think. Read over these stories carefully and consider Jesus's actions. Think about the lessons he was trying to teach with the things he said and did, and what impact they had.

# Faith and Discipleship

The disciples were Jesus's <u>devoted followers</u> during his lifetime. The <u>Twelve</u> were the most important.

## Jesus First Called **Four Disciples** to Follow Him (1:16-20)

1) Simon (later called <u>Peter</u>) and <u>Andrew</u> were brothers who were <u>fishermen</u> on the Sea of Galilee. Jesus said to them, "Come, follow me... and I will send you out to fish for people" (Mark 1:17 NIV). Jesus meant that they would <u>tell</u> people <u>God's message</u>. They immediately <u>left</u> their work behind and <u>went</u> with him.

2) Jesus also called <u>James</u> and <u>John</u>, two more fishermen, to go with him. They "left their father Zebedee in the boat" (Mark 1:20 NIV) — their faith was so <u>strong</u> that they left both <u>work</u> and <u>family</u> behind.

## Discipleship Means **Learning** and **Following**

1) The number of disciples grew — there were <u>twelve</u> who were especially <u>important</u> to Jesus. Twelve was <u>symbolic</u> of the twelve <u>tribes</u> of Israel in the <u>Old Testament</u>. By choosing twelve, Jesus suggested they were the <u>new chosen people</u> of God.

2) 'Disciple' meant the <u>pupil</u> of a teacher, or the <u>apprentice</u> of a master craftsman, so the disciples <u>learned</u> from <u>Jesus</u>. It also meant <u>following</u> his <u>life</u> and his <u>example</u>.

3) The first disciples show <u>modern Christians</u> the level of faith <u>expected</u> of them. They <u>sacrificed</u> their livelihoods and followed Jesus <u>without</u> asking any <u>questions</u>. People <u>nowadays</u> might be a disciple by following a <u>vocation</u> to work for <u>God</u>, for example being a <u>priest</u>. Others might carry out what Jesus <u>taught</u> people, for example by being <u>kind</u> and <u>helping</u> those in need.

## Jesus Told the **Twelve** to **Preach** and **Heal** (6:7-13)

1) Jesus told his disciples to go out in <u>pairs</u> to <u>preach</u>, <u>heal</u> the sick and drive out <u>demons</u>.

2) They took <u>no food</u>, <u>money</u> or <u>luggage</u> — they were to rely on the <u>hospitality</u> of others. If they <u>weren't</u> made <u>welcome</u> somewhere, Jesus said to <u>leave</u> and "shake the dust off your feet as a testimony against them" (Mark 6:11 NIV). These people had had their chance to hear the <u>message</u> — the disciples should spend <u>no more time</u> there.

3) Jesus spent most of his <u>ministry</u> like this, so the disciples were <u>sharing</u> his <u>mission</u>, showing their <u>faith</u> that God would <u>provide</u> for them.

4) Early Christians were <u>encouraged</u> by this during their <u>missionary journeys</u> throughout the <u>Roman Empire</u>.

5) Mission in the 21st century is <u>similar</u> — it usually involves <u>practical help</u> as well as <u>preaching</u>. <u>Christian Aid</u> and <u>CAFOD</u> are Christian organisations which give practical help where needed in <u>foreign countries</u>.

## Discipleship has **Costs** as well as **Rewards** (8:34-38 and **10:28-31**)

1) Jesus said his <u>disciples</u> must "take up their cross and follow me" (Mark 8:34 NIV). He was saying they might <u>suffer</u> and <u>die</u>, as he was going to.

2) But anyone who showed <u>faith</u> and <u>gave</u> things <u>up</u> for Jesus would be <u>rewarded</u> both on <u>Earth</u> and in <u>heaven</u>. Although they'd given up family, they'd have a huge <u>new family</u> of Jesus's followers. They may have been treated <u>badly</u> on Earth, but in <u>heaven</u> it'd be them, rather than their persecutors, who were <u>respected</u>. Early Christians would have been <u>comforted</u> by this.

> "...no one who has left home... for me and the gospel will fail to receive a hundred times as much in this present age... and in the age to come eternal life. But many who are first will be last, and the last first" Mark 10:29-31 NIV

3) Those who opted for an easy life instead would <u>lose</u> their <u>future life</u> in the <u>kingdom of God</u>. Anyone who <u>disowned</u> him would <u>later</u> be disowned by <u>Jesus</u> on the <u>Day of Judgement</u>.

4) Modern Christians are less likely to face the same <u>suffering</u> as Jesus's early followers, but they must still be prepared to <u>give up</u> their own <u>wishes</u> and be ready for <u>hardship</u> rather than an <u>easy life</u> when they "take up their cross".

# Faith and Discipleship

## Jesus Heals a **Woman** who is **Bleeding Heavily (5:24-34)**

1) A woman who had been suffering from a haemorrhage (excessive bleeding) for 12 years approached Jesus in a crowd and secretly touched his cloak. She believed it would heal her and it did.

2) Jesus felt power leave him. He asked who had touched him and the woman owned up.

3) The bleeding meant the woman would have been seen as unclean, and by touching Jesus she would have made him unclean too, but that didn't concern him. Jesus said to her: "Daughter, your faith has healed you. Go in peace and be freed from your suffering" (Mark 5:34 NIV).

4) The woman in the story was healed because she had faith. Jesus often said this when he healed people. Faith in Mark's Gospel means trusting God — and acting on that trust. The woman acted by seeking out Jesus and touching him. This story shows the importance of faith for Christians.

## Peter **Denies** He is One of Jesus's **Disciples (14:27-31, 66-72)**

1) Just before his arrest, Jesus predicted that all of the disciples would desert him. Peter insisted he wouldn't, even if everyone else did. But Jesus said "today... before the cock crows twice you yourself will disown me three times" (Mark 14:30 NIV). Each disciple swore he would rather die than desert Jesus.

2) After Jesus was arrested, Peter was challenged three times in the courtyard outside where Jesus was being held. Each time, he denied being one of Jesus's disciples.

> "I don't know this man you're talking about."
> Mark 14:71 NIV

3) Then he heard the cock crow twice, and recalled what Jesus had said. He was very upset: "he broke down and wept" (Mark 14:72 NIV).

Mark considered Peter to be the unofficial leader of the disciples — he was the first to declare Jesus as the Messiah. But out of fear, even Peter deserted Jesus in his hour of need. This is a warning for Christians of the need for God's help to remain faithful. It reassures them that even the best Christians fail sometimes.

## Jesus **Sent** his **Disciples** Out and **Ascended** to Heaven (16:14-20)

1) Jesus appeared to the disciples after his resurrection. There were only eleven of them — Judas (who had betrayed him) had gone.

> "he rebuked them for their lack of faith" Mark 16:14 NIV

2) Jesus told them off for not believing the people who had seen him alive.

3) He commissioned them to tell everyone about the gospel and to baptise converts. He said, "Whoever believes and is baptised will be saved, but whoever does not believe will be condemned" (Mark 16:16 NIV). He predicted many miraculous signs would accompany their preaching.

4) Then Jesus ascended to heaven to be with God. The disciples did as he had commanded and miraculous things did happen — e.g. St Paul was bitten by a poisonous snake, but survived.

5) This encourages modern Christians to continue the disciples' work — God will protect them while they do so.

### Mark's Gospel Suggests **Only Christians** will be **Saved**

1) Jesus's commission to his disciples could be understood to mean that only Christians will be saved. However, verses 9-20 weren't included in some original versions of the Gospel.

2) Many modern Christians reject this idea. They think that other religions can also be paths to God. They also respect good people who have no religion.

3) Excluding some people could encourage prejudice and discrimination. The rest of Mark's Gospel is against both of these, and there are laws in the UK making discrimination illegal (see p.157).

**EXAM TIP**

## And that's the end of Mark's Gospel

You need to refer to specific Gospel quotes in some of your answers, so be sure you know a few.

# Worked Exam Questions

Over the next few pages are some exam-style questions to help you get ready for the exams you'll be sitting. On this page the answers have been completed, then the next two pages are left blank for you to complete.

1    Which of the following did a woman pour over Jesus's head at Bethany?
Put a tick (✓) in the correct box.

    A    Perfume    ✓

    B    Water    ☐

    C    Vinegar    ☐

    D    Wine    ☐

*[1 mark]*

2    Give the names of two of Jesus's disciples who were originally fishermen.

    1) Andrew

    2) John

*[2 marks]*

3    Explain two contrasting views seen in St Marks's Gospel about the status of children.

    People brought their children to Jesus because they wanted him to bless them. This shows that they cared about their children greatly.

    The disciples, however, were angry with the people who brought their children. This suggests that they didn't think children were important enough to take up Jesus's time.

*[4 marks]*

4    Explain two ways in which the story of Jesus healing the Gentile woman's daughter is important to Christians today. Your answer should refer to Mark's Gospel.

    In the first century, Jews and non-Jews (like this woman who was "a Greek, born in Syrian Phoenicia" (Mark 7:26 NIV)) did not mix, and Gentiles were sometimes discriminated against. Jesus ignored this fact and healed the Gentile woman's daughter anyway. Modern Christians interpret this to mean that they should follow Jesus's example and treat all people equally.

    The woman calls Jesus "Lord" even though she has never met him before. This shows that even Gentiles were starting to recognise the divinity of Jesus, so Christians can come from any background as long as they accept Jesus as the Son of God.

*[5 marks]*

**5** Which of the following is the reason Jesus healed the woman with a haemorrhage? Put a tick (✓) in the correct box.

A She had faith ☐

B He pitied her ☐

C She begged him to ☐

D The crowd asked him to ☐

*[1 mark]*

**6** Explain two ways in which the idea of discipleship found in Mark's Gospel is important to Christians today. Your answer should refer to Mark's Gospel.

.......................................................................................................................

.......................................................................................................................

.......................................................................................................................

.......................................................................................................................

.......................................................................................................................

.......................................................................................................................

.......................................................................................................................

.......................................................................................................................

*[5 marks]*

**7** 'The kingdom of God means a physical place on earth.'

SPaG MARKS

Evaluate this statement. Your answer should include the following:
• references to Mark's Gospel
• arguments that support the statement
• arguments that disagree with the statement
• a conclusion.

*Write your answer on a separate sheet of paper.*

*[12 marks]*

# Exam Questions

8    Which of the following is **not** a reason why many people think Mark's Gospel is an accurate source?  Put a tick (✓) in the correct box.

   A    It contains similar information to the other gospels.    ☐

   B    It was probably written within 50 years of Jesus's death.    ☐

   C    It was written by an anonymous author.    ☐

   D    Historians at the time mentioned events from Mark's Gospel.    ☐

   *[1 mark]*

9    Give two things Christians can learn about the kingdom of God from the parable of the mustard seed.

   ........................................................................................................................................................

   ........................................................................................................................................................

   ........................................................................................................................................................

   ........................................................................................................................................................

   *[2 marks]*

10    Explain two contrasting views about the story of Jesus driving out a demon from a boy.

   ........................................................................................................................................................

   ........................................................................................................................................................

   ........................................................................................................................................................

   ........................................................................................................................................................

   ........................................................................................................................................................

   ........................................................................................................................................................

   ........................................................................................................................................................

   *[4 marks]*

11    'People who live a good life will go to heaven, even if they are not Christian.'    ⓢ SPaG MARKS

   Evaluate this statement.  Your answer should include the following:
   • references to Mark's Gospel
   • arguments that support the statement
   • arguments that disagree with the statement
   • a conclusion.

   *Write your answer on a separate sheet of paper.*

   *[12 marks]*

# Revision Summary

That's Theme H finished — the <u>last section</u> in the book.  But before you leave, have a go at these <u>revision questions</u>.

- Try these questions and <u>tick off each one</u> when you <u>get it right</u>.
- When you've done <u>all the questions</u> for a topic and are <u>completely happy</u> with it, tick off the topic.

## The Kingdom of God (p.153-156) ☑

1) What is meant by the kingdom of God?
2) What do the seeds in the parable of the sower represent?
3) In the parable of the sower, some of the seeds fell on the path
   — what happened to them and what does this represent?
4) Briefly recap the parable of the growing seed.
5) In the parable of the growing seed, what does the harvest represent?
6) Give one interpretation for what the birds represent in the parable of the mustard seed.
7) What did Jesus say to the rich man who asked what he must do to get eternal life?
8) How did Jesus's teachings on wealth differ from the beliefs held by Jews at the time?
9) Give one example of a modern interpretation of Jesus's teachings on wealth.
10) What was Jesus's response when his disciples tried to stop children from seeing him?
11) What did Jesus say were the two greatest commandments?
12) How did Jesus's teachings on the Golden Rule differ from the Jewish understanding at the time?

## People Disregarded by Society (p.157-159) ☐

13) Why were the ill isolated from others and not allowed to worship in 1st century Jewish society?
14) Why were tax collectors disliked in 1st century Jewish society?
15) Give an example of how Jesus's welcoming of outcasts can be reflected in our modern society.
16) Give an example of how Jesus's healing of the leper inspired the actions of early Christians.
17) What was significant about Jesus choosing Levi as his disciple?
18) Why did Jesus heal the daughter of the Gentile woman?
19) Why did Jesus speak harshly to a man who brought his son who was possessed to him?
20) Why was the money the widow donated to the temple more valuable
    than the money donated by the rich?
21) Why did Jesus defend the actions of the woman who tipped expensive perfume over his head?

## Faith and Discipleship (p.160-161) ☑

22) What was the profession of Jesus's first four disciples?
23) Why did Jesus choose twelve important disciples?
24) What does disciple mean?
25) What did Jesus mean when he said his disciples must "take up their cross"?
26) Why, according the Jesus, was the woman who was suffering a haemorrhage healed?
27) How many times did Peter deny Jesus?
28) Why is the story of Peter denying Jesus important to Christians?
29) What did Jesus tell his disciples to do after his resurrection?
30) What is a modern Christian view on who will be saved?

# Do Well in Your Exam

You've learnt all the <u>facts</u> — now it's time to get those <u>grades</u>.

## You'll Sit **Two Exams** Which are Worth **50% Each**

This information is for the <u>full course</u>. For the <u>short course</u> you'll just sit <u>one exam</u>.

1) You'll sit <u>two</u> exam papers: <u>Paper 1</u> is about religious <u>beliefs</u>, <u>teachings</u> and <u>practices</u>, and <u>Paper 2</u> is about the <u>thematic studies</u>.

2) Both papers are <u>1 hour and 45 minutes</u> long, and they're each worth <u>50%</u> of your <u>overall mark</u>.

### Paper 1

- For Paper 1, you'll be given <u>two booklets</u>, one for each of the <u>two religions</u> you've studied.
- There'll be <u>2</u> questions in <u>each</u> booklet, with each <u>broken down</u> into <u>5</u> parts.
- Try to spend around <u>50 minutes</u> on each religion.

### Paper 2

- In Paper 2, you need to answer the questions for the <u>four themes</u> you've studied.
- There'll be <u>1</u> question <u>per</u> theme, which will be <u>divided</u> into <u>5</u> parts.
- Aim to work on <u>each</u> theme for roughly <u>25 minutes</u>.

3) If you've done the textual studies on <u>St Mark's Gospel</u> (Themes G and H), you'll answer questions on <u>Christianity</u> or <u>Catholic Christianity</u>, plus <u>one other religion</u> in <u>Paper 1</u>. In <u>Paper 2</u>, you'll choose questions on the <u>two</u> religious, philosophical and ethical studies themes you've covered (Themes A-F), then the <u>two</u> themes on Mark's Gospel.

## The **Basics** — **Read** the Questions

1) <u>Read</u> the questions <u>carefully</u>. Remember to answer <u>all the parts</u> of the questions.

2) Be aware of how much <u>time</u> you're using. Leave plenty of time for the long-answer questions. The more <u>marks</u> a question's worth, the <u>longer</u> you should be spending on it — for these exams, allow around <u>1 minute per mark</u>. Try to leave yourself 5 minutes at the end to <u>check your work</u>.

3) Some questions will have extra marks available for <u>Spelling, Punctuation and Grammar</u> (SPaG) — there are <u>6 SPaG marks</u> available in <u>Paper 1</u> and <u>3 SPaG marks</u> in <u>Paper 2</u>. The exam paper will tell you which questions offer SPaG marks — so make your writing for these the <u>best</u> it can be (see p.169-171 for more).

4) Don't use any fancy colours — write <u>only</u> in <u>black</u> ink.

## 1-Mark Questions are Always **Multiple Choice**

The 1-mark questions are pretty <u>straightforward</u> — read <u>all</u> the options before you make your choice. If you're <u>not sure</u>, guess — you won't lose any marks.

> Which of the following is the Jewish concept of charity?
>
> a) Shekhinah          b) Tikkun olam          c) Tallit          d) Tzedakah

The correct answer is d) <u>Tzedakah</u>.

## Make sure you know which religions and themes you've studied

After you've done all your revision, make sure you get a good night's rest before your exam — you won't be able to do your best if you're half asleep.

# Do Well in Your Exam

There are some subtle differences between the question types, so make sure you're clear what's what.

## 2-Mark Questions Just Need Two Brief Points

1) The two-mark questions will ask for two points on a particular topic. You could be asked for two beliefs, examples, reasons, ways — e.g. examples of how religious believers might act, reasons why something is important or influences believers, or ways that believers celebrate something.

2) Keep your answers short and to the point — you don't need to write in full sentences.

> Give two religious beliefs about divorce.

> Many religious people think that divorce should be the last resort. Roman Catholics think that divorce is impossible.

Don't be tempted to write lots.

For the Paper 2 questions, your points can be general or about a specific religion.

## 4-Mark Questions Might Ask How Beliefs Influence People

1) The four-mark question in the 'Beliefs' section of Paper 1 will ask you to explain how a particular belief influences religious people.

2) Make two points, but you'll have to develop them in order to get full marks.

> Explain two ways in which believing in the Trinity influences modern Christians.

The first sentence here introduces the influence, and the second sentence builds on that point.

> Christians believe that Jesus set the example for how Christians should act. By reading the Gospels, they can learn more about his life and how they should behave.
> Christians believe the Holy Spirit guides them personally and the Church as a whole. They think the Spirit can help them to follow God's teachings and to live in the way God intended.

## 4-Mark Questions Might Ask for Similar or Contrasting Views

1) The four-mark questions in the 'Practices' section of Paper 1 and all of Paper 2 will ask you to explain either two similar or two contrasting views about a topic.

2) Be sure to read the whole question. For some 'contrasting' questions on Themes A-F, you'll be asked to write about views from one or more religious traditions — you can pick the religions.

3) For others you must answer about the main religious tradition in the UK (Christianity) and another religious tradition. You don't have to write about different religions here — you could write about two contrasting views from within Christianity, e.g. from different denominations.

> Explain two contrasting beliefs in Britain today about forgiveness.
> You must refer to the main religious tradition in the UK and at least one other religious viewpoint.

> Forgiveness is important to many Christians. They believe that God is always prepared to forgive sins, and Christians should accept his forgiveness and follow his example.
> In Islam, some sins are seen as being so terrible that they can't be forgiven. For example, if someone commits shirk, this is considered unforgivable.

## Don't let exam nerves get the better of you

Make sure your revision includes practising doing exam-style questions under timed conditions. It'll pay off in the end — you'll be less likely to run out of time in the real exam, and you'll know what to expect.

# Do Well in Your Exam

## For 5-Mark Questions You Must Be Able to Refer to Sacred Texts

1) The <u>five-mark</u> questions ask you to <u>explain</u> two things, such as beliefs, teachings, ways that believers act, or reasons why something is important.

2) You need to give two points and <u>develop</u> them, but for full marks you must <u>refer</u> to a <u>sacred text</u> or religious <u>teaching</u>. This could be by including a <u>quotation</u>, or by <u>paraphrasing</u> (explaining what's said in your own words). You'll need to say which text or teaching the information <u>comes from</u> — e.g. the <u>Bible</u> or the <u>Qur'an</u>.

> Explain two Muslim teachings on jihad.
> Your answer should refer to religious texts.

There's only <u>one mark</u> available for referring to religious texts, so <u>one quote or reference</u> will do.

> Greater jihad is the struggle to live life according to Allah's teachings. It's a personal struggle, and individuals must work to be the best Muslims they can be. Lesser jihad can involve defending Islam. This could be in a peaceful way, or by fighting a threat to Islam in self-defence. The Qur'an says: "Permission [to fight] has been given to those who are being fought".

You could also write something like 'The Qur'an gives Muslims permission to defend themselves if they're being fought'.

## For 12-Mark Questions You Need Both Sides of the Argument

1) For the <u>12-mark</u> question, you'll need to write a <u>longer answer</u>. You'll be given a <u>statement</u> and a <u>list</u> of bullet points — these tell you what to put in your answer.

2) You need to give arguments <u>for</u> and <u>against</u> the statement, so read it carefully, then make a rough list of all the <u>views</u> on each side that you can think of.

3) <u>Plan</u> out your answer <u>before</u> you start writing — it needs to be <u>clear</u> and <u>organised</u> for the examiner.

> 'Animal experimentation should be allowed if it benefits humanity.'
> Evaluate this statement. Your answer should include the following:
> • religious arguments that support the statement
> • religious arguments that disagree with the statement
> • a conclusion
> You can also include non-religious points of view in your answer.

The points in <u>Paper 1</u> are a bit <u>different</u>. They'll ask you to include <u>teachings</u> from the <u>religion</u> you've studied, arguments <u>for</u> and <u>against</u> and a <u>conclusion</u>.

> Many religious believers share this point of view. They believe that animal testing is acceptable if it is for valid reasons, such as producing life-saving medicines. Testing cosmetics on animals wouldn't be considered acceptable. They also think that the animals must be treated humanely, and no unnecessary pain caused. Many religious people see themselves as stewards of the Earth, and believe they must look after animals.
>   Some religious teachings allow animal experimentation. The Catechism of the Catholic Church says that animal testing is allowed if it brings about scientific or medical advances, but the animals shouldn't be allowed to suffer. The Jewish idea of pikuach nefesh, saving human lives no matter what, could be used to argue that animal experimentation is tolerable if it could save someone's life.
>   Some people might look at animal testing from a utilitarian point of view. If testing on animals would produce the best balance of good and bad outcomes, they would argue it is allowed.
>   However, not all religious believers would support this view. Some people, such as the Society of Friends (Quakers), are against causing any kind of suffering to animals. They would think it's wrong to inflict pain on animals just to further our knowledge of science and medicine.
>
>   I think that, although allowing animals to suffer is wrong, if the experiments could benefit humanity then they should be allowed. As for what is considered beneficial, any medical or scientific advances that could save human lives would be acceptable, but testing non-essential products such as cosmetics would not be a good enough reason to carry out animal testing. The Bible and the Qur'an say that animals should be looked after well, so any inessential suffering in the experiment would be unacceptable.

This answer starts by giving some <u>general views</u> that <u>agree</u> with the statement.

The second paragraph gets more specific and references <u>religious ideas</u> and <u>texts</u>.

The third paragraph explains how <u>ethics</u> influence views.

This paragraph discusses arguments <u>against</u> the statement. You would need to include <u>more</u> here — this part of the answer <u>isn't finished</u>.

Finish with a <u>conclusion</u> — say what <u>you</u> think, and <u>back it up</u> with ideas you've discussed. These sentences should give you an idea — but you'd need to say a bit <u>more</u> in the real thing.

# Spelling, Punctuation and Grammar

You get marks in your exams for having good <u>spelling</u>, <u>punctuation</u> and <u>grammar</u> (SPaG).  It might not be particularly thrilling but if you can get it right, it's <u>easy marks</u>.  This page is about checking your work...

## Some **12-Mark** Questions Have **3 Extra Marks** for SPaG

1) In <u>Paper 1</u>, <u>3 marks</u> are available for spelling, punctuation and grammar in the <u>12-mark question</u> on '<u>Beliefs</u>', for <u>each</u> of your two religions — so that's <u>6 SPaG marks</u> available in total for Paper 1. For <u>Paper 2</u>, up to <u>3 SPaG marks</u> are available for <u>each</u> 12-mark question — but it's only the <u>highest</u> SPaG mark you get across your four 12-mark questions that's counted.  So that's <u>3 SPaG marks</u> available for Paper 2, meaning you could get <u>up to 9 marks</u> across the two exams just for SPaG.

2) The examiner will look at your spelling, punctuation and grammar in <u>general</u>, but they'll also look at how many <u>technical terms</u> you use and how <u>accurately</u> you use them.

3) Leave <u>5 minutes</u> at the end of the exam to <u>check your work</u>.  That <u>isn't</u> long, so there <u>won't</u> be time to check <u>everything</u> thoroughly.  Look for the <u>most obvious</u> mistakes.

4) <u>Start</u> by checking the <u>12-mark</u> questions since they're the <u>only ones</u> that award SPaG marks.  <u>Only</u> check the rest of your answers if you've got <u>time</u>.

## Check for Common **Spelling Mistakes**

When you're writing under pressure, it's <u>easy</u> to let <u>spelling mistakes</u> creep in, but there are a few things you can watch out for:

*Check for missing words as well as misspelt words.*

1) Look out for words which <u>sound the same</u> but <u>mean different things</u> and are <u>spelt differently</u>. Make sure you've used the correct one.  For example, 'their', 'there' and 'they're':

| | | |
|---|---|---|
| The Bible says that wives should do what <u>their</u> husbands say. | <u>There</u> are many conditions that must be met for a war to be 'just'. | Some people might commit crime because <u>they're</u> living in poverty. |

2) <u>Don't</u> use text speak, and always write words out <u>in full</u>.  For example, use '<u>and</u>' instead of '&' or '+'. <u>Don't</u> use '<u>etc.</u>' when you could give <u>more examples</u> or a <u>better explanation</u>.

3) Make sure you've used the appropriate <u>technical terms</u> (like 'euthanasia', 'sacrament' or 'shari'ah'). If they're <u>spelt correctly</u>, it'll really <u>impress</u> the <u>examiner</u>.

## Make Sure Your **Grammar** and **Punctuation** are **Correct**

1) Check you've used <u>capital letters</u>, <u>full stops</u> and <u>question marks</u> correctly (see p.171).

2) Make sure your writing <u>isn't too chatty</u> and doesn't use <u>slang words</u>.  It should be <u>formal</u>.

3) Watch out for sentences where your writing switches between <u>different tenses</u>.  You should usually use <u>one tense</u> throughout your answer (don't worry if you've used a quote that's in a different tense though).

4) Check that you've started a <u>new paragraph</u> every time you make a new point. It's important that your answer <u>isn't</u> just <u>one long block</u> of text (see p.171).

5) Watch out for tricksy little <u>grammar mistakes</u>:

- Remember — '<u>it's</u>' (with an apostrophe) is short for '<u>it is</u>' or '<u>it has</u>'. '<u>Its</u>' (without an apostrophe) means '<u>belonging to it</u>'.

- It's always '<u>should have</u>', not 'should of' (the same goes for 'could have' and 'would have' too).

If you know that you <u>often</u> confuse two words, like 'it's' and 'its', <u>watch out</u> for them when you're checking your work in the exam.

## Make sure you use correct punctuation

There's a lot of stuff to check, which is why it's really important to get to grips with it all and practise before the exam.  That way you'll start to do it automatically, and make fewer errors in the first place.

# Spelling, Punctuation and Grammar

Making a mistake in your exam is <u>not</u> the end of the world.  Just correct it and you won't lose any marks.

## Make Your Corrections **Neatly**

1)  If the mistake is just <u>one word</u> or a <u>short phrase</u>, cross it out <u>neatly</u> and write the correct word <u>above</u> it.

> A stable family can give a child a sense of identity and a feeling of security, teaching him
>
> receive
> or her how to behave in different social situations and how to give and ~~recieve~~ love.

2)  If you've <u>forgotten</u> to start a <u>new paragraph</u>, use a <u>double strike</u>
    (like this '///') to show where the new paragraph should <u>begin</u>:

> The Third Pillar of Islam commands that Muslims give 2.5% of their wealth to charity.  The money is collected and distributed by the mosque. **//** Christians feel it is their duty to be charitable.  This doesn't always mean donating money, but could mean giving time (e.g. by visiting the sick), or effort (e.g. helping in a charity shop).

## Use an **Asterisk** to Add **Extra Information**

1)  If you've <u>missed something out</u>, think about whether you have space to write the missing bit <u>above</u>
    the line you've already written.  If you <u>can</u>, use a '∧' to show <u>exactly where</u> it should go.

> is a
> Jews greet each other by saying 'shalom', which means 'peace'.  Generally, they believe that war ∧ bad thing, but may be necessary in some circumstances, for example in self-defence or to help neighbouring countries.

2)  If the bit you've missed out <u>won't</u> fit above the line, use an <u>asterisk</u>
    (like this '*') to show the examiner <u>where</u> the missing bit should go.

3)  Write the <u>missing words</u> at the <u>end</u> of your answer with another asterisk next to them.

> Christianity teaches that animals should be treated kindly.* Some Christians
> believe that animal testing is wrong because they think it is unhelpful.
> * and shouldn't be made to suffer unnecessarily.

## **Cross Out** Anything You **Don't** Want to be **Marked**

1)  If you've written something that you <u>don't</u> want the examiner to mark, <u>cross it out neatly</u>.

2)  Cross out any <u>notes</u>.  But — if you don't <u>finish</u> your answer <u>in time</u>, don't cross out
    your <u>plan</u> — the examiner might look at it to see what you were <u>going to write</u>.

3)  Don't <u>scribble things out</u> without thinking — it'll make your answers look <u>messy</u>.

## Spell **Technical Words** Correctly

1)  There are a lot of <u>technical words</u> in RS.  You need to be able to <u>spell</u> them <u>correctly</u>.

2)  <u>Learn</u> these examples to start you off.  The <u>coloured letters</u> are the tricky bits to watch out for.

| | | |
|---|---|---|
| reconciliation | euthanasia | deterrence |
| omniscient | pacifism | justice |
| procreation | sanctity | contraception |
| revelation | environment | transcendent |

Make sure you know the specific technical words for your topics.  For example, if you're studying views on marriage, you would need to know words like 'kiddushin' (part of a Jewish wedding ceremony) and 'nikah' (a Muslim wedding ceremony). There's a list of technical terms in the glossary on p.207-210.

# Spelling, Punctuation and Grammar

This page is full of tips for good <u>punctuation</u> and <u>grammar</u> to help you keep silly mistakes at bay.

## You Need to **Punctuate Properly**...

1) Always use a <u>capital letter</u> at the start of a <u>sentence</u>.
   Use capital letters for <u>names</u> of <u>particular people</u>, <u>places</u> and <u>things</u>. For example:

   > Many <u>J</u>ews live in <u>I</u>srael, where the official language is <u>H</u>ebrew.

   All sentences start with capital letters.
   The name of a group of religious believers.
   A country.
   The name of a language.

2) <u>Full stops</u> go at the end of <u>sentences</u>, e.g. 'Muslims worship Allah<u>.</u>'
   <u>Question marks</u> go at the end of <u>questions</u>, e.g. 'What is divorce<u>?</u>'

3) Use <u>commas</u> when you use <u>more than one adjective</u> to describe something or to separate items in a <u>list</u>:

   > Christians believe in a <u>benevolent</u>, <u>compassionate</u> God. They believe <u>the Father</u>, <u>the Son</u> and <u>the Holy Spirit</u> make up the Trinity.

4) <u>Commas</u> can also <u>join two points</u> into one sentence with a joining word (such as '<u>and</u>', '<u>or</u>', '<u>so</u>' or '<u>but</u>'):

   > Salah ideally takes place in a mosque, <u>but</u> it can be done anywhere.

   > The Earth is seen as being a product of the love of Allah, <u>so</u> we should treat it with love.

5) <u>Commas</u> can also be used to separate <u>extra information</u> in a sentence:

   > The Big Bang theory, <u>the idea that the universe began in an explosion of matter and energy</u>, was first put forward by a priest.

   *When you use commas like this, the sentence should still make sense when the extra bit is taken out.*

## ...and Use **Grammar Correctly**

1) <u>Don't change tenses</u> in your writing by mistake:

   > Muslims only <u>allow</u> animal testing if there <u>is</u> a good reason for it.

   This sentence is correct because <u>both</u> verbs are in the <u>present tense</u>.
   Writing '<u>was</u>' instead of '<u>is</u>' would be wrong.

2) <u>Don't</u> use <u>double negatives</u>. You should only use a negative <u>once</u> in a sentence:   *Don't put 'no' here.*

   > Creatures with fins and scales are kosher, but Jews keeping kosher shouldn't eat <u>any</u> other seafood.

3) Write longer answers in <u>paragraphs</u>. A paragraph is a <u>group of sentences</u> which talk about the <u>same thing</u> or <u>follow on</u> from each other. You need to start a <u>new paragraph</u> when you start making a <u>new point</u>. You show a <u>new paragraph</u> by starting a <u>new line</u> and leaving a gap (an <u>indent</u>) before you start writing:

   This gap shows a new paragraph.

   > Weapons of Mass Destruction (WMDs) are weapons that can destroy large areas of land or lots of people at once. They harm anyone in their path, both soldiers and civilians.
   >     Nuclear weapons are one type of WMD. All Christian denominations are against the indiscriminate killing they cause, but some people think that possessing them keeps the peace.

   When <u>planning</u> long answers, remember that you should write a <u>new paragraph</u> for each main point.

## Don't forget those 3 extra SPaG marks on 12-mark questions

Having good SPaG is a great way to get marks in the RS exams, and it might even make a difference to your grade. That's why it's really important that you learn everything on the last few pages.

# GCSE Religious Studies

## Paper 1: Beliefs, Teaching and Practices

| Centre name | | | | | | Surname | |
|---|---|---|---|---|---|---|---|
| Centre number | | | | | | Other names | |
| Candidate number | | | | | | Candidate signature | |

**Time allowed:**
• 1 hour 45 minutes

**Instructions to candidates**
• Write your name and other details in the spaces provided above.
• Write in black ink or ballpoint pen.
• Answer **all** questions on the two religions you have studied.
• Do all rough work on your answer paper.
  Cross through any work you do not want marked.

**Information for candidates**
• The marks available are given in brackets at the end of each question.
• There are 102 marks available for this paper.
• There are 3 marks available for spelling, punctuation and grammar
  for the Beliefs question on each religion.

**Advice to candidates**
• Aim to spend around 25 minutes on each question (so 50 minutes on each religion).
For multiple choice questions:
• Clearly tick the box next to your chosen answer. For example: ✓
• If you wish to change your answer, put a cross through your original
  answer. For example: ☒
• If you wish to change your answer back to one that you have previously
  crossed out, draw a circle around the answer. For example: ⊗

# CHRISTIANITY — Beliefs

If you are studying Christianity, answer **all** the questions on this page

**1.1** Which of the following is **not** a Christian belief about evil?
Put a tick (✓) in the correct box.

| | | |
|---|---|---|
| **A** | There are two types of evil in the world. | ☐ |
| **B** | Natural evil includes things like earthquakes and floods. | ☐ |
| **C** | Moral evil comes from human beings. | ☐ |
| **D** | Evil is always more powerful than good. | ☐ |

*[1 mark]*

**1.2** Give two Christian beliefs about Jesus's ascension.

*[2 marks]*

**1.3** Explain two ways in which the idea of judgement influences Christians today.

*[4 marks]*

**1.4** Explain two ways in which the creation story influences
the way Christians understand God and the universe.
Your answer should refer to specific Christian teachings or sacred texts.

*[5 marks]*

**1.5** 'Jesus's death on the cross is more important to Christians than his resurrection.'

Evaluate this statement. Your answer should include the following:
• examples from Christian teachings
• arguments that support the statement
• arguments that disagree with the statement
• a conclusion.

*[12 marks]*
*[+3 SPaG marks]*

## CHRISTIANITY — Practices
If you are studying Christianity, answer **all** the questions on this page

**2.1** Which of the following is the first day of Lent?
Put a tick (✓) in the correct box.

| | | |
|---|---|---|
| **A** | Easter Sunday | ☐ |
| **B** | Shrove Tuesday | ☐ |
| **C** | Ash Wednesday | ☐ |
| **D** | Good Friday | ☐ |

*[1 mark]*

**2.2** Give two examples of popular destinations for Christian pilgrims.

*[2 marks]*

**2.3** Explain two contrasting views on the importance of evangelism.

*[4 marks]*

**2.4** Explain two ways in which the Lord's Prayer is important to Christians.
Your answer should refer to specific Christian teachings or sacred texts.

*[5 marks]*

**2.5** 'The presence of the actual body and blood of Christ is what makes the Eucharist important.'

Evaluate this statement. Your answer should include the following:
• examples from Christian teachings
• arguments that support the statement
• arguments that disagree with the statement
• a conclusion.

*[12 marks]*

## CATHOLIC CHRISTIANITY — Beliefs

If you are studying Catholic Christianity, answer **all** the questions on this page

3.1 Which of the following is the place where people are purified after death?
Put a tick (✓) in the correct box.

A   Heaven     ☐

B   Purgatory   ☐

C   Immortality  ☐

D   Hell        ☐

*[1 mark]*

3.2 Give two Christian beliefs about Jesus's ascension.

*[2 marks]*

3.3 Explain two ways in which the idea of judgement influences Christians today.

*[4 marks]*

3.4 Explain two ways in which the creation story influences
the way Christians understand God and the universe.
Your answer should refer to specific Christian teachings or sacred texts.

*[5 marks]*

3.5 'Jesus's death on the cross is more important to Christians than his resurrection.'

Evaluate this statement. Your answer should include the following:
• examples from Christian teachings
• arguments that support the statement
• arguments that disagree with the statement
• a conclusion.

*[12 marks]*

*[+3 SPaG marks]*

176

## CATHOLIC CHRISTIANITY — Practices
If you are studying Catholic Christianity, answer **all** the questions on this page

**4.1** Which of the following is a description of the 'Stations of the Cross'?
Put a tick (✓) in the correct box.

| | | |
|---|---|---|
| **A** | Pictures of Jesus's suffering | ☐ |
| **B** | A necklace of beads | ☐ |
| **C** | Locations on a pilgrimage | ☐ |
| **D** | The place where Jesus was crucified | ☐ |

*[1 mark]*

**4.2** Give two examples of popular destinations for Christian pilgrims.

*[2 marks]*

**4.3** Explain two contrasting views on the importance of evangelism.

*[4 marks]*

**4.4** Explain two reasons why Catholic Christians perform the sacrament of anointing the sick.
Your answer should refer to specific Christian teachings or sacred texts.

*[5 marks]*

**4.5** 'Informal prayer is more important to Christians than formal prayer.'

Evaluate this statement. Your answer should include the following:
• examples from Christian teachings
• arguments that support the statement
• arguments that disagree with the statement
• a conclusion.

*[12 marks]*

## ISLAM — Beliefs

If you are studying Islam, answer **all** the questions on this page

**5.1** Which of the following do Muslims believe was a prophet?
Put a tick (✓) in the correct box.

**A** Jibril ☐

**B** Mika'il ☐

**C** Ibrahim ☐

**D** Iblis ☐

*[1 mark]*

**5.2** Give two articles of faith in Sunni Islam.

*[2 marks]*

**5.3** Explain two ways in which belief about the Qur'an may influence Muslims today.

*[4 marks]*

**5.4** Explain two Muslim beliefs about the nature of God.
Your answer should refer to specific Muslim teachings or sacred texts.

*[5 marks]*

**5.5** 'It is impossible to believe in both predestination and free will.'

Evaluate this statement. Your answer should include the following:
• examples from Muslim teachings
• arguments that support the statement
• arguments that disagree with the statement
• a conclusion.

*[12 marks]*
*[+3 SPaG marks]*

# ISLAM — Practices

If you are studying Islam, answer **all** the questions on this page

**6.1** Which of the following is the name given to the celebration of the 'Night of Power',
the commemoration of Muhammad first receiving the Qur'an?
Put a tick (✓) in the correct box.

    **A**    Laylat al-Qadr    ☐

    **B**    Zakah    ☐

    **C**    Ashura    ☐

    **D**    Id ul-Adha    ☐

*[1 mark]*

**6.2** Give two of the Ten Obligatory Acts.

*[2 marks]*

**6.3** Explain two contrasting ways in which Salah is performed.

*[4 marks]*

**6.4** Explain two reasons why Id ul-Fitr is important to Muslims.
Your answer should refer to specific Muslim teachings or sacred texts.

*[5 marks]*

**6.5** 'Jihad should be the main duty in a Muslim's life.'

Evaluate this statement. Your answer should include the following:
• examples from Muslim teachings
• arguments that support the statement
• arguments that disagree with the statement
• a conclusion.

*[12 marks]*

## JUDAISM — Beliefs

If you are studying Judaism, answer **all** the questions on this page

**7.1** Which of the following words means that God is all-powerful?
Put a tick (✓) in the correct box.

**A** Eternal ☐

**B** Omnipotent ☐

**C** Omnipresent ☐

**D** Immanent ☐

*[1 mark]*

**7.2** Name two ways in which the mitzvot can be grouped.

*[2 marks]*

**7.3** Explain two ways in which beliefs about the nature of God influence Jews today.

*[4 marks]*

**7.4** Explain two Jewish beliefs about God's presence on Earth.
Your answer should refer to specific Jewish teachings or sacred texts.

*[5 marks]*

**7.5** 'Belief in one God is a Jew's most important duty.'

Evaluate this statement. Your answer should include the following:
• examples from Jewish teachings
• arguments that support the statement
• arguments that disagree with the statement
• a conclusion.

*[12 marks]*
*[+3 SPaG marks]*

## JUDAISM — Practices
### If you are studying Judaism, answer all the questions on this page

**8.1** Which of the following describes the Jewish food laws?
Put a tick (✓) in the correct box.

A    Challot    ☐

B    Simchat bat    ☐

C    Kavanah    ☐

D    Kashrut    ☐

*[1 mark]*

**8.2** Give two ways in which Jews mark Rosh Hashanah.

*[2 marks]*

**8.3** Explain two contrasting features of Orthodox and Reform synagogue buildings.

*[4 marks]*

**8.4** Explain two ways in which prayer is important for Jews.
Your answer should refer to specific Jewish teachings or sacred texts.

*[5 marks]*

**8.5** 'Jewish rituals are more significant for boys than for girls.'

Evaluate this statement. Your answer should include the following:
• examples from Jewish teachings
• arguments that support the statement
• arguments that disagree with the statement
• a conclusion.

*[12 marks]*

## Practice Paper 2

For this practice paper, answer the question on **each** of the **four themes** you have studied —
so you need to answer **four questions** in total. Each question has **five parts**. If you have studied
**St Mark's Gospel**, answer the questions on **Themes G** and **H**, as well as **two** other questions from
**Themes A-F**. If you **haven't** studied St Mark's Gospel, answer **four** questions from **Themes A-F**.
You'll need some paper to write your answers on.

# GCSE Religious Studies

## Paper 2: Thematic Studies

| Centre name | | | | | |
|---|---|---|---|---|---|
| Centre number | | | | | |
| Candidate number | | | | | |

| Surname |
|---|
| Other names |
| Candidate signature |

### Time allowed:
* 1 hour 45 minutes

### Instructions to candidates
* Write your name and other details in the spaces provided above.
* Write in black ink or ballpoint pen.
* Answer **all** questions on the four themes you have studied.
* Do all rough work on your answer paper.
  Cross through any work you do not want marked.

### Information for candidates
* The marks available are given in brackets at the end of each question.
* There are 99 marks available for this paper.
* There are 3 marks available for spelling, punctuation and grammar for each 12-mark question,
  but only your highest SPaG mark across all four answers will count towards your overall mark.

### Advice to candidates
* Aim to spend around 25 minutes on each theme.
For multiple choice questions:
* Clearly tick the box next to your chosen answer. For example: ✓
* If you wish to change your answer, put a cross through your original
  answer. For example: ☒
* If you wish to change your answer back to one that you have previously
  crossed out, draw a circle around the answer. For example: ⊗

## Theme A — Relationships and Families
If you are studying Theme A, answer **all** the questions on this page

**1.1** Which of the following terms describes a family where a couple live together with their children? Put a tick (✓) in the correct box.

   **A**   Nuclear  ☐

   **B**   Extended  ☐

   **C**   Beanpole  ☐

   **D**   Single-parent  ☐

*[1 mark]*

**1.2** Give two religious beliefs about gender discrimination.

*[2 marks]*

**1.3** Explain two contrasting beliefs regarding cohabitation.
You must refer to the views of at least one religious group.

*[4 marks]*

**1.4** Explain two religious beliefs about contraception.
Your answer should refer to specific religious teachings or sacred texts.

*[5 marks]*

**1.5** 'Divorced people should not be allowed to remarry.'

Evaluate this statement. Your answer should include the following:
• religious arguments that support the statement
• religious arguments that disagree with the statement
• a conclusion.
You can also include non-religious points of view in your answer.

*[12 marks]*
*[+3 SPaG marks]*

**Theme B — Religion and Life**

If you are studying Theme B, answer **all** the questions on this page

2.1 Which of the following is the idea that humans have power over nature?
Put a tick (✓) in the correct box.

**A** Creation ☐

**B** Stewardship ☐

**C** Dominion ☐

**D** Humanism ☐

*[1 mark]*

2.2 Give two arguments against the existence of an afterlife.

*[2 marks]*

2.3 Explain two contrasting beliefs in British society today about the sanctity of life.
You must refer to the main religious tradition in the UK
and at least one other religious viewpoint.

*[4 marks]*

2.4 Explain two religious beliefs about the origins of human life.
Your answer should refer to specific religious teachings or sacred texts.

*[5 marks]*

2.5 'Abortion is acceptable in certain circumstances.'

Evaluate this statement. Your answer should include the following:
• religious arguments that support the statement
• religious arguments that disagree with the statement
• a conclusion.
You can also include non-religious points of view in your answer.

*[12 marks]*

*[+3 SPaG marks]*

## Theme C — The Existence of God and Revelation
### If you are studying Theme C, answer **all** the questions on this page

**3.1** Which of the following is the meaning of the word 'transcendent'?
Put a tick (✓) in the correct box.

| | | |
|---|---|---|
| **A** | All-powerful | ☐ |
| **B** | Part of the physical world | ☐ |
| **C** | Able to travel anywhere at any time | ☐ |
| **D** | Separate from the world | ☐ |

*[1 mark]*

**3.2** Give two examples of miracles found in major religious texts.

*[2 marks]*

**3.3** Explain two contrasting beliefs about why evil and suffering exist in the world.
You must refer to the views of at least one religious group.

*[4 marks]*

**3.4** Explain two religious beliefs about revelation in scripture.
Your answer should refer to specific religious teachings or sacred texts.

*[5 marks]*

**3.5** 'The First Cause argument is proof that God exists.'

Evaluate this statement. Your answer should include the following:
• religious arguments that support the statement
• religious arguments that disagree with the statement
• a conclusion.
You can also include non-religious points of view in your answer.

*[12 marks]*
*[+3 SPaG marks]*

## Theme D — Religion, Peace and Conflict
If you are studying Theme D, answer **all** the questions on this page

4.1 Which of the following means deliberately causing harm or injury
while campaigning for a cause? Put a tick (✓) in the correct box.

    **A**    Tribalism ☐

    **B**    Discrimination ☐

    **C**    Violent protest ☐

    **D**    Conversion ☐

*[1 mark]*

4.2 Give two examples of how religious people might support
victims of war without visiting the war zone themselves.

*[2 marks]*

4.3 Explain two similar religious beliefs about terrorism.
You must refer to the views of at least one religious group.

*[4 marks]*

4.4 Explain two religious beliefs about the use of weapons of mass destruction.
Your answer should refer to specific religious teachings or sacred texts.

*[5 marks]*

4.5 'Religion should never be used to justify violence.'

Evaluate this statement. Your answer should include the following:
• religious arguments that support the statement
• religious arguments that disagree with the statement
• a conclusion.
You can also include non-religious points of view in your answer.

*[12 marks]*

*[+3 SPaG marks]*

## Theme E — Religion, Crime and Punishment
If you are studying Theme E, answer **all** the questions on this page

5.1 Which of the following means breaking one of God's laws?
Put a tick (✓) in the correct box.

**A**    Mitzvot        ☐

**B**    Sin             ☐

**C**    Judgement    ☐

**D**    Restitution    ☐

*[1 mark]*

5.2 Give two reasons that religious believers might give to justify punishing criminals.

*[2 marks]*

5.3 Explain two contrasting beliefs in British society today about forgiveness.
You must refer to the main religious tradition in the UK
and at least one other religious viewpoint.

*[4 marks]*

5.4 Explain two religious beliefs about corporal punishment.
Your answer should refer to specific religious teachings or sacred texts.

*[5 marks]*

5.5 'Responsibility for breaking the law lies entirely with the person who commits the crime.'

Evaluate this statement. Your answer should include the following:
• religious arguments that support the statement
• religious arguments that disagree with the statement
• a conclusion.
You can also include non-religious points of view in your answer.

*[12 marks]*
*[+3 SPaG marks]*

## Theme F — Religion, Human Rights and Social Justice
If you are studying Theme F, answer **all** the questions on this page

**6.1** Which of the following is a key idea behind social justice?
Put a tick (✓) in the correct box.

    **A**    People can follow any faith. ☐

    **B**    People should have the right to a fair trial. ☐

    **C**    Criminals should do community service. ☐

    **D**    Everyone should be treated fairly. ☐

*[1 mark]*

**6.2** Give two religious beliefs about human rights.

*[2 marks]*

**6.3** Explain two similar religious beliefs about freedom of belief.
You must refer to the views of at least one religious group.

*[4 marks]*

**6.4** Explain two religious beliefs about giving money to the poor.
Your answer should refer to specific religious teachings or sacred texts.

*[5 marks]*

**6.5** 'Religion should lead the way on equality.'

Evaluate this statement. Your answer should include the following:
• religious arguments that support the statement
• religious arguments that disagree with the statement
• a conclusion.
You can also include non-religious points of view in your answer.

*[12 marks]*
*[+3 SPaG marks]*

## Theme G — St Mark's Gospel: the Life of Jesus
### If you are studying Theme G, answer **all** the questions on this page

**7.1** Which of the following is the reason Pilate offered to release Jesus?
Put a tick (✓) in the correct box.

A     The chief priests asked him to ☐

B     It was Passover ☐

C     He was afraid of the crowd ☐

D     Barabbas was too dangerous ☐

*[1 mark]*

**7.2** Give two reasons why it is important to Christians that Mark calls Jesus 'the Messiah'.

*[2 marks]*

**7.3** Explain two contrasting views about the truth of the miracle stories in Mark's Gospel.

*[4 marks]*

**7.4** Explain two reasons why the story of James and John's request is important to Christians.
Your answer should refer to Mark's Gospel.

*[5 marks]*

**7.5** 'Jesus voluntarily sacrificed himself for the sake of mankind.'

Evaluate this statement. Your answer should include the following:
• references to Mark's Gospel
• arguments that support the statement
• arguments that disagree with the statement
• a conclusion.

*[12 marks]*
*[+3 SPaG marks]*

**Theme H — St Mark's Gospel as a Source of Religious, Moral and Spiritual Truths**
If you are studying Theme H, answer **all** the questions on this page

**8.1** Which of the following asked Jesus about the most important commandment?
Put a tick (✓) in the correct box.

A    A young child            ☐

B    One of the disciples     ☐

C    A Roman soldier          ☐

D    A teacher of the law     ☐

*[1 mark]*

**8.2** Give two reasons why sick or disabled people were excluded from first century society.
*[2 marks]*

**8.3** Explain two contrasting beliefs about Peter's denial of Jesus.
*[4 marks]*

**8.4** Explain two reasons why the story of the rich man is important to modern-day Christians.
Your answer should refer to Mark's Gospel.
*[5 marks]*

**8.5** 'Jesus's treatment of the poor and sick is the most important part of his teaching.'

Evaluate this statement.  Your answer should include the following:
• references to Mark's Gospel
• arguments that support the statement
• arguments that disagree with the statement
• a conclusion.

*[12 marks]*
*[+3 SPaG marks]*

## Mark Schemes

The answers provided here are just examples of points you could make. Other answers are acceptable, as long as they are relevant and correct.

Use this mark scheme for all 4-mark questions:

- *Marks can be awarded for up to two correct points.*
- *For each correct point, award 2 marks for a detailed explanation, or 1 mark for a simple explanation.*
- *If the question asks how a belief influences people, the answer must discuss influences, not just the belief itself. If the question asks for similar points, the second point can only receive marks if it's similar to the first one. For a contrasting question, the second point must contain a contrasting idea to the first.*
- *If the question specifies that the views of the main religious tradition in the UK (Christianity) must be discussed, a maximum of 2 marks can be awarded if no Christian viewpoints have been given.*

Use this mark scheme for all 5-mark questions:

- *Marks can be awarded for up to two correct points.*
- *For each correct point, award 2 marks for a detailed explanation, or 1 mark for a simple explanation.*
- *Award 1 additional mark if the answer contains a suitable and correct reference to a sacred text or specific religious teaching.*

12-mark questions are level marked — read the level descriptions below, and work out which level best suits the answer. Then decide whether the answer deserves a lower or higher mark within the range, depending on the quality of the answer.

Use this mark scheme for all 12-mark questions:

Level 0: There is no relevant information. *[0 marks]*

Level 1: The answer contains one point of view, with one or more reasons given to support it. *[1-3 marks]*

Level 2: A careful consideration of one point of view is given. The response should be logical and well-reasoned, demonstrating knowledge and understanding of evidence for that point of view. *[4-6 marks]*
OR The answer contains more than one point of view. One or more reasons are given in support of each. *[4-6 marks]*

Level 3: A careful consideration of more than one point of view is given. The response should be logical and well-reasoned, demonstrating knowledge and understanding of evidence for each point of view. There must be a clear reference to one or more religions. *[7-9 marks]*

Level 4: A well-argued answer, with careful consideration of more than one point of view and a conclusion. The response should be logical and well-reasoned, demonstrating knowledge and understanding of evidence for each point of view. There must be clear references to one or more religions. *[10-12 marks]*

Some 12-mark questions have 3 extra marks available for spelling, punctuation and grammar. This is highlighted on the relevant questions — use this mark scheme to award marks for spelling, punctuation and grammar:

*[3 marks]* for accurate spelling, punctuation and grammar throughout, including correct spelling and use of a wide range of specialist terms.

*[2 marks]* for generally accurate spelling, punctuation and grammar. A good range of specialist terms are used correctly.

*[1 mark]* for reasonably accurate spelling, punctuation and grammar. Limited range of specialist terms used.

*[0 marks]* for no response, an answer that is not relevant to the question, or one in which the spelling, punctuation and grammar are so poor that the meaning is unclear.

## Beliefs, Teachings and Practices — Christianity and Catholic Christianity

### Page 10

5   Grace *[1 mark]*

6   - When God created the world, it was purely good.
- When Adam and Eve disobeyed God, evil came into the world. This is known as 'the Fall'.
- Adam and Eve were tempted by Satan, who is evil.
- God created humans with free will, so they can choose whether or not to commit evil.
*[2 marks available, 1 mark for each correct point]*

7   - God created humans "in his own image" (Genesis 1:27 NIV). This means that humans are special when compared to the rest of creation, so they should all be treated with respect.
- Since humans are created in God's image, they should try to be more like God — they should be benevolent and just.
- God created Adam and Eve individually — he made Adam from dust and Eve from Adam's rib. Christians believe that this shows God's special love for human beings, and the personal relationship they can have with him.
*[4 marks available — see p.190 for mark scheme]*

8   Arguments that support the statement:
- Believing in the Trinity means believing that Jesus is divine. This belief is necessary to understand how the story of Jesus's death and resurrection, as told in the Gospels, leads to the salvation of Christians. So without an understanding of the Trinity, Christian belief is impossible.
- A belief in the Trinity is the only way that Christians can make sense of what God is like in the Bible, the main text of the religion. The Father is the God of the Old Testament who created the universe and spoke to Adam, Abraham and Moses. The Son is Jesus who lived as a human being on earth. The Holy Spirit is the unseen presence of God that guides people.
- The idea of the Trinity was a major issue at the Councils of Nicaea and Constantinople, and a description of it makes up the Nicene Creed. This shows how important the belief is to Christians.
Arguments against the statement:
- Some Christians, like Christadelphians and Jehovah's Witnesses, do not believe in the Trinity. However, they still consider themselves Christians, which shows that this belief is not the most important for all Christians.
- Belief in the salvation of mankind through Jesus's death on the cross is more important than a belief in the Trinity. Without it, the religion would not exist. It is possible to believe that Jesus was the Son of God without believing in the Trinity.
- There is no direct reference to the Trinity in the Bible, although the Father, the Son and the Holy Spirit are all referred to. This suggests that the Trinity is not the most important belief for Christians, because there are other teachings which appear repeatedly in the Bible like Jesus's teachings on the kingdom of God or the importance of loving others.
*[12 marks available — see p.190 for mark scheme]*

### Page 21

5   A baptism *[1 mark]*

6   - During Lent, the 40 days before Easter, some Christians fast or choose to give something up. They do this to remember the story in the Gospels of Jesus fasting in the desert for 40 days.
- On Good Friday, the day Jesus was crucified, Christians go to church services to remember his suffering. Sometimes these services last three hours — according to Mark's Gospel, this was the amount of time the sky was dark just before Jesus died: "At noon, darkness came over the whole land until three in the afternoon" (Mark 15:33).
- Some churches have services at sunrise on Easter Day to represent Mary Magdalene's discovery of Jesus's empty tomb at sunrise as told in the Gospels.

- In some churches, a Paschal candle is lit on Easter Day. The light of the candle represents the resurrection of Jesus, who said he was "the light of the world" (John 8:12 NIV).
*[5 marks available — see p.190 for mark scheme]*

7 Arguments that support the statement:
- In recent years, shrines like Lourdes have become very commercialised and busy. Some Christians argue that they will be closer to God if they stay at home and go on an inner journey of faith instead.
- Some Christians argue that God is omnipresent — in Jeremiah, he asks "Do not I fill heaven and earth?" (Jeremiah 23:24 NIV). This suggests that there is no need to travel to get closer to him.
- There are no passages in the New Testament which tell Christians to go on pilgrimages, so some Christians argue that they are not important.
Arguments against the statement:
- Many Catholics consider pilgrimage to be important because it represents people's journey towards God. In the Catechism of the Catholic Church (2691), it says that pilgrimages "evoke our earthly journey toward heaven".
- Some Christians go on pilgrimages to escape everyday life and concentrate on their faith in peace. For example, they might go to Taizé or Iona. Modern life can be very fast-paced and hectic, so pilgrimages to calm locations are arguably more important to Christians today.
- The large number of people visiting shrines like Lourdes proves that pilgrimage remains important to Christians in the modern day. They still travel to distant locations in the hope that they will be healed or their faith will be strengthened.
*[12 marks available — see p.190 for mark scheme]*

## Beliefs, Teachings and Practices — Islam

### Page 30

5 Malaikah *[1 mark]*

6 - The angel Israfil will sound the trumpet.
- The dead will be resurrected.
- Allah will judge all people according to their deeds.
- Those judged to have lived good lives will go to paradise, those judged to have lived immoral lives will go to hell.
*[2 marks available, 1 mark for each correct point]*

7 - Muslims will not accept that there may be more than one god. To do so would be shirk, which is considered to be the gravest of all sins. For example, Muslims disagree with the Christian concept of the Holy Trinity, as it goes against Tawhid.
- Muslims will affirm this belief through the shahadah. Many Muslims repeat this belief through the shahadah several times throughout the day, as well as at key events such as birth, deaths and marriages.
- Muslims will avoid making images of Allah as this risks shirk. Worshipping images and statues is similar to the forbidden worship of idols. Instead, Islamic art has found other ways of representing Allah visually, e.g. through depicting some, or all, of the ninety-nine names of Allah.
- When explaining Islam to non-Muslims, Muslims may tell them about Tawhid.
*[4 marks available — see p.190 for mark scheme]*

8 Arguments that support the statement:
- In the first revelation, Muhammad was commanded by the angel Jibril to "Recite!" what would become Surah 96. Receiving the revelations that would become the Qur'an took the next twenty-three years of Muhammad's life. The task was not completed quickly, but continued over time, suggesting it was his main role.
- The teaching of messengership (risalah) explains that the role of a prophet is to receive the message of Allah through angels. The Qur'an identifies 25 prophets who have taken on this role, including Muhammad. As such, messengership could be seen as his primary role.

- Muhammad was Allah's final prophet (the 'seal of the prophets') with no more to follow. His life centred around receiving and reciting the Qur'an, and ensuring his scribes recorded the teachings, suggesting this role took precedence over all others.
Arguments against the statement:
- Muhammad's main role was to be a model for how to live according to Allah's wishes. Preaching the Qur'an was one aspect of this role, but living in accordance to Allah's wishes was Muhammad's main role, as it is for all Muslims.
- Muhammad's role cannot be reduced to just a single element. It included preaching and recording what was revealed to him as well as exemplifying these teachings and becoming a spiritual and political leader in Makkah.
- Muhammad played an important role in the spread and preservation of Islam. He helped to establish Islam across the Arab world and acted to defend both the Islamic faith and Muslim communities from hostile forces.
*[12 marks available — see p.190 for mark scheme]*

### Page 37

5 Ihram *[1 mark]*

6 Ibrahim *[1 mark]*

7 The Ka'aba and/or the black stone, Zamzam Well, Safa and/or Marwa, Mount Arafat, Muzdalifa, the three pillars at Mina.
*[2 marks available, 1 mark for each correct point]*

8 - Sawm symbolises physical and spiritual discipline in obedience to Allah. It encompasses more than simply fasting, but abstaining from sexual relations, wasting time and harmful actions.
- It is required by the Qur'an: "O you who have believed, decreed upon you is fasting as it was decreed upon those before you that you may become righteous" (Qur'an 2:183).
- For Sunni Muslims, sawm is one of the Five Pillars. For Shi'a Muslims, it is one of the Ten Obligatory Acts.
- It is an expression of thanksgiving for the Qur'an, which is believed to have first been given to Muhammad on the Night of Power: "Indeed, We sent the Qur'an down during the Night of Decree" (Qur'an 97:1) / "The Night of Decree is better than a thousand months" (Qur'an 97:3). Many Muslims will read the Qur'an from start to finish while fasting during Ramadan to mark this key point in Muslim history.
- It is a reminder for Muslims to prioritise spirituality and religious responsibilities. The annual demands of sawm act to aid Muslims in re-aligning their lives to the will of Allah:
"...Whoever fasts during the month of Ramadan out of sincere faith and hoping to attain Allah's rewards, then all his past sins will be forgiven" (Sahih al-Bukhari Volume 1, Book 2, Hadith 37).
*[5 marks available — see p.190 for mark scheme]*

## Beliefs, Teachings and Practices — Judaism

### Page 45

5 Exodus *[1 mark]*

6 - God made a covenant with Abraham, agreeing to give Abraham land, descendants and his blessing: "The whole land of Canaan... I will give as an everlasting possession to you and your descendants... and I will be their God" (Genesis 17:8 NIV). In return, Abraham and his descendants had to obey God and live their lives as an example to others.
- The sign of the covenant between Abraham and God was the circumcision of all of Abraham's male descendants: "every male among you shall be circumcised" (Genesis 17:10 NIV).
- The covenant meant Abraham and his family moved to Canaan, as God told Abraham to leave and go to the "land I will show you" where "I will make you into a great nation" (Genesis 12:1-2 NIV). This meant Canaan became known as the 'promised land' and represents a very important aspect of the covenant for Jews.

- As part of the covenant, God promised to give Abraham and his wife, Sarah, a child. Jews believe this direct male descendant of Abraham and Sarah was Isaac: "your wife Sarah will bear you a son, and you will call him Isaac. I will establish my covenant with him as an everlasting covenant for his descendants after him" (Genesis 17:19 NIV).
- Jews believe that the covenant is a binding agreement between God and the Jewish people. The covenant with Abraham was followed by other covenants — for example, with Moses.

*[5 marks available — see p.190 for mark scheme]*

7  Arguments that support the statement:
- Prophecies in the Tenakh support the claim that the Messiah will bring peace and prosperity: "a King who will reign wisely and do what is just and right" (Jeremiah 23:5 NIV). Prophecies in Ezekiel state that God will send the Messiah during a period of strife, to "rid the land of savage beasts" (Ezekiel 34:25 NIV). This clearly illustrates the Messiah's role in achieving peace on Earth.
- Only the Messiah can achieve this as one chosen by God. Jews believe that while the Messiah will be human, he will be descended from King David and have a perfect understanding of God's law. Only this person, sent by God, could possibly achieve peace and prosperity on Earth.
- Achieving peace on Earth can only be done by spreading God's law across the land to both Jews and non-Jews. This means an unparalleled political leader. Jews believe the only person who could do this is the Messiah, to whom other world leaders will look to for guidance and leadership: "He will judge between the nations and will settle disputes for many peoples" (Isaiah 2:4 NIV).
Arguments against the statement:
- While the Messiah may play a part in achieving peace and prosperity on Earth, ultimately this can be achieved by God alone. The Messiah will achieve peace through the power of God as Moses led the Israelites to freedom through the power of God: "The Spirit of the Lord will rest on him" (Isaiah 11:2).
- Many Reform and Progressive Jews believe that the idea of a Messiah bringing peace on Earth should be interpreted metaphorically. Rather than being a literal prediction, it is a positive vision of how the world could be under the right circumstances.
- It isn't right to just rely on a Messiah. Each person has a responsibility to work towards peace and prosperity.
This underlines the importance of compassion, charity and making good use of the free will gifted to people by God.

*[12 marks available — see p.190 for mark scheme]*

## Page 54

5  Atonement *[1 mark]*

6  - The couple receive blessings and share wine.
This may include the seven blessings (sheva b'rakhot) during the wedding ceremony itself.
- Giving blessings for Israel and Jerusalem.
- The groom gives the bride a ring and states the wedding vow. In some Progressive Jewish weddings this ritual is reciprocated by the bride.
- A marriage contract (ketubah) is read out.
- Holding the wedding ceremony (nisuin) under a canopy (huppah).
- The breaking of a glass (which is often covered first).

*[2 marks available, 1 mark for each correct point]*

7  - The body of the deceased is treated with the utmost respect as the former host of the person's soul. For this reason the body is buried rather than cremated, and procedures such as autopsies are avoided as far as possible.
- However, some Reform Jews have allowed cremations, though this is not universal within the movement. This stems from the belief that while burial is often a preference, cremation is not identified anywhere within the law as a sin.
- Progressive Jews are also more likely to accept cremation, as they do not believe the body will be physically resurrected — they believe that the body is just a vessel for the soul.

- The mourning for the loss of a parent (avelut) lasts a year. Mourners avoid joyous occasions during this time, avoid buying new clothing and, for the first month at least, do not shave or cut their hair.
- In contrast, the mourning for the loss of other relatives is restricted to one month after the funeral (sheloshim). During this time, they are not expected to bear some of their normal communal responsibilities, such as attending festival meals. After this time, a person is expected to participate in the community again.

*[4 marks available — see p.190 for mark scheme]*

8  Arguments that support the statement:
- The Tenakh contains the Torah, which contains the core Jewish laws and teachings. Through the Torah, the Tenakh is a complete record of all 613 mitzvot (commandments). This includes the Ten Commandments, and so provides all the necessary guidance for living according to the Covenant, e.g. "Remember the Sabbath day by keeping it holy" (Exodus 20:8 NIV).
- While there are other teachings outside of the Tenakh which may be helpful to know, the Tenakh contains the essential teachings that Jews need to know. Abiding by the Covenant recorded in the Tenakh is fundamentally what is required by God: "Now if you obey me fully and keep my covenant, then out of all nations you will be my treasured possession" (Exodus 19:5 NIV).
- Guidance on the Torah can be found within the Tenakh itself. The other parts of the Tenakh, the Prophets (Nevi'im) and Writings (Ketuvim), provide helpful advice and clarification of the mitzvot such as how and when to pray: "Evening, morning and noon I cry out in distress, and he hears my voice" (Psalm 55:17 NIV).
Arguments against the statement:
- The study of the oral law (the Talmud) is important for living daily life well. The Tenakh, while sacred, is an ancient document, which requires interpretation in the context of modern life. Many Orthodox Jews try to do more than what the mitzvot require so that none are broken accidentally and the Talmud is helpful for this.
- Daily life can be unpredictable and occasionally the laws contained in the Tenakh may not be appropriate. For instance, there may be times when preserving the lives of others is at odds with the demands of the Tenakh. In these circumstances, the Talmud is needed to give guidance: "Every danger to human life suspends the [laws of the] Sabbath" (Talmud Yoma 83a).
- While the Tenakh contains essential teachings, Jewish children also need the living example of prayer and worship in the home. The Shema states that children should learn not only from the Tenakh but from their parents: "These commandments that I give you today are to be on your hearts. Impress them on your children" (Deuteronomy 6:6-7 NIV).
- Living well in daily life comes from a combination of studying the Tenakh, the Talmud and learning from others. Often this can be done in study groups in the synagogue or by discussing difficulties with a rabbi. Out of this arises a range of additional principles and responsibilities from the sanctity of life (pikuach nefesh) to acting as custodians of the environment.

*[12 marks available — see p.190 for mark scheme]*

# Theme A — Relationships and Families

## Page 64

4  Adultery *[1 mark]*

5  - Roman Catholics believe that divorce is impossible due to marriage being a sacrament.
- Some Christians, such as many from the Church of England, believe people should be given second chances and so should be allowed to divorce.
- In Islam, divorce is permitted but has to be requested three times over a three-month period.
- According to Muslims, Allah does not take divorce lightly.
- In Judaism, divorce is allowed but is always viewed as a last resort.

- For Jews, marriage is a very serious commitment and should be intended to be permanent.
*[2 marks available, 1 mark for each correct point]*

6   Viewpoints that oppose homosexuality:
- The book of Leviticus states: "If a man has sexual relations with a man as one does with a woman, both of them have done what is detestable" (Leviticus 20:13 NIV). Some Christians use this to argue that homosexuality is wrong.
- Some Muslims believe homosexual relationships are forbidden by Islam due to teachings in the Qur'an, such as the story of Sodom and Gomorrah.
- The Torah teaches that homosexuality is a sin, so many Orthodox Jews believe that homosexual relationships are wrong.
Viewpoints that support homosexuality:
- Jesus taught about equality and stood up for people in the minority. Some Christians therefore see everyone as being equal, regardless of sexuality.
- The Qur'an only forbids homosexual actions, not feelings, so it doesn't condemn actually being homosexual.
- Reform Jews campaigned for the introduction of same-sex marriage. They use the teaching that we are all made in the image of God to support the idea that everyone, regardless of sexuality, should be treated equally.
*[4 marks available — see p.190 for mark scheme]*

## Page 71

2   Gender inequality *[1 mark]*

3   Viewpoints that support same-sex parenting:
- In the UK, same-sex couples can adopt, foster and legally use a surrogate to create a family. Therefore, some people completely support same-sex parenting.
- Some believers hold the view that the most important aspects of a family are security and love. They consider these values to be more important than the sexual orientation of the parents and accept that the most loving thing is to adapt religious teachings to the modern world.
- Some less traditional believers think that an individual's happiness is at the heart of a relationship. They therefore support same-sex parenting as long as the couple are in a loving relationship.
Viewpoints that oppose same-sex parenting:
- Some traditional believers hold the view that heterosexual relationships provide the role models children need to grow and develop within a family. They see this as being are part of God's plan. They argue that same-sex parenting cannot provide the same role models.
- The Roman Catholic Church teaches that same-sex parenting is wrong. This is due to their beliefs that God created men and women to form a family, and due to their rejection of homosexuality.
- Most Muslims do not support the idea of same-sex parenting because they believe homosexuality is wrong.
- The Torah forbids a sexual relationship between two people of the same sex. In traditional Jewish families, men and women have specific parenting roles. So same-sex parenting is opposed, particularly by Orthodox Jews.
*[4 marks available — see p.190 for mark scheme]*

4   - Many Christians believe that children are a gift from God, and that parents have a responsibility to teach them to live how God would want them to: "bring them up in the training and instruction of the Lord" (Ephesians 6:4 NIV).
- Christian parents might teach their children key passages from the Bible such as the Ten Commandments or The Lord's Prayer. Parents are encouraged to do this in the Old Testament: "These commandments that I give you today are to be on your hearts. Impress them on your children." (Deuteronomy 6:6-7 NIV).
- In Judaism, birth rituals concerning male circumcision and the naming of girls ensure that Jewish children are connected to the faith from birth. Children must learn about Judaism in preparation for bar and bat mitzvah ceremonies.

- As Jewish families believe that family life is a training ground for the Jewish way of life, the home plays a vital role in educating children. For example, the home is where children can learn about Jewish worship, such as the weekly Shabbat celebration or marking of Jewish festivals. Proverbs 22:6 says "Start children off on the way they should go, and even when they are old they will not turn from it" (NIV).
- Muslim parents believe that educating their children about Islam is a crucial part of their role: "And Abraham instructed his sons [to do the same] and [so did] Jacob, [saying], 'O my sons, indeed Allah has chosen for you this religion, so do not die except while you are Muslims'" (Qur'an 2:132).
- Rituals such as the naming ceremony (aqiqah) and the bismillah ceremony (where a child first starts to learn about Islam) are considered crucial in ensuring Muslim children have clear understanding of their faith.
*[5 marks available — see p.190 for mark scheme]*

## Theme B — Religion and Life

### Page 79

2   The Big Bang theory *[1 mark]*

3   Only human life is sacred *[1 mark]*.

4   - The Universe was created by God.
- The Universe was created in six days.
- After creating the Universe, God rested for a day.
- The Universe was created according to the Big Bang theory but controlled by God.
- The creation story in the book of Genesis is a metaphor for how God created the Universe.
*[2 marks available, 1 mark for each correct point]*

5   - Christians believe that God gave humans the Earth to look after. This is known as stewardship. They believe that all Christians have a duty to take care of the environment.
- Jews also believe in stewardship. They believe that the Earth belongs to God, so humans should look after it.
- Jews believe that they should not only protect the world and the environment, they should also try to make it better. This is known as tikkun olam.
- Muslims believe that humans are khalifah (trustees or vice-regents) of the world. This means that they have a duty to act as stewards and to protect the environment.
*[4 marks available — see p.190 for mark scheme]*

### Page 86

4   Belgium *[1 mark]*

5   Believing in the afterlife is a comfort to people when someone dies *[1 mark]*.

6   - Before 24 weeks if continuing to be pregnant would be worse for the mother's physical and mental health (if two doctors agree).
- At any time if the mother's life is at serious risk.
- At any time if the foetus has a serious disability.
*[2 marks available, 1 mark for each correct point]*

7   Arguments that support the statement:
- Judaism teaches that, in the future, the Messiah will establish God's kingdom on Earth, and some or all people will be resurrected. Belief in resurrection is one of Maimonides' 13 principles of faith, so the afterlife is an important part of Judaism.
- Muslims believe that after death they will either go to paradise (jannah) or hell (jahannam). Their ultimate aim is to spend eternity in jannah in the afterlife, so it could be argued that it must be more important than life on Earth.
- A key part of the Christian faith is that Jesus was resurrected from death, and returned to heaven at the ascension to prepare a place there for those that believe in him. The afterlife is therefore central to Christianity, and ultimately joining Jesus in heaven is more important than any experience on Earth.

Arguments against the statement:
- The Torah focuses on life on Earth, and does not talk a lot about the afterlife. Jews are encouraged to live good lives for the sake of life on Earth, rather than to try to get to paradise in the afterlife. This leads many Jews to believe that life on Earth has greater meaning.
- According to Islam, the afterlife for the righteous will be like paradise — the word for heaven, 'jannah', actually means garden. However, to get there Muslims must lead a righteous life, so life on Earth is extremely important.
- Most Christians believe that they should aim to bring about the kingdom of God. Many Christians believe that the afterlife is extremely important because that is where the kingdom will come to be. However, some Christians believe that the kingdom can exist on Earth. Jesus said that "the kingdom of God is in your midst" (Luke 17:21 NIV). This means that life on Earth could be just as important as the afterlife.
- Non-religious people might not believe in an afterlife, so they would say that life on Earth is all that matters. Others might argue that even if an afterlife exists, we have little to no evidence of what it will actually be like. For this reason, it makes sense to live as if there is no afterlife, and focus only on life on Earth.
*[12 marks available — see p.190 for mark scheme]*

## Theme C — The Existence of God and Revelation

### Pages 98-99

5 Charles Darwin *[1 mark]*

6 Visions *[1 mark]*

7 - Many scientists believe that there is no need to explain the creation of the universe using a God. They believe that the Big Bang theory gives enough of an explanation that a God isn't needed.
- The theory of evolution can be used to explain how life and human beings came to be. There is no need for a creator God to form animals and humans.
- Science is based on the collection of physical evidence to test a hypothesis. Many scientists argue that, since God is claimed to be a supernatural being, there is just not enough physical evidence to show God exists, so it must then be concluded that he does not exist.
*[2 marks available, 1 mark for each correct point]*

8 Viewpoints that believe in revelation:
- Nature is considered a form of general revelation. Christians believe that the beauty of nature reveals the wonder and intelligence of God himself.
Viewpoints that do not believe in revelation:
- Some Christians believe that nature can be cruel, so it no longer reveals God's true nature.
- Atheists believe that the world can be explained by science, even if we have not discovered it yet. This means that there is no reason to see nature as a revelation from God.
*[4 marks available — see p.190 for mark scheme]*

9 They were written centuries ago *[1 mark]*

10 There isn't enough scientific evidence that they happened *[1 mark]*.

11 - Religious experiences are private, so it is impossible to prove to another person that they happened.
- People who claim to have had a religious experience might actually have a mental health issue or a condition of the brain that makes them believe they have seen something that isn't really there.
- Believers might choose to interpret their experience in a religious way whereas a non-religious person might interpret it differently.
*[2 marks available, 1 mark for each correct point]*

12 Arguments that support the statement:
- Visions are direct and powerful — they can often convince the person who experienced them that God exists, as this seems to be the only explanation for what they have been through.

- Many visions occur in scripture, and they often predict things that then happened. For example, in the Qur'an, the angel Jibril appeared to Maryam to tell her she was going to have a son, which she then did. The large number of stories of visions throughout history convinces people that God must exist for so many people to have had direct experiences of him.
- Some visions completely change the lives and beliefs of even people who don't believe in God. In the Bible, Saul persecuted Christians, but one day he saw a vision of Jesus. He completely changed his life as a result, and dedicated his life to God. Some Christians argue that if a vision could change someone's mind so completely, it must show that God exists.
Arguments against the statement:
- Visions might be powerful to those who experience them, but they are almost always personal. No one else can experience the same thing, so they might only convince one person that God exists.
- Some progressive Jews believe that the visions described in the Tenakh should be seen as metaphors rather than actual events that happened to people. This makes them weaker forms of revelation and less likely to convince people that God exists.
- Sufi Muslims claim to experience visions and other direct experiences of Allah. However, some other Muslims are sceptical of these claims, and do not believe these experiences are real. If even people from the same religion are sceptical of claims, they cannot be used to prove that Allah exists.
*[12 marks available — see p.190 for mark scheme]*

## Theme D — Religion, Peace and Conflict

### Page 111

4 Forgiveness *[1 mark]*

5 Indiscriminate *[1 mark]*

6 - It must be started by a proper authority, e.g. government or head of state.
- There must a good reason, e.g. self-defence or protection of others/innocents.
- All alternatives to conflict or war must have been attempted.
- The war must have a reasonable chance of success.
- The harm caused must be proportionate to the harm or evil the war is trying to prevent.
*[2 marks available, 1 mark for each correct point]*

7 Arguments that support the statement:
- Some religious believers may argue that each person's first responsibility is to build and preserve their relationship with God. No person is without sin and so individuals ought to focus on their own actions before becoming involved in the conflicts of others.
- Many Muslims believe that the struggle to obey Allah and become a better Muslim (greater jihad) is given priority over the struggle to make the world a better place (lesser jihad): "no bearer of burdens will bear the burden of another" (Qur'an 35:18).
- Some Jews may argue that it is vital to follow the 613 mitzvot and that this ought to be a person's priority.
- Some Christians may argue that while making peace with others is to be encouraged, developing their faith is the most important thing, as it is through that they'll receive God's grace. They believe that salvation comes through belief in Jesus as saviour: "I am the resurrection and the life. The one who believes in me will live, even though they die" (John 11:25 NIV).
Arguments against the statement:
- Many religious believers would argue that peace is always to be preferred over violence. There are many religious teachings which consistently identify peace, reconciliation and forgiveness as central features of God's creation.
- For Christians, those who seek peace and try to help others achieve peace are identified positively by Jesus in the Sermon on the Mount: "Blessed are the peacemakers, for they will be called children of God" (Matthew 5:9 NIV).

- The promotion of peace and reconciliation is central in Judaism: "Learn to do right; seek justice. Defend the oppressed" (Isaiah 1:17 NIV). Various Jewish groups seek to resolve conflicts between others, through means of active non-violence such as negotiation (e.g. the Jewish Peace Fellowship).
- Many religious leaders, such as Archbishop Desmond Tutu, were successful in resolving conflicts between others. By following their example and working towards the same goal it could be said that people may also be building their own relationship with God.
- Muslims may follow the example of the Prophet Muhammad who worked to restore peace between others: "And not equal are the good deed and the bad. Repel [evil] by that [deed] which is better; and thereupon the one whom between you and him is enmity [will become] as though he was a devoted friend" (Qur'an 41:34).
- Atheists and non-religious people may argue that there is no higher goal than working towards a peaceful world. They may believe that it is wrong to focus on oneself over helping others.
*[12 marks available — see p.190 for mark scheme]*

## Theme E — Religion, Crime and Punishment

### Page 122

5   Poverty *[1 mark]*

6   - Christians believe that people should obey God's law as well as obeying the laws of the state they are in: "Then Jesus said to them, 'Give back to Caesar what is Caesar's and to God what is God's.' And they were amazed at him" (Mark 12:17 NIV).
- Christians believe that where the laws of the state conflict with God's law, people should obey God's law first: "We must obey God rather than human beings!" (Acts 5:29 NIV).
- Muslims believe that God's law should be obeyed. The law, which is called shari'ah, is contained in the Qur'an and other teachings: "Allah orders justice and good conduct and giving to relatives and forbids immorality and bad conduct and oppression" (Qur'an 16:90). Many Muslim countries base the state law on the shari'ah law.
- Muslims believe that breaking God's law will result in punishment on the Day of Judgement, if criminals do not seek forgiveness from God: "He admits whom He wills into His mercy; but the wrongdoers — He has prepared for them a painful punishment" (Qur'an 76:31).
- Jews should follow the state laws of the country they reside in, alongside the 613 mitzvot outlined in the Torah. It may be justified to ignore state laws, but only when they are clearly unjust, such as when Jewish midwives disobeyed the King of Egypt's command to murder baby boys (Exodus 1:16-17).
- The Torah teaches that breaking God's law will result in punishment unless Jews seek forgiveness from God: "...the Lord's anger will burn against you, and he will shut the heavens so that it will not rain and the ground will yield no produce, and you will soon perish" (Deuteronomy 11:17 NIV).
*[5 marks available — see p.190 for mark scheme]*

7   Arguments that support the statement:
- Prison should be a form of retributive punishment for criminal wrongdoing. If it is a positive experience, it undermines this idea — if a criminal enjoys their time in prison then it's not really a punishment.
- The Qur'an states that the punishment should fit the crime "...an eye for an eye" (Qur'an 5:45), and so some Muslims believe that criminals who have committed terrible crimes should have an unpleasant experience in prison.
- For Jews, one of the Noahide Laws requires justice to be carried out in society, suggesting that serious crimes require a similarly serious punishment.

- For Jews and Christians, teachings in the Torah and Old Testament reinforce the idea that crime requires punishment: "Whoever does not obey the law of your God and the law of the king must surely be punished by... imprisonment" (Ezra 7:26 NIV).
- Some people believe that if prison were a positive experience, it would not act as a deterrent to other criminals. They might argue that prison should be, and should be seen as, an unpleasant punishment for people who have inflicted suffering on others. This will then discourage other potential criminals from committing crimes.
- Similarly, in relation to rehabilitation, prisons can only reform criminals if they understand that there are negative consequences to committing crimes. If prison is a positive experience, it could undermine the effectiveness of prisons in discouraging criminals from re-offending after they are released.
Arguments against the statement:
- Prison is a punishment as it deprives criminals of their freedom, so they're still being punished just by being in prison.
- Christians look to the parable of the sheep and the goats, in which Jesus blesses those who show compassion towards prisoners: "Truly I tell you, whatever you did for one of the least of these brothers and sisters of mine, you did for me" (Matthew 25:40 NIV). The experience of being in prison should be made positive in order to demonstrate this compassion.
- The Qur'an is also clear that prisoners are vulnerable members of society and should be treated fairly and with compassion: "And they give food in spite of love for it to the needy, the orphan, and the captive" (Qur'an 76:8).
- The main aims of prisons should be to protect society, punish criminals and reform them. Keeping prisoners locked up achieves the first two and making prison a more positive experience makes reformation more effective in the long run by promoting rehabilitation.
*[12 marks available — see p.190 for mark scheme]*

## Theme F — Religion, Human Rights and Social Justice

### Page 131

4   The Equality Act *[1 mark]*

5   Conversion *[1 mark]*

6   Any two from: age, sex/gender, disability, gender reassignment, marriage and civil partnership, pregnancy/maternity, race, religion or belief, sexual orientation.
*[2 marks available, 1 mark for each correct point]*

7   Arguments that support the statement:
- Many Christians would support people's right to choose their own beliefs. The Catechism of the Catholic Church 1747 says "The right to the exercise of freedom, especially in religious and moral matters, is an inalienable requirement of the dignity of man."
- Jews have been persecuted for their faith many times in their history, so tend to be supportive of the right not to be oppressed for one's choice of belief.
- Jews do not try to convert people, so support people's right to choose their faith. People can convert to Judaism if they want to.
- The Qur'an says "There shall be no compulsion in [acceptance of] the religion" (Qur'an 2:256), so most Muslims feel people should be allowed to choose whether to follow Islam.

- It could be argued that everyone should be allowed to make up their own mind about their beliefs, without pressure from believers speaking to them forcefully, e.g. in schools or on the street.

Arguments against the statement:

- Jesus said: "I am the way and the truth and the life. No one comes to the Father except through me" (John 14:6 NIV). Some Christians therefore believe that non-Christians need to be converted to Christianity to be saved, so do not encourage freedom of religion.

- In Islam, many believe that converting away from Islam or becoming an atheist (apostasy) is a terrible sin. So freedom of religion might not be seen as possible in Islam.

- Some might argue that people shouldn't have the right to express religious beliefs that discriminate against others, such as criticism of homosexual relationships. They might therefore feel that complete religious freedom should not be allowed.

*[12 marks available — see p.190 for mark scheme]*

## Page 138

2  Amnesty International *[1 mark]*

3  National living wage *[1 mark]*

4  Unemployment, lack of skills, lack of fair pay, high living costs, war, exploitation
   *[2 marks available, 1 mark for each correct point]*

5  - Christians view human trafficking as slavery and believe that they have a duty to prevent it happening. The Bible tells people to support and speak up for those who are poor and can't protect themselves.

   - Jews, from their own historical struggles, feel very strongly about human trafficking. Due to the success of Moses moving the Israelites to freedom out of slavery, Jews feel that they should also aim to abolish slavery.

   - Islam prohibits human trafficking. The Qur'an says that people who set slaves free are righteous, and condemns anyone who forces women into prostitution.

   - The Global Freedom Network has been created collectively by Catholic, Anglican and Sunni Islam leaders. The aim of this is to eradicate people trafficking on an international level.

   *[4 marks available — see p.190 for mark scheme]*

## Theme G — St Mark's Gospel: the Life of Jesus

### Pages 150-151

5  John *[1 mark]*

6  Bethany *[1 mark]*

7  - He would be delivered to the chief priests and teachers of the law.
   - He would be condemned to death.
   - He would be handed over to the Gentiles/Romans.
   - He would be mocked/spat at/flogged.
   - He would be killed, but he would rise again after three days.
   *[2 marks available, 1 mark for each correct point]*

8  - The paralysed man's friends couldn't get him inside the house because the crowd was too large. They carried him onto the roof and made a hole to lower him down. This shows their determination, and suggests to Christians that if they have faith in Jesus and show determination, they will be rewarded.

   - Jesus said to the man, "Son, your sins are forgiven" (Mark 2:5 NIV). It is only after some teachers of the law began to question his ability to forgive sins that he showed his power by healing the man's paralysis. This shows that, to Jesus, forgiving sins is more important than healing the body.

   - When the teachers of the law questioned how Jesus could forgive sins, Jesus replied that "the Son of Man has authority on earth to forgive sins" (Mark 2:10 NIV). For Christians, this is evidence that Jesus was the Son of Man.

   *[5 marks available — see p.190 for mark scheme]*

9  The temple curtain ripped *[1 mark]*

10  - Jesus's clothes became a dazzling white.
    - Elijah and Moses appeared and spoke to Jesus.
    - A cloud appeared to cover them.
    - God spoke to the disciples.
    *[2 marks available, 1 mark for each correct point]*

11  - Some Christians believe that Jesus's crucifixion was the only way that human beings could be forgiven for their sins and therefore get to heaven.

    - In contrast, some Christians believe that Jesus's death wasn't necessary for God to forgive humanity. A God who is loving, merciful and omnipotent should be able to forgive people's sins anyway.

    - Some Christians believe that Jesus's crucifixion is important because it shows how much God loves human beings — he gave his only son to save us.

    - In contrast, some Christians believe that the crucifixion was important because it led to the resurrection, which shows that God is so powerful that he can triumph over death.

    *[4 marks available — see p.190 for mark scheme]*

12  Arguments that support the statement:

    - Mark's Gospel doesn't contain any information about Jesus's birth. It begins with John the Baptist and Jesus's baptism. This suggests that this story is important because it is the beginning of Jesus's ministry — the beginning of the 'good news' that Mark wanted to tell in the Gospel.

    - The appearance of the Holy Spirit in the form of a dove, and the sound of the voice of God, shows that Jesus is the Son of God. Jesus's identity as the Son of God is central to Christianity, so the story where this is first declared could be seen as the most important.

    - The story is the most important because Christians are still baptised today. Their baptism marks them joining the church and becoming Christians, following in the footsteps of Jesus.

    Arguments against the statement:

    - The story of Jesus's death and resurrection is the most important. It is through this that the sins of mankind are forgiven, which means that Christians can go to heaven.

    - The parables of Jesus are the most important stories in Mark's Gospel. They tell Christians what the kingdom of God will be like, which is the basis of the Christian faith.

    - The story of Jesus's baptism isn't the most important because it only marks the beginning of Jesus's teachings. Christians use the gospels as guides to show them how to act. The baptism only tells them they should be baptised. It is the rest of the gospel which shows them what to do to follow Jesus's example.

    *[12 marks available — see p.190 for mark scheme]*

## Theme H — St Mark's Gospel as a Source of Religious, Moral and Spiritual Truths

### Pages 163-164

5  She had faith *[1 mark]*

6  - To become a disciple, Jesus said that people must "deny themselves and take up their cross and follow me" (Mark 8:34 NIV). This shows Christians that being true followers of Jesus will require sacrifice and suffering.

   - The word 'disciple' means pupil or apprentice. Jesus acted as a teacher, teaching his pupils about the kingdom of God. This shows Christians that they need to study religion and keep trying to understand their faith and God better.

   - When Jesus called the first disciples, Peter and Andrew, they immediately "left their nets and followed him" (Mark 1:18 NIV). This teaches Christians that nothing is more important than following Jesus, not even everyday life or a career.

- In Mark 16, Jesus sent his disciples out to other towns to preach the Gospel, convert people by baptising them and perform miracles. This shows Christians that they should spend time preaching the Gospel to others, and that they can do miraculous things if they have faith in Jesus.
*[5 marks available — see p.190 for mark scheme]*

7    Arguments that support the statement:
- In the parable of the mustard seed, Jesus described the kingdom of God growing from a small seed. Christians interpret this to mean that his teachings are the small seed, which will then spread amongst the disciples and across the earth, making a physical kingdom.
- Some Christians argue that the kingdom is already partially here, because Jesus showed God's power over nature, sin and death through the miracles of Jesus. Although it is partly here as a physical location, it has not fully arrived yet.
- At the last supper, Jesus said that he would not drink wine again "until that day when I drink it new in the kingdom of God" (Mark 14:25 NIV). This suggests that the kingdom of God will be a physical place where Jesus will be in the future.
- The Lord's prayer (in Matthew and Luke) says "your kingdom come, your will be done, on earth as it is in heaven" (Matthew 6:10 NIV). This suggests that the kingdom of God will, at some point, be a real place on earth.
Arguments against the statement:
- When Jesus blessed the young children, he said that "anyone who will not receive the kingdom of God like a little child will never enter it" (Mark 10:15 NIV). Here he seems to imply that people can receive the kingdom into their hearts today. This suggests that the kingdom is a state of being rather than a physical place.
- When the teacher of the law agreed with Jesus about the greatest commandment, Jesus replied "You are not far from the kingdom of God" (Mark 12:34 NIV). The teacher of the law wasn't close to a physical kingdom, but to a mental state where he was close to God.
- When he tells his followers to take up their cross and follow him, Jesus says "some who are standing here will not taste death before they see that the kingdom of God has come with power" (Mark 9:1 NIV). Jesus knew that no physical kingdom would come about in the lifetime of anyone present, but this suggests that the kingdom would be present inside his disciples and followers.
*[12 marks available — see p.190 for mark scheme]*

8    It was written by an anonymous author *[1 mark]*.

9    - At first it will be very small.
- It will grow to be very large.
- It will include non-Jews (the birds) as well as Jews.
*[2 marks available, 1 mark for each correct point]*

10   - In the first century, people believed that the symptoms the boy had meant he was possessed by an evil spirit. The boy's father asked Jesus to help his son by driving out the spirit. Some modern Christians believe that this is what really happened to the boy.
- In the modern day, we know that the boy's symptoms suggest that he had epilepsy. Many modern Christians believe that Jesus cured this disease rather than driving out a spirit.
*[4 marks available — see p.190 for mark scheme]*

11   Arguments that support the statement:
- In John's Gospel, Jesus says "My Father's house has many rooms" (John 14:2 NIV). Some Christians believe that this means there is room in heaven for people of different religions, and that Christianity is not the only way to heaven.
- Some Christians argue that although the commissioning of the disciples at the end of Mark's Gospel suggests that only Christians will go to heaven, the verses where this took place (verses 9-20) are not included in the original copies of the text.
- Some Christians argue that much of Jesus's teaching was about how wrong it was to reject people, and that we should love our neighbours as ourselves. They believe that this means good people would not be rejected from heaven just because they are not Christians.

Arguments against the statement:
- In order to be saved and go to heaven, people must ask for their sins to be forgiven. This requires a belief in Jesus — John says that Jesus died so "whoever believes in him shall not perish but have eternal life" (John 3:16 NIV). To believe that Jesus was resurrected and can forgive sins means that you are a Christian.
- Jesus commissioned his disciples to go and preach the Gospel, saying "Whoever believes and is baptised will be saved, but whoever does not believe will be condemned" (Mark 16:16 NIV). This suggests that only those who have been baptised as Christians can be saved and go to heaven.
- Christians believe that sin entered the world when Adam and Eve disobeyed God in Genesis. As a result, all humans are born with 'original sin'. The only way of being redeemed of this sin is through Jesus. This means that all people need to be redeemed by Jesus's death and resurrection, but only Christians who believe in him can be saved.
*[12 marks available — see p.190 for mark scheme]*

## Practice Paper 1

1.1 Evil is always more powerful than good *[1 mark]*.

1.2 - Jesus rose from the Earth to heaven to be with God.
- Jesus had finished his mission on Earth, so he could return to heaven.
- He went to prepare a place for his followers in heaven.
- It shows how powerful Jesus was — he rose to sit at God's right hand.
*[2 marks available, 1 mark for each correct point]*

1.3 - Christians believe that after death humans will be judged by God and be sent either to heaven or hell. This means that Christians should try to do good deeds in their lives so they will be sent to heaven.
- Christians believe that Jesus died on the cross so their sins can be forgiven and they can go to heaven. They therefore pray to Jesus for forgiveness if they have sinned.
- Christians believe all people will be judged — this encourages some to try to convert non-believers to Christianity, so they have the chance to get to heaven.
*[4 marks available — see p.190 for mark scheme]*

1.4 - The creation story describes how God "created the heavens and the earth" (Genesis 1:1 NIV) in only six days. This demonstrates to Christians that God is omnipotent — all powerful.
- In order to create the universe, Christians argue that God must have existed before it. This shows that he is eternal, as he existed before time began.
- God created the universe, and he "saw that it was good" (Genesis 1:25 NIV). He then created human beings to "rule over" his creation (Genesis 1:26 NIV). To Christians, this shows God's goodness — his benevolence — since he gave humans such an amazing gift.
- The creation story in Genesis says that God created the universe in six days, and then he rested on the seventh. Some Christians interpret this story literally, and so they do not accept the scientific view that the universe has developed over billions of years.
- Some Christians do not think the creation story is literally true — instead they believe that it is symbolic. It helps them to understand what God is like, but they are open to other theories about how the world came to be (like evolution and the Big Bang theory).
*[5 marks available — see p.190 for mark scheme]*

1.5 Arguments that support the statement:
- Just before he died, Jesus cried out, asking why God had abandoned him. This shows how much pain and suffering he was going through. This means that he can understand the pain and suffering experienced by humans, which is an important source of comfort for Christians.

- The idea of original sin — that all humans are born with sin as a result of Adam and Eve's disobedience — means that all humans need God's forgiveness to enter heaven. Jesus's death on the cross allows this forgiveness to take place.

- Jesus's death on the cross is the most important Christian belief because it shows that God loves mankind so much that he was willing to sacrifice his only son to save us: "For God so loved the world that he gave his one and only Son" (John 3:16 NIV).

Arguments against the statement:

- Jesus's resurrection is just as important as his death because it proves that Jesus has power over death — "death no longer has mastery over him" (Romans 6:9 NIV). It gives Christians hope that they will also be resurrected after death and live in heaven with God.

- For their sins to be forgiven, Christians need to have faith that Jesus is the Son of God. This fact is proved by Jesus's resurrection, so it gives Christians the faith they need.

- Jesus's resurrection is proof that Jesus is the Son of God, and therefore Christians should follow his example as described in the Gospels. Jesus told his disciples "I have set you an example that you should do as I have done for you" (John 13:15 NIV). This is more important than his death, which doesn't help Christians decide how to act.

- Jesus's resurrection is more important because without it, Christians' faith in Jesus is pointless as their sins cannot be forgiven. The Bible says, "And if Christ has not been raised, your faith is futile; you are still in your sins" (1 Corinthians 15:17 NIV).

*[12 marks available — see p.190 for mark scheme]*

2.1 Ash Wednesday *[1 mark]*

2.2 Lourdes, Walsingham, Lindisfarne, Iona, Taizé, Rome, Jerusalem
*[2 marks available, 1 mark for each correct point]*

2.3 Viewpoints that support the importance of evangelism:

- Many Christians believe that they have a duty to spread the gospel because Jesus told his disciples to "Go into all the world and preach the gospel to all creation" (Mark 16:15 NIV). For them, helping to save other people is a major part of their religion.

- Missionaries believe that evangelism is so important that they are willing to move to distant parts of the world to spread the gospel.

Viewpoints that see evangelism as less important:

- Some Christians believe that it is more important to have a good personal relationship with God than to spend time spreading the word about him to others.

- Some Christians might be careful about how much they evangelise because they might be worried about people being offended or even persecuting them for their faith. They might find other ways to spread the word of God, like living a life according to Biblical teachings which sets an example for others.

*[4 marks available — see p.190 for mark scheme]*

2.4 - The Lord's Prayer was how Jesus taught his disciples to pray in the gospels of Luke and Matthew, saying "This, then, is how you should pray" (Matthew 6:9 NIV), so Christians believe it is important that they also recite it.

- Christians all over the world and at different points in history have recited the Lord's Prayer, so it makes Christians feel connected to a wider community of worshippers.

- The Lord's Prayer is accepted by all Christian denominations and is said during church services all over the world. For example, it is in the Church of England's 'Book of Common Prayer'. It helps different denominations remember to focus on what they have in common rather than the disagreements that divide them.

- The Lord's Prayer includes several different types of prayer. For example, "hallowed be your name" is adoration (Matthew 6:9 NIV) and "Give us today our daily bread" is supplication (Matthew 6:11 NIV). It acts as a reminder of what prayer is for, and how Christians should address God.

*[5 marks available — see p.190 for mark scheme]*

2.5 Arguments that support the statement:

- Some Christians believe that the bread and wine at the Eucharist turn into the real body and blood of Christ. The Eucharist is a re-enactment of the suffering and death of Jesus, which then brings the power of Jesus's salvation into their bodies as they consume the bread and wine.

- The fact that ordinary bread and wine become the body of Jesus is a miracle, which strengthens the faith of those who believe in it. It adds to the proof that Jesus is the Son of God.

- The Catechism of the Catholic Church (1335) argues that the bread turning into Jesus's body and the wine turning into Jesus's blood echo the miracles of the feeding of the 5000 and Jesus turning water into wine. This links the Eucharist to the events of the Gospel even more strongly, linking the actions of modern Christians with the actions of Jesus during his life.

Arguments against the statement:

- Many Christians believe that the bread and wine do not literally become the body and blood of Jesus, but that the Eucharist is still a very important ceremony because it is a re-enactment of the Last Supper — the final meal Jesus shared with his disciples before his crucifixion.

- According to the Catechism of the Catholic Church (1334), the Eucharist is also important because it links Jesus to events in the Old Testament. The Last Supper took place on Passover, and the bread represents the manna that God gave the Israelites in the desert.

- Some Christians, such as Baptists, believe that the importance of the Eucharist is in Christians coming together as a community to celebrate Jesus's sacrifice. The bread and wine are simply symbols of Jesus's body being broken on the cross, and his blood being spilt as he died.

*[12 marks available — see p.190 for mark scheme]*

3.1 Purgatory *[1 mark]*

3.2 - Jesus rose from the Earth to heaven to be with God.

- Jesus had finished his mission on Earth, so he could return to heaven.

- He went to prepare a place for his followers in heaven.

- It shows how powerful Jesus was — he rose to sit at God's right hand.

*[2 marks available, 1 mark for each correct point]*

3.3 - Christians believe that after death humans will be judged by God and be sent either to heaven or hell. This means that Christians should try to do good deeds in their lives so they will be sent to heaven.

- Christians believe that Jesus died on the cross so their sins can be forgiven and they can go to heaven. They therefore pray to Jesus for forgiveness if they have sinned.

- Christians believe all people will be judged — this encourages some to try to convert non-believers to Christianity, so they have the chance to get to heaven.

*[4 marks available — see p.190 for mark scheme]*

3.4 - The creation story describes how God "created the heavens and the earth" (Genesis 1:1 NIV) in only six days. This demonstrates to Christians that God is omnipotent — all powerful.

- In order to create the universe, Christians argue that God must have existed before it. This shows that he is eternal, as he existed before time began.

- God created the universe, and he "saw that it was good" (Genesis 1:25 NIV). He then created human beings to "rule over" his creation (Genesis 1:26 NIV). To Christians, this shows God's goodness — his benevolence — since he gave humans such an amazing gift.

- The creation story in Genesis says that God created the universe in six days, and then he rested on the seventh. Some Christians interpret this story literally, and so they do not accept the scientific view that the universe has developed over billions of years.

- Some Christians do not think the creation story is literally true — instead they believe that it is symbolic. It helps them to understand what God is like, but they are open to other theories about how the world came to be (like evolution and the Big Bang theory).
*[5 marks available — see p.190 for mark scheme]*

3.5 Arguments that support the statement:
- Just before he died, Jesus cried out, asking why God had abandoned him. This shows how much pain and suffering he was going through. This means that he can understand the pain and suffering experienced by humans, which is an important source of comfort for Christians.
- The idea of original sin — that all humans are born with sin as a result of Adam and Eve's disobedience — means that all humans need God's forgiveness to enter heaven. Jesus's death on the cross allows this forgiveness to take place.
- Jesus's death on the cross is the most important Christian belief because it shows that God loves mankind so much that he was willing to sacrifice his only son to save us: "For God so loved the world that he gave his one and only Son" (John 3:16 NIV).

Arguments against the statement:
- Jesus's resurrection is just as important as his death because it proves that Jesus has power over death — "death no longer has mastery over him" (Romans 6:9 NIV). It gives Christians hope that they will also be resurrected after death and live in heaven with God.
- For their sins to be forgiven, Christians need to have faith that Jesus is the Son of God. This fact is proved by Jesus's resurrection, so it gives Christians the faith they need.
- Jesus's resurrection is proof that Jesus is the Son of God, and therefore Christians should follow his example as described in the Gospels. Jesus told his disciples "I have set you an example that you should do as I have done for you" (John 13:15 NIV). This is more important than his death, which doesn't help Christians decide how to act.
- Jesus's resurrection is more important because without it, Christians' faith in Jesus is pointless as their sins cannot be forgiven. The Bible says, "And if Christ has not been raised, your faith is futile; you are still in your sins" (1 Corinthians 15:17 NIV).
*[12 marks available — see p.190 for mark scheme]*

4.1 Pictures of Jesus's suffering *[1 mark]*

4.2 Lourdes, Walsingham, Lindisfarne, Iona, Taizé, Rome, Jerusalem
*[2 marks available, 1 mark for each correct point]*

4.3 Viewpoints that support the importance of evangelism:
- Many Christians believe that they have a duty to spread the gospel because Jesus told his disciples to "Go into all the world and preach the gospel to all creation" (Mark 16:15 NIV). For them, helping to save other people is a major part of their religion.
- Missionaries believe that evangelism is so important that they are willing to move to distant parts of the world to spread the gospel.

Viewpoints that see evangelism as less important:
- Some Christians believe that it is more important to have a good personal relationship with God than to spend time spreading the word about him to others.
- Some Christians might be careful about how much they evangelise because they might be worried about people being offended or even persecuting them for their faith. They might find other ways to spread the word of God, like living a life according to Biblical teachings which sets an example for others.
*[4 marks available — see p.190 for mark scheme]*

4.4 - Catholics believe that this sacrament allows the Holy Spirit to strengthen the sick person's faith and help them cope with their current illness (Catechism of the Catholic Church 1532).
- Catholics believe that anointing the sick links the sick person with Jesus's suffering (Catechism of the Catholic Church 1532). Remembering that Jesus suffered can help sick people endure their own suffering.

- The Catechism of the Catholic Church (1210) says that all of the seven sacraments are hugely important in a Christian's life — they "give birth and increase, healing and mission to the Christian's life of faith".
- The Catechism of the Catholic Church (1210) states that "Christ instituted the sacraments of the new law" — Christians perform them in order to follow Jesus's example. Also, when Jesus sent out his disciples they "anointed with oil many people who were ill and healed them" (Mark 6:13 NIV). Catholics follow this example by performing this sacrament.
*[5 marks available — see p.190 for mark scheme]*

4.5 Arguments that support the statement:
- Jesus said that instead of praying in full view of everyone else, people should "go into your room, close the door" (Matthew 6:6 NIV) and pray in private. Private prayer is often more informal, as people can have a personal conversation with God. This means informal prayer is more important to Christians, because it makes it easier to follow Jesus's instructions in Matthew to pray privately.
- Paul writes, "I want the men everywhere to pray, lifting up holy hands" (1 Timothy 2:8 NIV). This suggests that prayer shouldn't be structured and formal — people should pray whenever they want to.
- Some Christians argue that informal prayers are more important because they are part of an individual's personal relationship with God. They are a form of private communication which is more natural when it is informal.

Arguments against the statement:
- Formal prayer can be more important because it often happens in groups. Jesus said that "where two or three gather in my name, there am I with them" (Matthew 18:20 NIV). When Christians gather for formal church services, Jesus is present.
- Some formal prayers are performed all around the world, which gives Christians a sense of community. This can offer them comfort when they are suffering.
- Formal prayers often include all of the different types of prayer — thanksgiving, adoration, confession, supplication and intercession. These different types are important for believers' relationship with God and with other Christians, so it is important to include them regularly. Formal prayer makes sure this happens.
*[12 marks available — see p.190 for mark scheme]*

5.1 Ibrahim *[1 mark]*

5.2 - Belief that Allah is the one and only god (Tawhid)
- Belief in angels (Malaikah)
- Belief in the holy books
- Belief in Allah's prophets (Nubuwwah)
- Belief in the day of judgement
- Belief in predestination (al-Qadr)
*[2 marks available, 1 mark for each correct point]*

5.3 - The Qur'an guides Muslims. It tells them everything they need to know about Allah and how to lead their lives according to his wishes. Muslims try to live according to the instructions given in the Qur'an — for example, in what they eat, when, where and how they pray and giving to charity.
- Some Muslims may choose to learn the Qur'an by heart as they believe it is an exact record of Allah's words to Muhammad.
- Muslims may choose to live, and resolve disagreements and issues, according to the guidance of the shari'ah law contained in the Qur'an.
*[4 marks available — see p.190 for mark scheme]*

5.4 - God is one, undivided and the only god, without equal: "Say, 'He is Allah, [who is] One'" (Qur'an 112:1).
- God is merciful and kind and forgives people of their sins. The majority of chapters in the Qur'an begin with the assertion Allah is merciful (the bismillah): "In the name of Allah, the Entirely Merciful, the Especially Merciful" (Qur'an 1:1).
- God is all powerful (omnipotent). He created all things and is in control of all things. This includes people and their actions (predestination).

- God is infinitely good (benevolent) and just. Allah wishes people to live well and revealed how to do this to the prophets. He judges people fairly, rewarding the good and punishing the evil.
- God is present in the world (immanent) and yet above it and unfathomable to human beings (transcendent). Allah takes a personal interest in the lives of all people yet is without equal in the whole of existence: "And We have already created man and know what his soul whispers to him, and We are closer to him than [his] jugular vein" (Qur'an 50:16).
- God has many characteristics, indicated by the ninety-nine names of Allah. These ninety-nine names originate in the Qur'an and describe a combination of what God is, what he has done, what he can do and what he will do — e.g. Al-Khaaliq (the creator).
*[5 marks available — see p.190 for mark scheme]*

5.5 Arguments that support the statement:
- Predestination (al-Qadr) is an important teaching in Islam. It is stated repeatedly that a person cannot do other than what Allah has chosen for them. This belief is incompatible with human freedom as they logically contradict each other.
- Holding the belief of predestination is not compatible with free will as it can lead to people rejecting their own free will and responsibility to make good choices. This is illustrated by the Hadith in which a man asks whether he should tie up his camel so it doesn't walk off or whether he should leave it untied and have faith that Allah will ensure that the camel will remain there: "'Shall I tie it and rely (upon Allah), or leave it loose and rely (upon Allah)?' He said: 'Tie it and rely (upon Allah)'" (Jamil al-Tirmidhi 2517). This demonstrates that people must be responsible for their own actions and so must have free will.
Arguments against the statement:
- It must be possible to believe in these two ideas as the purpose of this life is to achieve an afterlife in paradise through good thoughts and deeds. This means not just doing the actions Allah has determined, but going about them with the right intention.
- Sunni Muslims typically believe that while Allah determines an individual's choices, they come into ownership of the choice when they consciously make it themselves.
- While everything that happens is predetermined by Allah, humans are in control of their own reactions and responses to events. Being outside of time, Allah knows in advance what these choices will be, and has planned the world accordingly.
*[12 marks available — see p.190 for mark scheme]*

6.1 Laylat al-Qadr *[1 mark]*

6.2 Any two from:
Salah, Zakah, Sawm, Hajj, Khums, Jihad, Amr-bil-Maroof, Nahi Anil Munkar, Tawalla, Tabarra
*[2 marks available, 1 mark for each correct point]*

6.3 - Sunni Muslims will give five sets of prayers at five separate points during the day. Prayer will be given at sunrise, around noon, in the late afternoon, at sunset and at night.
- Some Sunni Muslims may combine sets of prayers if they have a good reason that prevents them from praying five times a day, e.g. when travelling.
- In contrast, Shi'a Muslims give five sets of prayers but combine them into three points during the day, combining noon with afternoon prayers and sunset with night time prayers.
- Sunni Muslims typically carry out each rak'ah on a prayer mat and touch their foreheads directly onto the mat or the ground. When standing, they will cross their hands.
- Shi'a Muslims typically touch their heads to something natural (wood or clay) during each rak'ah and do not cross their hands when standing.
- During Friday prayers, men are often expected to pray at a nearby mosque.
- However, women will typically pray where they normally would throughout the week.
*[4 marks available — see p.190 for mark scheme]*

6.4 - The festival marks the end of the holy month of Ramadan. It celebrates strength in the face of adversity after a month of fasting: "O you who have believed, decreed upon you is fasting as it was decreed upon those before you that you may become righteous" (Qur'an 2:183).
- It is a festival of spiritual renewal. Many Muslims feel closer to Allah after completing the fourth pillar, sawm, and have spent time refocusing on their spiritual life: "...But to fast is best for you, if you only knew" (Qur'an 2:184).
- It marks the point by which charity for that month (Zakah ul-Fitr) must be given. For many Muslims, the importance of compassion and charity is a focus during the previous month of fasting.
- The festival was celebrated by Muhammad himself from 624 CE. Muslims believe Muhammad lived perfectly according to Allah's will, which suggests it is right to celebrate Id ul-Fitr.
*[5 marks available — see p.190 for mark scheme]*

6.5 Arguments that support the statement:
- Jihad represents the internal struggle of every Muslim to live according to Allah's teachings and be a good Muslim. As such, it may be argued that it encompasses a person trying to fulfil the whole range of duties required in Islam.
- The 'greater jihad' is personal and individual. Ultimately, each person will be held to account for their own thoughts and deeds, and jihad is the duty to live accordingly.
- For Shi'a Muslims, jihad is one of the Ten Obligatory Acts.
- Another interpretation of jihad is as the struggle to make the world a better place. This is a broader, higher duty than that which one owes oneself. It is rooted in care and compassion for others. This selflessness was exemplified in the life of Muhammad.
Arguments against the statement:
- While jihad is one of the Ten Obligatory Acts for Shi'a Muslims, no one duty is held to be more important than the others. Jihad is not one of the Five Pillars for Sunni Muslims, and so arguably should not be considered one of the main duties of a Muslim's life.
- It could be argued that Shahadah is the central duty. While none of the duties are more important than the others, Shahadah is the pre-requisite for the others.
- Salah is a very important duty as it brings a person in close contact with Allah. It is the chief discipline to avoid believing in other gods (shirk) which is the worst sin.
- Jihad can refer to physical struggle or conflict. While violence is sometimes necessary, in self-defence or defence of another for instance, it is not the overriding duty of a person's life.
- Jihad has been used by extremist groups to justify aggressive actions against innocents. The vast majority of Muslims condemn this interpretation of jihad and so would not view this interpretation as a duty.
*[12 marks available — see p.190 for mark scheme]*

7.1 Omnipotent *[1 mark]*

7.2 - Mitzvot between a person and God are referred to as ritual mitzvot, whereas between two people they are referred to as ethical (or moral) mitzvot.
- Mitzvot can be grouped as 'positive' (telling Jews what they should do) or 'negative' (telling Jews what they shouldn't do).
*[2 marks available, 1 mark for each correct point]*

7.3 - The belief in monotheism (God is one) means Jews will not worship other beings, including rejecting the Christian concept of the Trinity.
- The belief that God is a judge and omniscient may influence Jews to live and act ethically at all times, and according to the laws established in the covenant.
- The belief that God is omnipresent and immanent influences Jews to believe that God is physically present in the world around them. Many Jews travel to places where they believe they will be particularly close to God, such as the Western Wall in Jerusalem.
*[4 marks available — see p.190 for mark scheme]*

7.4 - Shekhinah is the belief that God is present in specific places on Earth. For example, it describes God's presence in the tabernacle used by Moses: "The glory of the Lord filled the tabernacle" (Exodus 40:35 NIV) — it represents the feminine aspect of God.

- God is still present in the remains of the Temple walls in Jerusalem (the Western Wall): "I saw the Lord, high and exalted, seated on a throne; and the train of his robe filled the temple" (Isaiah 6:1 NIV). Many Jews travel to the Western Wall to pray and worship.

- Some Jews believe that God is omnipresent and exists everywhere in the universe at all times. This can be a comfort as it suggests God shares in all suffering.

- The Talmud teaches that Shekhinah is present when a group of Jews pray together or read the Torah. Some Jewish prayers and services require at least ten Jewish people (minyan), although the Talmud states that God is present if just two are gathered in prayer.
*[5 marks available — see p.190 for mark scheme]*

7.5 Arguments that support the statement:
- The belief in one God, and no other god (monotheism), has been a central element of all covenants between God and man. In particular, it was a feature of the covenants made with both Abraham and Moses.

- The first of the Ten Commandments is to believe in God and the second is to have no other gods (Exodus 20:2-3 NIV), emphasising the central importance of this belief.

Arguments against the statement:
- The covenant between God and Jews demands the keeping of all 613 mitzvot. While belief in God is important, the agreement between God and Jews is binding on all duties. The Israelites agreed to "do everything the Lord has spoken", and so the agreement is binding as a whole.

- The principle of the sanctity of life (pikuach nefesh) suggests that at points moral obligations to other people can outweigh the obligations of the covenant and, temporarily at least, become a Jew's most important duty: "Every danger to human life suspends the [laws of the] Sabbath" (Talmud Yoma 83a). Examples given to illustrate this include doctors working to save lives on the Sabbath day or breaking down a wall or door to save a trapped child.

- Many Progressive Jews place an emphasis on adhering to the mitzvot between and one person and another, and follow other mitzvot less strictly. The Talmud lends some support to placing an emphasis on the moral relationship with others: "That which is despicable to you, do not do to your fellow, this is the whole Torah, and the rest is commentary, go and learn it" (Talmud Shabbat 31a).
*[12 marks available — see p.190 for mark scheme]*

8.1 Kashrut *[1 mark]*

8.2 - A ram's horn (shofar) is blown to mark the start of the new year.
- The day is spent largely in the synagogue where the Torah is read.
- Prayers focusing on God's judgement and forgiveness are said in the synagogue.
- Foods dipped in honey, such as bread and apples, are eaten.
- A ceremony (tashlich) may take place next to a body of water where special verses are recited.
- Many Jews will empty their pockets casting the contents into the water. Often these are breadcrumbs, representing the casting away of sins from the past year.
*[2 marks available, 1 mark for each correct point]*

8.3 - In Orthodox synagogues, there are separate sections for men and women, and the male and female areas may be separated by a screen.
- In contrast, men and women are seated together in Reform synagogues.
- In Orthodox synagogues, the reading platform (bimah) is in the centre.
- In contrast, in Reform synagogues, the bimah is normally close to the Ark at the wall facing Jerusalem.
*[4 marks available — see p.190 for mark scheme]*

8.4 - Prayer is important as it is a requirement of the Covenant, a (ritual) mitzvah: "Worship the Lord your God" (Exodus 23:25 NIV). Many Jews try to pray three times a day: "Evening, morning and noon I cry out in distress, and he hears my voice" (Psalm 55:17 NIV).

- The Jewish declaration of faith (Shema) is an especially important prayer, which affirms the belief in only one God: "Hear, O Israel: The Lord our God, the Lord is one" (Deuteronomy 6:4). Many Jewish men follow the instruction in the Shema to wear verses of the Torah in boxes (tefillin) bound to their arms and foreheads during morning prayer.

- Many Jews believe that God is present when they pray (Shekhinah). This is often associated with prayer in the synagogue but is also believed to take place whenever a group of Jews join together to pray or study.

- Prayer is an important part of an individual's relationship with God. Jews believe God hears prayers as he is present everywhere (immanent) and may forgive sins when forgiveness is asked for sincerely: "The Lord is good to all; he has compassion on all he has made" (Psalm 145:9 NIV).
*[5 marks available — see p.190 for mark scheme]*

8.5 Arguments that support the statement:
- The ritual circumcision of boys (brit milah) is derived from the Torah as a part of God's Covenant with Abraham. As such it is a mitzvah: "every male among you shall be circumcised" (Genesis 17:10 NIV). This is not true for the naming ceremony (simchat bat) of Jewish girls.

- In Orthodox Judaism, boys have a bar mitzvah ceremony at the age of thirteen to mark the point they become responsible for upholding the mitzvot. Most Orthodox Jews don't require girls to hold an equivalent bat mitzvah ceremony as girls are not under the same ritual obligations.

- Both the simchat bat and bat mitzvah ceremonies are recent developments. They are aimed at increasing equality between boys and girls in Judaism. However, this underlines the greater significance of rituals for boys which have been established for thousands of years.

Arguments against the statement:
- Within Progressive and Reform Judaism, the simchat bat naming ceremony is equivalent to the male brit milah ceremony. The ceremonies include blessings, as for boys, the reciting of the kiddush and the giving of a Hebrew name.

- Many Jewish girls have a bat mitzvah at twelve or thirteen. This marks entry into adulthood in the same way as the bar mitzvah does for boys. Just as boys are responsible for their actions and choices to God, so are girls. Judgement applies equally, regardless of gender: "God will bring every deed into judgment... whether it is good or evil" (Ecclesiastes 12:14 NIV).

- While Orthodox Jews do not hold a bat mitzvah for girls, many take part in the daughter of valour ceremony (bat hayil) instead. This means rituals are equally significant for boys and girls.

- Rituals around mourning make no distinction between genders. When mourning the loss of a parent or relative, the same rules of avelut and sheloshim apply, irrespective of gender.
*[12 marks available — see p.190 for mark scheme]*

## Practice Paper 2

1.1 Nuclear *[1 mark]*

1.2 - Roman Catholic and Orthodox churches won't allow women to be priests, so these denominations believe men and women can be treated differently.
- Anglican churches now allow women to be bishops, indicating that they are equal to men.
- In Orthodox Judaism, men and women sit separately in the synagogue, which might be seen as gender discrimination.
- Reform and Liberal Jews reject gender discrimination by allowing men and women to sit together in the synagogue and by having both male and female rabbis.

- Some Muslims believe that man was created first and therefore has authority over women.
- Many Muslims interpret the Qur'an as saying that men and women have different roles within the community, but do have equal status.

*[2 marks available, 1 mark for each correct point]*

1.3 Viewpoints that support cohabitation:
- Some people believe that cohabitation is perfectly acceptable in preparation for marriage, or as an alternative to it.
- Progressive Jews accept cohabitation as long as the decision to live together is based on a long-term commitment to one another.

Viewpoints that oppose cohabitation:
- Some traditional Christians believe that sex outside marriage is wrong and they therefore reject cohabitation.
- Many Muslims reject the idea of living together because they believe that sex outside marriage is a sin.
- Orthodox Jews hold traditional views believing that sex should only take place within a marriage.

*[4 marks available — see p.190 for mark scheme]*

1.4 - The Catholic Church teaches that one of the main reasons for marriage is to "be fruitful and increase in number" (NIV), as instructed by God in Genesis 9:7. They think artificial contraception is wrong because it goes against this teaching, and prevents life, which is a gift from God.
- Some Christians think family planning is important as it enables couples to only have children when they're ready.
- Some Jews avoid using contraception because the Tenakh teaches that children are gifts from God: "Children are a heritage from the Lord, offspring a reward from him" (Psalm 127:3 NIV). They feel that it is wrong to go against God's wishes.
- Many Progressive Jews accept the use of contraception but some avoid barrier methods such as condoms because of the teaching in Genesis 38:8-10 regarding Onan, son of Judah. He was killed for "spilling his semen on the ground" (NIV), which was seen as a waste. Therefore, some Jews prefer hormonal methods such as the pill.
- In Islam, any form of contraception has to be 'reversible', because Muslims should aim to have children at some point within their marriage. Therefore, sterilisation and vasectomies are not permitted.
- Muslims don't agree with any forms of contraception that cause an abortion, e.g. the morning after pill. Muslims believe that life is sacred and the Qur'an states that "whoever kills a soul... it is as if he had slain mankind entirely" (Qur'an 5:32).

*[5 marks available — see p.190 for mark scheme]*

1.5 Arguments that support the statement:
- Roman Catholics do not think divorce is possible and therefore neither is remarriage. They believe marriage to be permanent because it is a sacrament: "Therefore what God has joined together, let no-one separate" (Mark 10:9 NIV).
- Marriage ceremonies involve making a commitment by exchanging vows and rings. Some people hold the view that this commitment is permanent and you are married 'for life'.
- Some people believe that divorce and remarriage are damaging to children. They believe it can cause divisions and lack of stability for children, especially if they see one parent less frequently than the other. Remarriage can sometimes create problems for stepchildren and step-parents when trying to form relationships with one another.

Arguments against the statement:
- Protestants believe that Jesus's teaching on marriage and divorce in the New Testament shows the ideal way to which all Christians should aspire. They accept, however, that sometimes humans fall short of this ideal and make mistakes, so therefore they need to be given a second chance.
- The Church of England accepts that sometimes marriages fail and that people need to have second chances. They use Jesus's teachings about forgiveness to support their views (e.g. the story of the woman who had committed adultery in John 8:2-11). People can remarry in a Church of England church if the minister agrees to do the ceremony.

- In Islam, after a divorce, both men and women are considered to be free to re-marry.

*[12 marks available — see p.190 for mark scheme]*

2.1 Dominion *[1 mark]*

2.2 - There isn't any evidence of a life after death, so there is no reason to believe in it.
- Memories of previous lives could be false, so they do not count as evidence.
- Stories about ghosts can often be explained by people being mistaken, so there is not enough evidence to believe that they are people who are living after death.
- Much of the evidence for the afterlife comes from religious teachings, but if you do not believe in that religion, there is no reason to believe in the afterlife.

*[2 marks available, 1 mark for each correct point]*

2.3 Viewpoints that believe the sanctity of life is the most important factor:
- Some Christians believe abortion is undesirable since God "created mankind in his own image" (Genesis 1:27 NIV), so even unborn babies are the images of God.
- The Catholic Church strongly believes that all life is sacred, and therefore humans cannot end it deliberately. Most Catholics are against abortion and euthanasia for this reason. The Catechism of the Catholic Church describes euthanasia as "murder" (Catechism 2277).
- Muslims believe that life is sacred because Allah has a plan for all humans and only he can decide when humans die: "it is not [possible] for one to die except by permission of Allah" (Qur'an 3:145).

Viewpoints that believe other factors need to be considered:
- Some Christians believe that allowing a woman to choose whether she has an abortion or not is a way of showing Christian compassion.
- Atheists and humanists believe that we should weigh the sanctity of life against quality of life. For example, they might believe that abortion should be allowed if the quality of life of the baby once it's born will be very low.
- Jews believe in the principle of pikuach nefesh — that they should do everything they can to save a life. This means that they generally do not allow euthanasia, but in cases where the mother's life is at risk, they would allow abortion because they wish to save the mother's life.

*[4 marks available — see p.190 for mark scheme]*

2.4 - Christians believe the Biblical creation story in Genesis, which says that God "created mankind in his own image" (Genesis 1:27 NIV). This means that humans are special, and should respect each other.
- Christians believe that man was created "from the dust of the ground" (Genesis 2:7 NIV) and woman "from the rib he had taken out of the man" (Genesis 2:22 NIV). This shows the care and attention that God paid to creating humans, which suggested that humans are more important to God than animals.
- Judaism also teaches the creation story in Genesis. Ultra-Orthodox Jews believe that the creation story is literally true, and God created humans "from the dust of the ground" (Genesis 2:7 NIV). However, other Jews believe that the story is only a metaphor.
- The Qur'an says that Allah created humans "from clay" (Qur'an 32:7). The first man was Adam, and Allah breathed life and a soul into him. This shows that human life is sacred because it comes from Allah.
- Many religious people believe in the theory of evolution — that humans evolved from animals. They see the creation story as a metaphor for this — God created humans and animals using the process of evolution.

*[5 marks available — see p.190 for mark scheme]*

2.5 Arguments that support the statement:
  - Muslims believe that after 120 days of pregnancy, the soul enters the foetus (ensoulment) — "the soul is breathed into his body" (Sahih al-Bukhari 55:549). This leads some Muslims to believe that before this time abortion can be allowed in some circumstances, for example if the baby would be born with a serious disability.
  - Some Christians (for example the Church of England) argue that abortion should be allowed in certain situations such as when the mother's life is at risk. They believe that the situation should be approached with Christian compassion.
  - Many Jews believe that, although all human life is sacred as part of God's creation, abortion should be allowed in certain circumstances. If the mother's life is in danger, for example, abortion is allowed in order to save her. This fits with the principle of pikuach nefesh — that everything possible should be done to save a life because "anyone who saves a life is as if he saved an entire world" (Mishnah Sanhedrin 4:5).
  - Many humanists believe that abortion is undesirable, but that it should be the choice of the mother. They argue that women should be able to decide what happens to their bodies.
  Arguments that disagree with the statement:
  - The Qur'an teaches that killing is wrong, so some Muslims believe that abortion is always wrong as it involves ending a human life. The Qur'an says "do not kill your children... their killing is ever a great sin" (Qur'an 17:31).
  - Christians believe God created humans "in his own image" (Genesis 1:27 NIV), and some argue this makes abortion wrong.
  - Roman Catholic Christians believe that human life begins at conception, so all abortion is a form of murder. The Catechism of the Catholic Church says, "The deliberate murder of an innocent person is gravely contrary to the dignity of the human being... and to the holiness of the Creator" (Catechism 2261).
  - Some Jews believe that abortion is always wrong since God created each human being in the womb: "For you created my inmost being; you knit me together in my mother's womb" (Psalm 139:13 NIV). If God created humans with such care, humans cannot decide when to end a life.
  *[12 marks available — see p.190 for mark scheme]*

3.1 Separate from the world *[1 mark]*

3.2 - The feeding of the 5000 in the Bible.
  - Jesus turning water into wine.
  - The Qur'an itself.
  - God sending manna from heaven to the Israelites in the desert.
  - God parting the Red Sea so the Israelites, led by Moses, could escape Egypt.
  *[2 marks available, 1 mark for each correct point]*

3.3 - Christians believe that God gave humans free will to choose to do good or evil. St Augustine argued that the price to pay for free will was the suffering that sometimes happened as a result.
  - Judaism teaches that suffering is a test from God. Enduring it can strengthen a person's faith and bring them closer to God.
  - Muslims believe that suffering is part of Allah's plan, even if we do not understand it. We must trust that Allah has this plan, and tolerate the suffering that is part of it.
  - Some people argue that suffering is a punishment for sin. As a result of Adam and Eve disobeying God, all humans carry 'original sin'. Suffering is punishment for this and other sins committed in the believer's life.
  - Atheists and humanists might argue that evil and suffering can't be punishments for sin, because they are experienced by almost everyone. Also, animals suffer as well, and it doesn't make sense to say that these animals are being punished for sinning.
  *[4 marks available — see p.190 for mark scheme]*

3.4 - Muslims believe that the Qur'an was directly revealed to Muhammad. It contains the exact words of Allah as revealed to Muhammad, and this is the final revelation from Allah to humans. The Qur'an says, "he revealed to His Servant what he revealed. The heart did not lie [about] what it saw" (Qur'an 53:10-11).

  - Some Jews (Orthodox Jews) believe that the Torah was directly revealed by God to Moses. It has a divine origin and should be taken literally.
  - Progressive Jews believe that the Torah does contain a message from God, but passed on through humans — they may need to interpret it.
  - Many Christians believe that the Bible was written by humans, but inspired by God: "All Scripture is God-breathed" (2 Timothy 3:16 NIV). It contains his message, but it needs to be interpreted by humans.
  *[5 marks available — see p.190 for mark scheme]*

3.5 Arguments that support the statement:
  - The First Cause argument fits with Islamic, Jewish and Christian sacred texts, which describe the universe being created by God. God is the First Cause who makes the rest of creation happen.
  - Christianity teaches that God is "eternal" (Deuteronomy 33:27 NIV) and "everlasting" (Isaiah 40:28 NIV). This means he would have existed before the universe, so he could be the First Cause.
  - It could be argued that the Big Bang theory supports the statement. God could have caused the Big Bang and therefore been the First Cause of the universe.
  Arguments against the statement:
  - Even if we accept that there is a First Cause, this is not necessarily proof that God exists. The First Cause could be a different kind of being or thing. The argument certainly does not prove the existence of the kind of God described in Christian, Muslim and Jewish holy books and teachings.
  - Some people argue that the First Cause argument doesn't make sense. If everything needs to have a cause, they argue, why doesn't the First Cause also need to be caused by something?
  *[12 marks available — see p.190 for mark scheme]*

4.1 Violent protest *[1 mark]*

4.2 - By raising money where they live.
  - By providing essentials such as food and medical supplies to be delivered by other organisations.
  - By campaigning and putting pressure on governments and international organisations to intervene.
  - By acting as mediators between groups in conflict.
  - By organising or attending protests against conflicts.
  *[2 marks available, 1 mark for each correct point]*

4.3 - Terrorism contradicts one of the key Christian principles, the belief that they should treat others as they would wish to be treated, so it is never acceptable to harm innocents to further a cause.
  - Christians see passive resistance as a better way to achieve change or further a cause. For example, this can be seen in the efforts of Dr Martin Luther King who did not resort to violence.
  - Terrorism goes against the peaceful principles of Islam — the Qur'an instructs Muslims to reply peacefully when they are addressed harshly.
  - Muslims believe peaceful protest or passive resistance are the best ways to fight injustice — this was demonstrated by many Muslims in the 2011 Arab Spring.
  - While Islamic terrorists have sometimes used the term 'jihad' to justify their actions, the overwhelming majority of Muslims view this as wrong, because terrorism involves harming innocent people.
  - Judaism teaches that violence should only be used to save one's own life or another person's life, which means terrorism is wrong, as it harms innocent people. Terrorism also goes against the commandment "You shall not murder" (Exodus 20:13 NIV).
  - Non-violent protest against injustice is encouraged in Judaism — Jews do not respond to anti-Semitism with violence.
  *[4 marks available — see p.190 for mark scheme]*

4.4 - The use of weapons which may indiscriminately harm civilians, land and animals alike goes against Christian and Jewish principles of peace and respect for God's creation: "When you lay siege to a city for a long time... do not destroy its trees by putting an axe to them, because you can eat their fruit" (Deuteronomy 20:19 NIV).

- Jesus taught his followers to "love your enemies" (Luke 6:27 NIV), which many Christians believe prohibits the use of weapons of mass destruction. Similarly, they should not be used as a form of retaliation if others use them: "If anyone slaps you on your right cheek, turn to them the other cheek also" (Matthew 5:39 NIV).
- The use of weapons of mass destruction that involves the killing of innocents would be considered murder in Islam and so is prohibited: "...whoever kills a soul... it is as if he had slain mankind entirely" (Qur'an 5:32).
- Muslims believe that even if the use of violence could be justified, it is likely that weapons of mass destruction fall outside of the rules of jihad because they are indiscriminate: "Do not kill women or children or an aged, infirm person. Do not cut down fruit-bearing trees. Do not destroy an inhabited place" (Hadith Muwatta Malik 21:10).
- The Talmud says that if something will inflict harm on over a sixth of the population, then it is not allowed. Due to the extensive damage caused by weapons of mass destruction, this teaching could prevent countries from using them.
*[5 marks available — see p.190 for mark scheme]*

4.5 Arguments that support the statement:
- Some religious believers would support the pacifist ideals that the use of violence can never be justified by religion or any reason.
- The Bible teaches Christians to be peaceful: "all who draw the sword will die by the sword" (Matthew 26:52 NIV).
- Islam teaches that peace is to be preferred over violence: "And the servants of the Most Merciful are those who walk upon the earth easily, and when the ignorant address them [harshly], they say [words of] peace" (Qur'an 25:63).
- The promotion of peace over violence is of central importance for Jews, who believe that the Messiah will bring peace to the whole world: "They will beat their swords into ploughshares and their spears into pruning hooks" (Micah 4:3 NIV).
- Some believers may argue that while violence may be justified on some grounds, it should never be carried out for religious reasons. Many now reject the idea of Holy War and do not believe that a just war can have a religious justification.
- Some believers may argue that religious justification can't be used where the violence is indiscriminate or targets innocents. So the use of weapons of mass destruction or terrorism are not allowable, even if a conflict is otherwise justified by religion.
Arguments against the statement:
- Some religious believers may argue that religious principles involve defending the weak and vulnerable, and that this can sometimes involve violence. They may believe that, while non-violent opposition to injustice is preferable, it is sometimes necessary to resort to violence in order to preserve justice. Jesus seemed to condone some acts of violence for religious reasons when he threw the money lenders from the temple (Matthew 21:12).
- Some believers may refer to religious principles which dictate when and how violence should be used. Often this is with a view to bringing about peace through violent means when such a path is unavoidable. Violence can be justified on religious grounds within the concept of the lesser jihad: "Allah will punish them by your hands and will disgrace them and give you victory over them..." (Qur'an 9:14). Military jihad, however, is subject to very strict rules with many similarities to the Just War theory.
- Judaism teaches that sometimes violence, in the form of war, may be required — this is the concept of milchemet mitzvah. It is thought that God approves of such wars, which may be fought in self-defence or to protect others: "The Lord... shot his arrows and scattered the enemy" (2 Samuel 22:14-15 NIV).
- Traditionally, the concept of Holy War has been used to justify violence on religious grounds. Religious teachings on just war are found in the writings of St Augustine and St Thomas Aquinas, and are reflected in contemporary Christian teachings such as the Catechism of the Catholic Church (2265).
*[12 marks available — see p.190 for mark scheme]*

5.1 Sin *[1 mark]*
5.2 - Punishment is an important way to preserve justice.
- Punishment gives criminals a chance to reform.
- Punishment can provide rehabilitation for criminals.
- Punishment can be justified as a deterrent to others.
- Punishment can be used to protect the public from dangerous individuals.
- Punishment can be used to compensate the victim(s) of crime.
*[2 marks available, 1 mark for each correct point]*
5.3 - Christianity teaches that God is forgiving and that people should be forgiving too. This is demonstrated in many teachings and practices, from the Lord's Prayer to the Catholic sacrament of reconciliation.
- Christianity teaches that forgiveness depends on repentance. This means that forgiveness can only happen when a person is truly sorry and wishes to be forgiven.
- Islam teaches that it is always better to be forgiving than to seek retribution. The Prophet Muhammad exemplifies this in the Hadith and many Muslims aim to follow his example.
- Muslims believe that there are some sins which are so bad they cannot be forgiven. For example, the sin of believing in multiple gods (shirk).
- Judaism teaches that God is forgiving and that Jews should follow this example. This means they should allow criminals to repent for their crimes.
- Judaism also teaches that forgiveness may only be granted by the person who has been harmed. This means that God cannot forgive all crimes and so people must seek forgiveness from those they have harmed.
*[4 marks available — see p.190 for mark scheme]*
5.4 - Some Christians believe that corporal punishment should be avoided, as it involves the use of violence. Even when used as a punishment, it is still violence being used against other human beings: "all who draw the sword will die by the sword" (Matthew 26:52 NIV).
- Some Christians might argue that there could be circumstances where corporal punishment can serve a purpose. The Bible, especially Old Testament, contains many references to corporal punishment: "If the guilty person deserves to be beaten, the judge shall... have them flogged... with the number of lashes the crime deserves" (Deuteronomy 25:2 NIV).
- Corporal punishment is permitted under Islamic law (shari'ah) as way of punishing serious crimes. These crimes can include stealing, adultery and drinking alcohol: "[As for] the thief... amputate their hands in recompense for what they committed as a deterrent [punishment] from Allah" (Qur'an 5:38).
- Muslims believe that corporal punishment should only be carried out under very strict conditions. For example, where there are multiple witnesses to a crime to ensure that there is no doubt about the criminal's guilt.
- The Torah allows the use of corporal punishment and contains examples of it being used. Exodus 21:24-25 ("eye for eye, tooth for tooth, hand for hand, foot for foot, burn for burn, wound for wound, bruise for bruise" (NIV)) can be seen to justify matching physical punishments with physical crimes.
- Many modern Jews disagree with the use of corporal punishment. Some have argued that the harsh punishments in the Torah were not intended to be carried out, but instead were used to indicate the relative seriousness of different offences: "And it is preferable... that even a thousand guilty people be set free than to someday execute even one innocent person" (Maimonides, Sefer Hamitzvot, Negative Commandment no. 290).
*[5 marks available — see p.190 for mark scheme]*
5.5 Arguments that support the statement:
- People have free will and so if they choose to abuse free will by committing crime, the responsibility rests with the individual themselves. Both religious believers and non-religious people may agree with this if they accept that human beings are capable of making their own choices.

- Part of what makes crimes bad is the intention behind the criminal action. If a person chooses to break the law and understands what they are doing, they alone should bear responsibility for this.
- In the parable of the sheep and the goats, Jesus taught that people will be judged by God on their actions and how they treated others in life. They are held to account for their actions, and so are responsible for any crimes they may have committed.
- Muslims believe that each person's deeds and intentions are recorded by angels, and that Allah will judge each person on how they spent their time on Earth. So they are held responsible for their own actions, including crimes.
- For Muslims, this hadith on intention means that if a crime was intended then a person will be judged on that intention: "The reward of deeds depends upon the intentions and every person will get the reward according to what he has intended" (Hadith Sahih al-Bukhari 1:1).
- For Jews, serious crimes such as theft and murder are prohibited under the Ten Commandments and the Noahide law, which apply to all people. Breaking these laws will result in punishment by God unless a person seeks forgiveness and makes amends for their actions — so God holds them and them alone accountable for their crimes.

Arguments against the statement:
- There are some reasons why a person may not be responsible for a crime they committed. For example if a person commits a crime because of mental illness, most people would not regard this as their fault.
- Sometimes, responsibility for crime might be placed with society. For example, many people believe that poverty, addiction and a troubled upbringing can all contribute to the likelihood that a person will commit crime. While this might not excuse criminal activities entirely, the failure of society to deal with these problems could be seen as a mitigating factor.
- Muslims acknowledge that many factors can contribute to criminal activity, including poverty and addiction, and may give zakah to charities which reduce the effects of these factors.
- Judaism recognises the influence of factors such as poverty and addiction, and Jews can try to alleviate the effects of these factors by giving financial aid (tzedakah) to appropriate charities.
- Some people believe that, when faced with an unjust law, a person has no choice but to break it in order to stick to a higher moral law or God's law. Responsibility for crime may lie with the law itself. Many Christians have consciously defied unjust laws where they conflicted with God's law, for example Rosa Parks and Dr Martin Luther King.
*[12 marks available — see p.190 for mark scheme]*

6.1 Everyone should be treated fairly *[1 mark]*.

6.2 - The Catholic Church teaches that every individual has a responsibility to ensure that human rights are protected.
- The Torah indicates that following justice is commanded by God. This means people should be treated fairly, and so human rights are important.
- The Qur'an says "Allah orders justice and good conduct" (Qur'an 16:90), so Muslims think justice and human rights are very important.
*[2 marks available, 1 mark for each correct point]*

6.3 Points that show support for freedom of belief:
- Although many Christians believe that Christianity is the true religion, they recognise and accept people's right to practise any faith.
- People can convert to Judaism if they choose to do so, although Jews themselves do not try to convert people, showing that they support people's right to choose their beliefs.
- Most Muslims feel people should be allowed to choose whether to follow Islam, and even though they believe Islam is the true religion, they believe that Allah accepts all righteous people.

Points that suggest a lack of support for freedom of belief:
- Some Christians believe that only Christians will be saved and reach heaven, so try to convert non-Christians to Christianity. This shows they do not encourage freedom of religion.
- In Islam, many believe that converting away from Islam or becoming an atheist (apostasy) is a terrible sin (some even believe this deserves the death penalty). So this seriously discourages people from choosing different beliefs.
*[4 marks available — see p.190 for mark scheme]*

6.4 - The story of the widow's offering (Mark 12:41-44) suggests that people have a duty to give as much to the poor as they can afford. It is not the amount they give that matters, but the fact that they are being generous with what they have.
- Christians should have a positive attitude to giving to the poor: "God loves a cheerful giver" (2 Corinthians 9:7 NIV).
- Jews refer to the teaching in the Torah which states that "If anyone is poor... be open handed and freely lend them whatever they need" (Deuteronomy 15:7-8 NIV). They believe God has instructed people to help the poor.
- Jews are warned in the Torah that if they don't help those in financial need, then God will be displeased. God indicates that he "will certainly hear their cry" (Exodus 22:23 NIV), meaning he will be aware of the suffering of those who haven't been helped.
- Jews follow the principle of tzedakah which literally means 'charity'. In Judaism, this act of giving to charity is very important because it makes society a better and fairer place.
- One of the Five Pillars of Islam (zakah) states that Muslims should give 2.5% of their wealth each year to those in need.
- In the hadith, Muslims are instructed to help those in poverty: "A man is not a believer who fills his stomach while his neighbour is hungry" (Al-Adab al-Mufrad 6:112).
*[5 marks available — see p.190 for mark scheme]*

6.5 Arguments that support the statement:
- Jesus said to "Love your neighbour as yourself" (Mark 12:31 NIV), meaning that everyone should be treated as you would expect to be treated yourself. So it could be argued that Christians have been instructed to work for equality.
- The teachings of the Torah specifically indicate that all races are equal. Leviticus 19:34-35 says, "The foreigner residing among you must be treated as your native-born. Love them as yourself..." (NIV). So Jewish teaching sets an example of racial equality, suggesting Jews should work to achieve this.
- The Torah and the Bible teach that humans all come from God: "God created mankind in his own image" (Genesis 1:27 NIV). This makes it clear that all humans should be treated with respect, so believers should aim to achieve equality.
- In Islam, the principle of the Muslim community, the ummah, sets an example of equality. All Muslims (regardless of race, gender or age) are seen as one united community. There are different types of Muslims, such as Shi'a and Sunni, but these are all part of the universal principle of ummah. This principle suggests that Muslims should support equality.

Arguments against the statement:
- Leadership on equality doesn't only come from religion. The Equality Act of 2010 was set up to promote the view that everyone is equal. This means it is against the law for anybody to treat others unequally. It could be argued that government should lead the way on equality.
- Although some of St Paul's writings preach equality, 1 Corinthians 6:9-10 forbids homosexuality, and 1 Timothy 2:12 says women shouldn't teach or have authority over a man. So the message from the Bible isn't always one of equality, and some Christians may not believe in working for equality in all areas.
- Some traditions in Judaism suggest that men and women cannot be treated equally due to the differing roles they have in worship. For example, female rabbis are generally not allowed in Orthodox Judaism. So some Jews may not believe in working for gender equality in all forms.

- Some Muslims believe that whilst equality is important due to the ummah, certain conditions may mean that individuals do not have to be treated equally. For example, some Muslims reject homosexuality, so may not believe in working for full equality in the area of sexual orientation.

*[12 marks available — see p.190 for mark scheme]*

7.1 It was Passover *[1 mark]*

7.2 - It links Jesus to Old Testament prophesies about the Messiah.
- It means 'anointed one', which shows how special Jesus is.
- The title 'Messiah' was given to kings of Israel, which shows how important Jesus is.
- The Messiah was supposed to save the Jews from their enemies.

*[2 marks available, 1 mark for each correct point]*

7.3 - Some Christians believe that the miracle stories are literally true. Jesus broke the laws of nature, showing his power, which must have come from God.
- Others believe that the miracle stories are just metaphors which teach spiritual truths, and shouldn't be taken literally.
- Some atheists believe that the miracles didn't happen at all — the events can be explained by science or the events didn't happen as they were described.

*[4 marks available — see p.190 for mark scheme]*

7.4 - James and John both wanted to sit in important places to the left and right of Jesus, but Jesus told them that to be first, they must "be slave of all" (Mark 10:44 NIV). This teaches Christians to be humble and to put others before themselves.
- This story shows Christians that Jesus is humble, and wished to serve mankind rather than be a military or political leader. He said he "did not come to be served, but to serve" (Mark 10:45 NIV). This leads Christians to worship Jesus, and to try to follow his example.
- Jesus predicts that James and John "will drink the cup I drink" (Mark 10:39 NIV). This means that they will have to suffer persecution in a similar way to Jesus. This is important to Christians because when they are suffering, they can feel less alone as Jesus understands what they are going through, and Christians in the past have also experienced the same suffering.

*[5 marks available — see p.190 for mark scheme]*

7.5 Arguments that support the statement:
- Jesus predicted his death many times in Mark's Gospel, for example at Caesarea Philippi. If he had wanted to avoid being arrested, he could have stopped teaching, or travelled somewhere else to teach. He did not, so he chose to accept his own death.
- It is important that Jesus chose to die for the sins of humanity. He had no sins himself, but loved humanity so much that he sacrificed himself to save us. If Jesus had not deliberately chosen to die, humanity would not have been saved.
- Jesus knew that one of his disciples would betray him. At the last supper he told them all that "one of you will betray me" (Mark 14:18 NIV). He could have named Judas and had him sent away to stop the betrayal, but he chose to let Judas organise his arrest.
Arguments against the statement:
- It is clear that Jesus wanted to hide the fact that he was the Son of God and the Messiah. For example, he told Jairus not to tell anyone that he had brought his daughter back from the dead. Some people argue that this is because he did not want to be arrested and killed.
- In the Garden of Gethsemane, Jesus first asks that his suffering be removed, and then submits to God's will, saying "Yet not what I will, but what you will" (Mark 14:36 NIV). This shows that Jesus knows he must be killed because it is the will of God.
- Jesus's death fulfilled prophecies from the Old Testament. Jesus had no choice but to let himself be arrested, saying "the Scriptures must be fulfilled" (Mark 14:49 NIV).

*[12 marks available — see p.190 for mark scheme]*

8.1 A teacher of the law *[1 mark]*

8.2 - Some people saw illness and disability as punishments from God, so the sick and disabled were seen as sinners.
- Some diseases were believed to be passed on by touching, so people suffering from them were isolated to protect others.
- Some diseases were thought to make people ritually unclean, so they couldn't worship God, and other people wouldn't touch them because they were afraid of becoming unclean too.

*[2 marks available, 1 mark for each correct point]*

8.3 - It shows that anyone can lose their faith. Peter was one of Jesus's closest disciples, and if he can betray Jesus, anyone is capable of it. It shows how difficult it is to keep faith and that Christians need God's help to do it.
- In contrast, Peter's failure is an example of how we all may fail. However, it is an opportunity for Peter to repent and be forgiven and it demonstrates to us the extent of God's forgiveness, showing us that all sins can be forgiven.

*[4 marks available — see p.190 for mark scheme]*

8.4 - Jesus told the rich man to "give to the poor" (Mark 10:21 NIV), which leads many modern day Christians to give to charity and volunteer for causes which help the poor.
- Jesus told the rich man to "sell everything you have" (Mark 10:21 NIV). Some modern Christians like nuns or monks believe that this means they should try to live completely without wealth or personal possessions.
- Jesus told the rich man that it is "easier for a camel to go through the eye of a needle than for someone who is rich to enter the kingdom of God" (Mark 10:25 NIV). Some Christians believe that Jesus's comparison of a rich man and a camel passing through the eye of a needle means that they can still own possessions, but that money should not be their main focus in life.
- Some modern Christians see this story as important because it shows Jesus as a humble leader. He was happy to remain poor and didn't need wealth or possessions. This makes him worthy of their worship.

*[5 marks available — see p.190 for mark scheme]*

8.5 Arguments that support the statement:
- During his life, Jesus spent a lot of time with the poor, the sick and other outcasts from society. If this wasn't a major part of his teaching, he would have spent this time with others instead.
- Jesus himself said that the most important commandment was "Love your neighbour as yourself" (Mark 12:31 NIV). This would have been hardest when it came to the poor and the sick, so it shows that Jesus's treatment of the poor and the sick is the most important part of his teaching.
- Even people who don't believe in the Christian God, like some atheists, might agree that Jesus was a very moral man — just not the Son of God. They might also agree that people should follow his example about how to treat the poor and the sick. This part of his teaching is the most important because it relates to everyone, not just to Christians.
- The protection of the poor and the sick, through a free healthcare system and benefits, is part of modern British society so it's clear that this part of Jesus's teaching has had a huge effect on the world.
Arguments against the statement:
- Jesus spent a long time teaching people about the kingdom of God, and how people can get there. Treating the poor and the sick with compassion is only part of Jesus's teaching on how humans can enter the kingdom of God, so it cannot be the most important part of his teaching.
- As well as the poor and sick, Jesus spent a lot of time with sinners like prostitutes and tax collectors — for example, he chose Levi to be his disciple. This suggests that his treatment of other outcasts from society is equally important.
- When Jesus was asked to heal the paralysed man, he instead forgave his sins, only healing him afterwards. This suggests that forgiving people's sins was a more important part of Jesus's teaching than improving their physical health.

*[12 marks available — see p.190 for mark scheme]*

# Glossary

Definitions relevant to **Christianity** and **Catholic Christianity**:

| | |
|---|---|
| **Advent** | The period of time that begins four Sundays before Christmas. |
| **the ascension** | When Jesus rose up to heaven to be with God again. |
| **catechism** | A series of statements laying down the official teachings of the Roman Catholic Church. |
| **confirmation** | The act of 'confirming' your faith, often at an age when you can decide for yourself. |
| **creed** | Statement of religious beliefs. |
| **disciples** | Followers of Jesus. This can refer to just his followers in the Bible or to all Christians. |
| **dominion** | The belief that people have power over God's creation and can use it as they like. |
| **the Eucharist** | When Christians remember the Last Supper with bread and wine. |
| **evangelism** | Spreading the Christian message in order to convert people. |
| **Gethsemane** | The garden where Jesus prayed before his arrest. |
| **Golgotha** | The 'place of the skull' where Jesus was crucified. |
| **grace** | God showing favour to those who haven't earned it. |
| **holy orders** | Ordination to a deacon, priest or bishop. |
| **incarnation** | The act by which Christians believe God became human, in the form of Jesus. |
| **the kingdom of God** | The time and place where God rules. |
| **Lent** | The period spent remembering Christ's 40 days of fasting in the desert. |
| **liturgical** | Worship that follows a set pattern that's been written out by the Church. |
| **original sin** | The flawed nature that humans have been born with since Adam and Eve first sinned. |
| **parable** | A story about daily life which has a message about spiritual truth. |
| **Purgatory** | A place where Catholics believe sins are paid for before going to heaven. |
| **the Rosary** | A string of beads used by Catholics when praying. |
| **sacrament** | A ceremony, or outward sign, of the direct communication of God's saving grace. |
| **salvation** | The soul being saved from death and sin so it can reach heaven. |
| **Second Coming** | The belief that Jesus will return to Earth. |
| **Sermon on the Mount** | A summary of Jesus's teachings on how to live a Christian life — Matthew 5-7. |
| **Stations of the Cross** | Pictures in church of Jesus's suffering, used by Catholics as a focus for contemplation. |
| **transfiguration** | An event in which Jesus's appearance changed miraculously, making his clothes 'dazzling white'. |
| **transubstantiation** | Transformation of the Eucharistic bread and wine into the flesh and blood of Christ. |
| **the Trinity** | The belief that God exists in three 'persons' — the Father, the Son and the Holy Spirit. |

# Glossary

Definitions relevant to **Islam**:

| | |
|---|---|
| **al-Adab al-Mufrad** | A collection of hadith. |
| **al-Akhirah** | The concept of life after death. This is a key Islamic belief. |
| **al-Qadr** | Predestination — the idea that Allah has already decided everything that will happen. |
| **barzakh** | Where souls wait for Yawm ad-Din (the Day of Judgement). |
| **hadith** | Islamic scripture containing a collection of things the Prophet Muhammad said and did. |
| **hajj** | The pilgrimage to Makkah. |
| **jahannam** | The place where people who have done bad deeds will be sent in the afterlife. |
| **jannah** | The afterlife paradise — described as "gardens of pleasure" in the Qur'an. |
| **jihad** | The struggle to be a good Muslim (greater jihad) and to make the world better (lesser jihad). |
| **khalifah** | The belief that Muslims must look after the Earth as vice-regents or trustees. |
| **Muwatta Malik** | A collection of hadith. |
| **Sahih al-Bukhari** | A collection of hadith. |
| **Sahih Muslim** | A collection of hadith. |
| **salah** | The action of praying five times a day. |
| **sawm** | The Muslim obligation to fast during daylight hours through the month of Ramadan. |
| **shahadah** | A Pillar of Islam — the Muslim declaration of faith. |
| **shari'ah** | The Islamic religious law. |
| **shirk** | Believing there are other gods or that anything is equal to Allah — it's considered the worst sin. |
| **Sunan Abi Dawud** | A collection of hadith. |
| **Tawhid** | Belief that Allah is the one and only God. |
| **wudu** | The ritual washing of exposed body parts before prayer. |
| **Yawm ad-Din** | The day when everyone will be judged by Allah based on their actions. |
| **zakah** | A Pillar of Islam — all Muslims must donate 2.5% of their wealth to charity. |

Definitions relevant to **Judaism**:

| | |
|---|---|
| **bar/bat mitzvah** | The coming of age ceremony — bar mitzvah for boys, bat mitzvah for girls. |
| **brit milah** | The circumcision of baby boys when they're 7 days old. |
| **Gan Eden** | Garden of Eden or paradise — where good people spend the afterlife. |
| **Gehinnom** | The place where souls go before Gan Eden. The truly wicked never move on from there. |
| **gemilut hasadim** | Kind and compassionate actions towards others. |
| **kashrut** | The food laws written in the Torah. |
| **ketubah** | The marriage contract, which sets out the couple's rights and responsibilities. |
| **kiddushin** | Betrothal — the first part of the marriage ceremony. |
| **kosher** | Food that is permitted under kashrut. |
| **Maimonides** | A Jewish scholar — he wrote the 13 principles of faith and compiled a lot of mitzvot. |

# Glossary

| | |
|---|---|
| **Mishnah** | The part of the Talmud that explains how the mitzvot in the Torah should be applied. |
| **Mishneh Torah** | The list of mitzvot from the Torah compiled by Maimonides. |
| **mitzvot** | Jewish laws — there are 613 mitzvot in total. |
| **omnibenevolent** | Being all-good. |
| **oral Torah** | Jewish teachings passed down orally and recorded in the Talmud. |
| **pikuach nefesh** | The principle of saving a life, even if it means breaking mitzvot. |
| **Pirkei Avot** | Part of the Talmud. |
| **Shabbat** | Also called the Sabbath, it is the Jewish day of rest (Saturday). |
| **shekhinah** | God's presence in a particular place on Earth. |
| **tikkun olam** | The belief that Jews should 'mend the world', e.g. by caring for the environment and the poor. |
| **tzedakah** | The practice of giving 10% of your wealth to charity. |

**General** definitions:

| | |
|---|---|
| **abortion** | Removing a foetus from the womb before it is able to survive, ending the pregnancy. |
| **adultery** | A married person having sex with someone who isn't their husband or wife. |
| **atheism** | A complete denial of the existence of a god. |
| **atonement** | Making amends for wrongdoing — often refers to people repairing their relationship with God. |
| **benevolent** | Being kind and loving. |
| **capital punishment** | The death penalty as punishment for a crime. |
| **celibacy** | Not taking part in any sexual activities. |
| **cohabitation** | Living together in a sexual relationship without being married. |
| **confession** | Admitting sins to God. |
| **conscience** | An inner feeling of what's right and what's wrong. |
| **contraception** | Also known as birth control, it stops a woman from conceiving. |
| **corporal punishment** | Punishing a criminal through physical pain. |
| **covenant** | A formal agreement between two or more people. |
| **discrimination** | Treating different people, or groups of people, differently (usually unfairly). |
| **euthanasia** | Ending someone's life to relieve their suffering, especially from an incurable, painful illness. |
| **fasting** | Not eating and/or drinking for a set time. |
| **free will** | The ability to choose how to behave. All three religions believe humans have free will. |
| **holy war** | A war where people believe that God is 'on their side'. |
| **homophobia** | Prejudice against people who are homosexual. |
| **human dignity** | The idea that all human life is valuable and everyone has the right to be treated with respect. |
| **humanism** | The belief that God doesn't exist, and humans should live good lives based on their knowledge. |
| **human rights** | The moral, legal and political rights that every human being on Earth is entitled to. |

# Glossary

| | |
|---|---|
| **humanity** | The entire human race. |
| **immanent** | God/Allah is present in the human world. |
| **justice** | The idea of each person getting what they deserve, and maintaining what's right. |
| **just war** | A war that meets certain conditions to be classed as necessary. |
| **Last Judgement** | The Day of Judgement when all of humanity's actions will be judged by God/Allah. |
| **Messiah** | A leader who will bring peace to Earth. Christians believe that Jesus is the Messiah. |
| **miracle** | An event believed to be the work of God, that can't be explained by the laws of science. |
| **mourning** | A period of deep sorrow for someone who has died. |
| **nuclear family** | A family made up of a mother, a father and their children living together. |
| **omnipotent** | Having unlimited powers — all-powerful. |
| **omniscient** | Knowing everything — in the past, present and future. |
| **pacifism** | The idea that war and physical violence are wrong under any circumstances. |
| **pilgrimage** | A journey to a place of religious significance. |
| **polygamy** | Marriage to multiple people. |
| **prejudice** | Judging something or someone with no good reason, or without full knowledge of a situation. |
| **procreation** | Having children. |
| **promiscuity** | Having many sexual partners. |
| **prophet** | A person on Earth who communicated God/Allah's will. |
| **racism** | Discrimination against people of other races — often based on unfair stereotypes. |
| **reconciliation** | Returning to harmony and friendship after conflict. |
| **reformation** | The idea that punishment should aim to change criminals so that they won't reoffend. |
| **reincarnation** | The rebirth of a soul in a new body after death. |
| **resurrection** | Being brought back to life after death. |
| **retribution** | Punishing a criminal by making them 'pay' for what they've done. |
| **revelation** | An experience that reveals God's presence. |
| **sanctity of life** | The belief that all life belongs to God/Allah, so it is holy. |
| **sexism** | Discrimination based on someone's gender (male or female). |
| **sin** | An act that breaks a religious law, i.e. when God's teaching is disobeyed. |
| **situation ethics** | An ethical principle where decisions are made based on what is best in individual cases. |
| **social justice** | The idea of fairness in society and putting the principles of human rights into practice. |
| **stewardship** | Taking care of the Earth as God's creation, so it can be passed on to the next generation. |
| **transcendent** | A characteristic of God/Allah — he is beyond this world. |
| **usury** | Charging high rates of interest on a loan. |
| **utilitarianism** | The idea that the correct course of action has the best balance of good and bad outcomes. |
| **vision** | A religious experience where a person sees something sacred. |

# Index

# Index

RAS41